The Genocide Convention Sixty Years after its Adoption

The Genocide Convention Sixty Years after its Adoption

edited by

Christoph Safferling
and
Eckart Conze

T•M•C• Asser press

ISBN 978-90-6704-315-1

www.asserpress.nl

FOREWORD

The Genocide Convention constitutes a milestone. To this day, it continues to be the principal legal instrument dealing with genocide. Motivated by the horrifying impressions left by the Holocaust, in 1948 the international community put the might of the law above the right of the mighty: For the first time, genocide was condemned in a binding document. And it was the first time that an international treaty provided for the establishment of an international criminal court.

The United Nations started preparations for the planned international criminal court as early as 1948. But the time was not yet ripe. During the first part of the 20th Century, state sovereignty in international relations meant almost everything. Consequently, it took almost 50 years before the first proceedings for genocide took place and the first sentences for genocide were passed at international level: In September 1998, for the first time, the Criminal Tribunal for Rwanda found an individual guilty of genocide. A further nine years later, the United Nations Tribunal for the first time pronounced a state guilty of violating the Genocide Convention.

It was the work of the *ad hoc* criminal tribunals for the former Yugoslavia and for Rwanda that paved the way for the establishment of the permanent International Criminal Court. It commenced work five and a half years ago now and its inception marked the beginning of a new chapter in the history of international criminal law. Crimes of the most serious nature which affect the international community as a whole can now be tried by an independent body.

Germany vigorously supported the establishment of the International Criminal Court right from the beginning. We played an active role in the drafting of the Rome Statute and joined forces with the group of like-minded states to fight for a well-functioning and thus reliable international court.

In future, too, the federal government will continue to do everything in its power to ensure that the Court can work effectively and that the support it receives from the international community is as widely based as possible – as we are convinced that it can make a substantial contribution in the struggle for peace and justice. At the Review Conference to be held in 2010, Germany will advocate establishing the crime of aggression, the details of which are currently the subject of intense debate among the Assembly of States Parties to the Rome Statute. Unfortunately, the political environment remains difficult. It appears unlikely under the Obama administration, as well, that the United States will accede to the Rome Statute any time in the foreseeable future.

The development of international criminal law as well as the establishment of the International Criminal Court have always been accompanied by a fundamental doubt: Can the law, and especially criminal prosecution, actually make any contribution to ensuring peace? Isn't it the case that punishments are more a source of disruption to new beginnings in society?

In my opinion, the answer is clearly no! Serious human rights violations must not go unpunished. Nobody should be allowed to place themselves above the law, and no perpetrator should be allowed to hide behind the protective shield of state sovereignty. This is not a question of retribution or revenge, but a question of prevention and of protection of legal interests. International criminal law and the prosecution of the most serious crimes without exception serve as a warning to all warmongers. In this way, international criminal law makes an important contribution towards asserting human rights and securing peace. I can't see any equivalent alternatives.

Amnesties, at any rate, are not a suitable means of conflict resolution. They don't resolve conflicts; at best they merely postpone them. The Spanish Amnesty Law of 1977 is a striking example of this. It meant that the crimes committed during the Franco dictatorship were prevented from being investigated for decades. This in no way contributed to any reconciliation between victims and perpetrators – as the current discussions make clear.

So-called 'truth and reconciliation commissions' can constitute a useful complement to the international criminal law system; however, they cannot replace it. Let us recall the much-cited example of the South-African Truth and Reconciliation Commission. Its successes are due to being closely interlinked with criminal prosecution. The Commission did not function outside international criminal law, but instead utilised the threat of criminal law sanctions for the purpose of carrying out its work. As a result of its authority to dispense with a criminal sanction, it was linked to the criminal procedure. And it was in fact this threat of criminal prosecution that led many members of the South-African security forces to co-operate with the Truth Commission.

Resolute criminal prosecution of serious crimes also serves another purpose that is very important to me: it gives victims a face. When a newspaper reports that someone, somewhere, has become a victim of a war crime, the human tragedy often gets almost completely lost. In a trial, however, a victim doesn't just have a name. They can also be certain that their individual view of the events, their pain and their suffering will become part of that which the international community condemns and prosecutes.

And, ultimately, establishing the facts of what happened by means of criminal proceedings also ensures that events are not ignored or forgotten.

Resolute criminal prosecution can, of course, only constitute one part of the effort to secure peace and justice. In addition to the process of coming to terms with what has happened in the past, it is essential that reconciliation takes place. Given the degree of suffering sustained, this does not always prove to be possible.

This is why it is all the more important to identify and combat the causes of such serious crimes as genocide. The United Nations have engaged a special adviser on this issue for the 'Responsibility to Protect.' It is Professor Edward Luck whom the federal government will be actively supporting.

I would like to end by quoting Kofi Annan, who said: 'There can be no healing without peace; there can be no peace without justice; there can be no justice without respect for human rights and the rule of law.' The Genocide Convention has subjected the world's most powerful to the rule of law. The anniversary of its existence is truly an occasion to celebrate.

Berlin, March 2010 *Lutz Diwell*

ACKNOWLEDGEMENTS

The Genocide Convention is a remarkable document, 60 years and also 62 years after its adoption. Collecting and editing the papers presented at the Conference commemorating the 60th anniversary of the Genocide Convention, which took place from 4 to 6 December 2008 at the International Research and Documentation Centre War Crimes Trials (ICWC) and was so splendidly co-ordinated by Dr. Albrecht Kirschner, took much more time than previously envisaged. It would not have been possible at all without many helping hands. First and foremost we must express our deepest gratitude to Ms Marie Scheffler, who with the precious help of Mr Konstantin Nareyek took most of the tiresome editing work onto her shoulders and co-ordinated the assistance of several other staff members of the ICWC, Ms Alena Hartwig, Ms Wencke Meteling, Ms Andrea Wiegeshoff, Mr Patrick Donath, Mr Timo Ide, Mr Philipp Graebke, Mr Sascha Hörmann, Mr Simon Menz, Mr Sebastian Nussbaum, and Mr Tobias Scholz. The language editing was performed with the invaluable assistance of Mr Lars Büngener (ICWC), Ms Jane Britten and Ms Ulrike Seeberger. We are mostly indebted to all of the authors who have entrusted us with the publication of their papers and shown enormous patience during the editing process. Likewise, we are immensely grateful to Philip van Tongeren and Marjolijn Bastiaans at T.M.C. Asser Press for publishing this volume and in particular for their endurance in waiting for a publishable document.

Finally, we wish to thank the German Ministry of Foreign Affairs, the Ministry of Justice of the Federal State of Hesse, the city of Marburg and the Fritz-Thyssen-Foundation for sponsoring the '60th anniversary of the Genocide Convention'-Conference and giving us the opportunity to bring together such a great variety of internationally renowned researchers and practitioners. Many thanks also go to the Dr. Reinfried Pohl-Foundation, which supported the editing process financially.

Marburg, March 2010 *Christoph Safferling* and *Eckart Conze*

SUMMARY OF CONTENTS

Part Three: Interpretation of the Crime of Genocide

Part Four: Case Studies

Part Five: Genocide and the International Court of Justice

Part Six: Historic Cases

TABLE OF CONTENTS

LIST OF ABBREVIATIONS

AJCL	American Journal of Comparative Law
AJIL	American Journal of International Law
All ER	All England Law Reports
BFSP	British and Foreign State Papers
BGBl.	Bundesgesetzblatt
BGHSt	Entscheidungen des Bundesgerichtshof in Strafsachen
CCL No. 10	Control Council Law No. 10
CDU	Christlich Demokratische Union
CERD	Committee on the Elimination of Racial Discrimination
CLF	Criminal Law Forum
Cmdr.	Commander
Col.	Colonel
Colum.L.R.	Columbia Law Review
Cr. App. R.	Criminal Appeal Report
CrimLR	Criminal Law Review
DC-Cam	Documentation Centre of Cambodia
ECCC	Extraordinary Chambers in the Courts of Cambodia
ECHR	European Convention on Human Rights
ECOSOC	UN Economic and Social Council
ECtHR	European Court of Human Rights
EJIL	European Journal of International Law
ETS	European Treaty Series
FDP	Freie Demokratische Partei
FDR	Franklin D. Roosevelt
FO	Foreign Office
FRG	Federal Republic of Germany
FRY	Federal Republic of Yugoslavia
GA	General Assembly
GDR	German Democratic Republic
Gen.	General
Harv. HRLJ	Harvard Human Rights Law Journal
HRRS	Höchstrichterliche Rechtsprechung-Strafrecht
IACL	International Association of Criminal Law
ICC	International Criminal Court
ICCPR	International Covenant on Civil and Political Rights
ICCSt	Rome Statute for the International Criminal Court
ICJ	International Court of Justice
ICLR	International Criminal Law Review
ICLQ	International and Comparative Law Quarterly
ICTR	International Criminal Tribunal for Rwanda
ICTY	International Criminal Tribunal for the Former Yugoslavia
ICWC	International Research and Documentation Centre for War Crimes Trials
IDF	Israel Defence Forces
IGC	Intergovernmental Committee on Refugees
ILC	International Law Commission
ILC Yearbook	Yearbook of the International Law Commission

ILM	International Legal Materials
IMT	International Military Tribunal
IRA	Irish Republican Army
JAG	Judge Advocate General
JCE	Joint Criminal Enterprise
JICJ	Journal of International Criminal Justice
JuS	Juristische Schulung
LeidenJIL	Leiden Journal of International Law
Lt.	Lieutenant
MDR	Monatsschrift für Deutsches Recht
MK	Münchener Kommentar Strafgesetzbuch
MLR	Modern Law Review
n.d.	no date
New Eng. L. Rev.	New England Law Review
NGO	Non-Governmental Organisation
NJW	Neue Juristische Wochenschrift
NSDAP	Nationalsozialistische Deutsche Arbeiterpartei
OGHBrZ	Oberster Gerichtshof für die Britische Zone
OMGUS	Office of Military Government for Germany
OSS	Office of Strategic Services
PLO	Palestine Liberation Organisation
POW	Prisoner of War
RGC-UN Agreement	Royal Government of Cambodia – United Nations Agreement
RSHA	Reichssicherheitshauptamt
RTLM	Radio Télévision Libre des Mille Collines
SBZ	Sowjetisch besetzte Zone
SD	Sicherheitsdienst (der SS)
SPD	Sozialdemokratische Partei Deutschlands
SS	Schutzstaffel
StGB	Strafgesetzbuch
UN	United Nations
UNCHR	United Nations Commission on Human Rights
UNSC	United Nations Security Council
UNTS	United Nations Treaty Series
UNWCC	United Nations War Crimes Commission
USLW	United States Law Week
USSR	Union of Soviet Socialist Republics
VRS	Vojska Republike Srpske (Bosnian Serb Army)
WRB	War Refugee Board
WWI	World War I
WWII	World War II
YaleLJ	Yale Law Journal
YBIHL	Yearbook of International Humanitarian Law
ZIS	Zeitschrift für Internationale Strafrechtsdogmatik
ZStW	Zeitschrift für die gesamte Strafrechtswissenschaft

Introduction

THE GENOCIDE CONVENTION SIXTY YEARS AFTER ITS ADOPTION

Christoph Safferling and Eckart Conze

On 9 December 1948, the General Assembly of the United Nations adopted one of its most important documents: the 'Convention on the Prevention and Punishment of the Crime of Genocide' (so-called 'Genocide Convention'),[1] fulfilling the promise given two years earlier by Resolution 96(1).[2] In the immediate aftermath of the Second World War as the greatest catastrophe of civilisation, the adoption of this convention marked a new beginning in that it formulated an international crime

> 'involving a denial of the right of existence of entire human groups, a denial which shocks the conscience of mankind and results in great losses to humanity, and which is contrary to moral law and to the spirit and aims of the United Nations (Resolution 96(1) of the General Assembly, December 11th 1946).'[3]

The Convention thus formulated a criminal norm which would be applicable to individual persons even if they acted in an official capacity (Art. IV of the Genocide Convention), and created an international obligation which would trigger state responsibility in the case of a violation by a state (Art. IX of the Genocide Convention). Despite its groundbreaking contents, this convention did not gain much practical importance for more than 50 years, as there was no mechanism established which would help executing the Convention even against heads of state. In the absence of an international criminal court, which Article VI of the Genocide Convention did envisage, state ordered genocide could only be prosecuted after a change in regime by revolution or after a military prostration by the victors.[4] Nevertheless,

---

[1] Adopted by Res. 260(III)A of the United Nations General Assembly on 9 December 1948.

[2] UN GA Res. 96(1) of 11 December 1946, headed 'The Crime of Genocide,' in which the Member States were invited to 'enact the necessary legislation for the prevention and punishment of the crime' and requested the Economic and Social Council to prepare a draft convention. This resolution was voted on immediately after the adoption of the so-called Nürnberg Principles by GA Resolution 95(1): 'Affirmation of the Principles of International Law recognized by the Charter of the Nürnberg Tribunal.'

[3] ICJ, *Reservations to the Convention on the Prevention and Punishment of the Crime of Genocide*, Advisory Opinion, Reports 1951, p. 23.

[4] Alfred Verdross & Bruno Simma, *Universelles Völkerrecht* [Universal Public International Law], 3rd edn. (Berlin, Duncker & Humblot 1984), para. 433.

C. Safferling and E. Conze (eds.), The Genocide Convention Sixty Years after its Adoption

the Genocide Convention gained an immense moral force and reminded the international community of its imperfection with regard to international law.

It was only after the end of the 'Cold War' in the early 1990s that the practical implications of the Genocide Convention boosted. The International Criminal Tribunal for the Former Yugoslavia,[5] established by the UN Security Council in the wake of the segregation of the former Yugoslavia, applied the criminal norm of genocide according to the Statute of the ICTY, which for its part is a verbatim citation of the Genocide Convention, in one of its first decisions in the case against Karadzić and Mladić, confirming, among others, counts of genocide in a decision pursuant to Rule 61.[6] Two years later, the International Criminal Tribunal for Rwanda[7] issued the first conviction on the grounds of genocide in the case against Akayesu.[8] At around the same time, Bosnia-Herzegovina invoked the ICJ charging Serbia and Montenegro with violations of the Genocide Convention.[9]

Fifty years after its adoption, the Genocide Convention has arrived at the top of the ladder: it is one of the few international conventions which is not only executable through the ICJ, but is also applied by international criminal tribunals holding individuals responsible for its violations. *Sixty* years after the adoption of this eventually successful document, it is high time to take a critical look and reflect not only on the successes but also on the failures.

It is the aim of this book to combine different approaches in one volume. At first, there is the legal approach. As the Genocide Convention is a legal document, lawyers mostly discuss the difficulties in applying the norm. But also lawyers take different approaches. The practitioner, who has a certain case to handle, will urge for a practicable method in applying the criminal norm of genocide. A legal scholar will focus more on a systematic approach and aim to develop a concise concept of genocide on a theoretical basis. Furthermore, we need to differentiate between the criminal norm of genocide and the public international norm – individual responsibility is conceptually different from state responsibility.

Secondly, there is the historical analysis. The history of the UN Genocide Convention is not limited to its precedent history, its genesis and the history of its application alone. Indeed, it goes beyond the history of international law and even legal history as such. The present volume can merely hint at this fact; however, by means of the contributions with historical viewpoints, it aims at underlining the importance of this topic and shedding some light on its various dimensions.

Thirdly, social sciences analyse the coming about of situations in which genocide can erupt and which role the legal concept can play in preventing such eruption

---

[5] Hereinafter, ICTY.

[6] ICTY, Review of the indictment pursuant to Rule 61 of the Rules of Procedure and Evicende, *Karadzic* and *Mladic*, 11 July 1996, Case No. IT-95-5-R61 and IT-95-18-R61.

[7] Hereinafter, ICTR.

[8] ICTR, *Prosecutor* v. *Akayesu*, ICTR-96-4-T, 2 September 1998.

[9] The application on behalf of Bosnia and Herzegovina dates 20 March 1993, see ICJ, *Application of the Convention on the Prevention and Punishment of the Crime of Genocide*, Preliminary Objections, Judgment, 11 July 1996, Reports 1996, p. 595.

or healing the wounds in the aftermath of genocide. Political sciences deal with the importance of the term genocide in international relations.

We have compiled a set of 22 authors from different backgrounds and traditions, in order to take a look onto the Genocide Convention from the different angles outlined above.

I. Legal remarks

In the context of international criminal law, the crime of genocide now takes a central role. Not only does it take the first place in the list of Article 5(1) of the Rome Statute for the International Criminal Court,[10] it is also called the 'crime of all crimes' both by scholars[11] and courts:[12]

> 'The Chamber holds that crimes against humanity, already punished by the Nuremberg and Tokyo Tribunals, and genocide, a concept defined later, are crimes which particularly shock the collective conscience.'[13]

It has thus taken the place of the crime of aggression, which in the Nuremberg IMT was considered the 'crime of all crimes.' According to the Nuremberg chief-prosecutor Justice Robert H. Jackson:

> '... to start or wage an aggressive war has the moral qualities of the worst of crimes.'[14]

Likewise, the International Military Tribunal held in its judgment that

> '[t]o initiate a war of aggression, therefore, is not only an international crime; it is the supreme international crime differing only from other war crimes in that it contains within itself the accumulated evil of the whole.'[15]

Genocide as a crime was, despite all the efforts of Raphael Lemkin, who is often called the father of the Genocide Convention and who was at times a member in the

---

[10] Hereinafter, ICCSt.

[11] Barbara Lüders, *Die Strafbarkeit von Völkermord nach dem Römischen Statut für den IStGH* [The Crime of Genocide according to the Rome Statute for the ICC] (Berlin, Berliner Wissenschaftsverlag 2004), p. 263; Robert Cryer, Hakan Friman, Darryl Robinson & Elisabeth Wilmshurst, *An Introduction to International Criminal Law and Procedure* (Cambridge, Cambridge University Press 2007), p. 165; Hans Vest, *Gerechtigkeit für Humanitätsverbrechen?* [Justice for Crimes against Humanity?] (Tübingen, Mohr Siebeck 2006), p. 143;

[12] ICTR, *Prosecutor* v. *Kambanda*, Case ICTR-97-23-S, 4 September 1998, para. 16; *Prosecutor* v. *Serashugo*, ICTR-98-39-S, 2 February 1999, para. 15.

[13] ICTR, *Prosecutor* v. *Kambanda*, ibid., para. 14.

[14] Robert H. Jackson in his Opening Address given at Nuremberg on 21 November 1945; IMT Nuremberg, *Trial of the Major War Criminals*, Vol. 2 (1947), p. 155.

[15] IMT Nuremberg, Vol. 1 (1947), p. 186.

US prosecution team at Nuremberg, neither mentioned in the Statute of the International Military Tribunal nor in the Nuremberg judgment. The term, having been discussed in other incidents like the Armenian genocide,[16] does however appear in the indictment at Nuremberg, though not as an independent criminal norm, but rather as a part of war crimes in occupied territories according to Article 6(b) of the IMT Statute:

> 'They [i.e., the armed forces] conducted deliberate and systematic genocide, viz., the extermination of racial and national groups, against the civilian populations of certain occupied territories in order to destroy particular races and classes of people and national, racial, or religious groups, particularly Jews, Poles, and Gypsies and others.'[17]

It is interesting to note that the crime of genocide experienced a rather steep career as an international norm, accepted as a customary rule[18] and even as *ius cogens*,[19] and *erga omnes* obligation,[20] after the adoption of the Genocide Convention in 1948, while at the same time states could not, and still cannot, agree on a proper definition of the crime of aggression.[21] The focus in the perception and the remembrance of the Second World War has shifted from the aggressive war of Nazi-Germany to the 'final solution' and the Holocaust. Maybe it was even the very lack of the Nuremberg Trial to put the systematic destruction of Jews, Sinti and other minorities, organised by the Nazi-regime in Auschwitz and dozens of other concentration camps all over Europe, at the heart of the criminal prosecution of those who were responsible, which fuelled international efforts to define a special crime which could cover such systematic extermination. Indeed, the criminal norm called 'genocide' was modelled *ex post* in order to cover the Holocaust;[22] in that sense it was drafted in a backwards-looking attitude rather than with a view to future cases. Given these historic circumstances, the ICTR Trial Chamber produced a circular argument when stating:

> 'The Chamber notes in this regard that the crimes prosecuted by the Nuremberg Tribunal, namely the holocaust of the Jews or the "Final Solution," were very much constitutive of genocide …'[23]

---

[16] See, e.g., Boris Barth, *Genozid* [Genocide] (Munich, C.H. Beck 2006), pp. 62-77.

[17] IMT Nuremberg, Vol. 1 (1947), p. 43.

[18] See ICJ, Case concerning application of the Convention on the Prevention and Punishment of the Crime of Genocide (*Bosnia and Herzegovina* v. *Yugoslavia (Serbia and Montenegro)*), 26 February 2007, para. 161.

[19] ICJ, *Reservations to the Convention on the Prevention and Punishment of the Crime of Genocide*, Advisory Opinion, Reports 1951, p. 23: the principles underlying the convention are 'binding on States, even without any conventional obligation.' See also Bernhard Kempen & Christian Hillgruber, *Völkerrecht* [Public International Law] (Munich, C.H. Beck 2007), § 10, MNs 2 et seq.

[20] ICJ, Case concerning the Barcelona Traction, Light, and Power Company, Limited (*Belgium* v. *Spain*), 5 February 1970, para. 34.

[21] Despite attempts as in General Assembly Resolution 3314 (XXIX) of 14 December 1974.

[22] B. Barth, *supra* n. 16, p. 14.

[23] ICTR, *Prosecutor* v. *Kambanda*, *supra* n. 12, para. 14.

The legal term of genocide still suffers from this historical role model. Modern tribunals find it difficult to apply the norm to individual cases. This is mainly because of two flaws in the formulation of the Genocide Convention: Firstly, the crime of genocide is restricted as concerns the victim-side. It only pertains to 'national, ethnical, racial or religious groups as such.' The approach taken by the Genocide Convention is thus much narrower than the one laid down in GA Resolution 96(1) of 11 December 1946, which speaks of 'racial, religious, political and other groups.'

Secondly, the special intent requirement, i.e., the intent to destroy a protected group in whole or in part, is both too wide and too narrow. On the one hand, it comprises an individual perpetrator acting on his own, even if his wish to destroy even part of the group is highly unrealistic; on the other, it establishes a subjective element which is often difficult to prove, particularly for high-ranking leaders.

The operability of the norm is further blurred by the fact that 'genocide' has also become a political term. Accusations of genocidal conduct are often used in the political debate on the international level, where legal parameters and general principles of criminal law do not matter.[24]

II. Historical remarks

After the adoption of the Genocide Convention on 9 December 1948, it took 50 years until on 2 September 1998 the International Criminal Tribunal for Rwanda, in the *Akayesu* case, handed down the first international judgment that was legally based on the Convention; indeed, Jean Paul Akayesu was the first person prosecuted for genocide by an international tribunal in history. This fact, however, should not lead to the conclusion that the Genocide Convention between 1948 and 1998 did not play a distinctive role in the practice of international law, in international politics and also within national states and societies.

The precedent history and genesis of the UN Genocide Convention have been thoroughly analysed in the past few years. The focus of research lay, on the one hand, predominantly on the significance of the First World War as marking an historical turning point. On the other, the emergence of the Genocide Convention was discussed as a topic of international politics in the years around 1945, above all in the context of the United Nations. In connection with the First World War and the attempt to implement a stable international post-war order, the importance of protecting national minorities was emphasised. As early as May 1915, the Turkish genocide of the Armenians, which claimed hundreds of thousands of victims in the years between 1915 and 1918, evoked a joint declaration by the governments of Great Britain, France and Russia, condemning the 'new crimes of Turkey against humanity and civilization' and announcing that they would 'hold personally re-

24 See also the contribution of Stefan Kirsch in this volume, who rightly differentiates between the 'social' and the 'legal' concept of genocide.

sponsible for the said crimes all members of the Ottoman Government as well as those of its agents who are found to be involved in such massacres.'[25]

The end of the war and the imperative of the right to self-determination of peoples, which dominated the debates at the Paris Peace Conference and also determined the national and territorial re-shaping of Eastern Central as well as South Eastern Europe, increased the need for the protection of national and ethnical minorities even more. The principle of ethnically homogenous national states, which was predominant during the inter-war years, as well as the frequent persecution of national and ethnical minorities gained international legal relevance insofar as they led to a number of international treaties for the protection of national minorities; these treaties, however, did not provide effective protection in most cases. There was no mechanism for sanctions in case of their violation, even though in 1937 the League of Nations, which the German Empire had already left by then, passed a convention on the creation of an international criminal court. The failure to create an effective protection of national minorities was certainly one of the basic motivations of *Raphael Lemkin*, whose thoughts on the protection of human rights were fundamentally based on his experiences and reflections during the inter-war years.[26]

The initiative of the United Kingdom to hold an international trial for war crimes committed in the First World War, however, was not so much motivated by the will to prosecute the crimes of the Ottoman Empire (even though the treaty of Sèvres of 10 August 1920 did contain provisions concerning this matter), but rather by the attempt to hold responsible German soldiers and civilians suspected of having committed war crimes, and place them before allied military courts or even an international tribunal, as envisaged by Articles 228 and 229 of the Versailles Treaty. The proximity of these provisions to the famous Article 231, by which, in connection with the provisions concerning reparations, the sole responsibility for the war was imposed upon Germany, is quite telling. The Allies were more concerned with sanctioning Germany than with the implementation of a general international criminal jurisdiction. The project was, however, not successful. Since the Netherlands refused to extradite Emperor William II, and also because the Allied and Germany soon agreed that German war crimes suspects should be tried before the Supreme Court of the German Empire in Leipzig instead, the establishment of an international criminal tribunal did not take place. In the Leipzig Trials of 1921 and 1922, however, while originally a number of about 900 defendants had been envisaged by the Allies, in the end only 17 persons stood trial, of which only ten were convicted and sentenced to imprisonment.[27]

---

[25] Cited according to W.A. Schabas, *Genocide in International Law: The Crime of Crimes* (Cambridge, Cambridge University Press 2000), p. 16.

[26] Ibid., pp. 22 et seq.

[27] See on the Leipzig Trials in general Gerd Hankel, *Die Leipziger Prozesse. Deutsche Kriegsverbrechen und ihre strafrechtliche Verfolgung nach dem Ersten Weltkrieg* [The Leipzig Trials. German War Crimes and their Criminal Prosecution after the First World War] (Hamburg, Hamburger edition 2003); see also Gerd Hankel, 'Verleugnung oder Auseinandersetzung? Zum Umgang mit Völkermord und staatlichen Gewaltverbrechen', in V. Radkau, et al. (eds.), *Genozide und staatliche Gewaltverbrechen im 20. Jahrhundert* [Genocide and State Crimes in the 20th Century] (Vienna, StudienVerlag 2004), pp. 40-51.

Finally, the importance of National Socialism and its crimes for the emergence of the Genocide Convention cannot be overestimated. In view of the Nazi crimes, whose magnitude became increasingly apparent as the war went on, the international efforts to effectively prosecute war crimes and crimes against humanity, a term which shifted more and more towards the centre of reflections concerning international law and international politics, were intensified. The more clearly the eventual German defeat became obvious, starting with the turn of the years 1942/43, the more intensive the efforts to prosecute and punish those responsible for the crimes became.

III. The legal and historical reflections

III.1 Historical development and public policy considerations

Part One of the book addresses historical issues concerning the Genocide Convention. At the outset, *William A. Schabas* gives an overview of the historical development of the Convention from the Second World War to its adoption and discusses critically whether the importance attributed to the 1948 Convention really ever existed or still exists. Schabas makes a case arguing that the disappointment about the judgment at Nuremberg, as the extermination of the European Jews was not accepted by the judges as constituting a genuine crime (against humanity), was the driving force and personal motivation for Lemkin to canvass for the adoption of a new criminal norm called 'genocide.' The flaws of Nuremberg thus turn into developing an entirely new system of international crimes, separating persecution from war crimes. In this regard the Genocide Convention was an immense step forward and the acceptance of the national states to a certain extent buttressed the certainty of the law regarding mass atrocities. Yet today it seems that the importance of the crime of genocide has declined, as other concepts like the ICC have appeared on the international stage, putting genocide and crimes against humanity on the same footing. The only substantive difference between crimes against humanity and genocide now seems to be the accessibility to the ICJ by virtue of Article IX of the Genocide Convention.

John Barrett takes issue with Raphael Lemkin, the father of the Genocide Convention, in greater detail focusing in particular on his role in and around Nuremberg. Lemkin is described as a difficult personality, egoistic, obsessive and often enough an annoyance to many, who never managed to get into the inner circle of legal experts surrounding Justice Robert H. Jackson's team preparing the Nuremberg Trial. He remained an outsider, the 'unofficial.' Yet even if Lemkin crafted the word 'genocide,' the development of the crime of genocide depended on many more and also people like Murray Bernays, Sidney Alderman, Francis Shea, Robert Jackson and their many other allies and colleagues along the way contributed immensely to this process. In fact the indictment at Nuremberg was the first international document containing the term 'genocide.'

The genesis of the United Nations is strongly intertwined with the efforts to establish an international criminal jurisdiction. *Jost Dülffer* demonstrates in his contribution how indeed the emergence of the UN Genocide Convention and the genesis of the United Nations as such are intrinsically connected, and how therefore the Genocide Convention is also related to the development of international politics in the wake of the increasing tensions between the East and the West. Dülffer however states that one should not blame the Cold War alone for the difficulties in applying and enforcing the Genocide Convention. His paper also points to the tense relations between the world powers, particularly the United States and the Soviet Union, on the one hand, and the rest of the world on the other. These tensions are also reflected in the conflicts between the UN Security Council and the UN General Assembly. According to his argument, national interests of the world powers prevented better results. Not until 40 years after its adoption, in 1988, the United States ratified the Genocide Convention; and only in 1998 the International Criminal Court was established by the adoption of the Rome Statute.

The contribution of *Wolfgang Form* brings the developments on the level of international politics and of the international systems around the year of 1945 down to the individual states' strategies of criminal prosecution taking the United Kingdom as an example. He takes issue with the political – and moral – imperatives of the United Kingdom after 1945 and how they where implemented. He does so not only with a view to the International Military Tribunal in Nuremberg, but also with a view on the trials which were held by the British occupying power in its zone of occupation. The paper stresses the efforts to prosecute also Nazi perpetrators of the centre of society apart from the top Nazis in government, the Nazi Party, in the administration and the military. It also emphasises that the British – other than the American – occupying power transferred the responsibility to prosecute crimes against humanity onto German courts.

Herbert Reginbogin identifies as the greater problem the lack of moral outrage as a reaction to mass atrocities, which he sees as the primary aim of the UN Genocide Convention, compared to the undecidedness of the Convention in judicial terms often criticised by lawyers. After all, the Convention in all its ambiguity clearly calls for a moral outcry against state crimes. Indeed, Reginbogin sees in the moral failure of the international community of states with regards to the persecution of Jews in Germany even before the beginning of the war, which he exemplifies by looking at the Conference of Evian in 1938, an important condition for the political motivation to adopt the Genocide Convention in 1948.

In Part Two, several societal issues concerning genocide are addressed. The first paper by *Ulrich Wagner* and *Thorsten Bonacker* takes a socio-psychological approach. The contribution analyses intergroup behaviour, in particular the eruption of massive violence equal to genocide, and the influence of media exposure from a sociological point of view. In addition to this, the authors point out what implications for third party interventions in intergroup conflicts can be derived from their analysis. They argue in favour of an early intervention from the outside which should carefully integrate 'insiders,' i.e., local participants, into the healing process and take heed to the respective narratives and needs both of victims and perpetrators. Most prominently Wagner and Bonacker identify the communication process between the intervening third party and the antagonists of a conflict as indispensable for the peace building process. 'Outreach' thus becomes an indispensable feature in transitional justice processes.

Annette Weinke in her paper analyses the prosecution of Nazi perpetrators in Germany as it happened in the immediate post war period – the Nuremberg trial against the German major war criminals and its subsequent trial may stand as *pars pro toto* in this regard – and how it relates to the Germans' dealing with the past both in East and West. Following up on theses brought forward by David Cohen[28] she concludes that the West German society in particular was more critical towards its Nazi past and crimes, and was therefore in a position to deal with itself, as soon as the efforts to prosecute Nazi war criminals on the international level became less important. The shadows of 'Nuremberg' needed to fade, one could say, before Germany and the Germans were ready not only to remember the Nazi crimes, but also to question the political and social conditions and circumstances for these crimes to come about in the first place.[29] The contribution of Weinke therefore stands for the crucial question as to the impact of international criminal law measures in the context of transitional justice processes in a wide understanding. It calls implicitly for a differentiated analysis of external and internal factors in Transitional Justice processes and for a historical and sociological appraisal both of their interplay and their influences.

Treatises like the one at hand need to embrace the discursive level for their analysis in a systematic manner. This is shown in a slightly different context by the paper of the Israeli historian *Moshe Zimmermann*, who takes issue with the meaning both of the term 'genocide' and the Genocide Convention for society and politics in Israel. Zimmermann directs the reader's attention to the efforts of constructing the Genocide Convention and its aim as protecting solely and exclusively Jews from genocidal persecution. The 'Law Concerning the Prevention and Punishment of the Crime of Genocide' of 26 December 1949, which transformed the UN Genocide Convention into Israeli law, is of crucial importance in this context. Visibly not only in this law, but in the entire political discourse up until today, Jews would only be seen as potential victims of genocidal persecution and never as potential offenders. The author deals with the problems resulting from this approach by discussing the example of the latest inner-Israeli debates on the Arab-Israeli conflict and the dealing with the Arab population in the territories occupied by Israel.

The paper thereby also refers to the use of the term 'genocide' as a synonym for Holocaust, i.e., the homicide of the European Jews during the Second World War,

---

[28] David Cohen, 'Öffentliche Erinnerung und Kriegsverbrecherprozesse in Asien und Europa', in C. Cornelißen, et al. (eds.), *Erinnerungskulturen. Deutschland, Italien und Japan seit 1945 im Vergleich* [Cultures of Remembrance. Germany, Italy and Japan since 1945 in Comparison] (Frankfurt a.M., Fischer 2003), pp. 51-69.

[29] A similar argument is put forward by Donald Bloxham, *Genocide on Trial. War Crimes Trials and the Formation of Holocaust History and Memory* (Oxford, Oxford University Press 2003).

which implies a comparative perspective. But is the singularity of the Holocaust as a historic incident thereby not diminished? What does it mean, if not only the Holocaust as the extermination of Jews in Europe is named genocide, but if all historic genocides of different times and different places are more and more often named 'Holocaust'? The non differentiated use of the terms 'Holocaust' and 'genocide' is presumably unavoidable, taking into account the process of universalisation of the Holocaust and its implementation into the conscience of mankind, which we have observed over the last couple of decades.

However, this problem points at another question leading back to the Genocide Convention of 1948. The Nazi murder of the European Jews marks not only the historical background but also constitutes the substantive basis stemming from this very experience, for the deliberation, the drafting and the adoption of the Genocide Convention in the years following 1945. It is exactly this perspective which forms the UN Convention, and partially also its transformation into national laws. The development and legislation in Israel is but one example in this regard. In fact the question arises, whether and to what extent such a perspective, which is so strongly determined historically, exacerbates the application of the Convention to different cases and different circumstances. Israel is only one example alongside many other different national settings and substantially different macro-crimes which question the effects of such a distinct historical positioning of the Genocide Convention. Does for example the 'intent to destroy' according to Article II of the Genocide Convention comprise all the different possibilities of genocidal conduct? In over six decades of research into National Socialism and into the Holocaust, and of controversial debates, the international historical science has dealt extensively with the question of intentionality, and has differentiated, maybe even diminished, the assumption of an individually imputable, indeed a premeditated, intent for conducting Nazi crimes and the murdering of the Jews in particular.

Crimes against humanity and genocides which were committed since 1945, prove that the Holocaust is but one possible manifestation of the crime of genocide. Moreover, historical research in National Socialism and its crimes exact today a new – and always different – look at the genesis, the execution and the offenders of genocides. A historical view is therefore unavoidable for a serious discussion of the relevance and the application of the UN Genocide Convention in public international and international criminal law at the beginning of the 21st century, as it is for the dealing of the international community with genocide and state-crimes in general, both in political and in legal terms.

III.2 **Legal issues**

After these historical and public policy considerations, the legal term of 'genocide' is made an issue in Part Three, and several difficulties in the interpretation and application of the crime of genocide in international criminal law are being discussed.

In the first paper by *Antonio Cassese*, the author discusses the perception of the policy element as a basic legal requirement for the notion of genocide in contemporary theory and practice. He concludes that the policy element, i.e., a general plan to destroy a protected group in whole or in part, is not a necessary requirement at least with regard to two categories of genocide, killing and causing bodily or mental harm, but to be a strong indicator and therefore serving the evidentiary examination of the situation at hand. With regard to the other three categories, inflicting destructive life conditions, birth prevention and forced transfer of children, however, the policy element is inherent in the criminal conduct.

The second paper by *Stefan Kirsch* points out the dire need for a precise qualification of the interplay between systematic and individual conduct pertaining to genocidal acts, and aims to clarify factual criteria in order to reach a uniform standard as set out by the ICJ. Both the 'ordinary' understanding of genocide, as well as the legal concept of genocide relate to macro phenomena. While the former seems obvious, only a proper analysis of the intent requirement of the crime of genocide, clearly reveals that genocide as a legal concept describes a systemic crime. Nevertheless, individual criminal responsibility for genocide cannot be determined by simply referring to the existence of a system of genocide or a genocidal campaign on its own.

Linked to the macro phenomenon of genocide is the question of how to deal with multi-perpetrator crimes. *Henning Radtke* examines the degrees of participation in genocidal acts according to Article 25 ICCSt and discusses the provision's ability to serve as an instrument to determine an actual qualitative differentiation. Despite the confusion about the many different forms of participating in genocide, the author underpins the need to define these as a prerequisite for proper sentencing in accordance with the principle of guilt.

The final paper by *Christoph Safferling* takes up the mental element requirement of the crime of genocide. The author stresses the importance of the special (genocidal) intent marking the main purpose of the criminal prohibition of genocide. This specific mental element can be derived from objective criteria and circumstances, but it must be shown that the perpetrator himself embraced a genocidal plan as a driving force behind his act in order to convict him of genocide.

III.3 **Case studies**

In Part Four, the focus lies on different situations amounting to genocide, which are or were being dealt with by international or internationalised tribunals. The first situation is that of Cambodia and the Khmer Rouge-regime. *Jürgen Assmann* deals with the numerous and severe obstacles of political, social and judicial nature faced by the Extraordinary Chambers in the Courts of Cambodia (ECCC), but nonetheless emphasises the importance and obligation of the ECCC to succeed in order to facilitate a new beginning for Cambodian justice.

The International Criminal Court (ICC) was established only a few years ago and has not yet dealt with a case of genocide. Judge *Hans-Peter Kaul* elaborates on the provisions of the Rome Statute for the International Criminal Court (ICCSt) and their legal scope regarding genocide, as well as their practical application in the exemplified Darfur situation. Furthermore, his contribution acknowledges a clear impact of the inclusion of genocide in the ICCSt on national jurisdictions.

The ICTY and the ICTR have already handed down several convictions for the crime of genocide. The jurisprudence of the UN tribunals thus deserves particular attention. *Matthias Schuster* approaches the legal problems revolving around the special intent requirement by evaluating the recent judicature of the *ad hoc* tribunals, in particular on the jurisprudence of the Appeals Chamber common to the ICTY and the ICTR. Judge *Inés Weinberg de Roca* and *Margaret Patten Knowlan* present three case studies from her own experience as a judge at the ICTR, showing the manifold facets of personal background and human conduct pertaining to the genocide which took place in Rwanda in 1994.

III.4 Genocide and the International Court of Justice

In Part Five we turn to the implications the Genocide Convention has for public international law, namely for state responsibility and human rights law. The main focus of the two papers contained in this part lies on the latest judgment of the International Court of Justice (ICJ) in the *Bosnian Genocide* case of 2007, which was the first decision of the ICJ rendering a comprehensive substantive decision on the prohibition of genocide. *Anja Seibert-Fohr* discusses whether or not the ICJ has jurisdiction regarding the crime of genocide, and offers a response to the negation of the concept of state responsibility. The author criticises the restrictive approach taken by the ICJ in that it has factually applied criminal law standards to a case of state responsibility, and makes a case for a broader understanding of state responsibility.

Judge *Bruno Simma* analyses the legal findings of the ICJ's 2007 judgment and its repercussion in international law regarding the perception of genocide. Similar to the paper before, Judge Simma would have preferred a more innovative approach linking the Genocide Convention more directly to the 'responsibility to protect'-requirement in modern human rights law. The ICJ will soon have the opportunity to further refine the approach taken in the *Bosnian* case, as it has just admitted a case of Croatia brought against Serbia claiming violation of the Genocide Convention.

IV. Historic cases: contemporary witnesses

In the final Part Six of the book we present three voices from contemporary witnesses who took active part in spectacular cases against different Nazi war criminals. The first is by *Gabriel Bach*, who speaks about the trials of Eichmann and of Demjanjuk in Israel. He sees the main achievement of the Eichmann trial in that it triggered the prosecution of Nazi crimes in Germany and other countries, and brought the Holocaust to public attention in Israel and elsewhere. The former Eichmann prosecutor also stresses the difficulties of the trials in particular with regard to the availability of evidence decades after the committal of the crimes.

One of the trials that were an immediate follow-up of the Eichmann trial was the so-called 'Auschwitz-Trial' in Germany. *Heinz Düx*, former investigative judge in this trial which took place in Frankfurt/Main, describes the difficulties he had in prosecuting this case against several concentration camp guards, and complains of a lack of support on the side of the Federal Government. His report is a perfect practical example of how difficult *Vergangenheitsbewältigung* in Germany was.

The final address is by *Whitney Harris*, former prosecutor in the Nuremberg Trial against the major Nazi war criminals. He describes the road to the first international criminal trial and the many practical problems which needed to be solved in organizing the prosecution. As a particular turning point in the ten months of trial at Nuremberg, the author identifies the testimony of Otto Ohlendorf, chief of *Einsatzgruppe A*, admitting the killing of 90,000 Jews in the year 1941, and the testimony of Rudolph Höss, commander of Auschwitz concentration camp, on the murder of two and a half million Jews in Auschwitz. Despite its general focus on the crime of aggression, it was in situations like these that the genocide organised by the Nazis was documented in the records of the trial at Nuremberg.

V. Future prospects

It is most obvious that a volume like the one at hand cannot cover all aspects of the Genocide Convention, its historical roots, its implications for today and its future prospects. This book nevertheless hopefully contributes to the future discourse on the controversial concept of the crime of genocide and encourages interdisciplinary approaches and debates on the issue which are, in our humble view, yet underdeveloped.

We consider it a privilege having been in a position to invite contemporary witnesses to contribute to our discussion. After all, to commemorate and learn takes a key position in the struggle both for reconciliation and prevention.

Part One
Historical Development

GENOCIDE IN INTERNATIONAL LAW AND INTERNATIONAL RELATIONS PRIOR TO 1948

William A. Schabas

'The blackest day of my life' is how Raphael Lemkin described the delivery of the verdict in the Nuremberg trial.[1] War crimes prosecutor Henry T. King Jr., who met Lemkin in the lobby of Nuremberg's Grand Hotel at the beginning of October 1946, described him as 'very upset.'[2] 'At the time, Lemkin was unshaven, his clothing was in tatters, and he looked dishevelled.'[3] According to King:

> 'When I saw him at Nuremberg, Lemkin was very upset. He was concerned that the decision of the International Military Tribunal (IMT) – the Nuremberg Court – did not go far enough in dealing with genocidal actions. This was because the IMT limited its judgment to wartime genocide and did not include peacetime genocide. At that time, Lemkin was very focussed on pushing his points. After he had buttonholed me several times, I had to tell him that I was powerless to do anything about the limitation in the Court's judgment.'[4]

Lemkin had recently learned that essentially his entire family had perished, victims of the crime to which he had given its name. He had been hospitalised in Paris,[5] and was evidently going through a period of great physical and emotional turmoil. According to biographer John Cooper, from his hospital bed 'he happened to hear on the radio about the forthcoming meeting of the General Assembly of the United Nations in New York' and was 'electrified by the news, believing that here at last was a forum which would listen to him.'[6] He organised a passage on a troop transport back to New York, and went immediately to the General Assembly, then meeting in a disused factory in Lake Success, on Long Island, in the suburbs of New York City.

---

[1] W. Korey, *An Epitaph for Raphael Lemkin* (New York, Jacob Blaustein Institute for the Advancement of Human Rights 2001), p. 25.

[2] H.T. King Jr., 'Origins of the Genocide Convention', 40 *Case Western Reserve Journal of International Law* (2008), p. 13.

[3] *Idem.*

[4] Ibid., at pp. 13-14.

[5] J. Cooper, *Raphael Lemkin and the Struggle for the Genocide Convention* (Basingstoke, United Kingdom, Palgrave Macmillan 2008), p. 73.

[6] Ibid., pp. 74-75.

C. Safferling and E. Conze (eds.), The Genocide Convention Sixty Years after its Adoption

Lemkin launched a campaign at what was the first session of the United Nations General Assembly that led to the adoption of a resolution to condemn genocide as an international crime.[7] Two years earlier, in his seminal book *Axis Rule in Occupied Europe*, he had lamented the shortcomings of existing international law, and called for the recognition of a new crime, to which he gave the name 'genocide.' 'New conceptions require new terms,' explained Lemkin. 'Genocide' referred to the destruction of a nation or of an ethnic group, he explained, describing it as 'an old practice in its modern development.'[8] At the General Assembly, Lemkin quickly obtained the support of three delegations, India, Cuba and Panama, for a proposed resolution on genocide that he had drafted.[9] Explaining why the resolution was necessary, the Cuban delegate, Ernesto Dihigo, said it was to address a shortcoming in the Nuremberg trial by which acts committed prior to the war were left unpunished.[10] Nazi atrocities had been prosecuted at Nuremberg under the heading 'crimes against humanity,' and this concept was applied by the International Military Tribunal so that it applied only to acts perpetrated subsequent to the outbreak of the conflict, in September 1939, in other words, to 'wartime genocide' but not 'peacetime genocide,' as Henry King reported.

One of the preambular paragraphs in the draft resolution stated:

> 'Whereas the punishment of the very serious crime of genocide when committed in time of peace lies within the exclusive territorial jurisdiction of the judiciary of every State concerned, while crimes of a relatively lesser importance such as piracy, trade in women, children, drugs, obscene publications are declared as international crimes and have been made matters of international concern …'[11]

This paragraph never made it to the final version of Resolution 96(I) because the majority of the General Assembly was not prepared to recognise universal jurisdiction for the crime of genocide. Nevertheless, the resolution, somewhat toned down from the text that Lemkin had prepared, launched a process that concluded two years later with the adoption of the Convention on the Prevention and Punishment of the Crime of Genocide.[12]

Thus, the recognition of genocide as an international crime by the General Assembly of the United Nations, and its codification in the 1948 Convention, can be understood as a reaction to the Nuremberg judgment of the International Military

---

[7] UN Doc. A/RES/1/96(I), 11 December 1946.

[8] R. Lemkin, *Axis Rule in Occupied Europe: Laws of Occupation, Analysis of Government, Proposals for Redress* (Washington, Carnegie Endowment for World Peace 1944), p. 79.

[9] J. Cooper, *supra* n. 5, pp. 76-87. For Lemkin's account, see R. Lemkin, 'Totally Unofficial Man', in S. Totten & S.L. Jacobs (eds.), *Pioneers of Genocide* Studies (New Brunswick, Transaction Publishers 2002), pp. 365-399 at pp. 384-387. Also S. Power, *A Problem from Hell: America and the Age of Genocide* (New York, Basic Books 2002), pp. 51-54.

[10] UN Doc. A/C.6/SR.22.

[11] UN Doc. A/BUR/50.

[12] *Convention on the Prevention and Punishment of the Crime of Genocide* (1951), 78 *UNTS* p. 277.

Tribunal. It was Nuremberg's failure to recognise the international criminality of atrocities committed in peacetime that prompted the first initiatives at codifying the crime of genocide. Had Nuremberg recognised the reach of international criminal law into peacetime atrocities, we might never therefore have seen a Genocide Convention. Raphael Lemkin would probably be no more than an obscure and eccentric personality, as Henry King remembered him in the Grand Hotel in Nuremberg, rather than the distinguished 'Father of the Genocide Convention.'[13]

The Convention itself was adopted by the General Assembly on 9 December 1948. It can be described as the first human rights treaty of the modern area. A few hours later, the General Assembly adopted what is assuredly the centrepiece of modern international human rights law, the Universal Declaration of Human Rights.[14] Over the decades, the commemoration of the Genocide Convention has been overshadowed by that of the Universal Declaration. It is a bit like the child who has the misfortune to be born on 25 December, and who is forced to share his or her birthday with a much larger celebration. At the Palais de Chaillot in Paris, where the two instruments were adopted, there is a memorial plaque for the Universal Declaration but nothing for the Genocide Convention. That situation is being remedied in a few weeks, by French foreign minister Bernard Kouchner. Increasingly, the importance of the Genocide Convention is being acknowledged, not only in its own right as a source of important norms in international criminal law, but also as a defining text within the overall system of international human rights law. By insisting that 'peacetime genocide' be condemned as an international crime, the General Assembly took a giant step in the protection of human rights. It made the violation of the right to life or to existence of a national, ethnic, racial or religious minority both an internationally unlawful act and an international crime. It also proposed, in Article VI, the establishment of an international criminal court to ensure the enforcement of the Convention.

The Convention entered into force in 1951, but remained in obscurity for the next half-century. It may well have arrived ahead of its time, a vehicle for radical concepts in international law that the world could barely accept in the euphoria of the post-Second World War context, but that became unworkable during the Cold War. Only in the 1990s was there a renaissance in international criminal law. The result was a certain revival of the Genocide Convention, accompanied by recognition of its role at the origins of the system. The ideas and concepts conveyed by the Convention became more fully developed in newer and more modern institutions and instruments, like the International Criminal Tribunal for the former Yugoslavia and the Rome Statute of the International Criminal Court.

---

[13] The words are engraved on his tombstone in New York's Mount Hebron Cemetery.

[14] Universal Declaration of Human Rights, GA Res. 217A(III), UN Doc. A/810.

I. Human rights, the United Nations and the drive for war crimes prosecutions

There are many possible starting points for a discussion of the origins of the Genocide Convention. Each has its own ancestors, in such sources as the law of armed conflict, the international legal protection of refugees and national minorities, and the aborted efforts at international criminal justice in the aftermath of the First World War. They both share a common DNA that first becomes recognisable in the early years of the Second World War. Unlike the First World War, whose origins and whose *raison d'être* still remain clouded in the machiavellian wrangling, confusion and misunderstanding of aging empires committed to colonialism, the Second World War was an international struggle against barbarism, genocide, totalitarianism and national oppression. Tens of millions were roused to enormous sacrifice by the urgency of defeating fascism coupled with the promise of a new world order. The Second World War was associated with a moral authority its predecessor had lacked.

The Atlantic Charter, signed by the United Kingdom and the United States only a few months before the latter's entry into the war, contained human rights proclamations of a general nature.[15] It acknowledged the right of all peoples to choose the form of government under which they wished to live, called for 'improved labour standards, economic advancement, and social security,' and declared that all states should abandon the use of force.[16] The Atlantic Charter was agreed to by Roosevelt and Churchill aboard the British battleship Prince of Wales in Placentia Bay, just off the coast of Newfoundland. Earlier that year, in his state of the union address, Roosevelt had proclaimed that the post-war system would be built upon 'four essential human freedoms':

> 'The first is freedom of speech and expression – everywhere in the world.
> The second is freedom of every person to worship God in his own way – everywhere in the world.
> The third is freedom from want – which, translated into world terms, means economic understandings which will secure to every nation everywhere a healthy peacetime life for its inhabitants everywhere in the world.
> The fourth is freedom from fear – which, translated into international terms, means a world-wide reduction of armaments to such a point and in such a thorough fashion that no nation will be in a position to commit an act of physical aggression against any neighbour – anywhere in the world.'

---

[15] *Atlantic Charter*, [1942] CTS 1; signed on 14 August 1941 by Franklin D. Roosevelt and Winston Churchill (both signatures in the original are in Roosevelt's handwriting). No official version exists: *New Cambridge Modern History*, Vol. XII (Cambridge, Cambridge University Press 1968), pp. 811-812.

[16] On the role of the *Atlantic Charter* in the development of international human rights, see E. Borgwardt, *A New Deal for the World, America's Vision for Human Rights* (Cambridge and London, Harvard University Press 2005), pp. 14-45.

Franklin D. Roosevelt's stirring and immortal words were reprised in the preamble of the Universal Declaration of Human Rights:

> 'Whereas disregard and contempt for human rights have resulted in barbarous acts which have outraged the conscience of mankind, and the advent of a world in which human beings shall enjoy freedom of speech and belief and freedom from fear and want has been proclaimed as the highest aspiration of the common people.'[17]

As the war was drawing to a close, diplomats meeting in San Francisco adopted the Charter of the United Nations,[18] which placed unprecedented emphasis on human rights. The Charter provided several references to human rights, and declared that 'promoting and encouraging respect for human rights and for fundamental freedoms for all without distinction as to race, sex, language, or religion' was among the purposes of the United Nations. To the dismay of many, however, the great powers reneged on earlier commitments to include a declaration of human rights within the Charter itself. Well before the San Francisco Conference in June 1945, at which the United Nations Charter was adopted, foreign ministries, academics and non-governmental organisations were at work preparing draft declarations of human rights designed to form part of the post-war legal regime and, ideally, to be contained within the constitutive document of the new organisation.[19] The compromise at San Francisco was to make perfunctory references to human rights in the Charter but to postpone adoption of anything substantive. Moreover, a poisonous exception was also incorporated: in pursuit of the principles of the United Nations, nothing contained in the Charter authorised the United Nations 'to intervene in matters which are essentially within the domestic jurisdiction of any state.'[20] Three years later, a few hours after endorsing the text of the Genocide Convention, the United Nations General Assembly adopted the Universal Declaration on Human Rights, in effect completing the work it had left unfinished at San Francisco. During its third session, which was held in Paris from October to December 1948, distinct subsidiary bodies of the General Assembly had laboured over the two texts, the Third Committee crafting the Universal Declaration while the Sixth Committee prepared the Genocide Convention. Both instruments were focused, in different and complementary ways, on the prevention of atrocities committed by a state against its own civilian population.

---

[17] *Universal Declaration of Human Rights*, GA Res. 217A(III) UN Doc. A/810.

[18] *Charter of the United Nations* (1946) Cmd. 7015, P. (1946-1947) XXV 1, 145 *BFSP* 805.

[19] L.B. Sohn, 'How American International Lawyers Prepared for the San Francisco Bill of Rights', 89 *AJIL* (1995), p. 540; J. Morsink, 'World War Two and the Universal Declaration', 15 *Human Rights Quarterly* (1993), p. 357; H. Lauterpacht, *An International Bill of the Rights of Man* (New York, Columbia University Press 1945).

[20] *Charter of the United Nations*, Art. 2(7).

II. Crimes against humanity and the drafting of the 1948 Genocide Convention

When the text of the Genocide Convention was being negotiated in the Sixth Committee of the General Assembly, there was frequent controversy about the relationship between genocide and crimes against humanity, an issue provoked by the judgment of the International Military Tribunal at Nuremberg. The United Nations Secretariat had prepared a note addressing the relationship between genocide and crimes against humanity that insisted upon the utility of a distinct crime of genocide principally because it would enable avoidance of the *nexus* with armed conflict that had featured at Nuremberg.[21] There was considerable discussion as to whether genocide was an autonomous infraction or a form of crime against humanity. France put forward a rival draft convention. Article I of its text began by affirming that '[t]he crime against humanity known as genocide is an attack on the life of a human group or of an individual as a member of such group, particularly by reason of his nationality, race, religion or opinions.'[22] This was, of course, connected with the idea, included in the final version of Article I, that genocide was a crime that could be committed in time of peace or of war.[23] Brazil's representative to the Sixth Committee said that crimes against humanity, as defined in the Nuremberg Charter, did encompass genocide, but only to the extent they were committed during or in connection with the preparation of war. Genocide, however, had to be defined as a crime that could also be committed in time of peace.[24] The Brazilian delegate noted the confusion at Nuremberg about the scope of the term 'crimes against humanity' and said: 'In view of the vagueness about the concept of crimes against humanity, it would be well to define genocide as a separate crime committed against certain groups of human beings as such.'[25] The debate also arose in the context of the preamble. Venezuela submitted a draft preamble that it explained had omitted any reference to the Nuremberg Tribunal, as genocide was distinct from crimes against humanity.[26] France had its own proposals for the preamble, of which the most significant was addition of a reference to the Nuremberg judgment.[27] Ultimately, of

[21] 'Relations Between the Convention on Genocide on the one hand and the Formulation of the Nurnberg Principles and the Preparation of a Draft Code of Offences Against Peace and Security on the other, Note by the Secretariat', UN Doc. E/AC.25/3.

[22] UN Doc. A/C.6/211, Art. I. See also UN Doc. A/C.6/SR.67 (Chaumont, France). France had been concerned that its own proposal would be forgotten if the Committee studied the *ad hoc* Committee draft. The chair assured the French representative that this was not the case: UN Doc. A/C.6/SR.66 (Alfaro (chair)).

[23] See, e.g., the following comments: UN Doc. A/C.6/SR.67 (Morozov, Soviet Union); and UN Doc. A/C.6/SR.68 (de Beus, Netherlands).

[24] UN Doc. A/C.6/SR.63 (Amado, Brazil).

[25] *Idem.*

[26] UN Doc. A/C.6/SR.109.

[27] UN Doc. A/C.6/267. '3. Substitute the following for the third sub-paragraph: "Having taken note of the legal precedent established by the judgment of the International Military Tribunal at Nürnberg of 30 September-1 October 1946."' The Soviet preamble, UN Doc. A/C.6/215/Rev.1, included a similar paragraph: 'Having taken note of the fact that the International Military Tribunal at Nuernberg in its

course, no allusion either to Nuremberg or to crimes against humanity was incorporated in the final text of the Convention, which was adopted by the General Assembly on 9 December 1948.

The Genocide Convention represents an attempt to provide a prospective definition of the crimes addressed at Nuremberg, but using different terminology. Necessarily, it is the result of compromises. The Nuremberg precedent, by which crimes against humanity did not apply to peacetime atrocities, was no aberration or oversight. Rather, it was a carefully conceived legal formulation aimed at addressing Nazi atrocities that were previously beyond the pale of international law, without at the same time threatening those who established the tribunal. These same great powers were prepared to agree to prosecution of peacetime atrocities only if they were defined much more narrowly than in the Charter of the International Military Tribunal. In other words, the Nuremberg definition of crimes against humanity covers a relatively broad range of acts, but only to the extent they are associated with aggressive war, while the *Genocide Convention* covers a much narrower set of acts, although these may take place in peacetime.

In the beginning, however, it seems that the terms genocide and crimes against humanity were used as if they were synonyms. Within months of publication of *Axis Rule in Occupied Europe* in November 1944, Lemkin's neologism was being widely used to refer to Nazi atrocities. There are several references to it in the record of the London Conference and the proceedings. In his 'Planning Memorandum distributed to Delegations at Beginning of London Conference, June 1945,' Justice Robert Jackson outlined the evidence he planned to adduce in the trial. Referring to 'Proof of the defendant's atrocities and other crimes,' he included: 'Genocide or destruction of racial minorities and subjugated populations by such means and methods as (1) underfeeding; (2) sterilization and castration; (3) depriving them of clothing, shelter, fuel, sanitation, medical care; (4) deporting them for forced labour; (5) working them in inhumane conditions.'[28] The indictment of the International Military Tribunal charged the Nazi defendants with 'deliberate and systematic genocide, viz., the extermination of racial and national groups, against the civilian populations of certain occupied territories in order to destroy particular races and classes of people, and national, racial or religious groups, particularly Jews, Poles, and Gypsies.'[29] The United Nations War Crimes Commission later observed that '[b]y inclusion of this specific charge the Prosecution attempted to introduce and to establish a new type of international crime.'[30] During the trial, Sir David Maxwell-Fyfe, the British prosecutor, reminded one of the accused, Von Neurath, that he had been charged with genocide, 'which we say is the extermination of racial and na-

judgments of 30 September-1 October 1946 has punished under a different legal description certain persons who have committed acts similar to those which the present Convention aims at punishing.'

[28] *Report of Robert H. Jackson, United States Representative to the International Conference on Military Trials* (Washington, US Government Printing Office 1949), p. 6.

[29] *France, et al.* v. *Goering, et al.*, 22 IMT 203 (1946), pp. 45-46.

[30] United Nations War Crimes Commission, *History of the United Nations War Crimes Commission and the Development of the Laws of War* (London, His Majesty's Stationery Office 1948), p. 197.

tional groups, or, as it has been put in the well-known book of Professor Lemkin, 'a co-ordinated plan of different actions aiming at the destruction of essential foundations of the life of national groups with the aim of annihilating the groups themselves.'[31] In his closing argument, the French prosecutor, Champetier de Ribes, stated: 'This is a crime so monstrous, so undreamt of in history through the Christian era up to the birth of Hitlerism, that the term "genocide" had to be coined to define it.'[32] He spoke of 'the greatest crime of all, genocide.'[33] The British prosecutor, Sir Hartley Shawcross, also used the term in his summation: 'Genocide was not restricted to extermination of the Jewish people or of the gypsies. It was applied in different forms to Yugoslavia, to the non-German inhabitants of Alsace-Lorraine, to the people of the Low Countries and of Norway.'[34] Shawcross referred to how '[t]he aims of genocide were formulated by Hitler.'[35] He went on to explain: 'The Nazis also used various biological devices, as they have been called, to achieve genocide. They deliberately decreased the birth rate in the occupied countries by sterilization, castration, and abortion, by separating husband from wife and men from women and obstructing marriage.'[36] Although the final judgment in the Trial of the Major War Criminals, issued 30 September-1 October 1946, never used the term, it described at some length what was in fact the crime of genocide. Lemkin later wrote that '[t]he evidence produced at the Nuremberg trial gave full support to the concept of genocide.'[37]

But genocide was not, in fact, a crime under the Charter of the International Military Tribunal. Instead, what must at the time have been viewed as a cognate concept, crimes against humanity, formed the legal basis of prosecutions, along with 'crimes against peace' and 'war crimes.' After considerable debate, the drafters of the Charter had agreed to add crimes against humanity in order to fill an obvious gap in existing international law applicable to the Nazi atrocities, namely persecution of the civilian population *within* Germany. The efforts at definition of this new category of international crime reveal why the fabled *nexus* with armed conflict – limiting the tribunal's jurisdiction to 'wartime genocide' – was inserted into the crimes against humanity provision used at the Nuremberg trial.

In the Legal Committee of the United Nations War Crimes Commission, which met in 1944 and 1945, the United States representative Herbert C. Pell had used the term 'crimes against humanity' to describe offences 'committed against stateless persons or against any persons because of their race or religion.'[38] More frequently,

---

31 17 IMT (1947), p. 61.

32 19 IMT (1947), p. 531.

33 *Idem.*

34 Ibid., p. 497.

35 19 IMT (1947), p. 496.

36 Ibid., p. 498. Also, pp. 509, 514.

37 R. Lemkin, 'Genocide as a Crime in International Law', 41 *AJIL* (1947), p. 145 at p. 147.

38 'Resolution moved by Mr. Pell on 16th March 1944', United Nations War Crimes Commission, Committee II, Doc. III/1, 18 March 1944; United Nations War Crimes Commission, *supra* n. 30, p. 175; A.J. Kochavi, *Prelude to Nuremberg, Allied War Crimes Policy and the Question of Punishment* (Chapel Hill, and London, University of North Carolina Press 1998), p. 143.

the concept was described using terms like 'atrocity' and 'persecution.' In May 1944, the Legal Committee submitted a draft resolution to the plenary Commission urging it to adopt a broad view of its mandate, and to address 'crimes committed against any persons without regard to nationality, stateless persons included, because of race, nationality, religious or political belief, irrespective of where they have been committed.'[39] Lord Simon, who was the British Lord Chancellor, explained the problem this might pose for his government:

> 'This would open a very wide field. No doubt you have in mind particularly the atrocities committed against the Jews. I assume there is no doubt that the massacres which have occurred in occupied territories would come within the category of war crimes and there would be no question as to their being within the Commission's terms of reference. No doubt they are part of a policy which the Nazi Government have adopted from the outset, and I can fully understand the Commission wishing to receive and consider and report on evidence which threw light on what one might describe as the extermination policy. I think I can probably express the view of His Majesty's Government by saying that it would not desire the Commission to place any unnecessary restriction on the evidence which may be tendered to it on this general subject. I feel I should warn you, however, that the question of acts of this kind committed in enemy territory raises serious difficulties.'[40]

The United States Department of State was decidedly lukewarm to the idea that war crimes prosecutions might innovate and hold Germans accountable for crimes committed against minority groups within their own borders.[41] This was reminiscent of the position taken in 1919 by Robert Lansing and James Brown Scott as representatives of the United States during attempts to prosecute atrocities perpetrated during the First World War.[42]

Later in 1944 and in early 1945, the position of the major powers, including the United States, evolved. A draft from the United States government dated 16 May 1945, and developed during the San Francisco conference, provided for a tribunal with jurisdiction to try '[a]trocities and offences committed since 1933 in violation of any applicable provision of the domestic law of any of the parties or of [*sic*] Axis Power or satellite, including atrocities and persecutions on racial or religious grounds.'[43] At the London Conference, which began on 26 June 1945, the United

---

[39] United Nations War Crimes Commission, *History of the United Nations War Crimes Commission and the Development of the Laws of War* (London, His Majesty's Stationery Office 1948), p. 176.

[40] 'Correspondence Between the War Crimes Commission and HM Government in London Regarding the Punishment of Crimes Committed on Religious, Racial or Political Grounds', UNWCC Doc. C.78, 15 February 1945, National Archives of Canada RG-25, Vol. 3033, 4060-40C, Part Four.

[41] A.J. Kochavi, *supra* n. 38, p. 149. See also S. Aronson, 'Preparations for the Nuremberg Trial: The OSS, Charles Dworak, and the Holocaust', 12 *Holocaust & Genocide Studies* (1998), p. 257.

[42] *Violations of the Laws and Customs of War, Reports of Majority and Dissenting Reports of America and Japanese Members of the Commission of Responsibilities, Conference of Paris, 1919* (Oxford, Clarendon Press 1919).

[43] 'Executive Agreement, Draft No. 2', in B.F. Smith, *The American Road to Nuremberg, The Documentary Record, 1944-1945* (Stanford, Hoover Institution Press 1982), p. 195.

States submitted a text that drew upon the Martens clause of the Hague conventions of 1899 and 1907. But the reference to 'the principles of the law of nations as they result from the usages established among civilized peoples, from the laws of humanity, and from the dictates of the public conscience' was linked to the crime of aggression.[44] The record of the meetings leaves no doubt that the four powers insisted upon a *nexus* between the war itself and the atrocities committed by the Nazis against their own Jewish populations. It was on this basis, and this basis alone, that they considered themselves entitled to proceed. The distinctions were set out by the head of the United States delegation, Robert Jackson, at a meeting on 23 July 1945:

> 'It has been a general principle of foreign policy of our Government from time immemorial that the internal affairs of another government are not ordinarily our business; that is to say, the way Germany treats its inhabitants, or any other country treats its inhabitants is not our affair any more than it is the affair of some other government to interpose itself in our problems. The reason that this program of extermination of Jews and destruction of the rights of minorities becomes an international concern is this: it was a part of a plan for making an illegal war. Unless we have a war connection as a basis for reaching them, I would think we have no basis for dealing with atrocities. They were a part of the preparation for war or for the conduct of the war in so far as they occurred inside of Germany and that makes them our concern.'[45]

Speaking of the proposed crime of 'atrocities, persecutions, and deportations on political, racial or religious grounds,' Jackson indicated the source of the lingering concerns of his government:

> '[O]rdinarily we do not consider that the acts of a government toward its own citizens warrant our interference. We have some regrettable circumstances at times in our own country in which minorities are unfairly treated. We think it is justifiable that we interfere or attempt to bring retribution to individuals or to states only because the concentration camps and the deportations were in pursuance of a common plan or enterprise of making an unjust or illegal war in which we became involved. We see no other basis on which we are justified in reaching the atrocities which were committed inside Germany, under German law, or even in violation of German law, by authorities of the German state.'[46]

Jackson himself was surely not very proud of the 'regrettable circumstances' in the United States 'in which minorities are unfairly treated.' But as a representative of his government, he could not agree with anything by which international law would recognise as a crime acts of persecution based on racial origin, because this might, at least in theory, expose United States officials to prosecution. Jackson's views manifest a candour lacking among the delegations of the United Kingdom, France

---

[44] 'Revised Draft of Agreement and Memorandum Submitted by American Delegation, 30 June 1945', in *Report of Robert H. Jackson, United States Representative to the International Conference on Military Trials* (Washington, US Government Printing Office 1949), p. 121.

[45] 'Minutes of Conference Session of 23 July 1945', in ibid., p. 331.

[46] Ibid., p. 333.

and the Soviet Union, but we can readily surmise that each had concerns about circumstances equivalent to or worse than the *apartheid* regime that then prevailed in parts of the United States. The result was an agreement by the four 'Great Powers' at the London Conference by which Nazi leaders could be prosecuted for such atrocities because they were committed in association with the war.

Article IV(c) of the Charter of the International Military Tribunal defines 'crimes against humanity' as 'murder, extermination, enslavement, deportation, and other inhumane acts committed against any civilian population, before or during the war, or persecutions on political, racial or religious grounds in furtherance of or in connection with any crime within the jurisdiction of the International Tribunal, whether or not in violation of the domestic law of the country where perpetrated.'[47] In the final judgment of the Nuremberg Tribunal, addressing implicitly the issue of the *nexus* between crimes against humanity and the war itself, something that appeared fundamental in order to comply with the Charter of the tribunal, the judges noted that '[i]t was contended for the Prosecution that certain aspects of this anti Semitic policy were connected with the plans for aggressive war.'[48] The tribunal made a distinction between pre-war persecution of German Jews, which it characterised as 'severe and repressive,' and German policy during the war in the occupied territories. Although the judgment frequently referred to events during the 1930s, none of the accused was found guilty of an act perpetrated prior to 1 September 1939, the day the war broke out.

This was the situation about which Raphael Lemkin was so exorcised in October 1946 when he met Henry King in the lobby of Nuremberg's Grand Hotel. The issue is one manifestation of a broader debate about the extent to which international law might breach the wall of state sovereignty when serious violations of human rights are perpetrated. By 1944, reports of the Nazi atrocities made it virtually unthinkable that these go unpunished due to the rigorous application of a traditional view by which states had no business interfering in the treatment of a civilian population by another state. The architects of the Nuremberg Tribunal finessed this matter by declaring Nazi crimes to be punishable to the extent that there was a *nexus* with international armed conflict. Their hypocrisy was transparent enough to other states, many of whom had historically found themselves on the receiving end of the same victorious powers who were prepared to punish the Nazis yet ensure that the underlying principles not apply to their own acts. The Genocide Convention was the initial fruit of this dissatisfaction, just as the Universal Declaration was the first important result of the failure to incorporate substantive human rights norms in the Charter of the United Nations.

---

47 *Agreement for the Prosecution and Punishment of Major War Criminals of the European Axis, and Establishing the Charter of the International Military Tribunal (IMT)*, annex, (1951) 82 *UNTS* 279.

48 *France, et al.* v. *Goering, et al.*, 22 IMT 203 (1946), p. 492.

III. Closing the impunity gap

It is often said that crimes against humanity were recognised as part of customary international law prior to Nuremberg. This is one way of answering the charge that the International Military Tribunal breached the principle of legality (*nullum crimen sine lege*). Reference to the debates in the United Nations War Crimes Commission and the London Conference should be enough to show just how unclear the state of customary law actually was. Whether it was unfair to prosecute the Nazis for their atrocities is another matter altogether. The Nuremberg judges famously said that *nullum crimen* was a 'principle of justice': 'To assert that it is unjust to punish those who in defiance of treaties and assurances have attacked neighbouring states without warning is obviously untrue, for in such circumstances the attacker must know that he is doing wrong, and so far from it being unjust to punish him, it would be unjust if his wrong were allowed to go unpunished.'[49]

The principle of legality was most adequately addressed with respect to the crime of genocide through the adoption of General Assembly Resolution 96(I) in December 1946 and, two years later, the Genocide Convention itself. The legal certainty that this codification accomplished no doubt contributed to the stability of the definition over the ensuing six decades. Although academics and human rights activists frequently criticised the narrowness of the definition, states rarely showed any inclination to consider amendment. They were given a golden opportunity at the 1998 Rome Conference to fix any 'blind spots' in the definition of genocide set out in Article II of the Convention but declined to do so. In debate in the Committee of the Whole at the Rome Conference, only Cuba argued again for amendment of the definition, so as to include social and political groups.[50] Otherwise, there was a chorus of support for the original text adopted by the General Assembly some fifty years earlier.[51]

Crimes against humanity, on the other hand, lingered on after Nuremberg in a fog of uncertainty. In sharp contrast with genocide, whose definition has remained unchanged for nearly six decades, it seems that each time crimes against humanity is defined the result is different. As one of its first projects, the United Nations International Law Commission had been given the task both of identifying the 'Nuremberg Principles' and developing a 'Code of Offences Against the Peace and Security of Mankind.' Principle VI of the 'Principles of International Law Recognized in the Charter of the Nürnberg Tribunal and in the Judgment of the Tribunal,'

[49] 22 IMT 461 (1948).

[50] UN Doc. A/CONF.183/C.1/SR.3, para. 100.

[51] Ibid., paras. 2, 18, 20 (Germany), 22 (Syria), 24 (United Arab Emirates), 26 (Bahrain), 28 (Jordan), 29 (Lebanon), 30 (Belgium), 31 (Saudi Arabia), 33 (Tunisia), 35 (Czech Republic), 38 (Morocco), 40 (Malta), 41 (Algeria), 44 (India), 49 (Brazil), 54 (Denmark), 57 (Lesotho), 59 (Greece), 64 (Malawi), 67 (Sudan), 72 (China), 76 (Republic of Korea), 80 (Poland), 84 (Trinidad and Tobago), 85 (Iraq), 107 (Thailand), 111 (Norway), 113 (Côte d'Ivoire), 116 (South Africa), 119 (Egypt), 122 (Pakistan), 123 (Mexico), 127 (Libya), 132 (Colombia), 135 (Iran), 137 (United States of America), 141 (Djibouti), 143 (Indonesia), 145 (Spain), 150 (Romania), 151 (Senegal), 153 (Sri Lanka), 157 (Venezuela), 161 (Italy), 166 (Ireland), 172 (Turkey), 174.

adopted by the Commission in 1950,[52] concerned subject matter jurisdiction. Crimes against humanity were defined as 'Murder, extermination, enslavement, deportation and other inhuman acts done against any civilian population, or persecutions on political, racial or religious grounds, when such acts are done or such persecutions are carried on in execution of or in connection with any crime against peace or any war crime.' The wording was not identical to that of the Charter of the International Military Tribunal. But it actually clarified and entrenched the significance and scope of the *nexus*. The Commission said it did not exclude the possibility that crimes against humanity could be committed in time of peace, but only to the extent that they took place 'before a war in connexion with crimes against peace.'[53]

Critics of the *nexus* often point to Control Council Law No. 10,[54] which was adopted by the Allies for the purpose of prosecutions within Germany. The famous *nexus* had disappeared from the definition of crimes against humanity. But this can be easily explained by the fact that the Allies believed they were enacting national law applicable to Germany rather than international law with the potential to apply to themselves, which had been the case at Nuremberg. Speaking of the Control Council Law prosecutions by American military tribunals, United States prosecutor Telford Taylor observed in his final report to the Secretary of the Army that '[n]one of the Nuremberg judgments squarely passed on the question whether mass atrocities committed by or with the approval of a government against a racial or religious group of its own inhabitants in peacetime constitute crimes under international law.' Taylor said that the practical significance of this problem could hardly be overstated, and cited the 1948 Genocide Convention, whose drafting had just been completed when he penned these words, as a manifestation of the interest in this question.[55]

Eventually, the *nexus* disappeared from the definition of crimes against humanity, but it would take half a century for the evolution to become evident. In 1995, the Appeals Chamber of the International Criminal Tribunal for the former Yugoslavia declared that the requirement that crimes against humanity be associated with armed conflict was inconsistent with customary law.[56] It offered the rather unconvincing explanation that the Security Council had included the *nexus* in Article 5 of the Statute of the International Criminal Tribunal for the former Yugoslavia as a jurisdictional limit only.[57] The more plausible explanation is that the lawyers in the

---

[52] II *Yearbook of the International Law Commission* (1951), UN Doc. A/CN.4/SER.A/1950/Add. 1, paras. 95-127.

[53] Ibid., para. 123.

[54] Control Council Law No. 10, Punishment of Persons Guilty of War Crimes, Crimes Against Peace and Humanity, 20 December 1945, *Official Gazette of the Control Council for Germany*, No. 3, Berlin, 31 January 1946.

[55] Telford Taylor, *Final Report to Secretary of the Army on the Nuernberg War Crimes Trials Under Control Council Law No. 10* (Washington, US Government Printing Office 1951), pp. 224, 226.

[56] ICTY, *Prosecutor* v. *Tadić*, Case IT-94-1-AR72, Decision on the Defence Motion for Interlocutory Appeal on Jurisdiction, 2 October 1995, para. 141; ICTY, *Prosecutor* v. *Tadić* Case IT-94-1-A, Judgment, 15 July 1999, para. 251; ICTY, *Prosecutor* v. *Kordić, et al.*, Case IT-95-14/2-T, Judgment, 26 February 2001, para. 23.

[57] ICTY, *Prosecutor* v. *Šešelj*, Case IT-03-67-AR72.1, Decision on the Interlocutory Appeal Concerning Jurisdiction, 31 August 2004, para. 13.

United Nations Secretariat who drafted the Charter believed the *nexus* to be part of customary law, and the Council did not disagree.[58] Nevertheless, there can today be no doubt that the flaw in the Nuremberg concept of crimes against humanity, something that prompted Lemkin's genocide-related initiatives at the General Assembly, has been corrected. The authoritative definition appears in Article 7 of the Rome Statute, which contains no reference to armed conflict as a contextual element. The only real remaining uncertainty is precisely when the *nexus* disappeared from the elements of crimes against humanity. As far as the International Law Commission was concerned, it was present as late as 1950, and perhaps after that. In 1954, the commission experimented by removing the *nexus*, replacing it with another contextual element, the state plan or policy.[59] There is also some recent authority from the European Court of Human Rights supporting the view that the *nexus* was absent as early as the 1950s.[60] In a September 2008 decision, a Grand Chamber of the Court said cautiously that a *nexus* with armed conflict 'may no longer have been relevant by 1956.'[61] The issue directly confronts the Extraordinary Chambers of the Courts of Cambodia in their current efforts to prosecute Khmer Rouge atrocities.

IV. Conclusions

The horrors of Auschwitz, Dachau and Treblinka set the context for the development of human rights law in the years following the Second World War. Prosecution of war crimes perpetrated against civilians had hitherto been confined to cases where the victims resided in occupied territories. What a country did to its own citizens had been deemed a matter that did not concern international law and the international community. Nuremberg appeared to take this bold step forward, but strings were attached. Although the Nazi persecution of Jews, even those within the borders of Germany, was deemed an international crime, the drafters of the Nuremberg Charter insisted upon a *nexus* between the crime against humanity and the international conflict. In effect, they were holding the Germans accountable for atrocities committed against Germans, but resisting a more general principle that might hold them responsible for atrocities perpetrated within their own borders or in their colonies. This imperfect criminalisation of crimes against humanity mirrored the ambiguities of the Charter of the United Nations, adopted in June 1945,

---

[58] See the Secretary-General's report: 'Crimes against humanity are aimed at any civilian population and are prohibited regardless of whether they are committed in an armed conflict, international or internal in character.' 'Report of the Secretary-General Pursuant to Paragraph 2 of Security Council Resolution 808 (1993)', UN Doc. S/25704 (1993), para. 47; L.D. Johnson, 'Ten Years Later: Reflections on the Drafting', 2 *JICJ* (2004), p. 368 at p. 372.

[59] II *Yearbook of the International Law Commission* (1954), UN Doc. A/CN.4/SER.A/1954/Add.l, p. 150.

[60] ECHR, *Kolk* v. *Estonia*, Application No. 23052/04; ECHR, *Kislyiy* v. *Estonia*, Application No. 24018/04, Admissibility Decision, 17 January 2006; ECHR, *Penart* v. *Estonia* Application No. 14685/04, Admissibility Decision, 24 January 2006.

[61] ECHR, *Korbely* v. *Hungary*, Application No. *9174/02*, Judgment, 19 September 2008, para. 82.

that pledged to promote and encourage respect for human rights yet at the same time promised that the United Nations would not intervene in matters which were 'essentially within the domestic jurisdiction of any state.'

The recognition of genocide as an international crime by the United Nations General Assembly in December 1946 and the adoption of the Genocide Convention two years later were a reaction to dissatisfaction with the restrictions on crimes against humanity imposed at Nuremberg. It is impossible to understand the codification of the crime of genocide, and the interest it created in international law, without appreciating this situation. If the law of Nuremberg had recognised what Lemkin called 'peacetime genocide,' there would probably have been no General Assembly Resolution and no Convention. Neither would have been necessary. There would have been no legal gap to fill.

Two streams converged in December 1948, at the General Assembly of the United Nations: the standard-setting of international human rights manifested in the Universal Declaration of Human Rights, and the individual accountability for violations of human rights, of which the Convention on the Prevention and Punishment of the Crime of Genocide was the modest beginning. The Genocide Convention established that in the case of a particular form of strictly defined atrocity there was no longer any *nexus*, and that the crime could be committed in time of peace as well as in wartime. The Universal Declaration laid the groundwork for steady progress in both standard setting and a growing recognition of the right of the international community in general and United Nations bodies such as the Commission on Human Rights in particular to breach the wall of the *domaine reservé* by which states historically sheltered atrocities from international scrutiny.

The legal significance of the Genocide Convention has declined over the past decade or so, but not because it is inapplicable to specific circumstances or out of a perceived conservativism of diplomats and judges. Rather, new instruments and new institutions have emerged. Foremost among them is the International Criminal Court. In a different way, it accomplishes much the same thing as the Genocide Convention, but in a manner applicable to crimes against humanity as well. Moreover, the recent 'responsibility to protect' doctrine extends the duty of prevention found in Article I of the Genocide Convention to crimes against humanity. A recent report by a high-level panel of experts in the United States, including Madeleine Albright and William Cohen, entitled *Preventing Genocide*, demonstrates the blurring of distinctions between genocide and crimes against humanity. It contains a section on 'Avoiding Definitional Traps' that offers the following explanation:

> 'To avoid the legalistic arguments that have repeatedly impeded timely and effective action, the task force has defined its scope in this report as the prevention of "genocide and mass atrocities," meaning large-scale and deliberate attacks on civilians. The victims of genocide and mass atrocities are typically targeted because of their identification as members of a group. In defining its scope, the task force has not attempted to circumscribe which kinds of groups deserve special protection or to articulate how these groups should be defined. The colloquial description of large-scale and deliberate attacks on civilians is buttressed by a framework in international law that has been

> accepted by the United States and other governments and that defines serious crimes meriting special international concern. We use the term genocide in this report as a shorthand expression for this wider category of crimes. Moreover, the central purpose of our effort being prevention, we are advocating the adoption of measures before acts of massive violence have been committed or labeled.'[62]

A footnote at the end of the penultimate sentence says:

> 'Those crimes are: (1) genocide as defined in the Convention on the Prevention and Punishment of the Crime of Genocide (1948) and (2) crimes against humanity as described in the Nuremberg Charter (1945) and most recently defined in the Rome Statute creating the International Criminal Court (1998). Many of the specific acts constituting these crimes are also proscribed by the Geneva Conventions of 1949 and in customary international law; war crimes can include individual criminal acts, but generally become a matter of international concern if they are committed as part of a plan or policy or as part of a large-scale commission of such crimes.'[63]

In other words, another definition or meaning for genocide is used: 'large-scale and deliberate attacks on civilians.' Even a summary review of the post-Second World War period shows just how much this view has evolved. Sixty years ago, the distinction between genocide and crimes against humanity was fundamental to American policy.

Today, the only real legal consequence of describing an atrocity as genocide rather than as crimes against humanity is the relatively easy access to the International Court of Justice offered by Article IX of the 1948 Convention. But Article IX has generated more heat than light, and the recent ruling of the Court in *Bosnia* v. *Serbia* should discourage resort to this remedy except in the very clearest of cases.[64] In a legal sense, there is now slight importance, if any, to the distinction between genocide and crimes against humanity. The importance of the Genocide Convention probably can be found not so much in its contemporary potential to address atrocities, something that is largely superseded by more modern texts, as its historic contribution to the struggle for accountability and the protection of human rights. We celebrate it today not for its legal effectiveness, which is now overshadowed by major normative developments, as for its symbolic role as the beginning of a system that has only really begun to thrive in the final years of the twentieth century and the first years of the twenty-first.

---

[62] M.K. Albright & W.S. Cohen, *Preventing Genocide, A Blueprint for US Policy-Makers* (Washington, United States Holocaust Memorial Museum, The American Academy of Diplomacy, Endowment of the United States Institute of Peace 2008), pp. xxi-xxii.

[63] *Idem.*

[64] ICJ, *Case concerning Application of the Convention on the Prevention and Punishment of the Crime of Genocide (Bosnia and Herzegovina* v. *Serbia and Montenegro)*, Judgment, 26 February 2007. On the judgment, see W.A. Schabas, 'Genocide and the International Court of Justice: Finally, a Duty to Prevent the Crime of Crimes', 2 *Genocide Studies and Prevention* (2007), p. 101.

RAPHAEL LEMKIN AND 'GENOCIDE' AT NUREMBERG, 1945–1946

John Q. Barrett*

Dr. Raphael Lemkin fathered the concept of genocide as a defined international crime.[1] His efforts to get the nations of the world to comprehend and then to outlaw this crime occurred in five phases:

- his own living, thinking and writing, culminating in his 1944 book, *Axis Rule in Occupied Europe*,[2] which coined the new word 'genocide' to communicate the systematic evil of acts committed with intent to destroy national, ethnic, racial or religious groups;
- his 1945-46 work relating to the prosecution in Nuremberg of the principal surviving Nazi leaders for crimes including genocide;
- his work at the United Nations in late 1946, culminating in the General Assembly's December 11, 1946, adoption of a resolution condemning genocide as a crime under international law;
- his continuing work at the UN during the next two years, culminating in the General Assembly's December 9, 1948, Resolution urging states to agree to a Genocide Convention by which they would commit to prosecute any perpetrator of the crime; and
- his subsequent efforts to persuade states to ratify the Convention on the Prevention and Punishment of the Crime of Genocide, which a sufficient number did to bring it into force in 1951.

Of these phases, Raphael Lemkin's work relating to the 1945-46 Nuremberg recognition and prosecution of Nazi genocidal conduct is the least studied and understood. Some accounts of this period, including Lemkin's own, are brief and imprecise.

---

* I thank St. John's law students Andrew W. Dodd and Virginia C. Dowd for excellent research assistance.

[1] See generally J. Cooper, *Raphael Lemkin & the Struggle for the Genocide Convention* (Houndsmills, Palgrave Macmillan 2008); Tanya Elder, 'What you see before your eyes: documenting Raphael Lemkin's life by exploring his archival Papers, 1900-1959', 7 *Journal of Genocide Research* (2005), p. 469; S. Power, *'A Problem from Hell': America & the Age of Genocide* (New York, Basic Books 2002); W. Korey, *An Epitaph for Raphael Lemkin* (New York, Jacob Blaustein Institute 2001, as reissued 2009).

[2] R. Lemkin, *Axis Rule in Occupied Europe: Laws of Occupation, Analysis of Government, Proposals for Redress* (Carnegie Endowment for International Peace 1944).

Some accounts are inaccurate. This chapter, based in contemporaneous documents, chronicles where Lemkin actually was, what he did, and how his concept and word 'genocide' advanced, fitfully and not by Lemkin's efforts alone, during the Nuremberg trial year.

I. Lemkin in Washington, spring 1945

In the late afternoon on Wednesday, May 2, 1945, President Harry S. Truman announced at a press conference that he had appointed Robert H. Jackson, an Associate Justice serving on the Supreme Court of the United States, to serve as US representative and chief of counsel to prepare and prosecute before an international military tribunal the European Axis powers and their agents on charges of atrocities and war crimes. Radio, newspapers and newsreels reported Jackson's appointment prominently.

Raphael Lemkin, a Pole, a Jew, a lawyer and a refugee from Nazism who then was working as a War Department consultant, heard the news and acted upon it. On May 4, he typed a letter to Justice Jackson and sent it, along with a magazine issue containing Lemkin's most recent article, to Jackson at the Supreme Court.[3]

Lemkin's short letter to Jackson, which apparently was their first contact, contained three distinct messages. First, it pointed out that the enclosed April 1945 issue of *Free World* magazine, a pro-Allies, internationalist magazine published in New York City, contained Lemkin's article, 'Genocide – A Modern Crime.'[4] Second, the letter highlighted that the article contained a chilling statement that recently captured German Army Generalfeldmarschall Gerd von Rundstedt had made in 1943 and urged that this statement, 'in connection with other specific acts, points to the particular responsibility of this man as a major war criminal' who, presumably, Jackson should prosecute.[5] Third, Lemkin's letter alerted Jackson to the Carnegie Endowment for International Peace's publication 'three months ago' – in fact it had been twice that long – of Lemkin's book *Axis Rule in Occupied Europe*, 'which contains also some legal evidence as to war crimes.' Lemkin added that he would be delighted to give a copy of the book to Jackson but for Lemkin's discov-

---

[3] See Dr. Raphael Lemkin letter to Honorable Robert Jackson, 4 May 1945, in Robert H. Jackson Papers, Library of Congress, Manuscript Division, Washington DC, Box 98, Folder 9. On this letter, Jackson's secretary jotted his instruction to 'ackn[owledge]' it to Lemkin. *Idem.*

[4] See R. Lemkin, 'Genocide – A Modern Crime', 9 *Free World* (1945), p. 39. The article contained much of chapter nine from Lemkin's then recently published book.

[5] *Idem.* In Jackson's hard copy of the magazine, which survives today as he or an assistant filed it, someone – probably Jackson – marked this quotation in pencil with lines and a large 'X.' Two pages later, the same person marked with pencil lines in the margin Lemkin's statement that 'the Jews in the overcrowded ghettos were forbidden the use of public parks' and the start of the next sentence, which refers to '[t]he authoritative report of the War Refugee Board published in November 1944, and the overwhelming new evidence that appears daily …' Ibid., at pp. 39, 42. I conclude that the pencil wielding reader was Justice Jackson, both because he regularly made pencil marks in printed items as he read them, and because the issue of *Free World* that Lemkin sent to him contains, at the first page of the Lemkin article, a blue paper Library of the US Supreme Court bookmark.

ery 'only today' that the book's first printing 'is exhausted' and that the Carnegie Endowment was undertaking a second printing. 'I am sure however,' Lemkin closed, 'that the Library of the Supreme Court has a copy.'[6] Justice Jackson, thanks to his habit of reading daily newspapers and other materials, might well have known already of Raphael Lemkin and his book. Jackson might have noted, for example, that the Washington Post had, in November 1944, published a prominent editorial, headlined 'Genocide,' which discussed a report that the Roosevelt Administration's War Refugee Board (WRB) had issued publicly that month. The WRB had reported then, months prior to Allied liberation of Nazi concentration camps, that Germany had used poison gas to kill approximately 1.7 million Jews at the Auschwitz and Birkenau extermination camps. The Post editorial also explained that 'a noted Polish scholar and attorney, Prof. Raphael Lemkin,' had recently coined the word 'genocide' to describe such conduct. The editorial, applying Lemkin's definition of the term, stated flatly that 'the Germans have committed genocide in virtually all of the countries of Europe which they occupied' and endorsed his call for 'international agreement now on the outlawing of genocide.'[7] Jackson also might have noticed another Washington Post editorial, published in early May 1945. It actually was published just one day after Jackson had received Lemkin's letter introducing himself and supplying the complimentary copy of *Free World* magazine containing his article. The Post editorial thus might have reinforced the significance of Lemkin's direct communication with Jackson. Titled 'Retribution,' this editorial described the war-ruined condition of Germany and argued that the Nazis had caused this devastation and their soon-to-become-official military defeat by unleashing 'terror and systematic destruction … in a world where men still place value on human life and freedom …' This editorial also cited Lemkin's *Free World* article and printed from it the quote from von Rundstedt's 1943 speech to the Reich War Academy in Berlin, which Lemkin had flagged in his letter to Jackson:

> 'One of [Germany's] great mistakes of 1918 was to spare the civil life of the enemy countries, for it is necessary for us Germans to be always at least double the numbers of the peoples of the contiguous countries. We are therefore obliged to destroy at least a third of their inhabitants. The only means is organized underfeeding which in this case is better than machine guns.'[8]

(It seems reasonable to suspect that Lemkin, who courted the press energetically, played an important role in calling first his 1944 book and, later, his spring 1945 magazine article to the newspaper's attention, and in persuading it to publish these editorial stances. Years later, Lemkin wrote in a summary of his proposed autobiography that he had in the late 1944-early 1945 time period won the support of Washington Post publisher Eugene Meyer.)[9]

---

6 Lemkin to Jackson, 4 May 1945, *supra* n. 3.

7 'Genocide', *Washington Post*, 3 December 1944, p. B4 (editorial).

8 'Retribution', *Washington Post*, 6 May 1945, p. B4 (editorial).

9 See 'Chap 8 summary', n.d., in Raphael Lemkin Papers, New York Public Library, Manuscripts & Archives Division, New York, NY, Reel 2.

Lemkin was, in his written surmise to Jackson, correct – the US Supreme Court Library, supplied by the Library of Congress, did have a copy of Lemkin's book *Axis Rule in Occupied Europe*. Jackson borrowed it from the Court's Library, took it to London that summer, kept it in his office there, took it to Nuremberg for the ensuing trial year, and finally returned it more than a year later, after he had completed his chief of counsel assignment.[10]

Within about ten days of receiving Lemkin's letter and the enclosed magazine, Jackson's secretary followed his instruction to prepare a letter of response, which Jackson signed and sent. Jackson wrote that he had read both the 'Genocide' article and the book and he thanked Lemkin for calling them to Jackson's attention.[11] (Jackson's ultimate and lasting familiarity with Lemkin's book is demonstrable: years after Nuremberg, Jackson recalled Lemkin accurately as 'one who had followed closely the Axis rule in occupied countries and had got out a book showing their decrees and rules.)'[12]

From the April 1945 start of Justice Jackson's assignment as US Chief of Counsel, his work followed, perhaps more closely than even he realised, Lemkin's conceptual lead. In his book *Axis Rule*, Lemkin described and analysed the SS, Gestapo and various other Nazi Party entities as criminal organisations. Inside the War Department during the second half of 1944 (i.e., months before Jackson's chief of counsel appointment), an advance copy of Lemkin's book and in particular his description of Nazism as organised criminality became a basis for the plan, developed by Colonel Murray C. Bernays (US Army, General Staff Corps Executive), a War Department attorney, to try Nazi leaders and their organizations before an international tribunal for the crime of conspiracy. Bernays's plan was approved, first by Secretary of War Henry L. Stimson and later by Secretary of State Cordell Hull and Attorney General Francis Biddle.[13] This plan became the basis for President Truman's appointment of Jackson and a central part of the position description and job guidance that he received. Bernays's conspiracy concept of Nazi criminality then became Jackson's blueprint for what came to be the August 1945 London Agreement and, in time, the Nuremberg trial itself.

---

[10] See 'Books Requested for Use Overseas By Members of Justice Jackson's Staff to Prosecute the Major Axis Criminals', n.d. (est. July 1945) (listing Lemkin's book as one of the 'Books Now On Loan to Justice Jackson Via Supreme Court Library'); Memorandum from Mary Burns to Lt. Col. [Leonard] Wheeler, 'Subject: Books and Publications in Justice Jackson's [London] Office', 27 August 1945, p. 2 (listing Lemkin's book), & 'Library of Congress', 15 October 1946 (listing Lemkin's book, with Jackson secretary Elsie Douglas noting that it had been 'Ret'd'), all in Jackson Papers, *supra* n. 3, Box 104, Folder 1; see also 'O.C.C. [Office of Chief of Counsel] Information Bulletin No. 155, Nurnberg, Germany, 30 July 1946' ('urgently request[ing] that all books borrowed during the preparation of the case from Justice Jackson's office,' some of which were missing and came 'from the Supreme Court Library and the Library of Congress, be returned to his secretary'), in Jackson Papers, *supra* n. 3, Box 105, Folder 8.

[11] Robert H. Jackson letter to Dr. Raphael Lemkin, 16 May 1945, in Jackson Papers, *supra* n. 3, Box 98, Folder 9.

[12] H.B. Phillips (ed.), *The Reminiscences of Robert H. Jackson* (New York, Columbia University Oral History Research Office 1955), p. 1211.

[13] See R.E. Conot, *Justice at Nuremberg* (New York, Carroll & Graf Publishers, Inc. 1984), pp. 11-12; J. Cooper, *supra* n. 1, pp. 62-63.

In May 1945, Justice Jackson assembled the core legal staff that would assist him as international tribunal negotiator and war crimes prosecutor. Jackson's lawyers, who came for the most part from existing government offices and/or military service, included a number of men who had been working already on war and war crimes-related matters. Jackson's first underling and executive officer was, from the War Department, Col. Bernays. They quickly became affiliated with leadership personnel from the Army's Judge Advocate General (JAG) Corps Department and from the Office of Strategic Services (OSS). Lieutenant James B. Donovan (US Navy Reserve), OSS's general counsel, became a principal participant. With President Truman's permission, Jackson recruited the head of the OSS, Major General William J. Donovan (US Army), to be Jackson's deputy. With the permission and support of Attorney General Biddle, Jackson recruited his close friend and former Department of Justice colleague, Assistant Attorney General (Claims Division) Francis M. Shea. Jackson also recruited Sidney S. Alderman, the general counsel of the Southern Railway System, who Jackson admired as an advocate before the Supreme Court. Col. Telford Taylor (General Staff Corps), Commander Sidney J. Kaplan (US Coast Guard) and other lawyers were detailed to the staff. One of these was Jackson's son, Ensign William E. Jackson (USNR), who became the Justice's executive assistant.

From the start, Raphael Lemkin's intellectual work was known to and influenced Jackson and his staff. During the week of May 7, 1945, Sidney Alderman obtained, from Jackson or elsewhere, a copy of Lemkin's book *Axis Rule* and read much of it over the May 12-13 weekend.[14] Col. Bernays, who knew his War Department colleague Lemkin's book and had conceptualised prosecuting Nazi criminal conspirators along the organisational lines it documented, drafted during this same period two memoranda for discussion with Jackson and his legal team. In one, an 11-page draft entitled 'Planning Memorandum,' Bernays wrote that the Allies' trial proof of the atrocities and other crimes that Nazi war criminals committed before and during their illegal wars of aggression would include evidence of '[d]ecimation of racial minorities and subjugated populations' by methods including '(1) underfeeding; (2) depriving them of clothing, shelter, fuel, sanitation, medical care; (3) deporting them for forced labor; [and] (4) working them in inhuman conditions.'[15] At a May 16 meeting at the Supreme Court, Jackson and most of his senior lawyers, going over this document paragraph by paragraph,[16] changed Bernays's draft to include – Jackson added in his own hand – Lemkin's word 'genocide.' The trial proof of these crimes, Jackson wrote, would include evidence of

---

14 See H.B. Phillips (ed.), *The Reminiscences of Sidney S. Alderman* (New York, Columbia University Oral History Research Office 1955), p. 817 ('I had procured a copy of this book the previous week [i.e., 7-11 May 1945] and had read the first half of it, Part I, over the [12-13 May] weekend.'). Alderman's oral history is a recitation of entries from a diary that apparently no longer exists.

15 See 'Draft, 14 May 1945, Planning Memorandum', at p. 9, in Jackson Papers, *supra* n. 3, Box 107, Folder 5.

16 Robert H. Jackson diary entry, 16 May 1945, in Jackson Papers, *supra* n. 3, Box 95, Folder 5.

> 'genocide, sterilization, castration, or destruction of racial minorities and subjugated populations by such means and methods as (1) underfeeding; (2) depriving them of clothing, shelter, fuel, sanitation, medical care; (3) deporting them for forced labor; [and] (4) working them in inhuman conditions.'[17]

Jackson approved this Planning Memorandum as amended.[18] (A month later, when Jackson and most of his staff relocated to London to continue trial preparations there while negotiating with British, Soviet and French allies, Jackson distributed a later, but still 'genocide'-mentioning, version of this Planning Memorandum to the foreign delegations 'as an aid to their understanding of the proposed agreement.)'[19]

On Friday, May 18, 1945, Sidney Alderman met Raphael Lemkin in person. Brigadier General John M. Weir, Judge Advocate General of the US Army, who had attended the May 16 meeting, brought Lemkin to meet Alderman, who at that time was working in the JAG Corps War Crimes office in the Munitions Building on the Washington Mall. Alderman and Lemkin spoke, probably at length. Alderman was pleased to learn that Lemkin had for a time been a law professor at Duke University, Alderman's *alma mater*. That evening, Alderman wrote in his diary about this meeting. He noted (erring on some particulars) that 'Raphael Lemkin was a German [*sic*], a Jew, who had to flee from Germany [*sic*].' Alderman described Lemkin's *Axis Rule in Occupied Europe* as 'a very comprehensive and interesting book, one of the basic texts along with Dr. [Franz] Neumann's *Behemoth*.'[20] Alderman also wrote about Lemkin's new word, 'genocide':

> 'I might say at this point that Prof. Lemkin, I believe in this book, coined the word "genocide" as a term to refer to the deliberate attempt to extinguish whole races of people – obviously referring to the German attempt to extinguish the Jews of Eastern Europe. I immediately saw that he was very proud of this word.'[21]

During the ensuing weeks, Jackson's staff continued to have contacts with Lemkin. Late on the afternoon of Saturday, May 26, he was invited to attend a contentious meeting, hosted by Francis Shea at the Department of Justice, that concerned the ignorance and resulting anxiety of non-OSS lawyers on Jackson's staff about how and what OSS was doing with the evidence assembling and other trial preparations that it had been assigned.[22] (Bill Jackson, who was present at the meeting, wrote

---

[17] See 'Draft, 14 May 1945, Planning Memorandum', *supra* n. 15.

[18] See ibid., at p. 1 (Jackson's handwritten note: 'Conference of May 16th. Approved this with changes').

[19] See 'Planning Memorandum', n.d., in *Report of Robert H. Jackson, United States Representative to the International Conference on Military Trials* (Washington, US Government Printing Office 1949), p. 64.

[20] See F. Neumann, *Behemoth: The Structure & Practice of National Socialism, 1933-1944* (London, V. Gollancz Ltd. 1942). Dr. Neumann served in the OSS during World War II and in Fall 1945 headed Justice Jackson's research section at Nuremberg, which assisted and advised US lawyers.

[21] See *The Reminiscences of Sidney S. Alderman*, *supra* n. 14, at p. 818 (discussing events of 18 May 1945).

[22] See ibid., pp. 837-839.

afterward that Lemkin 'did not appear to have any idea of the type of case we are concentrating on, although he is no doubt a scholar of parts.)'[23] Shea and Alderman subsequently chose Lemkin to serve on a 'control squad' that would, by commissioning from OSS a micro-trial brief or some other sample of its work, take 'test borings' on what it was doing.[24] On Monday, May 28, Lemkin began to work officially under Gen. Weir in the JAG Corps War Crimes office.[25] Col. Taylor and Cmdr. Kaplan soon gave Lemkin what Alderman regarded as 'a complete waterhaul out' but they failed to get any information on how this proposed OSS-oversight committee would work. The US lawyers then decided to strike Lemkin from the committee roster, 'leaving him for encyclopedic purposes in the War Crimes office.'[26]

Lemkin thus remained in the War Department, near and in contact with, but not formally a member of, the Jackson project and staff. When Justice Jackson, Alderman and other senior personnel relocated to London in late June 1945, they left a 'rear echelon' group, headed by Col. Taylor, behind at the Pentagon. In a memorandum to Jackson as they were preparing to leave, Alderman suggested activities and possible new projects for Taylor and his staff. 'On genocide,' Alderman suggested, this team could review War Refugee Board materials they had already acquired, plus 'further materials' that Alderman believed 'are contained in Lemkin's book ...'[27]

II. LEMKIN IN LONDON, LATE SUMMER 1945

Although Raphael Lemkin was not present in London during the four-nation Allied negotiations that ran from late June until early August 1945, his linguistic and conceptual contributions were present. The Americans knew Lemkin, they knew of his book, article and related press, and they knew his word 'genocide.' The British, Soviet and French delegations perhaps also knew Lemkin's word and his legal concept, from his writings and from the Planning Memorandum that Jackson distributed to each delegation as the conference began.[28]

During the London negotiations, all four powers insisted that their right to prosecute Nazi atrocities derived from the connection between those acts and the central Nazi crime, the waging of aggressive war.[29] The resulting London Agreement

---

23 William E. Jackson note, 26 May 1945.

24 See *The Reminiscences of Sidney S. Alderman*, *supra* n. 14, at p. 818 (discussing events of 18 May 1945).

25 See William E. Jackson note, *supra* n. 23 (Lemkin 'reports to Weir's division Monday morning').

26 See *The Reminiscences of Sidney S. Alderman*, *supra* n. 14, p. 842.

27 Sidney S. Alderman, *Memorandum for Mr. Justice Jackson, Subject: Suggestion of specific tasks to be assigned to the rear echelon Task Force, to be carried on in Washington, 13 June 1945*, Inclosure One, pp. 1-2, in Jackson Papers, *supra* n. 3, Folder 107, Box 5.

28 See 'Planning Memorandum', *supra* n. 19, p. 64.

29 See W.A. Schabas, *Genocide in International Law: The Crime of Crimes*, 2nd edn. (Cambridge, Cambridge University Press 2009), pp. 39-42.

and Charter of the International Military Tribunal (IMT), signed on August 8, 1945, identified Crimes against Peace, War Crimes and Crimes Against Humanity, along with 'participating in the formulation or execution of a common plan or conspiracy to commit any of the foregoing crimes,' as the offenses within the IMT's jurisdiction.[30] Although these instruments did not use the word 'genocide,' they in substance adopted much of Lemkin's insight, legal definition and argument for the future of international law. In particular, the Allies defined Crimes Against Humanity as

> 'murder, extermination, enslavement, deportation, and other inhumane acts committed against any civilian population, before or during the war, or persecutions on political, racial or religious grounds in execution of or in connection with any crime within the jurisdiction of the Tribunal, whether or not in violation of the domestic law of the country where perpetrated.'[31]

Indeed Jackson, describing near the end of his life the significance of the London Agreement, used Lemkin's word to summarise part of this legal achievement: 'here was a clear-cut declaration by four of the dominant powers of the world, which nineteen others joined, that aggressive war is a crime, and that these crimes against humanity, such as genocide, are crimes.'[32]

Lemkin's work in London occurred after the London Agreement had been signed. He came at the invitation of Col. Bernays, representing the War Department. In late July, Bernays lobbied to have Lemkin detailed to London, bringing with him materials 'on spoliation and exploitation' that he had been assembling.[33] When Bernays told OSS general counsel and newly-promoted US Navy Commander James Donovan of his (Bernays's) idea to bring Lemkin to London, Donovan objected. He told Bernays that OSS had considered employing Lemkin on several occasions, but that each time it had not done so based on a general agreement at OSS that Lemkin's scholarship, including his book *Axis Rule*, was 'inadequate,' that 'better Polish scholars [were] available,' and that Lemkin had 'an emotional approach to problems, personality difficulties, etc.' Bernays nonetheless decided to go forward, presumably with approval from Shea, Alderman or Justice Jackson, agreeing 'that if Lemkin came he would be his (Bernays's) responsibility.'[34] As events unfolded that summer, however, Bernays soon left London – he retired from Jackson's staff in August. As a result, although Lemkin arrived and was nominally affiliated with

---

30 'Charter of the International Military Tribunal', Art. 6, in *Report of Robert H. Jackson, supra* n. 19, p. 423.

31 Ibid., as amended by 'Protocol to Agreement and Charter', 6 October 1945, in *Report of Robert H. Jackson, supra* n. 19, p. 429.

32 *The Reminiscences of Robert H. Jackson, supra* n. 12, p. 1641.

33 M.C. Bernays, 'Notes for Mr. Shea and Ensign Jackson', in *Francis M. Shea Journal*, US Holocaust Memorial Museum Archives, Washington DC (25 July 1945), pp. 1-2.

34 Memorandum from Commander [James B.] Donovan to Colonel [Telford] Taylor, cc: Justice Jackson, 'SUBJECT Dr. Lemkin', 24 September 1945, p. 2, in Jackson Papers, *supra* n. 3, Folder 106, Box 4.

the Jackson staff – Lemkin's name was added in pencil to the Jackson staff roster, but Lemkin did not have an assigned office or a telephone number[35] – he was largely unsupervised.

It seems that Lemkin arrived in London from Washington in late August 1945.[36] In Washington, he had been working to complete an extensive report on General Karl Haushofer, a German former geopolitical theorist and teacher who the US then was considering for addition to the list of prospective Nazi war crimes defendants.[37] Lemkin's report, which reached Jackson's London office in late August or early September 1945, impressed Shea and Alderman; in the second week of September, they arranged for a copy to be delivered in Washington to Justice Jackson, who was back in the US for consultations with President Truman and others.[38] Shea also ordered, from the War Department for Jackson's London office, six more copies of Lemkin's book.[39]

In London, Lemkin had some involvement in Jackson office discussions of evidentiary matters. By late August, he had told Jackson staff colleagues, who had reported it to the Justice, that he (Lemkin) had 'information that a very large amount of evidence of atrocities in Poland [was] accumulated in Warsaw,'[40] to which the Soviet Union controlled access. Jackson followed up by putting Lemkin in contact with the senior USSR official at the London Conference, General I.T. Nikitchenko,[41] but apparently nothing came of Lemkin's claimed lead to evidence. Lemkin also made contact in London, it seems on his own initiative, with members of the United Nations War Crimes Commission (UNWCC), with World Zionist Organization president Chaim Weizmann and his colleague Moshe Shertok (Sharrett), and with Rabbi Stephen Wise and attorney Jacob Robinson, president and legal adviser, respectively, of the World Jewish Congress.

In September 1945, Lt. Col. Joseph V. Hodgson (JAGD, US Army), the US representative to the UN War Crimes Commission in London and a supportive friend of Justice Jackson and his team, complained to Cmdr. James Donovan about Lemkin.

---

[35] See 'Alphabetical Roster of Personnel, OCC', n.d. (est. late August 1945), in Jackson Papers, *supra* n. 3, Box 106, Folder 7. On this typewritten roster, Lemkin's name is added in pencil and Bernays's is crossed out.

[36] See 'Record of Telephone Conference 15 August 1945 at 1803 Hours British Time' (Francis Shea and Telford Taylor in London speaking with Lt. Col. John W. Griggs and Lt. Cmdr. Charles A. Horsky (US Coast Guard) in Washington), p. 4, in Jackson Papers, *supra* n. 3, Box 110, Folder 9.

[37] See Dr. E.A. Walsh, 'Report on Professor Karl Haushofer of the University of Munich and the Influence of his Geopolitics', 6 February 1946, p. 1 (describing 'Lemkin's report … prepared in Washington' as 'a complete survey of the subject, with many exhibits, charts and photostats … bound in heavy cardboard covers'), in Jackson Papers, *supra* n. 3, Box 104, Folder 10.

[38] See 'Record of Telephone Conference 10 September 1945 at 1800 Hours British Time' (Shea and Sidney Kaplan in London speaking with Gen. Weir, Lt. Cmdr. Horsky, Lt. Col. Griggs and Lt. Col. John F. Richter in Washington), pp. 3-4, in Jackson Papers, *supra* n. 3, Box 110, Folder 9.

[39] Ibid., at p. 5.

[40] Lt. Col. Leonard Wheeler, Jr., 'Notes of Staff Meeting, 31 August 1945', p. 2, in Jackson Papers, *supra* n. 3, Box 110, Folder 1 (cited in Michael Salter, *Nazi War Crimes, US Intelligence & Selective Prosecution at Nuremberg* (Abingdon, Routledge-Cavendish 2007), p. 339 & n. 117).

[41] See Jackson diary entry, 31 August 1945, in Jackson Papers, *supra* n. 3, Box 95, Folder 5.

Hodgson reported that Lemkin had been complicating Hodgson's diplomatic responsibilities by meeting with UNWCC members. Worse, Lemkin had been telling them 'of the tremendous amount of work which has been done by him and others' and of the 'excellent evidence' that has been assembled in Gen. Weir's JAG Corps War Crimes office – evidence that the UNWCC members had never seen from Hodgson. He also reported that Lemkin had put Hodgson on the spot at a luncheon with UNWCC members by expressing amazement that he had never given them copies of Lemkin's book, which forced Hodgson to order copies for them through the War Department. Hodgson also reported that Lemkin was discussing war crimes issues with reporters. When Donovan arrived in Washington shortly after receiving these complaints, he sent a reporting memorandum back to Col. Taylor in London. Donovan understood that Taylor was the War Department official who was supervising Lemkin in London following Bernays's departure. In his memorandum, after reporting Hodgson's complaints, Donovan included his account of OSS's unimpressed history with Lemkin. Donovan closed by conveying Hodgson's 'sole suggestion that the sooner Lemkin is out of London, the more Col. Hodgson will be pleased.'[42]

Although Justice Jackson received a copy of Donovan's memorandum, there is no indication that Jackson read it. Years later, Jackson recalled inaccurately that Lemkin had been one of Gen. William Donovan's OSS experts who had studied the problem of prosecuting Nazi war criminals and assembled and studied relevant evidence.[43] Decades after that, Taylor repeated Jackson's error[44] – Lemkin was not OSS.

III. 'Genocide' in the Nuremberg Indictment, October 1945

During September and into October 1945, senior lawyers on Jackson's staff worked in London with British counterparts to draft what would become the Nuremberg Indictment.[45] The Americans included Lt. Col. Benjamin Kaplan (US Army), Cmdr. Sidney Kaplan, Col. Telford Taylor and Sidney Alderman. The British participants included G.D. ('Khaki') Roberts, K.C., and Wing Cmdr. Peter Calvocoressi. Alderman, the ranking official among the Americans, later recalled that Raphael Lemkin was

> 'constantly coming to see me, trying to be sure that his word genocide was used in the indictment. Finally, over some opposition from other members of our staff, I got the

[42] Donovan to Taylor, *supra* n. 34. Donovan's biography contains no information about Lemkin in London or this controversy. See P.J. Bigger, *Negotiator The Life and Career of James B. Donovan* (Bethlehem, PA, Lehigh University Press 2006).

[43] *The Reminiscences of Robert H. Jackson*, *supra* n. 12, p. 1211.

[44] See T. Taylor, *The Anatomy of the Nuremberg Trials A Personal Memoir* (New York, Alfred A. Knopf 1992), p. 49.

[45] For a good summary account, see A. Tusa & J. Tusa, *The Nuremberg Trial* (London, BBC Books 1995), pp. 112-114.

word genocide into the last draft of the indictment, and I am quite certain that Prof. Lemkin has always been greatly pleased that it appeared in that document. The British particularly thought it was too fancy a word to put in a legal document, and some of their graduates of Oxford University said that they couldn't understand what the word meant.'[46]

Lemkin, drafting in the late 1950s an autobiography that never was published, gave credit to his London contacts from the World Jewish Congress, Stephen Wise and Jacob Robinson, for being 'very helpful in obtaining the support of the British Government for the inclusion of the charge of Genocide in the Nuremberg Trials.'[47] British participant Calvocoressi, however, in his post-Nuremberg book chapter on the relevant portion of the Indictment, mentioned neither the inclusion of the word 'genocide' nor any Lemkin role in preparing the Indictment.[48] US participant Taylor, in his Nuremberg book, identified Roberts as the British lawyer who objected to the word 'genocide,' properly credited Lemkin – who Taylor described as 'at that time a member of the American prosecution staff' – with coining the word, and wrote ambiguously that 'we,' which probably meant the Americans, 'used the word' in the Indictment.[49]

The last-minute, improvised nature of the addition of the word 'genocide,' along with (for the unfamiliar) its definition, to the Indictment was and is revealed by its odd location – it was placed not where it would seem most relevant, in Count Four charging Crimes Against Humanity, but in Count Three, charging War Crimes. The specific sentence, as located within that Count, was as follows:

'COUNT THREE – WAR CRIMES

Statement of the Offense

All the defendants committed War Crimes between 1st September, 1939, and 8th May 1945, in Germany and in all those countries and territories occupied by the German armed forces since 1st September, 1939, and in Austria, Czechoslovakia, and Italy, and on the High Seas.

...

(A) Murder and Ill-Treatment of Civilian Populations of or in Occupied Territory and on the High Seas

Throughout the period of their occupation of territories overrun by their armed forces the defendants, for the purpose of systematically terrorizing the inhabitants, murdered and tortured civilians, and ill-treated them, and imprisoned them without legal process.

The murders and ill-treatment were carried out by divers means, including shooting, hanging, gassing, starvation, gross over-crowding, systematic under-nutrition, system-

---

46 *The Reminiscences of Sidney S. Alderman*, *supra* n. 14, p. 818.

47 Lemkin draft autobiography, '1st chapter?', n.d., in Lemkin Papers, *supra* n. 9, Reel 2, p. 4.

48 See P. Calvocoressi, *Nuremberg: The Facts, the Law and the Consequences* (London, Chatto & Windus 1947), pp. 45-60.

49 T. Taylor, *supra* n. 44, p. 103.

> atic imposition of labor tasks beyond the strength of those ordered to carry them out, inadequate provision of surgical and medical services, kickings, beatings, brutality and torture of all kinds, including the use of hot irons and pulling out of fingernails and the performance of experiments by means of operations and otherwise on living human subjects. In some occupied territories the defendants interfered in religious matters, persecuted members of the clergy and monastic orders, and expropriated church property. *They conducted deliberate and systematic genocide, viz., the extermination of racial and national groups, against the civilian populations of certain occupied territories in order to destroy particular races and classes of people and national, racial, or religious groups, particularly Jews, Poles, Gypsies and others.*
>
> ...
>
> Such murders and ill-treatment were contrary to international conventions, in particular to Article 46 of the Hague Regulations, 1907, the laws and customs of war, the general principles of criminal law as derived from the criminal laws of all civilized nations, the internal penal laws of the countries in which such crimes were committed, and to Article 6(b) of the [London] Charter ...'[50]

Lemkin in later years took full credit for this development. In a summary of his planned autobiography, which he proposed to call *Totally Unofficial* and then *The Unofficial Man*, he wrote, 'I was sent after the war by the U.S.A. Government to London and Nuremberg to help prepare the indictment against the Nazi war criminals. I included the charge of Genocide in this indictment.'[51] In a draft of the first chapter, Lemkin wrote, 'In 1945, I went to London and succeeded in having inserted the charge of Genocide against the Nazi war criminals in Nuremberg.'[52] In a draft summary of his life's activities that he prepared to make the case that he deserved to receive the 1958 Nobel Peace Prize, Lemkin, writing about himself in the third person, stated that '[h]e included the charge of genocide in the indictment against the [Nazi] war criminals.'[53]

On October 18, 1945, the International Military Tribunal, meeting in Berlin, held its first public session and received the Indictment officially. The British chief prosecutor, Attorney General Hartley Shawcross, announced that the Allied chief prosecutors had agreed on the Indictment. At his request, three senior attorneys, Roman Rudenko of the USSR, Francis Shea of the US and a French lawyer, then read the Indictment to the judges. Each lawyer took a turn reading in his respective native tongue and interpreters then sequentially recited translations of that material in the other two languages. When this slow, lengthy proceeding was over, 'genocide' had appeared for the first time in an 'official document of international

[50] Indictment, *The United States, et al.* v. *Hermann Wilhelm Göring, et al.*, in Robert H. Jackson, *The Case Against the Nazi War Criminals* (New York, Alfred A. Knopf 1946), App. II, pp. 111, 137-138 [emphasis added].

[51] Summary, n.d., in Lemkin Papers, *supra* n. 9, at Reel 2, p. 1.

[52] Lemkin draft autobiography, '1st chapter?', n.d., in Lemkin Papers, *supra* n. 9, at Reel 2, pp. 3-4.

[53] Summary of Activities of Raphael Lemkin, n.d., in Lemkin Papers, *supra* n. 9, at Reel 2. Although the prior sentence antecedent of this Lemkin use of 'He' is 'the U.S.A. Chief Prosecutor at the Nurenberg trial' (i.e., Jackson), it is clear from context that this is a reference to Lemkin.

stature ...'[54] Lemkin, who at this time was in London, sent a cable the next day to the Washington Post. He claimed that its December 3, 1944, 'Genocide' editorial, which had more recently been distributed in reprint form, had 'contributed greatly' to the inclusion of 'genocide' in the Indictment's Count Three.[55]

IV. Lemkin and 'Genocide' during the Nuremberg trial, November 1945-September 1946

When the Nuremberg trial began on November 20, 1945, Lemkin's word 'genocide' was uttered for the first time in a courtroom litigation proceeding. An assistant prosecutor representing France, Pierre Mounier, read Count Three, including 'genocide,' to introduce the charged particulars of Nazi crimes in occupied France.[56] Soviet assistant prosecutor Lt. Col. J.A. Ozol also read 'genocide' later on that day when he introduced Count Three's charged particulars of Nazi crimes in Soviet Republics.[57]

It is not clear when Lemkin first came to Nuremberg. One memoir, by Jackson's first executive trial counsel Col. Robert G. Storey (US Army), reported that Lemkin was one of the experts who conducted an evening seminar for the staff's education during the fall months before the trial began.[58] I know of no evidence that Lemkin was in Nuremberg during this pretrial period – he himself later wrote that he 'return[ed from London] to Washington to help prepare the War Crimes Trials in Tokyo.'[59] During winter 1946, Lemkin's specific work in Washington included proposing that the US should prosecute Haushofer in Japan because his geopolitical thinking linked intellectually the aggressive war making of Nazi Germany and Imperial Japan.[60] (Lemkin, a bachelor of apparently some public prominence in Washington, also was interviewed during this period by a Washington society news writer about the attractive qualities of local women.)[61]

Lemkin definitely was in Nuremberg, perhaps for the first time, during late Spring 1946, as the trial approached its conclusion. A private note by Bill Jackson indicates that Lemkin and a JAG Corps officer met there with Justice Jackson on

---

[54] D.A. Sprecher, *Inside the Nuremberg Trial: A Prosecutor's Comprehensive Account*, Vol. 1 (Lanham, Maryland, University Press of America 1999), p. 101. Sprecher, who was a prosecutor on Jackson's US staff at Nuremberg during 1945-46, does not mention Lemkin in this two-volume book.

[55] Dr. Raphael Lemkin, 'Genocide', *Washington Post*, 23 October 1945, p. 6 (publishing Lemkin's cable as a letter to the editor).

[56] II *Trial of the Major War Criminals before the International Military Tribunal* (Nuremberg, 1947), pp. 45-46.

[57] Ibid., p. 60.

[58] See R.G. Storey, *The Final Judgment?: Pearl Harbor to Nuremberg* (San Antonio, TX, The Naylor Co. 1968), p. 96. Storey wrote erroneously that 'Dr. Lempkin [*sic*]' was 'from Germany' and 'on our [i.e., the US] staff.' *Idem*.

[59] Raphael Lemkin, 'Outline for "Totally Unofficial"', in Lemkin Papers, *supra* n. 9, at Reel 2.

[60] See J. Cooper, *supra* n. 1, pp. 67-69.

[61] See G. Reynolds, 'Cosmopolites Clock the American Femme: Nice, But Too Honest to Be Alluring', *Washington Post*, 10 March 1946, p. S4. Lemkin's conclusion: 'I'll settle for one.' *Idem*.

June 2, 1946. They told Jackson that they had been visiting or at least learning about prisoner of war camps. They reported that over 25,000 SS men had already been released. Lemkin and his colleague said they were in Germany to see the effect of that. Jackson was puzzled and surprised that such prisoner releases could be occurring while the IMT case, including against the SS as a criminal organisation, was ongoing. Lemkin and his colleague also reported to Jackson that in most camps, the German prisoners who remained were being guarded by only a handful of US soldiers and a few Poles. Jackson thought this a dangerous, ludicrous situation. Lemkin also said, or at least Jackson took away the (apparently incorrect) impression and soon repeated to his son, that Lemkin had been 'in Japan.' He reported that Joseph B. Keenan, Jackson's former Department of Justice colleague who then was US Chief of Counsel for Japanese War Crimes Prosecutions, was getting more documents than he (Keenan) had been previously, and that defendants in Japan were denying nothing that was stated in a document. Jackson seems to have commented that the IMT defendants on trial in Nuremberg were behaving the same way.[62]

Almost three weeks later, Lemkin was still in, or he was back in, Nuremberg. According to another note, he reported to Jackson at that time that US military review boards were, based on erroneous determinations of non-dangerousness, releasing 500 former SS men per day without taking their photographs or giving them identification papers. By contrast, Lemkin reported, more ordinary (i.e., non-SS) prisoners were still being held. Lemkin also told Jackson that the US military had released 25,000 German civilians from internment, and that their former camps were being returned to German control. Lemkin stated that Lt. Gen. Lucius D. Clay (US Army), Deputy Military Governor, Office of Military Government for Germany (US), had told him that these releases of former SS men were based on economic grounds – the US could not afford to keep these prisoners indefinitely. Jackson observed that the entirety of the SS, not merely its leadership, was an organisation that still was on trial at Nuremberg.[63]

If Lemkin also was lobbying Jackson at this time to use the word 'genocide' in the trial, he was unsuccessful. Lemkin's apparent contacts with British prosecutors seem, on this measure, to have been more fruitful. On June 25, 1946, British deputy prosecutor Sir David Maxwell Fyfe, while cross-examining defendant Constantin von Neurath, read a memorandum about the 'Germanisation' of Czechoslovakia,

---

[62] See William E. Jackson note, 2 June 1946 ('Lemkin + Col. from War Crimes office of JAG, Washington, call on RHJ – they over here to see effect of release of SS from camps – over 25,000 SS already released (how can they be before this case settled?) – in most camps guarded by only handful of US soldiers, plus a few Poles – dangerous + ludicrous situation[.] Lemkin was in Japan – says Keenan getting more docs. than formerly – and, as here, Japs deny nothing if stated in a doc. –').

[63] See William E. Jackson note, 21 June 1946 ('Lemkin came in – re release of SS men – 500 a day being released by boards who decide they are not dangerous, tho ordinary non SS P/W's not released – also 25,000 civilian internees released, + their camps being turned over to Germans to control – this on USFET [US Forces European Theater] orders[.] Clay told Lemkin real reason was economic – can't keep these people indefinitely – yet confused Leadership Corps of Nazi Party (we indict only top level) with SS (whole under indictment), and hence release all low rankers – a hell of a thing – no photographs or identification papers on them before releasing them – and they are killers – madness').

reminded the defendant that he and others were charged with 'genocide,' and read from Lemkin's book, by name, his definition of the crime.[64] On July 27, British chief prosecutor Sir Hartley Shawcross spoke in his closing argument of the defendants' crimes of 'genocide.'[65] On July 29, French chief prosecutor Auguste Champetier de Ribes argued that

> 'scientific and systematic extermination of millions of human beings and more especially of certain national or religious groups whose existence hampered the hegemony of the Germanic race … is a crime so monstrous, so undreamt of in history throughout the Christian era up to the birth of Hitlerism, that the term "genocide" has had to be coined to define it …'[66]

French deputy prosecutor Charles Dubost also spoke in his closing argument of 'genocide.'[67]

United States newspapers, led by the New York Times, took note of Lemkin's word's trial appearances at Nuremberg that summer. On August 26, 1946, the Times published, as the fifth of its six editorials that Monday morning, its institutional perspective on the word that it employed as the editorial's eye-catching title: 'Genocide.'[68] Nineteen months earlier, the Times had given a very big boost to Raphael Lemkin's book *Axis Rule in Occupied Europe*, its coinage of the word 'genocide' and that word's application to Nazi conduct by giving the book a full, front-page review in the Sunday Book Review section.[69] (This review, which led the 28-page section, ran on the high-readership Sunday that was the day following President Franklin Roosevelt's fourth inauguration.) Similarly, the Times in October 1945 had published a wire service summary of a longer London Sunday Times report, published at a time when Lemkin was in London, that the Nuremberg Indictment contained a charge that each defendant had 'conducted deliberate and systematic

---

64 See XVII *Trial of the Major War Criminals*, *supra* n. 56, at p. 61.

65 See XIX *Trial of the Major War Criminals*, *supra* n. 56, at pp. 497, 515.

66 Ibid., at p. 531.

67 See ibid., at p. 551.

68 See 'Genocide', *N.Y. Times*, 26 August 1946, p. 17 (editorial). Dr. William Korey's monograph on Lemkin, published decades later, mistakenly indicates that this editorial was published in 1945 (i.e., before the start of the Nuremberg trial) rather than in 1946 (i.e., near the trial's conclusion, as the IMT was drafting its Judgment). See W. Korey, *supra* n. 1, pp. 20 & 132 n. 40.

69 See O.D. Tolischus, 'Twentieth-Century Moloch: The Nazi-Inspired Totalitarian State, Devourer of Progress – and of Itself', *N.Y. Times Book Review*, 21 January 1945, p. 1. Interestingly, although reviewer Tolischus praised the book and explicitly noted Lemkin's coinage of genocide as 'a new term of gruesome significance,' ibid., at p. 24, the reviewer faulted Lemkin for various errors and other failings. These included Lemkin's failure to understand Nazism as an instance of 'that modern monstrosity known as totalitarian government,' and for faulting 'the entire German people' in a way that is 'too likely to feed that nazism-in-reverse which has done so much to prolong th[e] war.' Ibid., at p. 1. Two months earlier, the Times had reported on its Friday 'Books' page a one-paragraph notice that Columbia University Press had just published Lemkin's book. See 'Books and Authors', *N.Y. Times*, 17 November 1944, p. 17. That notice, which identified Lemkin as 'a Polish lawyer now in' the US, described the book as '[a]n analysis of the laws and decrees promulgated by the Nazis and their puppet governments in the conquered areas of Europe' but did not use the word genocide. See *idem*.

genocide,' and that this 'new word' had been coined by Lemkin.[70] On July 30, 1946, the Times also had published a wire service story from Nuremberg. This report quoted French prosecutor de Ribes's closing argument to the IMT and conspicuously added, in brackets, credit to Lemkin for coining the word.[71]

The 26 August New York Times editorial continued its practice of prominently supporting Lemkin, his word and his legal objective. Reflecting detailed knowledge of the nearly-completed IMT trial, the editorial reported in its first sentence that British prosecutors Shawcross and Fyfe each had used this 'new word ... to castigate the twenty-one German leaders who are on trial ...' The Times explained that 'Prof. Raphael Lemkin,' whom it identified, in keeping with the earlier press reports and generously, as 'of Duke University' and an 'adviser on foreign affairs to our War Department,' had 'coined' the word and defined it as 'the biological and cultural destruction of national, religious and other entities.' The editorial explained that preexisting words were inadequate to describe Nazi crimes – 'mass murder' failed 'because it says nothing about motives' and '[d]enationalization is no better because it has no connotation of biological destruction.' The editorial then explained Lemkin's coinage of 'genocide,' recited past genocides (by Czarist Russia, Rumania and Turkey) that the US government had protested, explained Lemkin's objective to codify genocide as an international crime punishable in any country, reported that he had 'half accomplished' his goal with the genocide charge against the Nuremberg defendants, and closed by urging use of Lemkin's word in the Nuremberg 'sentence.'[72] All of this was content that Lemkin and few, if any, others could have provided. Although the editorial might have reflected merely the contents of the Times's clippings files and perhaps input from its Nuremberg trial reporters and visitors,[73] it seems likely that Lemkin himself supplied most of the information and convinced someone important at the Times that the paper should take this editorial stance.

Lemkin's successful effort, if it in fact occurred, to persuade the New York Times to lobby the IMT judges to use the word 'genocide' in their imminent Nuremberg Judgment would have been consistent with his other efforts. On 26 August 1946, the same day as the Times's editorial, Lemkin, then back in London, wrote to Sir David Maxwell Fyfe in Nuremberg. Lemkin recounted that he had just given, at the International Association of Criminal Law (IACL) meeting in Cambridge, England, a well-received report on genocide. Indeed, Lemkin wrote that he had already telephoned this information to Fyfe's secretary in Nuremberg and was writing in case that message had not reached him. Lemkin thanked Fyfe for his support and told

---

70 See Associated Press report, 'New Word "Genocide" Used In War Crimes Indictment', *N.Y. Times*, 22 October 1945, p. 5.

71 United Press report, 'Jackson to Start Home Tomorrow', *N.Y. Times*, 30 July 1946, p. 2.

72 'Genocide', *supra* n. 68.

73 See, e.g., C.L. Sulzberger, *A Long Row of Candles: Memoirs and Diaries [1934-1954]* (New York, Macmillan 1969), pp. 306-307 (publishing the New York Times's Chief Foreign Correspondent's 6 March 1946, diary entry regarding his attendance at Nuremberg trial sessions and his 'long talk' that day with Justice Jackson).

him to communicate to those who might be interested, including in Nuremberg, the news of Lemkin's positive reception at the IACL. Lemkin closed his letter with an implicit request that prosecutor Fyfe, at this post-summation moment in the trial, seek to influence the IMT judges as they were reaching their verdicts and drafting their Judgment:

> 'I think that the inclusion of Genocide in the judgment would contribute to the creation of a preventive atmosphere against repetition of similar acts of barbarity. Indeed, we cannot keep telling the world in endless sentences: – Don't murder members of national, racial and religious groups; don't sterilize them; don't impose abortions on them; don't steal children from them; don't compel their women to bear children for your country; – and so on. But we must tell the world now, at this unique occasion, – don't practice Genocide.'[74]

On Monday, September 30, 1946, the IMT judges began to read, with each taking a turn at the microphone, their lengthy Judgment. It found that the evidence established that certain defendants had, as charged in Count One, engaged in a conspiracy to commit the crime charged in Count Two, aggressive war.[75] The tribunal also found that the overwhelming evidence established that defendants had, as charged in Count Three, committed War Crimes,[76] and that they had, following the start of Germany's aggressive war making in 1939, committed Crimes against Humanity as charged in Count Four.[77]

On other legal issues, the tribunal's rulings were adverse to the prosecutors. The IMT decided to disregard Count One's charges of conspiracy to commit War Crimes and Crimes against Humanity, for instance, because the tribunal concluded that the London Charter, which was binding on the IMT,[78] defined only aggressive war as a criminal object of conspiracy.[79] With regard to Count Four, Crimes against Humanity, the IMT, again construing the London Charter as limiting its jurisdiction, held that its power reached only those crimes committed after Germany began its military aggression (September 1939), and that such crimes were encompassed within the scope of Count Three, War Crimes:

> 'With regard to crimes against humanity, there is no doubt whatever that political opponents were murdered in Germany before the war, and that many of them were kept in concentration camps in circumstances of great horror and cruelty. The policy of terror was certainly carried out on a vast scale, and in many cases was organized and systematic. The policy of persecution, repression and murder of civilians in Germany

---

[74] Raphael Lemkin letter to the Right Honorable David Maxwell Fyfe, 26 August 1946, pp. 1-2, in Raphael Lemkin Collection, P-154, Box 1, Folder 18, American Jewish Historical Society, Newton Centre, MA and New York, NY. Published with permission.

[75] See Judgment of the International Military Tribunal, XXII *Trial of the Major War Criminals before the International Military Tribunal* (Nuremberg, 1948), pp. 427, 468-469.

[76] Ibid., p. 469.

[77] See ibid., pp. 469-498.

[78] See ibid., p. 461.

[79] Ibid., pp. 469, 496.

before the war of 1939, who were likely to be hostile to the Government, was most ruthlessly carried out. The persecution of Jews during the same period is established beyond all doubt. To constitute crimes against humanity, the acts relied on before the outbreak of war must have been in execution of, or in connection with, any crimes within the jurisdiction of the Tribunal. The Tribunal is of the opinion that revolting and horrible as many of these crimes were, it has not been satisfactorily proved that they were done in execution of, or in connection with, any such crime. The Tribunal therefore cannot make a general declaration that the acts before 1939 were Crimes against Humanity within the meaning of the Charter, but from the beginning of the war in 1939 war crimes were committed on a vast scale which were also crimes against humanity; and insofar as the inhumane acts charged in the Indictment, and committed after the beginning of the war, did not constitute war crimes, they were all committed in execution of, or in connection with, the aggressive war and therefore constituted crimes against humanity.'[80]

Finally, as to the War Crimes charged in Count Three (and, for that matter, as to the entirety of the Judgment), the IMT, while describing in fact, based on the enormous trial record, the crime of genocide,[81] did not use Lemkin's word.

Lemkin wrote later that he was in Paris when the IMT announced its Judgment:

'When the Nuremberg Judgment was pronounced I was not in Nuremberg. At that time, the Peace Conference with the Satellite Axis Powers was taking place in Paris. I went to Paris and tried to include Genocide in the clauses of the peace treaties. I came at the wrong time because there was a stalemate in the negotiations. The delegates to the Peace Conference listened to me, but their minds were elsewhere. Under the stress of this work, I became ill and was confined to the American military hospital in Paris. It was there that I listened over the radio to the Nuremberg judgment which condemned the Nazis but failed to take into account an international law, the full moral, social, and humanitarian implications of Genocide as international crime.'[82]

Lemkin 'returned hastily from Paris to New York' in October 1946 and then concentrated his efforts on the United Nations.[83] Although US assistant prosecutor Henry King decades later recalled seeing Lemkin at the Grand Hotel in Nuremberg in fall 1946 following the IMT Judgment,[84] it seems more likely that those were

[80] Ibid., p. 498.

[81] See W.A. Schabas, *supra* n. 29, p. 44. Indeed, Lemkin himself later wrote that '[t]he evidence produced at the Nuremberg trial gave full support to the concept of genocide.' *Idem*, quoting Lemkin, 'Genocide as a Crime in International Law', 41 *AJIL* (1947), p. 145 at p. 147.

[82] Lemkin draft autobiography, '1st chapter?', n.d., in Lemkin Papers, *supra* n. 9, at Reel 2, p. 5.

[83] Ibid., p. 6.

[84] See H.T. King, Jr., 'Genocide and Nuremberg', in R. Henham & P. Behrens (eds.), *The Criminal Law of Genocide: International, Comparative and Contextual Aspects* (Aldershot, Ashgate Publishing Ltd. 2007), p. 30; H.T. King, Jr., B.B. Ferencz & W.R. Harris, 'Origins of the Genocide Convention', 40 *Case Western Reserve Journal of International Law* (2007-08), p. 13 at pp. 13-14; J.Q. Barrett, W.R. Harris, H.T. King, Jr., & B.B. Ferencz, 'Nuremberg and Genocide: Historical Perspectives', in E. Andersen & D.M. Crane (eds.), *Proceedings of the Second International Humanitarian Law Dialogs* (Washington, American Society of International Law 2009), pp. 47-48. In our subsequent conversations, King, who lived in the Grand Hotel from his arrival in Nuremberg in May 1946 until he moved

memories of Lemkin in Nuremberg that spring and summer, before the IMT trial had concluded.

In the US that fall, Lemkin was present as the fledgling United Nations met for the first time in Lake Success, New York. Before the year was out, his efforts led delegates to introduce, and then the General Assembly to pass unanimously, a resolution calling genocide a crime under international law. Earlier that same day (11 December 1946), the General Assembly affirmed the legal principles of the August 1945 London Agreement and IMT Charter and the IMT's September 1946 Judgment. From 1947 through the end of his life, Lemkin then concentrated on and accomplished UN passage of the Genocide Convention and then its entry into effect through state ratifications.

In all of that, Nuremberg was for Lemkin an episodic, only somewhat productive, and thus personally transitional undertaking. In August 1947, Justice Jackson's son Bill, his former Nuremberg executive assistant who then was completing his first year in what ultimately would be a fifty-three year career practicing law in the Milbank, Tweed firm in New York City, wrote this in one of his regular letters to his father in Washington:

> 'Dear Dad:
> A strange voice came on the telephone this morning, and it turned out to be Dr. Lemkin, who is now a sort of part-time expert consultant to the UN, chiefly on the draft convention of genocide. I never could quite figure the bugger out when he was in London and then Nuremberg ...'[85]

V. Conclusion

There is a disjunction between the general greatness and historical significance of Raphael Lemkin and what his role really was in the process that led up to and included the international trial at Nuremberg of the principal Nazi war criminals. Lemkin conceptualised the crime of genocide and ultimately achieved its recognition in international law. He was only barely, and not centrally, involved, however, in the international diplomatic process and then the Nuremberg trial during 1945 and 1946.

For international law, those seventeen months of Nuremberg involved great events and significant advances toward global understanding of genocide and, ultimately, its criminalisation. The August 1945 London Agreement and Charter of the International Military Tribunal did not use Lemkin's word 'genocide,' but they codified

---

into a private house there late that fall, clarified that he could not recall whether his Grand Hotel encounters with Lemkin predated or followed the IMT's 30 September 1946, Judgment.

85 Bill [William E. Jackson] letter to Dad [Justice Robert H. Jackson], 11 August 1947, in Jackson Papers, *supra* n. 3, Box 2, Folder 8. I thank Jim Fussell for first calling this letter to my attention. This letter is, alas, cited and quoted in David Irving, *Nuremberg: The Last Battle* (London, Focal Point Publications 1996), pp. 335 n. 30 & 351 n. 29.

for the first time Crimes Against Humanity, an overlapping legal concept of great significance. The October 1945 Nuremberg Indictment was the first international legal agreement to use the word 'genocide.' During the Nuremberg trial proceedings in 1946, British, Soviet and French prosecutors used and defined the word in court, thus advancing its visibility and comprehension. The September 1946 IMT Judgment did not use the word, but the Judgment recognised legally the criminality of any individual planning, supervising or committing genocidal conduct as part of waging aggressive war and, related, the new category of Crimes against Humanity during such war making. And all of this gave Lemkin and his concept stature and credibility as he then turned his efforts to the United Nations and, in time, achieved its 1948 adoption of the Genocide Convention.

Yet Lemkin was involved in Nuremberg infrequently, from its periphery, somewhat unofficially, in focused but also egotistical, obsessive, at times annoying personal pursuit of anyone, in any venue, who might make use of the word that he had coined. He was, in the cascade of complex, human actions at Nuremberg during 1945 and 1946 that advanced the criminalisation of genocide, the precipitating agent. But he was not, in these actions, alone or even primary. Lemkin fathered the word 'genocide' and was the leading promoter of its comprehension, but many people, including Murray Bernays, Sidney Alderman, Francis Shea, Robert Jackson and their many other allies and colleagues along the way, contributed much to an essential part of what history properly recalls as Lemkin's achievement.

THE UNITED NATIONS AND THE ORIGINS OF THE GENOCIDE CONVENTION 1946–1948

Jost Dülffer

When the 'United Nations Organization' was founded during the San Francisco Conference of 1945, this was not the first institution of this name.[1] The war coalition of 26 nations which had been founded in early 1942 bore exactly the same name, 'United Nations,' and it was no accident that the new UN was formally only *renamed*, as the permanent, peacetime institution of the coalition which had defeated Nazi Germany and its allies. When re-examining the plans and expectations for a peaceful world and co-operation after the war, we have to state that there was a clear primacy of Great Power politics on the agenda of the new organisation. The most important impulses were derived from the meetings of the Big Three powers.[2]

From Tehran 1943 to Yalta 1945, the main driving force for these three powers was maintaining their unity into the post-war period. Joseph Stalin made the strongest remarks on this, when he argued[3] that 'the main thing was to prevent quarrels in the future between the three Great Powers and that the task, therefore, was to secure their unity for the future. The convent of the new World Organization should have this as its primary task.' Franklin D. Roosevelt also attached the greatest importance to the institutionalisation of this effort in the new world order of the United Nations system. The Security Council and the power of veto of the final five permanent member states, the basic principle of national sovereignty, codified in Article 2(7) of the UN Charter – all these go back to massive political interests of both

[1] R.C. Hilderbrand, *Dumbarton Oaks. The Origins of the United Nations and the Search for Postwar Security* (Chapel Hill, University of North Carolina Press 1990); G. Schild, *Bretton Woods and Dumbarton Oaks. American economic and political postwar planning in the summer of 1944* (Basingstoke, Macmillan 1996); E. Luard, *A History of the United Nations, Vol. I: The Years of Western Domination, 1945-1955* (London and Basingstoke, Macmillan 1982); H. Volger, *Geschichte der Vereinten Nationen*, 2nd edn. (Munich, Oldenbourg 2008), pp. 1-28; Paul Kennedy, *Parliament of Men. The United Nations and the Quest for a World Government* (New York, Random House 2006).

[2] J. Wheeler Bennett & A. Nicholls, *The Semblance of Peace. The Political Settlement after the Second World War* (London, Macmillan 1972); W. Loth, *Die Teilung der Welt. Geschichte des Kalten Krieges, 1941-1955*, 8th edn. (Munich, dtv 2000); J. Dülffer, *Jalta, 4. Februar 1945. Zweiter Weltkrieg und Entstehung der bipolaren Welt*, 2nd edn. (Munich, dtv 1999); D. Reynolds, W. Kimball & A. Chubarian (eds.), *Allies at War: The Soviet, American, and British Experience, 1939-1945* (Basingstoke, Macmillan 1994).

[3] Third Plenary Meeting, Yalta, 6 February 1945, *Foreign Relations of the United States. The Conferences of Malta and Yalta* (Washington, Government Printing Office 1955), pp. 666 et seq.

C. Safferling and E. Conze (eds.), The Genocide Convention Sixty Years after its Adoption

the Soviet Union and the United States. It was only because of the 1944 election campaign that President Roosevelt was willing to concede more authority to the General Assembly. It was Stalin in particular who had warned him in Tehran that the smaller states might want to have more rights, rather than simply expressing their opinion on the decisions taken by the Great Powers, as the US President had originally proposed.[4] This became the basis for the secondary competence of the General Assembly in the UN Charter. To be clear: the Great Powers[5] were there at the start and it was these states which made the new institution an instrument which must not interfere with their ideas of a collectively agreed new world order – mainly directed against a new 'fascist' aggression. Seen this way, the peace settlements with the former aggressor states were clearly reserved for the Great Powers first, and only at a later stage, did the smaller belligerents of World War II have the opportunity to add minor points to the Paris Peace Treaties of February 1947.

It is well known that soon the unity of the Great Powers and their common management of the major security problems, i.e., questions of war and peace, were to be superseded by the conflicts of the forthcoming 'Cold War.' But nevertheless, remnants of co-operation as well as status problems of the permanent members of the UN Security Council also played a major role when dealing with other topics on the early UN agenda. This can be shown for the origins of the Genocide Convention, too.

I. Chronological outline

The chronology of events is well known.[6] Briefly after the judgment of the tribunal of the major war criminals in Nuremberg was delivered on 30 September/1 October, 1946, the UN General Assembly on 11 December, 1946, passed Resolution 96(I), in which genocide was declared a crime. This resolution was passed to the Economic and Social Council for further consideration and proposals. As a conse-

---

[4] Roosevelt had proposed an all-states committee ('Executive committee') which could make recommendations, and the Great Powers, then called the 'Four Policemen,' should decide on the major questions. Stalin: 'He did not think that the small powers of Europe would like the organization composed of the Four Policemen.' Stalin to Roosevelt, 29 November 1943, in *Foreign Relations of the United States. The Conferences of Tehran and Cairo* (Washington, Government Printing Office 1961), pp. 529-531.

[5] Originally, China had been the fourth power. France was only accepted in Yalta as the fifth member with a permanent seat in the Security Council – a major concession to Great Britain, which preferred a continental European power as a counterweight against the Soviet Union. China's position is neglected here because the Guomindang government of Chiang Kai-shek, under the conditions of the civil war, could never really play a major role in this pertinent question.

[6] The best overviews and reference works: W.A. Schabas, *Genocide in International Law. The Crime of Crimes* (Cambridge, Cambridge University Press 2000), esp. pp. 51-101; J. Cooper, *Raphael Lemkin and the Struggle for the Genocide Convention* (Houndsmills, Palgrave Macmillan 2008); P. Drost, *The Crime of the State. United Nations Legislation on International Criminal Law,* Vol. II (Leyden, A.W. Sythoff 1959) a good, but general first overview; H. Abtahi & P. Webb (eds.), *The Genocide Convention. The Travaux Préparatoires (The Travaux Préparatoires of Multilateral Treaties)* (Leiden, Martinus Nijhoff, December 2008) is not yet available to this author.

quence, on 28 March 1947, ECOSOC returned the matter to the Secretary General and asked him to undertake the 'necessary studies.' His Human Rights Division commissioned three experts to prepare a draft, Raphael Lemkin (USA), Henri Donnedieu de Vabres (France), and Vespasian V. Pella (Romania). On 13 June 1947, this 'Secretariat's Draft' was sent by the Secretary General to the 'Committee on the Progressive Development of International Law and its Codification' and then to ECOSOC which, on 6 August, again passed it to the General Secretary and asked him to collect the opinions of states for the further consideration of ECOSOC. Then, on 21 November, 1947, the General Assembly under Resolution 180(II) returned the draft to its legal committee (Sixth Committee), together with comments by several states. ECOSOC created an *ad hoc* drafting committee consisting of seven states. After 28 sessions, their new draft was submitted with comments to the Commission on Human Rights in June 1948. Again via this committee and the ECOSOC, a new Draft Genocide Convention reached the General Assembly's Human Rights division, the Sixth Committee, which completed its examinations on 2 December 1948. Basically, this text was adopted by the General Assembly in the form of a resolution on 9 December 1948. This became known as the Genocide Convention and came in effect on 12 January 1951. Another convention, the Universal Declaration of Human Rights had been negotiated by separate bodies and was signed one day after the Genocide Convention, on 10 December 1948.[7]

II. Basic questions

The course of debates clearly shows that the convention did not have an easy birth, but one in which many tactical objections as well as questions of principle were raised, both in the open, and even more behind closed doors. Certainly, the genocide question was negotiated under the responsibility of the General Assembly where the permanent members of the Security Council held no veto power, but nevertheless a convention against the opposition of one or more of these powers would have made little sense. During this phase of building the United Nations, the position of each individual state or its representative depended mainly on *two tactical political reasons*: firstly, would the position taken further one's own country's national interests; and secondly, would it permit others to accuse one's own state of past, present or possible future violations of the convention, i.e., of genocide?

The positions adopted in the General Assembly and its commissions shall be analysed in this regard. I will limit myself to the four questions of greatest impact during these negotiations.[8] 1. Should there be a new international institution to

[7] P.G. Lauren, *The Evolution of International Human Rights, 1945-1995. Vision seen*, 2nd edn. (Philadelphia, University of Pennsylvania Press 1993), pp. 188-232; J. Morsink, *The Universal Declaration on Human Rights. Origins, Drafting and Intent* (Philadelphia, University of Pennsylvania Press 1999).

[8] A similar list, but also the debate in further research mostly by intellectuals: A. Curthoys & J. Docker, 'Defining Genocide', in D. Stone (ed.), *The Historiography of Genocide* (London, Macmillan Palgrave 2008), pp. 9-41.

judge the crime of genocide, i.e., a criminal court? 2. Should the problem of 'cultural genocide' be included in the definitions? 3. Should 'political genocide' be part of the definition of genocide? 4. Should there be precautions not only to punish genocide committed, but also to prevent it in earlier preparatory stages? (The fifth question would be whether *intention* forms an intrinsic factor of genocide. This question was discussed in detail only in later years. In this essay it will only be dealt with in passing).

At this stage not all United Nations procedures, rites and rules were fixed. To a certain extent, committee members could express their personal legal opinions, which might not have been bound by government instructions from home. This holds especially true for representatives of smaller or medium-sized states, which might not have had an established or political interest in a certain form of resolution or convention. These states could also be prone to outside influences exerted by pressure groups or individuals. In addition, the local atmosphere at the meeting places – Lake Success, Geneva, Paris, Washington – and the lobbyists, present unofficially, played an important role, as well as strong personal convictions regarding the development of international law or mankind in general, or even personal vanity. All these factors could intermingle, of course.

The situation was basically different, when the interests of the Great Powers came into play. Then the situation was completely different from that where only minor states stated their opinions. One possible attitude of a Great Power was that its government had a strong and active interest in the definition of the crime of genocide – either wanting to see genocide punished because it had been inflicted on the country in the past, present or possibly in a foreseeable future, or wanting to avoid any attempt to use the Convention against it for past or present politics, for whatever reason. Understandably, it was above all the Great Powers who might be guided by the idea that a certain phrasing of a Genocide Convention would be used against their government or state, even for past events. Nevertheless, even over this aspect, they sometimes displayed a wide-ranging lack of interest. This might have been the result of a haughty Great Power attitude, or even arrogance, because they saw themselves as standing above the negotiated clauses.

III. Great Power interests and the negotiations for the Genocide Convention

The staunchest opponent of a genocide convention was the *United Kingdom*. One of the arguments which were frequently repeated was the claim that the Nuremberg trial had already *de facto* condemned genocide – so that the principle was clear. At several other points, British delegates tried to move the deliberations on genocide to the International Law Commission. The majority of observers were convinced: these British measures were intended to stall the convention. Why? Sir Hartley Shawcross, the British chief prosecutor at Nuremberg who also became principal delegate of his country to the UN from 1945 to 1949 in November 1946, still publicly claimed a favourable attitude:[9] 'It was necessary ... that international law should limit the omnipotence of certain States over their citizens ... International conventions should be concluded, but the public denunciation of this crime would have to take place immediately.' But it was only two months later that the principal legal adviser of the FO reported to his government:[10] 'It is a complete waste of time, seeing that, if genocide takes place anywhere, it will take place under conditions where no international convention will be observed.' Indeed there were actual circumstances just at this time which had involved Britain in grave international conflicts. It was not the colonial past of the European powers, which might have caused some memory of massacres. Neither in the British nor in the French case is there any direct and explicit connection with this problem.

In spring 1947, Britain had returned its trusteeship of Palestine to the United Nations for further consideration.[11] In November 1947, the General Assembly proposed a separation between Jews and Arabs – a solution which was immediately rejected by the Arab states who fought a bitter war against Israel's declaration of independence in May 1948, when the British authorities finally left Palestine. Already in summer 1947, the Arab states began to oppose the idea of a Genocide Convention because it could be seen as an instrument to help the Zionist cause.[12] The United Kingdom, particularly from 1947, had a massive interest in remaining in a mediator's position between the Arab world, which was important for the future of the British Empire in the Middle East (Egypt, the Suez Canal and oil were the major issues), and the Zionists, who could be regarded as custodians of the cause of the European Jews, a logical follow-up to World War II and the genocide.

Besides the violent situation in Palestine which, among others, caused the British to prevent the landing of the ship 'Exodus' with more than 4000 Jewish survivors of World War II in Palestine in July 1947, there was massive British interest in not giving the Arab states a pretext for accusing Britain of being partisan in the Zionist cause. The question was not whether the character of the violence towards Jews or Arabs could have any meaningful connection with a definition of genocide, but for the Arab states, the fight against a Genocide Convention became a real and important tactical instrument in fighting British interests. At this stage, the United States refrained from helping the British government in this question – thus the former mandate was returned to the General Assembly of the UN. Clearly, Washington was prepared to step in for Britain on other issues – for example, the Truman Doctrine of March 1947 was aimed at stabilising Turkey and Greece against communist intervention –, but refrained from doing so in the Palestine case.

---

9 J. Cooper, *supra* n. 6, p. 84 (*Journal of the United Nations*, 2 December 1946).

10 J. Cooper, *supra* n. 6, p. 94 (Eric Becket in a report to his Government).

11 Good overview: D. Reynolds, *Britannia Overruled. British Policy and World Power in the 20th Century* (London, Longman 1991), pp. 145-172; J. Brown & W.R. Louis (eds.), *The Oxford History of the British Empire. The Twentieth Century* (Oxford, Oxford University Press 1999).

12 J. Cooper, *supra* n. 6, p. 96; B. Wasserstein, *The British in Palestine. The Mandatory Government and the Arab-Jewish Conflict,* 2nd edn. (Oxford, Oxford University Press 1991).

The Indian question and the violence following the independence of India and the partition of the South Asian subcontinent into the states of India and Pakistan after 15 August, 1947, was a different matter:[13] since 1946, violence between Hindus and Muslims had accelerated the planned British withdrawal. Now there was a chaotic migration: the flight and expulsion of millions of Muslims from India, and Hindus from East and West Pakistan. In the process, over 200,000 people, maybe half a million or even a million, died due to violence. In late 1946, the Indian ambassador to the UN, Vijaya Lakshmi Pandit, the sister of Congress Party leader Jawarhal Nehru, had been instrumental in moving the first UN resolution for genocide;[14] the following autumn brought bitter recriminations by the Pakistani delegate against India. According to him hundreds of thousands of people had been murdered for religious reasons, with the connivance of the Indian government – a reproach which the Indian delegate flatly rejected.[15] Without doubt, in this case, the debate on the Genocide Convention had entered the sphere of current politics and had become an instrument of war and then a political battle between two Commonwealth members. To make things worse, Pakistan accused India of genocide in at least four Security Council sessions, on 28 January, 7 May, 3 and 8 June, 1948.[16] The Pakistani foreign minister also raised this topic in the debates on genocide in the ECOSOC.[17] In the eyes of the proponents of a Genocide Convention, this event was a reason for increased urgency, while for British policy-makers it became a reason to try and bury this dangerous undertaking, because of Britain's leading, but declining role as a world power.

The *Soviet Union's* attitude towards a convention was ambivalent. On 20 November 1947, it formed an obstructive coalition with the United Kingdom, trying to adjourn the whole debate. But basically, the Socialist state followed a policy of co-operation in favour of a convention, but with its own specific aims. In the 1930s, the Soviet delegate and deputy Foreign Minister Andrey Vishinsky, had been the prosecutor in many of the Stalinist show trials (and later became Foreign Minister from 1949-1953). During this earlier period, he had published articles opposing 'counter-revolutionary intervention through criminal law.'[18] And of course the memory of the lethal Soviet policies against the 'kulaks' and their starvation policy in the Ukraine, with millions of dead, as well as their deportation policy during World War II, were commonly known facts, but not discussed in diplomatic circles. However, this does not seem to have overly influenced the Soviet Union's attitude.[19]

---

[13] R.J. Moore, *Escape from Empire. The Attlee Government and the Indian Problem* (Oxford, Oxford University Press 1983).

[14] J. Cooper, *supra* n. 6, p. 80.

[15] Ibid., p. 100.

[16] Ibid., p. 127.

[17] *Idem* (quotes letter form Zaffrulla Khan to Charles Malik, 4 February 1948).

[18] J. Cooper, *supra* n. 6, p. 83.

[19] Ibid., p. 102.

Maybe this was one reason, though, why the Soviet Union vehemently opposed the inclusion of political genocide in the convention.[20] However, the attitude of the Communist state seems to have had much more to do with the concrete situation in Eastern Europe in the years following World War II, where all political parties were more or less deprived of their independence, and where legal and illegal terror as well as other internal measures with mass killings took place.[21] In an ideology where class struggle was seen as a basic principle of history and where the communist party functioned as the avant-garde of the proletariat, the persecution of other parties, or bourgeois, capitalist governments even by means of force, was probably the reason for the massive Soviet fight against the inclusion of political genocide in a convention. Most western politicians (including the chief lobbyist and inventor of the notion of genocide, Raphael Lemkin) objected to the inclusion of political groups among those to be protected against genocide because they were regarded as too volatile. The delegates were especially impressed by the argument that people were free to decide both to join or leave such an organisation (political party).

On the contrary, the Soviet attitude seems to have been influenced by a much more essentialist or structurally based assessment of such groups. On the other hand, Soviet delegates repeatedly moved for a wider interpretation of racist groups. For them, the genocide of racial groups had been closely linked to Fascist Nazi theories[22] 'which preach racial and national hatred, the domination of the so-called superior races and the extermination of inferior races.' This was not exactly Marxist terminology. As far as can be seen, this attitude was not so much a tactical one, but during these years was frequently based on a hope of establishing a common basis with the Western powers (which, for example, had been included in the Potsdam Declaration of 1945).[23] And for obvious reasons, this had to do with the experience of racial war waged by Germany during World War II. 'Racism is [the] spiritual father of G[enocide]. Organic relationship between Fascism and Genocide.'[24] The Soviet Union also proposed a radical ban on propaganda and wanted to punish 'all forms of public propaganda (press, radio, cinema etc.) aimed at inciting racial, national or religious enmities or hatred or at provoking the commission of acts of genocide.'[25]

In reality, during these years, this pretended fight against any fascist propaganda had more and more been used as an arbitrary instrument to promote Soviet rule in

[20] There exists no special study on the Soviet attitude. The following observations are based on J. Cooper, *supra* n. 6, and W.A. Schabas, *supra* n. 6, *passim*.

[21] Good overview: G. Roberts, *Stalin's Wars. From World War to Cold War, 1939-1953* (New Haven and London, Yale University Press 2006); S. Creuzberger & M. Görtemaker (eds)., *Gleichschaltung unter Stalin? Die Entwicklung der Parteien im östlichen Europa, 1944-1949* (Paderborn, Schöningh 2002).

[22] J. Cooper, *supra* n. 6, p. 123; cf., UN Doc. A/C.6/273 (Soviet amendment 18 November 1948).

[23] Potsdam declaration, in *Foreign Relations of the United States: The Conference of Berlin*, Vol. II (Washington, Government Printing Office 1960), pp. 1481-1485 (This included the 'four Ds': democratisation, decentralisation, demilitarisation and denazification).

[24] J. Cooper, *supra* n. 6, p. 139.

[25] UN Doc. A/C.6/215 Rev 1, 9 October 1948.

Eastern Europe. It also became a pretext for abolishing political parties or other organisations which were labelled 'fascist.' But this does not seem to have been the main motive for Soviet proposals to legitimise the destruction of free opinion in the public sphere.[26] On the other hand, this process was dominant in the western assessment of the Soviet policy of abolishing freedom of expression. With this in mind, preparatory steps, such as propaganda or the incitement of hate, could not be made part of the new convention. 'If it were admitted that incitement were an act of genocide, any newspaper article criticising a political group, for example, or suggesting certain measures with regard to such a group for the general welfare, might make it possible for certain States' to claim an act of genocide, was the stated US attitude.[27]

The *United States'* attitude to a convention was probably the most complicated one.[28] Firstly, the US had a long tradition of human rights; powerful humanitarian groups especially Jewish and Christian ones, were agitating for a convention. Of course, the annihilation of the European Jews during World War II was their yardstick, and the US delegation made a point of sharing opinions with these groups or individuals very often. The *ad hoc* committee was headed by the American diplomat, John Maktos, and the delegation in some cases was prone to accepting very far-reaching regulations. Secondly, while diplomatic considerations of establishing a common position with the other great Western power, the United Kingdom, were not important in 1946, they gained some weight in the following two years. Thirdly, the questions of domestic legislation in regard to all problems of genocide, and new or far-reaching international obligations towards establishing a new international court were not clearly discussed. To summarise the argument: as in many other cases the United States developed two foreign policies: one which was more oriented towards domestic issues – a broad plea for human rights and punishment of violations – and one more oriented towards *foreign issues*. This was the case especially in the genocide question.

There was one matter on which the US was and remained strictly critical: the question of the inclusion of cultural genocide. Understandably, Raphael Lemkin and other people were guided by the image of German policies not only towards the Jews, but they focussed clearly on German racial policies against Poles and other Slav countries as well. To a large extent, Lemkin's 1944 book, *Axis Rule in Occupied Europe*, was a collection of data which could be interpreted in this sense, e.g., showing Germanisation policies etc.[29] During the deliberations on the 'Secretariat's Draft,' Lemkin had argued in favour of a multiplicity of cultures, so that 'cultural genocide' meant much more than forced assimilation. It could be inflicted also 'by

---

26 M. Lippman, 'A Road Map to the 1948 Convention on the Prevention and Punishment of the Crime Genocide', 4(2) *Journal of Genocide Research* (2002), pp. 177-195, esp. pp. 182-185.

27 W.A. Schabas, *supra* n. 6, p. 268.

28 L. LeBlanc, *The United States and the Genocide Convention* (Durham, Duke University Press 1991).

29 R. Lemkin, *Axis Rule in Occupied Europe. Laws of Occupation. Analysis of Government. Proposals for Redress* (Washington, Carnegie Endowment for International Peace 1944).

the involuntary transfer of children from one group to another, by the destruction of the nation's intelligentsia, by the prohibition of the use of a national language in private conversation, and by the burning of books and the destruction of religious monuments or their diversion to alien uses.'[30] This was, of course, very vague and in practice would have mostly been accompanied by other physical measures against people. As a consequence, cultural genocide as such was not included in the Secretariat's Draft, but only the issue of 'preventing its [a group's] preservation or development.'[31] Later, however, the notion of cultural genocide was included in the *ad hoc* committee's draft. Because it formed such a broad notion which might possibly be rather difficult to delimit, it was confined to a separate article. Delegates (such as the Danish one) could mock that the closure of libraries could not properly be regarded as genocide.

What was more important, of course, was the attitude of the *United States* towards this issue. In the summer of 1947, the State Department had accepted the inclusion of political groups and of cultural genocide in the Convention with the comment: 'The possibility exists that sporadic outbreaks against the Negro population of the United States may be brought to the attention of the United Nations,' but since the US authorities would retain their jurisdiction anyway, 'no possibility can be foreseen of the United States being held in violation of the treaty.'[32] Thus the reliance on national sovereignty on the one hand, enabled the US in 1947 to support wide-ranging efforts for a convention on the other hand. But the subtext of earlier US treatment of the Native Americans (Indians) or African Americans (Negroes) remained. In 1948, the US-President of the *ad hoc* committee, Matkos, even pleaded for a new world court – but under these new conditions the question of cultural genocide which had been included in the draft, was vehemently rejected by the US.[33]

In addition, the US delegation argued that primarily the persecution of individuals should be punished – cultural arguments belonged more to the protection of minorities, a matter where the League of Nations had already broken ground.[34]

---

[30] J. Cooper, *supra* n. 6, p. 91 (E 447).

[31] A.D. Moses, 'The Holocaust and Genocide', in D. Stone (ed.), *The Historiography of the Holocaust* (Houndsmills, Palgrave Macmillan 2004), pp. 533-551 at p. 541; cf., A.D. Moses, 'Empire, Colony, Genocide: Keywords and the Philosophy of History', in *idem*, *Empire, Colony, Genocide. Conquest, Occupation, and Subaltern Resistance in World History* (New York, London, Berghahn Books 2008), pp. 3-54 at pp. 17-20; A. Rabinbach, 'Raphael Lemkin's Concept of Genocide. Fifty Years later. The First Conviction was handed down', in *IP Magazine. Transatlantic Edition, Spring 2005*, pp. 70-75; C. Kraft, 'Völkermorde im 20. Jahrhundert. Raphael Lemkin und die Ahndung des Genozids durch das internationale Strafrecht', in J. Hösler & W. Kessler (eds.), *Finis Mundi. Endzeiten und Weltenden im östlichen Europa, Festschrift für Hans Lemberg* (Stuttgart, Steiner 1998), pp. 91-111.

[32] J. Cooper, *supra* n. 6, p. 99.

[33] Ibid., pp. 123, 124.

[34] W.A. Schabas, *supra* n. 6, pp. 179 et seq.; C. Fink, *Defending the Rights of Others. The Great Powers, the Jews, and International Minority Protection, 1878-1938* (Cambridge, Cambridge University Press 2004); as to the divergence of peace-making after the two world wars in regard to minorities: J. Dülffer, 'Die Diskussion um das Selbstbestimmungsrecht und die Friedensregelungen nach den Welt-

Other delegations argued that the question of cultural protection ought better be included in the human rights declaration, which finally, however, did not include this issue. On both questions – cultural genocide and a new international court – the US position ended up being a minority position. The underlying principle was: the more the US seemed ready to accept new international authorities or even a court, the less it would be ready to include broad provisions, such as cultural genocide, in the convention.

This position changed again in spring of 1948, when John Matkos was instructed by his government not to accept universal jurisdiction by an international tribunal and to confine the crime of genocide to governments only.[35] Among others, the Soviet Union continued to argue at this time that Nazi policies had also aimed at the cultural destruction of whole nations,[36] and pleaded for the inclusion of 'national-cultural genocide.' In a special draft for the *ad hoc* committee, the Soviet Union, together with other states, also wanted to include the definition of 'destroying, or preventing the use of, the libraries, museums, schools, historical monuments, places of worship or other cultural institutions and objects of the group' as cultural genocide.[37] This can be easily understood as a general circumscription of the sufferings of World War II, but also applies to some events which had just happened in Soviet-dominated Eastern Europe. In the decisive session of the UN assembly's Sixth Committee, on 25 October 1948, all the western Great Powers voted against the inclusion of cultural genocide.

With a majority of 25 to 16 votes (and four abstentions), cultural genocide was excluded.[38] The Soviet Union remained one of the proponents of cultural genocide. Probably, besides the United States with their Native American problem, the European colonial powers also felt that for them some problems might arise from such a wording.[39] Indeed the difference between cultural genocide on the one hand, and common assimilation of – as it was then seen – 'primitive cultures' was not easy to define. The delegate Gilberto Amado from Brazil warned that 'some minorities might have used it as an excuse for opposing perfectly normal assimilation in new countries.'[40] Thus it was preferable to delete this dangerous provision.

Similar to the United States, French delegates stressed their state's long-standing championship of human rights since the French Revolution. But in other aspects, the fourth Great Power, *France,* developed a position substantially different from that of the other three. Firstly, its representatives tried to see the Nuremberg principles and the Nuremberg judgment as precursors and consequently moved phrases connecting the Convention to this trial. Secondly, in the French view, the

---

kriegen des 20. Jahrhunderts', in J. Fisch (ed.), *Selbstbestimmung und Selbstbestimmungsrecht: Errungenschaft der Moderne oder kollektive Illusion?* [*Self-Determination and the Right of Self-Determination: Achievement of Modernity or Collective Illusion?*] (Munich, Oldenbourg 2010 – forthcoming).

35 J. Cooper, *supra* n. 6, p. 131.

36 Ibid., p. 153; W.A. Schabas, *supra* n. 6, p. 181.

37 W.A. Schabas, *supra* n. 6, p. 182 (quotes UN Doc. E/AC.25/SR 14, p. 13).

38 *United Nations, General Assembly, Sixth Committee, 1948* (Paris, no publisher 1948), p. 206.

39 J. Cooper, *supra* n. 6, p. 158; W.A. Schabas, *supra* n. 6, pp. 178-189.

40 W.A. Schabas, *supra* n. 6, p. 184 (UN Doc. A/C 6/SR. 135); M. Lippman, *supra* n. 26, p. 183.

question of the annihilation of a group as such or 'in part,' could also mean the killing of one person – if the intent was genocidal. Thirdly, cultural genocide was not a principle which the French would accept in any case. Further research would be needed to clarify whether this was a result of the French colonial doctrine of assimilation[41] which gave all subjects a chance to become French citizens by adopting the French language and culture.

In the light of its own recent history and therefore national interests, it is astonishing that the Soviet Union propagated the inclusion of 'cultural-national genocide' and also took a positive attitude towards the institution of a new world court. The fact that genocide was regarded as a crime under international law stood at the beginning of all deliberations. There was a common consensus in this assessment. The evasive or obstructive arguments which were, e.g., favoured by the British delegation, were that genocide had already been implicitly banned, and explicitly after the Nuremberg trials. Therefore no further action or resolution was needed. The fact that genocide as a notion had not literally been included at Nuremberg, was to be one of the main motives for Raphael Lemkin to lobby for a special Genocide Convention.[42] After declaring genocide a crime, this would lead to the logical conclusion that all states were obliged to prosecute this crime in their domestic laws. This would include individuals or groups. But from the beginning of the debate, it was evident that in most cases states themselves would be involved in genocidal crimes. How to deal with them or their representatives?[43] While some smaller states concluded from this the necessity to create a new international court, others warned that this would be an infringement of national sovereignty.

With hindsight, both positions can be logically accepted. The attitude of the Great Powers can best be explained by the idea that they themselves would never accept the accusation of genocide. At a very early stage, Sir Hartley Shawcross argued this: it was necessary that 'international law should limit the omnipotence of certain States over their citizens and in certain cases protect them against their own government.'[44] France also traditionally had a strong standing as the nation of human rights. Likewise, the Frenchman René Cassin was a central figure in the elaboration of the Human Rights Convention. And in 1948, the French delegate also supported the creation of an international court.[45] Thus a French proposal of 5 February 1948 went so far as to include detailed provisions for the establishment of an international court in the Hague which should have exclusive competence for

---

[41] Ch.-R. Ageron, *La decolonization française* (Paris, Armand Colin 1994), R. v. Albertini, *Dekolonisation. Die Diskussion über Verwaltung und Zukunft der Kolonien, 1919-1960* (Cologne, Westdeutscher Verlag 1966), pp. 307-538.

[42] W.A. Schabas, *supra* n. 6, pp. 37-42; J. Cooper, *supra* n. 6, pp. 73-83; A. Weinke, '"Von Nürnberg nach Den Haag"? Das Internationale Militärtribunal in historischer Perspektive', in Justizministerium Nordrhein-Westfalen (ed.), *Leipzig – Nürnberg – Den Haag. Neue Fragestellung und neue Forschungen zum Verhältnis von Menschenrechtsverbrechen, justizieller Säuberung und Völkerstrafrecht* (Recklinghausen, Justizakademie 2008), pp. 20-43.

[43] M. Lippman, *supra* n. 26, pp. 185 et seq.

[44] J. Cooper, *supra* n. 6, p. 84.

[45] Ibid., pp. 139, 156, 161.

genocide in relation to national courts.[46] In the Sixth Committee, France went so far as to propose:[47] Genocide 'is committed, encouraged or tolerated by the rulers of a State.' This could have had far-reaching consequences for a future court – and also for all states, including the Great Powers.

No other major power was prepared to follow this course. While the United States on its part refused to take on a clear responsibility for transforming the Genocide Convention into national, i.e., potentially state law, the other Great Powers, with the exception of France, were also negative: the Soviet Union, but also Britain, dismissed the idea of recognising such far-reaching world law. The compromise finally found in Article VI of the Convention ruled that, as an alternative to national courts, crimes may be judged 'by such international penal tribunal as may have jurisdiction with respect to those Contracting Parties which shall have accepted jurisdiction.' This left the way open to *ad hoc* tribunals, but did not create an *ad hoc* or permanent new court.[48] In the final stages of the negotiations, Great Britain and other states had argued that other UN organisations, such as the Security Council, might deal with genocide which was not punished nationally, and on other occasions, the British delegate had argued, that the punishment of states' crimes would normally mean war.[49]

In the last days before the unanimous adoption of the Genocide Convention by 56 states in December 1948, the United Kingdom once again worded its fundamental criticism that the Convention had started from the wrong end, namely from individual crimes, while France deplored the failure of the institution of a new court, but stressed that the principle had been accepted anyway. Soviet delegates again brought forward most of their earlier amendments which were rejected.

IV. Conclusion

After the signing ceremony, all proponents in the General Assembly underlined the great progress which had been made. What this paper has tried to emphasise is that this was indeed the case, but that General Assembly Resolution 260 also had to do with compromises in the political sphere. This was especially important for the Great Powers who had no right of veto in the deliberations, but were nevertheless decisive on the final extenuated versions of several central issues.

This paper could, of course, not deal with the matter in an exhaustive way, but only provide some examples. After ratification by the first 20 states, the Convention came into effect as planned in 1951. But nothing serves better to demonstrate the Convention's ultimate weakness than the fact that the United States was not among the ratifying states. In the first ratification debate in the US Senate on 24

---

46 W.A. Schabas, *supra* n. 6, p. 371 (UN Doc. E/623, Add.1.); new French proposal: UN Doc. A/C.6/211, 1 October 1948.

47 UN Doc. A/C.6/224 & Corr. 1, 8 October 1948.

48 W.A. Schabas, *supra* n. 6, pp. 418-424.

49 J. Cooper, *supra* n. 6, p. 161; W.A. Schabas, *supra* n. 6, pp. 419 et seq.

January, 1950, a member from Louisiana argued:[50] 'How can the United States be asked, or urged, to ratify this so-called Genocide Convention which is a direct encroachment on the domestic affairs of this country under the Constitution of the United States ... [Ratification would mean] a flagrant violation of one of the solemn provisions of its own charter, or a violation of that part of the international agreement by which the United States came into being.' Of course, this alluded to national sovereignty, guaranteed in Article 2(7) UN Charter. Basically, this refusal continued for the next decades under Republican as well as Democratic administrations. During the years between 1946 and 1948, the United States had been important in preparing the Convention, but it was only forty years later, one year before the fall of the Berlin Wall, that the US finally ratified the Convention, on 25 November 1988. But quite apart from that, during the entire period of the prolonged East-West conflict, the Convention went through a period of 'lengthy hibernation' as Matthew Lippman has called it. It lay 'largely dormant' as William Schabas argued.[51] Their assessments remind one of the old fairy tale, 'Snow White and the Seven Dwarfs'!

This paper has tried to show that at least during the years of negotiation, this sceptical diagnosis could not completely or even mainly be attributed to the rising 'Cold War,' i.e., to the antagonism between to enemy camps. The very negotiation of the Convention between 1946 and 1948 underlined the thesis that national interests, at least on the side of the United States, the United Kingdom and the Soviet Union, precluded a better and further-reaching result. What then does the minor impact of the Genocide Convention in the years until 1989 mean for the overall importance of this resolution? Was this related to a certain type of international system or was there a long period of collective learning in the community of states? Or was genocide as a crime really less important in the forty years following the signing of the Convention than in the past twenty years? In this author's opinion, the answers are anything but clear.

In the years after World War II, the world and thus the United Nations still felt the impact of the German genocide of the European Jews, and all member states felt obliged to make a new start to prevent similar developments in the future. Nevertheless, in 1948, the category of 'intent to destroy' (Art. II) was generally accepted[52] as a description of National Socialist crimes and thus transferred to the Genocide Convention. This hardly conforms with the serious contemporary historical scholarship which tries to explain the genocide of the European Jews.[53]

---

[50] L. Perez, in 29(12) *Congressional Digest* (December 1950), pp. 316-318 (http://web.ebscohost.com/ehost/detail?vid=9&hid=9&sid=7221e6ce-6572-4473-a5bc-acdf9b25bb29%40SRCSM1&bdata=JnNpdGU9ZWhvc3QtbGl2ZQ%3d%3d#db=a9h&AN=12177740).

[51] M. Lippman, *supra* n. 26, p. 191; W.A. Schabas, 'Preventing the "Odious Scourge": The United Nations and the Prevention of Genocide', 14 *International Journal on Minority and Group Rights* (2007), pp. 379-397 at p. 384.

[52] W.A. Schabas, *supra* n. 6, pp. 213-228; a good brief summary: C. Kreß, 'The Crime of Genocide under International Law', 6 *ICLR* (2006), pp. 461-502 at pp. 484-502.

[53] There has been a long scholarly and public debate which in the 1970s culminated in two schools of 'intentionalist' and 'structuralist' interpretations. Today, the prevailing interpretation is that radical

The United Nations, in the first years of its existence as a new world organisation could not be much more than a clearing house for the diverging interests of different states, not an active organisation in its own right. But during the following decades, the codification and sharpening of the universal determination that such crimes as committed during World War II should be punished, nevertheless led to a growing trust in new norms. Maybe during the intense period of East-West conflict up to 1989, such features were superseded by the special character of East-west relations – and this also holds true especially for the North-south conflict. But since then, major progress has been made in the indictment and punishment of genocidal crimes. Whether there was more genocidal violence after 1989 or whether the persecution of genocide has increased during this period, in my opinion is less than clear today. The 'gentle civilizer of nations' – that is how Martti Koskenniemi characterised International Law in general.[54] Undoubtedly, this effect did not unfold immediately after the signature of the UN Genocide Convention, but only in the decades since then.

---

anti-Semitism in Germany led to an escalation to genocidal mass murder only under the special situation of World War II. The older debate was conducted in G. Hirschfeld & W. Mommsen (eds.), *Der 'Führerstaat.' Anspruch und Realität. Studien zur Struktur und Politik des Dritten Reiches* [The 'Führer State': Myth and Reality] (Stuttgart, Klett-Cotta 1981); actual summary: R. Evans, *The Third Reich at War* (New York, Penguin Press 2008); good research overview: K. Hildebrand, *Das Dritte Reich,* 6th edn. (Munich, Oldenbourg 2003), pp. 327-444; D. Stone (ed.), *The Historiography of the Holocaust* (Houndsmills, Palgrave Macmillan 2004); my earlier interpretation: J. Dülffer, *Nazi Germany. Faith and Annihilation* (London, Edward Arnold 1996).

[54] M. Koskenniemi, *The Gentle Civilizer of Nations. The Rise and Fall of International Law 1870-1960* (Cambridge, Cambridge University Press 2001), esp. Chapter 6: 'Out of Europe: Carl Schmitt, Hans Morgenthau and the turn to "international relations"', pp. 413-508.

STRATEGIES FOR 'GENOCIDE TRIALS' AFTER WORLD WAR II – HOW THE ALLIED POWERS DEALT WITH THE PHENOMENON OF GENOCIDE IN OCCUPIED GERMANY

Wolfgang Form

I. Preliminary remarks: defining humanity

What moved the international community to desire the punishment of crimes against humanity and genocide? The discussion of recognising the inherent rights of all human beings runs like a thread through the history of the past two centuries. At the beginning of World War I, a crime horrified the world: the genocide committed on the Armenians.[1] From 1915 onwards, the Ottoman Empire began systematically liquidating a part of its population. Many hundreds of thousands of people perished in mass expulsions.[2] A phenomenon began to emerge that, though not exclusively related to military conflicts, chiefly occurred during times of war: the planned murder, humiliation, deportation or other kinds of inhumane treatment of civilians. In the preamble of the Hague Convention on the Laws and Customs of War on Land of 18 October 1907 we read:

> 'Until a more complete code of the laws of war has been issued, the High Contracting Parties deem it expedient to declare that, in cases not included in the Regulations adopted by them, the inhabitants and the belligerents remain under the protection and the rule of the principles of the law of nations, as they result from the usages established among civilized peoples, from *the laws of humanity*, and the dictates of the public conscience.'[3]

For many years, the question of how the term 'humanity' should be interpreted remained unanswered. In 1948, judging a case of repeated ill-treatment of Jewish prisoners in the era of National Socialism, the Supreme Court for the British Zone

---

[1] See T. Akçam, *Armenien und der Völkermord. Die Istanbuler Prozesse und die türkische Nationalbewegung* [Armenia and Genocide. The Istanbul Trials and the Turkish National Movement] (Hamburg, Hamburger Edition 2004).

[2] Yoshimura, *Total War and 'Genocide' – various Aspects of the Armenian Massacres, Comparative Genocide Studies*, Vol. 1 (2004), pp. 21-28.

[3] [Emphasis added]. The English translation is reprinted in A. Roberts & R. Guelff (eds.), *Documents on the Law of War*, 3rd edn. (Oxford, Oxford University Press 2000), p. 67.

C. Safferling and E. Conze (eds.), The Genocide Convention Sixty Years after its Adoption

of Occupation (*Oberster Gerichtshof für die Britische Zone*) relied in one of its first decisions on a mixed approach taking into account both individual and supra-individual aspects.[4] This supra-individual aspect according to the Court's opinion pertains to the 'undetachable value of personhood in the moral order of society.'[5] An action that affects a person in the depths of his or her personality is a violation of that individual's personhood.[6] Such violation amounts to an assault on that physical and mental sphere of every human being which constitutes this human being's value and dignity. Three levels of values mesh together to form a multidimensional network of relations, which is equivalent to a variable realm of values: life, physical integrity, and freedom.[7] A crime against humanity thus, consists in depriving a person of one or more of these attributes – for example, regarding certain individuals as base, inferior, or useless, eliminable if necessary. The line separating 'ordinary' violence and a crime against humanity is crossed when generally recognised values of humanity are concerned and supra-individual effects ensue.[8] Such crimes are virtually inconceivable without systematic state action, particularly if the disregard of the person's value is oriented toward persecution of an identifiable group.[9]

II. European experiences with mass violence

The necessity of a permanent protection of human beings is proven by the examples of Armenia, the murder of the European Jews, and the events in ex-Yugoslavia and Rwanda. As we know today, after World War I all international efforts to punish war crimes and crimes against humanity failed. As far as Germany goes, the so-called Leipzig trials can only be considered a fiasco.[10] The genocide of the Ar-

---

[4] As to the definition of crimes against humanity by the OGHBrZ see also K. Ambos, *Der Allgemeine Teil des Völkerstrafrechts* [General Principles of International Criminal Law] (Berlin, Duncker & Humblot 2002), pp. 164 et seq.

[5] 'Den unverlierbaren Wert des Menschseins in der sittlichen Ordnung', OGH decision of 4 May 1948 reprinted in *Entscheidungen des Obersten Gerichtshofes für die britische Zone in Strafsachen* [OGHBrZ], Vol. 1 (Hamburg and Berlin, De Gruyter 1949), p. 1 at p. 3.

[6] Ibid., p. 3.

[7] *Idem.*

[8] *Idem.*

[9] See W.A. Schabas, *Genocide in International Law. The Crime of Crimes*, 2nd edn. (Cambridge, Cambridge University Press 2009), p. 12; G. Werle, *Völkerstrafrecht* [International Criminal Law], 2nd edn. (Tübingen, Siebeck 2007), pp. 306-307; *Trials of War Criminals before the Nuremberg Military Tribunals*, Vol. 1 (Washington DC, US Government Printing Office 1949), p. 913: 'It is one of the very purposes of the concept of crimes against humanity, not only as set forth in Law no. 10 but also as long recognized by international law, to reach the systematic commission of atrocities and offenses by a state against its own people.'

[10] See G. Hankel, *Die Leipziger Prozesse. Deutsche Kriegsverbrechen und ihre strafrechtliche Verfolgung nach dem Ersten Weltkrieg* [The Leipzig Trials. German War Crimes and their Prosecution after the First World War] (Hamburg, Hamburger Edition 2003); H. Wiggenhorn, *Verliererjustiz – Die Leipziger Kriegsverbrecherprozesse nach dem ersten Weltkrieg* [Vanquished's Justice – The Leipzig War Crimes Trials after the First World War] (Baden-Baden, Nomos 2005).

menians, for its part, remained not only unpunished, but even minimised by the Turkish government until today.[11] An essential aspect of this failure was the gap between the will to prosecution and the materialisation of that will.[12]

World War II led Europe into an entirely different situation. This was no war of static warfare, but rather involved the conquest of entire nations through *Blitzkrieg* and the flight of the governments of the conquered nations into exile. Early on during World War II, the barbaric cruelty was visible. At the latest, from the time of the systematic deportation and subsequent 'industrial' extermination of the European Jews, the world was forcefully acquainted with the results of a policy of uninhibited state action. It is unrealistic to assume that Germany could have been transformed in only a few months of warfare, that a machinery of million-fold murder could in so short a span of time come into being. Numerous developmental steps were necessary in order to manifest the persecution of political, ethnic, national, and religious groups. Haunted by their discouraging experiences after World War I, the Allies, working in concert with the exile governments of countries occupied by Germany, committed themselves early on to the criminal prosecution of war crimes and crimes against humanity.

II.1 The path to Nuremberg

To understand the political and legal actions in response to war crimes and crimes against humanity – as well as genocide – after World War II,[13] it is necessary to study the (diplomatic) statements and conferences on the subject during the war.[14] Such statements, made by leading members of the governments of Great Britain, the Soviet Union, the United States and exile-governments of occupied countries serving on the United Nations War Crimes Commission (UNWCC), could not by themselves establish international law.[15] They did, however, clarify the views and intentions of these governments: Retribution for war crimes was first said to be essential by the United Kingdom, while the establishment of an international tribunal for major war criminals – which would focus on war crimes only – was put forward first by the Soviet Union in 1942. Nonetheless, all the Allies believed that the majority of cases should be tried by national courts of the states where the crimes had been committed.

---

[11] T. Akçam, *A Shameful Act: The Armenian Genocide and the Question of Turkish Responsibility* (New York, Metropolitan Books 2006).

[12] T. Akçam, *supra* n. 1.

[13] For a historical discussion of crimes against humanity, see I *Trials of War Criminals before the Nuremberg Military Tribunals* (1949), pp. 909-925.

[14] See also H.-H. Jescheck, *Die Verantwortlichkeit des Staatsorgane nach Völkerstrafrecht* [Accountability of State Organs according to International Criminal Law] (Bonn, Röhrscheid 1952), pp. 121 et seq.

[15] The term 'United Nations' here describes the allied states participating in a 1942-Conference in Washington and is to be separated from the international organisation 'United Nations' which was founded in June 1945 in San Francisco. See H. Ahlbrecht, *Geschichte der völkerrechtlichen Strafgerichtsbarkeit im 20. Jahrhundert* [History of International Criminal Jurisdiction] (Baden-Baden, Nomos 1999), p. 62.

Early in wartime, on 25 October 1941, Prime Minister Churchill declared his horror at the 'cold blooded execution of innocent people by the Nazis' in Poland, Yugoslavia, Norway, Belgium, and Russia. He demanded that: 'Retribution for these crimes must henceforward take its place among the major purpose of the war.' And: 'those who are guilty of Nazi crimes will have to stand up before tribunals in every land where their atrocities have been committed in order that an indelible warning may be given to future ages, and that successive generations of men may say,' Churchill declared, 'so perish all who do the like again.'[16]

In other words: German atrocities were considered an outrageous violation of the elementary principles of international law and international agreements signed by the representatives of Germany itself. Those guilty of these crimes were to be handed over to judicial courts for trial. Further, American President Franklin D. Roosevelt (in 1942) stated, addressing representatives of the occupied European states: 'it seems only fair that [Germans responsible for war crimes and crimes against humanity] shall have to stand in courts of law in the very countries they are now oppressing, and answer for their acts.'[17]

At the initiative of the USSR, the demands of the St. James Declaration were implemented.[18] An internal document of the British Foreign Office indicates that already in autumn 1942, the Allies had pondered how the punishment of war criminals could be administered internationally.

In October 1942 the USSR published a note which set out the views of the Soviet government as concerns war crimes, in response to a declaration by representatives of the occupied European states calling for the judicial punishment of all those guilty of crimes committed in occupied territories (13 January 1942).[19] The Soviet note contained three main points:

1. The Nazi leaders should be tried under criminal law before an international tribunal.
2. War criminals of a lesser calibre should be tried by national criminal courts.
3. The Soviet Union was willing to cooperate in the extradition and surrender of war criminals.[20]

In October 1942 the Lord Chancellor of the United Kingdom had announced that war criminals should be caught and handed over as a condition of an armistice, with

---

[16] The National Archive Kew, London Record Group FO 370/2899.

[17] *Idem.*

[18] The so-called St. James declaration of 12 June 1941 was adopted by the governments of the United Kingdom, of Canada, Australia, New Zealand and South Africa, the government of Belgium, the Provisional Czechoslovak government, the governments of Greece, Luxemburg, the Netherlands, Norway, Poland and Yugoslavia, and the Representatives of General de Gaulle, leader of Free Frenchmen. See Punishment for War Crimes, the Inter Allied Declaration Signed at St. James Palace on 13 January and Relative Documents (London, Her Majesty's Stationery Office 1942).

[19] As to the Soviet view on trying German war criminals, see also F. Hirsch, 'The Soviets at Nuremberg: International Law, Propaganda, and the Making of the Postwar Order', 113 *American Historical Review* (2008), p. 701 at pp. 703-710.

[20] The National Archives Kew, London Record Group FO 370/2899.

the right to require the delivery of others as soon as the supplementary investigations were complete. And – according to major allied politicians, regarding the mass execution of Jews in Europe (later known as genocide) – the governments of the occupied states reaffirmed their solemn resolution to ensure that those responsible for these crimes would not escape retribution. One year later (on 30 August 1943), the British government spoke of the need to punish the instigators and perpetrators of crimes committed in concentration camps. They declared that, as long as such atrocities continued to be committed by representatives and in the name of Germany, they had to be considered at the time of any armistice with Germany.[21] The most important statement on war crimes (as well as crimes against humanity – including atrocities later known as genocide) was made by representatives of Roosevelt, Churchill and Stalin on 30 October 1943. The statement became known as the Moscow Declaration. They declared:

> 'at the time of the granting of any armistice to any Government which may be set up by Germany, those German officers, men and members of the Nazi Party who have been responsible for, or have taken a consenting part in the above atrocities, massacres and executions, will be sent back to the countries in which their abominable deeds were done, in order that they may be judged and punished according to the laws of these liberated countries and of the Free Governments which will have been erected therein. Lists will be compiled in all possible detail from all these countries, having regard especially to the invaded parts of the Soviet Union, to Poland, to Czechoslovakia, to Yugoslavia and Greece including Crete and other islands, to Norway, Denmark, the Netherlands, Belgium, Luxembourg, France and Italy ... The above declaration is without prejudice to the case of the major criminals whose offences have no particular geographical location and who will be punished by a joint decision of the Government of the Allies.'[22]

There was no decision taken in favour of an international tribunal at Moscow, but the possibility therefore was established in the declaration.

At the same time – October 1943 –, a significant number of acts that we today would classify under international criminal law were excluded: all crimes against humanity committed by a state against its own population. It may thus be understandable why the Holocaust was not explicitly mentioned in the Moscow Declaration.[23] In national prosecutions, it was decided only to consider crimes which had occurred in the territories occupied by Germany. It is natural to inquire how the first part of this two-pronged procedure was to be realised. This is a significant aspect

---

[21] *Idem.*

[22] Moscow Declaration see G. Ueberschaehr, *Die alliierten Prozesse gegen Kriegsverbrecher und Soldaten 1943-1952* [Allied Prosecution against War Criminals and Soldiers 1943-1952], 2nd edn. (Frankfurt, Fischer 2000), pp. 287-288. In English: 28 *AJIL* (1944), Suppl. 7.

[23] This is of course apart from the fact that the 'final solution' of the Jewish question agreed upon in the Conference at Wannsee on 20 January 1942, was unknown at that time. Indeed the Wannsee-Protocol was discovered only in 1947 and introduced as evidence into the so-called *Wilhelmstraßenprozess* at Nuremberg, see K. Kastner, *Von den Siegern zur Rechenschaft gezogen* [Held Accountable by the Victors] (Nuremberg, Hoffmann 2001), p. 268.

because World War II reached its zenith in October 1943, at a time when the systematic murder of European Jewry had reached an unprecedented magnitude. If the Moscow Declaration is interpreted as the result of Allied concerns, the initiatives of the European governments-in-exile have to be interpreted as its complementary opposite pole.

The Moscow Declaration was the culmination of allied strategies to punish German atrocities – especially acts of violence inflicted upon civilians.[24] With their focus on civilians, these acts have nothing in common with the conceptions of wartime acts or political crimes, as understood by civilised nations under the Hague Convention of 1907. The claim was an (internationalised) punishment program, through the channel of organised justice for those responsible for these crimes, whether the offenders had ordered them, perpetrated them or participated in them. In the words according to the St. James-Meeting in January 1942, the Allies resolved to act in a spirit of international solidarity to ensure that the responsible persons, whatever their nationality, were sought out, handed over for trial, and judged, and that the sentences pronounced were carried out. The envisaged legal effects were interpreted differently in wartime. The representatives of the Polish government in exile, for instance, said that offences against common law should be treated as such. Representatives from France, however (General de Gaulle) said it meant that Germany alone was responsible for the outbreak of the war and that those shared with her allies and accomplices the responsibility for all the atrocities that proceeded from it. The Greek politicians opined that 'butchers, gaolers, and looters of every kind' would no longer be allowed individually to elude their individual responsibilities on the pretext that they were acting under orders from above. In consequence, the Allies and the representatives of the occupied states of Europe could not establish – in wartime – the practice of international law, but – and this is in my view already a very important step for the further development of international criminal law at this time – their recommendations provided the guidelines for future law.

II.2 Institutionalisation efforts

The first historical body in this development toward prosecuting the crimes of the nation-state was the 'International Commission on Penal Reconstruction and Development,'[25] which held a conference in Cambridge on 14 November 1941. Lawyers in attendance, who came from the United Kingdom and from many occupied states, discussed crimes against international public order. They concluded that war crimes could properly be defined as criminal, in the ordinary and accepted sense of the fundamental rules of warfare, by reason of their heinousness, brutality, ruthless disregard for the sanctity of human life and personality, or their wanton interfer-

---

24 G. Werle, *supra* n. 9, MN 17.

25 See *Historical Survey of the Question of International Criminal Jurisdiction.* Memorandum submitted by the Secretary-General of the United Nations (London, Her Majesty's Stationery Office 1949), p. 19.

ence with rights of property unrelated to military necessity. Later on, such atrocities were expanded to include as 'crimes against humanity' German atrocities against Germans. One of the main principles was that if a criminal claimed he had acted under superior orders, consideration would be given to his rank and the degree of duress in determining punishment, but superior orders would not absolve him from criminal liability for his illegal act.[26]

In 1943, it became more and more evident that crimes of extermination committed within and outside Axis countries for racial or for political reasons, were to be considered as war crimes in the sense of the Hague Conventions. The Allies increasingly accepted that the man who ordered the crime was as responsible as the man who committed it, and affirmed that some 'crimes against mankind' should be branded as such and made punishable by international law, even when they were not punished by local law. Allied politicians discussed atrocities before the war at this time, but solitary observers saw the connection between German pre-war and war policy. Dr. Ecer, a member of the Czechoslovakian exile-government in London, pronounced: 'Not only the aggressor States as such, but also their rulers and military leaders are personally responsible in the eyes of the law for the gigantic chain of crimes which compose this and which are punishable under criminal laws.'[27]

II.3 The United Nations War Crimes Commission

One consideration in 1944 was to bring crimes committed by Germans in Germany against allied nationals, stateless persons and German as well as non-German Jews – i.e., Holocaust, genocide – before an international court, because of the territorial designations in the Moscow Declaration. One year before, in 1942, under the auspices of the League of Nations (by Viscount Cecil of Chelwood), the London International Assembly had been created. By 1943, it had evolved into the United Nations War Crimes Commission (UNWCC).[28] The Commission had the status of an international organisation because the expenses of its administration were divided between members, and its staff had a degree of diplomatic immunity in the United Kingdom, where it met.[29] The UNWCCs work was divided between three committees. Committee I was called the Facts and Evidence Committee; it was concerned with examining information on war crimes submitted by the different states. Its job was to collect material to establish crimes and to name and identify the persons responsible for their perpetration. By 31 March 1948, 8,178 charges had been examined, involving 36,000 people, whose names had been compiled in eighty lists.[30]

---

[26] See, e.g., Art. 8 IMTSt.

[27] The National Archives Kew, London Record Group FO 370/2899.

[28] As to the legal basis of the UNWCC see K. Ambos, *supra* n. 4, pp. 141 et seq.

[29] As to the work of the UNWCC see also H. Ahlbrecht, *supra* n. 15, p. 63; H.-H. Jescheck, *supra* n. 14, pp. 128 et seq.; M.C. Bassiouni, in M.C. Bassiouni (ed.), *International Criminal Law*, Vol. III, 2nd edn. (The Hague, Nijhoff 1999), p. 31 at pp. 39 et seq.

[30] UNWCC (ed.), *History of the United Nations War Crimes Commission and Development of the Laws of War* (London, Her Majesty's Stationery Office 1948), Annex.

Committee II was concerned with enforcement: the detection, trials and war criminals. It was in contact with Supreme Headquarters Allied Expeditionary Force (SHAEF) and had a liaison team attached to the Commander in Chief of the US and the UK. Committee III had an advisory function, and, through this nature, the possibility of making proposals to the governments, was entrusted to the Commission.[31] The Soviet Union did not participate in the UNWCC due to the fact that the Soviet government had insisted on a member seat for each Soviet Republic.[32] This was unacceptable for the other countries.

The UNWCC did not harmonise the European and post-war politics in the different zones of occupation to punish war crimes and crimes against humanity. It did, however, rule that the occupying authority had the right to enquire into each case and decide on the action.[33] One of the important achievements of the UNWCC was to prepare a list of war crimes (32 items altogether) – actually made by the Commission of Responsibilities after World War I in 1919.[34] This catalogue was taken as a solid legal basis because Italy and Japan had helped to prepare the war crimes-list and Germany had not objected to the inclusion of any of the 32 proposed items. The UNWCC added two more war crimes: 1. Indiscriminate mass arrests for the purpose of terrorising the population, whether described as taking hostages or not; 2. Acts violating family hour and rights, the lives of individuals, religious convictions and liberty of worship, as provided for in the Hague Law. The preamble of the Hague Convention was also included: 'in cases not covered by the rules adopted ... the inhabitants and the belligerents remain under the protection and governance of the principles of the law of nation ... from the laws of humanity and from the dictates of the public conscience.' The UNWCC conceived of crimes against humanity as two types: '[t]hose of the "murder type" (Murder, extermination, enslavement, deportation and the like) and those of the "persecution type" committed on racial, political or religious grounds.'[35]

This definition includes very important circumstances: First, it was irrelevant whether a crime against humanity had been committed before or during the war. Second, neither the nationality of the victims nor the place where the crime had been committed mattered. Commission members, Dr. Zivkovic form Yugoslavia and Dr. Mayr-Harting from Czechoslovakia, who were both lawyers, said: '... the notion of crimes against humanity, as it evolved in the Commission, was based

---

[31] UNWCC, *supra* n. 30, pp. 120-126.

[32] See also W.A. Schabas, *supra* n. 9, pp. 35 et seq., and UNWCC, *supra* n. 30, pp. 112 et seq.

[33] Ethiopia asked the UNWCC to deal with war crimes in Italy's war with her in 1935; the commission refused to deal with any cases outside WWII at first, but in 1947 it agreed to investigate a few cases. See The National Archives Record Group FO 370/2899, FO 371/63171, FO 371/66583, FO 371/79515.

[34] The Commission of Responsibilities was founded on 25 January 1919 and consisted of representatives of of the five major Allied powers, Britain, France, Italy, USA and Japan, with the addition of Belgium, Greece, Poland, Rumania and Yugoslavia. See International Law Commission, *Historical Survey of the Question of International Criminal Jurisdiction* (New York, 1949) (UN Doc. A/CN.4/7/Rev.1).

[35] Annex B, The National Archives Record Group FO 370/2899.

upon the opinion that many offences committed by the enemy could not technically be regarded as war crimes *stricto sensu* on account of one or several elements … methods and principles must be brought into line with the principles expressed in the Allied declarations. [They were crimes committed] in violation of the criminal laws of the countries invaded or otherwise affected, of the laws and customs of war, of the general principles of criminal law as recognised by civilised nations, or of the laws of humanity and the dictates of the public conscience as provided in the Hague Preamble. Crimes committed against any person without regard to nationality, stateless person included, because of race, nationality, religious or political belief irrespective of where they had been committed.'[36]

Before the end of the war, on 13 February 1945, the UNWCC wrote to the United Kingdom's Foreign Secretary to ask whether he believed the UNWCC should be limited to considering crimes against Allied nationals. The United Kingdom did not answer at once, but in the London Charter (also known as Nuremberg Statute or IMT Statute) crimes against humanity had no such limitations, and were an inherent part of the IMT's jurisdiction – albeit with a link to war crimes and/or aggression. Moreover, the definition of crimes against humanity was almost identical to the definition given by the UNWCC.[37]

III. National jurisdictions after World War II

The majority of trials against war criminals and perpetrators of crimes against humanity were not held before international tribunals (Nuremberg and Tokyo) but in ordinary courts under the control of the occupying powers. Each of the powers had a different way of dealing with the prosecution of German war criminals. Yet, in general the Allies, i.e., the United Kingdom, the United States,[38] the Soviet Union[39] and France,[40] opted for a dual strategy: Military courts and special courts with jurisdiction for more than only war crimes.

III.1 **Military courts**

In the British Zone of Occupation, war criminals were tried under the Royal Warrant of 14 June 1945 for crimes that were violations of the laws and usages of war,

---

36 The National Archives Kew London Record Group FO 370/2899.

37 *Idem.*

38 M. Bryant, 'Dachau Trials – Die rechtlichen und historischen Grundlagen der US-amerikanischen Kriegsverbrecherprozesse, 1942-1947', in H. Radtke, D. Rössner, T. Schiller & W. Form (eds.), *Historische Dimensionen von Kriegsverbrecherprozessen nach dem Zweiten Weltkrieg* [The Historical Dimensions of War Crimes Trials] (Baden-Baden, Nomos 2007), pp. 111-122.

39 See A. Hilger, '"Die Gerechtigkeit nehme ihren Lauf?" Die Bestrafung deutscher Kriegs- und Gewaltverbrecher in der Sowjetunion und der SBZ/DDR', in N. Frey (ed.), *Transnationale Vergangenheitspolitik* [Transnational Politics of the Past] (Göttingen, Wallstein 2006), pp. 180-246.

40 C. Moisel, *Frankreich und die deutschen Kriegsverbrecher* [France and German War Criminals] (Göttingen, Wallstein 2004).

i.e., war crimes *stricto sensu*.[41] Crimes against humanity and crimes against peace were not included. The war criminals subject to military law were mostly tried by British Courts Martial. From July 1945 until 22 December 1949, around 420 military trials were held in Italy, Germany, the Netherlands, and Norway on a 'royal warrant' basis. The same rules which governed the US-American so-called Dachau trials also applied to the British proceedings: a charge of war crimes could only be maintained if the defendant's actions could be considered to some extent a crime against humanity. As one of many in this connection, the so-called 'baby home trials' conducted by British Royal Warrant Courts serve as an example. German civilians were charged with having been concerned in the killing by wilful neglect of a number of children. These children were almost exclusively children of Polish mothers brought to Germany from Poland in pursuance of the policy of deportation for slave labour.[42] Babies were taken away from their mothers eight to ten days after birth and were placed in a home. In that home they died in large numbers as the result of what the court found to have been criminal neglect.

III.2 Non-military courts under Control Council Law No. 10

Second, other courts with jurisdiction for aggression and crimes against humanity were established by Control Council Law No. 10 (CCL No. 10).[43] This decree also covered crimes committed by Germans against German victims. The CCL No. 10 created a trans-zonal criminal jurisdiction for all of occupied Germany. It consisted of two parts: (1) the applicability of the Nuremberg Charter for national trials; and (2) rules for extradition. CCL No. 10 was implemented in all Zones of Occupation in 1946. Article III No. 2 paragraph 1 stated: 'The tribunal by which persons charged with offences hereunder shall be tried and the rules and procedure thereof shall be determined or designated by each Zone Commander for his respective Zone.' The following sentence, however, eliminated any imperative: 'Nothing herein is intended to, or shall impair or limit the Jurisdiction or power of any court or tribunal now or hereafter established in any Zone by the Commander thereof, or of the International Military Tribunal established by the London Agreement of August 8, 1945.' Because the IMT Charter was an integral component of Law No. 10, it is unsurprising that the elements of the offence in both cases were largely the same. The description of crimes against humanity under CCL No. 10 was expanded beyond the IMT Charter to include false imprisonment, torture, and rape. The connection between crimes of aggression and war crimes, however, was erased; at the same time, CCL No. 10 was construed to cover the entire period of the Nazi regime, not only the war period.

---

[41] In greater detail: K. Hassel, *Kriegsverbrechen vor Gericht* [War Crimes at Trial] (Baden-Baden, Nomos 2009).

[42] H. Lauterpacht, 'Foreword', in G. Brand, *War Crimes Trials Vol. VII. The Velpke Baby Home Trial* (London/Edinburgh/Glasgow, Hodge 1950), p. XIII.

[43] Decreed on 20 December 1945.

III.3 The principle of non-interference in domestic affairs

With the prosecution of crimes committed by Germans against other Germans, a long time dogma of international law fell by the wayside: the non-interference into the domestic affairs of national states during peacetime. On account of the acknowledged freedom in applying the law, it was not necessary to extend the time period backward into the pre-war years. Rather, pragmatic concerns made it undesirable for the Allies to conduct all the trials under Control Council Law No. 10 themselves. Article III No. 1 d) offered another possibility: 'Such tribunal may, in the case of crimes committed by persons of German citizenship or nationality against other persons of German citizenship or nationality, or stateless persons, be a German Court, if authorized by the occupying authorities.' This would not have been possible in the absence of an independent charge of 'crimes against humanity.' If the bond between crimes against humanity and aggression and/or war crimes continued as a precondition to trial, German courts would have inevitably found themselves forced to joining these charges to their indictments. Such a situation would have been irreconcilable with the provision that only cases involving German victims could be prosecuted by German courts, because war crimes could not be committed on one's co-nationals. Furthermore, the crime of waging wars of aggression for similar reasons could not be tried in a German court. There was no other alternative remaining but to establish an independently chargeable offense of crimes against humanity.

III.4 Punishing crimes committed before the war

More importantly, it was in the Allies' interest to enable punishment of atrocities committed prior to the war – above all, those inflicted on political opponents at the onset of the Nazi regime, as well as the attacks carried out during the nationwide pogrom of 9 November 1938.[44] The US-American military administration decided against this option, while the British[45] and French[46] relied on German participation in the trials conducted under CCL No. 10. The Western occupation zones thus split into two geographic regions of punishment.

In the British zone, military government courts were the primary bodies by which Control Council Law No. 10 was applied – therefore also responsible for genocide matters. These courts adjudicated only a few cases involving crimes against humanity in Germany and Austria. Beginning on 1 January 1947, however, this situation fundamentally changed. Upon amendment of CCL No. 10 by the zonal administration at the end of 1946, control commission courts were convened, which

---

[44] The so-called *Reichskristallnacht* pogroms.

[45] *Military Government Gazette Germany British Zone of Control* (Printing & Distribution Unit, Control Commission for Germany B.E. 1946), No. 13, p. 306.

[46] C. Moisel, 'Résistance und Repressalien. Die Kriegsverbrecherprozesse in der französischen Zone und in Frankreich', in N. Frei (ed.), *Transnationale Vergangenheitspolitik* [Transnational Politics of the Past] (Wallstein, Göttingen 2006), p. 247.

also had to apply CCL No. 10. Until 1948, such courts held around 150 trials exclusively involving crimes against humanity, committed between 1933 and the end of the war and insofar as German or stateless victims were involved.[47] If the victims were nationals of states that participated in the war, the proceedings were generally conducted by Royal Warrant Courts.

As far as the background of the crimes was concerned, they involved the persecution of European Jews, Gypsies and political opponents, as well as forced sterilisation, homicidal crimes committed by civil offices like the Gestapo and police, and denunciations. They related to actions that prepared the way for genocide, constructing a sprawling network of destruction across all of Germany.

An example is the trial before a control commission court on 12 June 1947 at Aachen of 8 persons accused of burning down a synagogue in Aachen i the night of 8-9 November 1938. The accused were charged with having committed crimes against humanity under CCL No. 10. On the basis of this judgment, ordinary German courts in the British Occupation Zone were authorised to try persons charged with crimes against humanity against Jews or in cases involving Jews. The result was an intense debate among German lawyers on application of the *nulla poena sine lege* principle and the retroactive application of CCL No. 10. Sir Alfred Brown wrote a sharp memorandum rebutting this criticism. He said:

> 'Some of those German lawyers who ... frequently refer to "natural law" or "super statutory law" show ... a rigid formalism, which disregards the ethical basis of such principles and thereby deprives them of their inner justification. Such is the case with the principle "nulla poena sine lege." It is often ignored that the purpose of that maxim does not rest on itself, but that it is destined to carry out some superior purposes. It means to serve justice; in addition, it is also intended to guarantee certainty with regard to the law. In normal conditions, within a legal system based on the fundamentals of present world civilisation, the carrying out of the principle "nulla poena sine lege" will, in fact, contribute to attain the ideals of justice and legal certainty. But it is different with a system which had jettisoned those ethical fundamentals, which intentionally induced the German people to brutal inhumanity, subjecting the individual to the unrestricted discretion of a savage power which did not feel bound by any ethical principles, but aimed at cruelly destroying all that was not in conformity with its purpose. The horrible picture of such a system was realised by National Socialism in a way unique in modern world history. Under that system, men committed innumerable inhumane acts, which, according to National Socialist [ideology] ... were considered to be permitted and not punishable, which, however, for any person who knew only the most elementary conceptions of morality were forthwith recognisable as grave injustice. Among those acts are the misdeeds which in Control Council Law No. 10 are denoted as "Crimes against humanity." It would be the summit of injustice to let these acts remain for ever unpunished because at the time of their commission they could not be punished under the rule of a system of criminal tyranny and under the law based on that system ... The undermined sense of justice can only be restored if the public be-

[47] See The National Archives Kew, London Record Group FO/2899 Appendix D; 148 Person charged before British Military Tribunals with crimes: 88 acquitted, 10 sentenced to death, 50 sentenced to shorter terms of imprisonment.

> comes aware that the misdeeds committed under the National Socialist regime will not remain unpunished, that, on the contrary, "right must remain right," even if temporarily it had been suppressed by criminal force.'[48]

At the centre of the trials stood the daily acts of inhumanity committed by an enormous number of perpetrators throughout Europe. Herein lays a basic divergence from the US-American strategies in the punishment of crimes against humanity: the Nuremberg subsequent proceedings were concerned exclusively with the leadership of the German military, its political structure, and its industry. In the British Occupation Zone, Germans were also charged before German courts (state courts and approximately 570 appellate cases) with crimes against humanity committed against German nationals or stateless persons. We know of about 2,200 cases.

There is, however, a feature that the Western Allied courts shared. The national territories of Great Britain were not enmeshed in World War II apart from the heavy air raids. British territory was never occupied by German troops in contrast to Continental Europe. Hence, the British Isles were not mentioned in the list of territories given in the Moscow Declaration of 1943. Thus no prosecution took place for war crimes and crimes against humanity committed on the territory of Great Britain. The analysis of the post-war trials in Europe confirms this thesis, because in many of them men and women were tried who committed their crimes inside Germany. This applies particularly to crimes against humanity (including genocide). By prosecuting war criminals in military government courts, Great Britain filled a gap in the original Moscow Declaration of 1943.

---

[48] A. Brown, 'The Principle "nulla poena sine lege" and the Control Council Law No. 10.' The National Archives Kew, London Record Group FO 371/64865.

THE HOLOCAUST AND THE GENOCIDE CONVENTION OF 1948

Herbert Reginbogin

In reaction to and memory of the anguish perpetuated by the Nazis and their collaborators during World War II, nations of the General Assembly of the United Nations came together in New York and on 9 December 1948 drafted a treaty called *Convention on the Prevention and Punishment of the Crime of Genocide* (Genocide Convention), codifying genocide as an international crime. By 1951, the Genocide Convention Treaty had become binding international law once the required number of states had ratified it.

The Preamble of the Genocide Convention recognises that at all periods of history genocide has inflicted great losses on humanity and calls upon the international co-operation 'to liberate mankind from such an odious scourge,' mindful of the recent genocide of the Jews through the Holocaust.[1]

Article I makes genocide, whether committed in time of peace or war, 'a crime under international law, which [signatories to the Genocide Convention] undertake to prevent and to punish.' Article II, by far the most criticised provision of the Genocide Convention, defines the international crime of genocide. It reads:

> 'In the present Convention, genocide means any of the following acts committed with intent to destroy, in whole or in part, a national, ethnical, racial or religious group, as such:
>
> Killing members of the group;
> Causing serious bodily or mental harm to members of the group;
> Deliberately inflicting on the group conditions of life calculated to bring about its physical destruction in whole or in part;
> Imposing measures intended to prevent births within the group;
> Forcibly transferring children of the group to another group.'[2]

The focus of this paper is not on the reasons why lawyers, jurists and legal scholars criticise the imprecision and ambiguity of the definition of the crime of genocide.

[1] Convention on the Prevention and Punishment of the Crime of Genocide, 78 *UNTS* (1948), p. 277, www.preventgenocide.org/law/convention/text.htm, last visited on 31 May 2009.
[2] *Idem.*

C. Safferling and E. Conze (eds.), The Genocide Convention Sixty Years after its Adoption

Instead it looks towards the moral implications of the events which led to the Genocide Convention. While the world of nations recalled the millions dying in the fires of German death camps, why did the world community not prevent the Holocaust? What more could the world community have done to prevent the Holocaust? When looking at the historical backdrop to the meaning of the Holocaust, it has had little impact as we witness states of the world community today being long on rhetoric, but short on embracing action to prevent a genocide, let alone calling upon Article 8 of the 1948 Genocide Convention which says, 'Any Contracting Partner may call upon the competent organs of the United Nations to take such action under the Charter of the United Nations as they consider appropriate for the prevention and suppression of acts of genocide ...'[3]

I. Holocaust/Shoah and the legal term Genocide

Many understand Holocaust as a general term for the crimes and atrocities committed by the Nazis. It was, however, not until the 1950s that the term Holocaust was used as the corresponding term for Shoah. The biblical word Shoah (which has been used to mean 'destruction' since the Middle Ages) became the standard Hebrew word for the killing of European Jewry as early as the early 1940s when a discourse began about the destruction of European Jewry among leaders of the Zionist movement and scholars in Palestine, in which the Hebrew term Shoah was widely used.[4] The Holocaust is defined today as the sum of all anti-Jewish actions carried out by the Nazi regime between 1933 and 1945: from depriving German Jews of their legal and economic status in the 1930s, segregating and starving them in the various occupied countries, and eventually the murder of two-thirds of the 11 million Jews in Europe. Over the course of time, the term Holocaust has been overused to describe the mass murder of other large scale atrocities and the destruction of masses of human beings through various methods. Out of the experience of World War II, a legal term emerged called genocide, coined by Raphael Lemkin in his 1944 book, *Axis Rule in Occupied Europe*,[5] in which he combined the Greek word *genos* for a 'race' or 'tribe' and the Latin *-cide*, which means 'killer' or 'act of killing' as in homicide.[6] Thus, the word 'genocide' was born. However, the *Holocaust* remains unique among other genocides and has become synonymous with extreme evil and, as noted by William Schabas, the 'crime of crimes.'[7]

---

3 *Idem.*

4 www1.yadvashem.org/odot_pdf/microsoft%20word%20-%206419.pdf, last visited on 26 May 2009.

5 R. Lemkin, *Axis Rule in Occupied Europe* (Washington DC, Carnegie Endowment for International Peace 1947).

6 www.hawaii.edu/powerkills/genocide.ency.htm, last visited on 31 May 2009.

7 W.A. Schabas, *Genocide in International Law. The Crimes of Crimes* (Cambridge, Cambridge University Press 2000), p. 9. The phrase crime of crimes comes from opinions issued in two genocidal trials before the International Criminal Tribunal for Rwanda. *Idem.*

II. ANTI-SEMITISM

Today, the Second World War is claimed to be a war unlike others to defend human rights and to be so potent a catalyst to produce an unprecedented growth in human rights law. However, humanity lags behind. 'Anti-Semitism is still very much with us,' says the German born historian Walter Laqueur. There is no doubt that anti-Semitism existed in America and Europe as well as in many other countries of the world among the poor and the wealthy, the lower class and high-born aristocracy yearning to disparage Jews in public. 'Anti-Semites were not upset to be called anti-Semites,' as Walter Laqueur points out, 'until Hitler gave anti-Semitism a bad name …'[8]

Leading representatives of Corporate America and aid organisations in the 1920s and 30s revealed anti-Semitic bias in which they portrayed President Roosevelt as a Jew by calling him Rosenfeld and the New Deal as a Jew Deal.[9] Some American tycoons provided generous financial support to Americas own fascist organisations yearning for a fascist saviour who might rid America of its reds and thus restore prosperity and profitability to America.[10] On the humanitarian scene, diplomats like Carl Jakob Burckhardt, the League of Nations High Commissioner in the City of Danzig 1937-1939 and an influential person in the International Committee of the Red Cross, showed a slight unease with the social advancement of Jewish intellectual circles, suggesting, as the historians Urs Bitterli and Paul Stauffer point out 'that Burckhardts emotional aloofness towards Jews could well have been a barrier in terms of a more active commitment on his part to help persecuted Jews.'[11]

There is no reason to believe that anti-Semitism came to an end in 1945. Although anti-Semitic venom like *The Protocols of the Elders of Zion* is no longer in vogue today, there are still parts of the world that continue to spread anti-Semitism with leaders regularly denying that the Holocaust happened, as Iranian President Ahmadinejad has done. The vile stereotyping of Jews continues, like neo-Conservatives attempting to evoke legends of the all powerful Jewish lobby in Washington, Jewish globalism, capitalism and a secret Jewish organisation that aspires to control the world by means of war, revolution and economic ruin.[12] While there

---

[8] A.H. Joffe, 'A Spade Is No Longer Called A Spade. An Interview with Walter Laqueur', *Covenant. The Global Jewish Magazine* (November 2006). www.tomgrossmedia.com/mideastdispatches/archives/000808.html, last visited on 24 May 2009.

[9] N. Baldwin, *Henry Ford and the Jews. The Mass Production of Hate* (Public Affairs, 2002), p. 279; C. Higham, *Trading With the Enemy* (New York, Dell Publishing 1984), p. 161; see also J. R. Pauwels, Profits über Alles! American Corporations and Hitler (Review Essays/Notes Critiques), www.entrepreneur.com/tradejournals/article/102155396_9.html, last visited on 24 May 2009.

[10] W. Hofer & H. Reginbogin, *Hitler, der Westen und die Schweiz* [Hitler, the West and Switzerland] (Zürich, NZZ Publishing House 2003), pp. 585-586.

[11] U. Bitterli, 'Humanitärer Auftrag und politische Ambition. Paul Stauffers neues Buch über Carl J. Burckhardt', *Neue Züricher Zeitung*, 1 September 1998, p. 13; see also H.R. Reginbogin, *Faces of Neutrality. A Comparative Analysis of the Neutrality of Switzerland and other Neutral Nations during WWII* (Berlin, et al., LIT Publishing House 2009), p. 99.

[12] A.H. Joffe, *supra* n. 8; www.tomgrossmedia.com/mideastdispatches/archives/000808.html, last visited on 24 May 2009.

have been major achievements in fighting anti-Semitism, the journey continues. The Holocaust remains today part of a broader aggregate of acts of oppression and murder of various ethnic and political groups in Europe and the rest of the world due to the exceptional attitude with which its perpetrators – the Nazis – had regarded their Jewish victims.

A case in point would be the mobile killing squads known as *Einsatzgruppen.* After the invasion of the Soviet Union, they would operate over a wide area of Eastern Europe from the Baltic to the Black Sea just behind the advancing regular German army into newly conquered territory by rounding up and murdering all the Jews and other undesirables. The German army, known as the *Wehrmacht*, was also heavily involved in the killings, as were the police battalions later on.

One of the most notorious of such massacres happened on the 29 and 30 of September 1941. Thousands of Jews living in the Ukranian City of Kiev were ordered to appear at a specific location within the city wherefrom they were transported in groups of ten to a remote ravine named *Babi Yar*. There they were herded into barb-wired areas where men, women, and children were ordered to undress, beaten if they resisted, led down the side of the ravine, ordered to lie face down on the edge of a pit, and to be systematically shot dead by machine gun fire. Afterwards the riddled bodies were covered with a thin layer of earth and the next group was ordered to lie over them and was similarly killed.[13] Over the next two days, a unit of the *Einsatzgruppen* and with the support of a battalion of Waffen-SS soldiers, the military arm of the Nazi Party, and local Ukrainian collaborators, in an orgy of executions, systematically shot dead by machine gun fire around 34,000 Jews. Operational Situation Report No. 101, sent from the field to Berlin and captured after the war, states that at least 33,771 Jews from Kiev were killed at Babi Yar on 29 and 30 September 1941.[14] Raul Hilberg estimates that such Open-air shootings by the *Einsatzgruppen* squads and their local collaborators managed to murder approximately 1.4 million Jews as well as members of other religious, national, and political groups.[15] The portrayed scale of massive killings raised a new level of Nazi atrocities as the millions of Jews and other persecuted groups were brought by trains from all over Europe to death camps like Auschwitz, Sobibor, Treblinka and Belzec after being systematically rounded up. They were either murdered immediately upon arrival in gas chambers (usually children and babies, the frail and the elderly), or selected for work, from which they were expected to perish through extermination-through-labor (*Vernichtung durch Arbeit*).

Who were these men and women that systematically killed without conscience to have responsibility for the Holocaust? It was the ordinary man on the street as Christopher Browning portrays the *Einsatzgruppen,* who was transformed into a

---

[13] A.L Sachar, *The Redemption of the Unwanted* (New York, St. Martins/Marek 1983); www.jewishvirtuallibrary.org/jsource/Holocaust/babiyar.html, last visited on 4 June 2009.

[14] New World Encyclopedia; www.newworldencyclopedia.org/entry/Babi_Yar#The_massacres_of_September_29-30.2C_1941, last visited on 6 June 2009.

[15] www.nizkor.org/ftp.cgi/camps/auschwitz/victims/ftp.py?camps/auschwitz/victims//numbers.killed, last visited on 4 January 2010.

ruthless killer out of a basic obedience to authority and peer pressure, not blood-lust or primal hatred. On the contrary, as Daniel Goldhagen rebuts, the cause for the Holocaust was the German culture, infused with what he calls eliminatory anti-Semitism, a uniquely German hatred of Jews so strong that without it German society would not have supported Hitlers measures to eliminate the Jews from German society. Are the Germans unique or does the potential to kill men, women and children while appreciating the fine arts by listening to classical music lie within the dark side of every human being?[16] Today, the world community is supposed to prevent genocide in accordance with the Genocide Convention. Back in the 1930s, before the Second World War began, what could the world community have done to prevent the *Holocaust*?

III. 1938 – THE WORLD COMMUNITY AND THE EVIAN CONFERENCE

The powerful major democracies of the world knew of the violent crimes conducted by the German Reich against its Jewish minority since the Nazis assumption of power in 1933, and did not see any need to call for any act of intervention. The Third Reichs official statements about the conditions the Jewish population faced in Germany were accepted without any hesitation because the actions rendered against German Jews were seen as an internal affair of a sovereign country according to the understanding of a countrys sovereign rights at the time. Supporting the contention that Germanys treatment of Jews was a country's internal matter were the governments of various European countries, whose major interest was to strengthen economic ties with Germany. A critical policy calling to examine Germanys policy towards German Jews could only have counterproductive implications. When in 1935 Hitler issued the Nuremberg Laws denying Jews their civil rights, disbarring them from professional and public service and thus withdrawing their foundation to make a living, an only too well known practice was revived: See No Evil, Hear No Evil, Speak No Evil. Sovereignty was perceived as the ability of a state to conduct such activities that were directed towards the welfare of the people like building schools, hospitals, and roads and did not take into account a states willingness to mistreat and eventually kill millions of innocent people.[17]

Before the Nazi government decided to solve the Jewish problem finally through extermination, fellow Jewish citizens were offered an opportunity to emigrate, to escape German terror. The first wave of frantic emigration came in the wake of the terror perpetrated in the early months of Nazi rule. About 50,000 are estimated to have emigrated between the beginning of 1933 and spring of 1934.[18] However, it

---

[16] See C. Browning, *Ordinary Men. Reserve Police Battalion 101 and the Final Solution in Poland* (New York, Harper Collins 1992); see also D.J. Goldhagen, *Hitlers Willing Executioners. Ordinary Germans and the Holocaust* (New York, Knopf Publishing Group 1996).

[17] See S. Power, *A Problem From Hell. America and the Age of Genocide* (New York, Basic Books 2002).

[18] L. Yahil, *The Holocaust. The Fate of European Jewry 1932-1945* (New York, Oxford University Press 1991), p. 91.

would have been simply inconceivable to the German mind, if the German Jews could pursue living a pleasant life abroad. The Germans, therefore, took very effective measures to prevent it. Jews who wanted to leave the 'beloved' German Reich, were given a choice to stay or sell their property to the state, or privately to some German citizen generally at a price far below real market value. This meant that only a limited number of emigrations were possible, taking into account that other countries were generally unwilling to grant visas to impoverished Jews although it was well known that the Nazis terrorised their Jewish citizens to force them to leave the country. The western world only very reluctantly made up its mind to admit refugees. It was primarily the Jewish associations through their financial support and assurances to respective countries that welfare expenditures would not increase through the immigrants, who made this happen. But even these organizations did not dare to pressure their governments to make a greater commitment because they feared a rise in existing latent anti-Semitism among their own countrymen. Xenophobia in the countries providing refuge, together with the fear that the refugees would compete with the native population for jobs, prevented a quota increase to admit more refugees, leaving the international community idly watching as the Jewish population of Germany was held in a cage exposed to terror and hate.[19] Indeed, it can be said as Leni Yahil points out in his book, *The Holocaust, The Fate of European Jewry, 1932-1945,* that 'the Nazi authorities in Germany, the nations of the world and the Jewish people were equally confounded by the inherent contradictions in their attitudes towards the emigration of Jews from Germany, and this necessarily precluded the formulation of a clear and solid policy on an issue that ultimately became a matter of life and death.'[20]

The further expansion of the German Reich through the annexation of Austria on 15 March 1938, released a second wave of Jewish emigration through the Gestapos brutal violent clashes with Jews. Thousands fled. Political tension among European neighboring countries to Germany increased as they began to tighten their borders around 28 March 1938 against the impoverished migrants in fear of being overrun by refugees while remaining complacent towards the National Socialists. There was a common political practice, also beyond Europe, of putting your head in the sand and thereby helping Germany to prosper. In whole, this was exactly what the Nazis expected because 'in this way it would be made clear to the whole world that the expelled Jewish minority by Germany could also find no refuge elsewhere.'[21] So what was so different between the world community and the German Nazis, if no one wanted the Jews?

The inadequacy to deal with the Jewish refugee problem in Europe caused the American President Franklin Roosevelt 'to get out in front and attempt to guide a strategy to hold off pressure for more liberal immigration legislation by liberals and

[19] S. Heim, 'Deutschland muss ihnen ein Land ohne Zukunft sein. Die Zwangsemigration der Juden 1933 bis 1938', *11 Arbeitsemigration und Flucht: Beiträge zur nationalsozialistischen Gesundheits- und Sozialpolitik* (1993), p. 59.

[20] See *supra* n. 18.

[21] S. Heim, *supra* n. 19.

Jews by taking a too prominent part which would appear to resist refugees and on the other hand to be careful about losing crucial support among isolationists. It was crucial to find a means that would aid emigrants from Germany and Austria and enable their absorption elsewhere.'[22] He called for an international conference to chart solutions to the pressing refugee problem. From Roosevelts commendable idea emerged the Evian Conference.

IV. The conference begins

On 6 July 1938, in response to an invitation given by the President of the United States, 32 delegates representing countries from all over the world along with three other countries as observers including Germany, Poland and Rumania came to the lake shore resort of Evian in France.[23]

During the next ten days of continuous meetings, one delegate after another continuously professed their countrys solemn solidarity with the refugees. Apparently, there was not enough sympathy to increase the respective immigration quotas, as one country after another, including the United States and Great Britain, tried to outdo one another speaking of their great compassion for the Jewish refugees while declaring the difficulties to admit more refugees. The countries of the western world would have so gladly remained neutral and unscathed. But they were finally forced to take an official stand on an annoying problem concerning Jews fleeing Nazi terror. Finally, their criticism was done in the spirit of great indifference towards the suffering of Jewish refugees reflected by a diametrically opposite policy to the purpose of the conference.[24]

The *United States* continued its restrictive immigration quota whose limited number made it impossible to admit a larger annual number of immigrants from Central and Eastern Europe. Even the extreme suffering by Jewish men, women and children made no impression on the Washington bureaucrats. Nothing could motivate them to increase the immigration quota slightly. Great Britain did its best to make it impossible for Jews to travel or return home to Palestine by blocking all entry and limiting the number of entry visas. The western European delegates pointed out that in their highly industrialised countries there was overpopulation and a high unemployment rate. All offered to permit transit through their country as long as it was guaranteed that the refugees had a guarantee to remain in another country over-

---

[22] D.S. Wyman, *Paper Walls. America and the Refugee Crisis 1938-1941* (New York, Pantheon 1985), p. 44.

[23] S. Heim, *supra* n. 19, p. 61.

[24] About the Evian Conference see E. Ben-Elissar, *La Diplomatie du IIIe Reich et les Juifs, 1933-1939* (Paris, Juillard 1969); R. Weingarten, *Die Hilfeleistung der westlichen Welt bei der Endlösung der deutschen Judenfrage. Das Intergovernmental Committee on Political Refugees (IGC) 1938-1939* (Bern, 1981); Actes du Comité Intergouvernemental. Evian, du 6 au Juillet. Compte rendu des Séances plenières du Comité. Résolutions et Rapports (1938). For a general portrayal see A. Cattani, *Hitlers Schatten über Europa. Brennpunkte der Zeitgeschichte 1933-1945* [Hitlers shadow over Europe 1933-1945] (Zürich, NZZ Publishing House 1995), pp. 40-44.

seas permanently. The *British Dominions* referred to their ties to the motherland and more or less bluntly stated that besides Anglo-Saxon immigrants hardly anyone else had a chance of being admitted. The most unvarnished spoken words were those of the *Australian* representative who stated that his country until now had not known any racial problems and did not even think of importing it. Countries of South America, Canada and Australia, which were large enough to absorb such a large number of immigrants, pointed to their agrarian economy and the wish that farmers would immigrate while all other types of professions would have no chance in meeting the requirements for an entry permit. It was fairly grotesque. Only 2% of the German and Austrian Jews were qualified to work in farming and forestry. The Central and South American delegates emphasised their adherence to the Latin and Catholic identity of their countries. Perhaps immigrants were needed, but surely not Jews from Germany and Austria.

The results of the ten-day conference were sobering. In public meetings representatives of 32 countries declared in great detail why they were unable to admit a larger number of refugees. The reason was mostly economically related and the fear of being infiltrated by foreigners was always cited.

Substantially shorter than the presentations made by each national delegation, which during the course of several days had an opportunity to express their good will, the various hearings of the private organisations admitted to the conference were cancelled. Most of them were Jewish organisations, which above all were supposed to financially contribute to the emigration project. Although there were forty organisations concerned about the plight of the refugees, each was only permitted three minutes to speak on a single long afternoon.[25] It was a sad day. There was such a falling out among the associations that it was impossible for them to appear as a large group attracting greater attention to their cause. Not even the life threatening emergency situation of their religious brothers could alter the self-centered behavior and self-righteousness of these groups to put their differences aside. However, the Jewish organisations assumed that the governments of the countries present at the conference would find a constructive solution to the refugee problem, which was the purpose of all the effort. The Jewish associations were willing to join efforts to implement the agreed upon solutions with the resources available to them regardless of prevailing differences of opinion between individual associations.

Thirty-two countries had sent delegations to Evian to signal their interest that they were interested and willing to make a contribution in solving the refugee problem. By padding each other on the shoulder and reading their well-prepared speeches, the large meeting came to a conclusion. It had served its purpose of demonstrating to one and the other that the world had done something, but naturally the problem could not be solved alone without the others participating. They indeed did not participate. None of the important countries were prepared to break away from the existing regulations and to seize other additional measures, and the smaller countries followed their example. In order to give all the activities in the days of the

[25] A. Cattani, *supra* n. 24, p. 42.

conference a serious coat of paint, a conscientious decision was made to establish an international committee in London, which should negotiate possible solutions in reference to the refugee questions. The newly founded institution was called Intergovernmental Committee on Refugees (IGC). Roosevelts envoy came out on top in the founding of this committee against the fierce British opposition whose delegation leader, Lord Winterton, not only refused to give some thought to possibly liberalising the immigration policy to Palestine but also demonstratively showed his disinterest for the topic of the conference in general. Hardly worth mentioning was the fact that practically no financial resources were allocated to the committee, let alone that no place was made available to where the immigrants could have been sent. Besides, it appeared to critical observers that an enormous indifference was shown by electing of all people the anti-Semitic Lord Winterton as President of the committee, who would seek to undermine the committee's efficiency. As director of the committee a 70-year-old American lawyer by the name of George Rubble was selected. It turned out that the IGC besides all its activities could not substantially contribute to solving the refugee problems. Madagascar until 1940 was still considered a possible place of relocation for Jews of Poland and Germany. But France refused to tolerate German-speaking minorities living in its colonies although Hitler was inclined to accept this option.[26] A number of Jews immigrated to South American countries. 15,000 Jews found a safe haven in Shanghai, which afterwards locked its doors. Many other places were contacted such as the Philippines, British Guinea, Angola, etc. etc. Not one government that came into question was officially prepared to accept Jews of the German Reich. Only Rafael Trujillo, President of the Dominican Republic, was willing to invite a greater number of Jewish refugees to come. They should do the slave work that Haitians had done before he killed 20,000 of them in 1937.[27] But who paid any real attention to the entire matter? Everyone gave the best they could to handle the social issues of the world. Now they could rest assured that they had done their best and with a good conscience devote their efforts to domestic issues, especially those involving the economy and trade. It was business as usual.

The German government had followed the developments at the Evian Conference very closely and wrote with voluptuous sniping remarks, how surprising it was that other countries criticised Germany for the treatment of its Jews but weren't prepared to take charge of an opportunity and to open their own borders. Headlines of triumph appeared on the front page of the *Völkische Beobachter*: No One Wants Them.[28] Not even children…

---

[26] R. Hilberg, *Die Vernichtung der europäischen Juden*, 2nd edn. (Frankfurt/Main, Fischer 1992), p. 416; see A. Hillgruber, *Hitlers Strategie. Politik und Kriegsführung 1940-1941* (Düsseldorf, Bernard & Gräfe 1965), p. 245; J. Lukacs, *The Last European War September 1939 – December 1941* (New York, Anchor Press 1976), p. 432; Akten zur Deutschen Auswärtigen Politik 1918-1945 (ADAP), Series D XI, p. 635.

[27] H.L. Feingold, *Bearing Witness. How America and Its Jews Responded to the Holocaust* (New York, Syracuse University Press 1995), p. 192. Less than 600 Jewish refugees were admitted to the Dominican Republic.

[28] E. Ben-Elissar, *supra* n. 24, p. 251.

Also the efforts by many American citizens to admit at least children were destined to fail. The United States Senate refused between 1939 and 1940 to pass a piece of legislation called Wagner-Rogers, which would have permitted that 20,000 Jewish children be allowed to enter the United States.[29] The widely spread racism among Americans including anti-Semitic prejudice among leading civil servants of different departments bear to a great extent the responsibility of not increasing the quota to accept more Jewish refugees.

V. Conference failure and the consequences

The complete failure of the Evian Conference was primarily due to two reasons. At the *political* level it was the international community's unwillingness to start a fight with Germany or at least to take steps to save the victims of the Nazi regime and to present this case before its own people – a hopeless undertaking, since the leaders wanted to be re-elected. The general public of those countries participating at the Evian Conference were, if not candidly, then subliminally anti-Semitic cultivating strong xenophobic feelings and not prepared in any event to give jobs to foreigners, especially if they were Jews. From a perspective of *international law* there was at the time of the Evian Conference a complete lack of a set of international norms about the legal status of refugees, a factor which should not be underestimated. They were not considered individuals legally requiring a special type of protection, but instead were classified like other unwelcomed foreigners. The High Commission by the League of Nations which had been founded already in 1933 and been instituted to protect refugees, lacked the needed legitimate legal authority. Its sphere of influence was additionally hampered not only by the uncompromising attitude of Germany, which showed complete disregard for trying to find procedures to channel the exit of Jews (known as the *Entjudung Deutschlands*) or to get rid of the Jews from Germany in an organised manner, but also because of the dwindling respect for the authority of the League of Nations.

Already in April and May various countries like Switzerland, as an example, entered into bilateral negotiations with National Socialist Germany to find ways to gain control of the wave of Jewish refugees. Emigrating to oversea-destinations from Switzerland had become more difficult rather than easier following the Evian Conference.[30] Failing to find an international solution at Evian, Switzerland resumed negotiations with Germany. On 27 and 29 September 1938 the Germans and Swiss achieved a preliminary understanding to accept the J stamp, which the Ger-

[29] W. Benz (ed.), *Die Juden in Deutschland 1933-1945. Leben unter nationalsozialistischer Herrschaft* [The Jews in Germany 1933-1945. Life under National-Socialist Reign] (Munich, C.H. Beck 1989), p. 425.

[30] *12 Diplomatische Dokumente der Schweiz 1848-1945* (DDS), 1 January 1937-31 December 1938, préparé sous la direction d'Oscar Gauye par Gabriel Imboden et David Bourgeois, Document No. 363 (Bern 1994), pp. 833-835.

mans had already propagated to use in their passports, allowing Switzerland to determine who was Arian and non-Arian.[31]

Soon expulsion became almost the order of the day. After the Munich Pact and the territorial changes concerning the Sudetenland, Slovakia and Hungary, about 3000 Jews were expelled and left destitute in the new border areas while others living in Germany like Soviet Russians would be sent to concentration camps from which they would be released only upon emigrating. The inability of the world community to find a universal solution to the European refugee problem escalated when the Polish government decreed a renewal of the passports of their citizens abroad, but deliberately delayed processing passport papers of Jews, which were soon to expire at the end of October 1938. This would have deprived them of their citizenship and prevented their return to Poland especially from annexed Austria. The German Foreign Ministry negotiated with the Poles without any resolve meaning that Nazi Germany could be left with ten thousands of stateless Jews. Before the deadline for passport renewal expired, the Gestapo rounded up whole families of Polish Jews (17,000 people), and transported them into no-mans-land between Poland and Germany. The plight of these families was horrendous. Eventually 8,000 of them found shelter along a small border town called Zbanszyn. Finally, they were admitted to enter Poland because the Polish government was put under pressure by the Jewish organisations and communities that were providing needed supplies to help the refugees wither the appalling conditions.[32]

In reprisal for Germanys expulsion of his parents along with thousands of other Polish Jews, the young 17 year old teenager Hershel Grynszpan, then living in Paris, entered the German Embassy on 7 November and assassinated the third secretary, Ernst vom Rath, who died two days later. This was the event that served as the catalyst for the *Kristallnacht*, the infamous night of broken glass, that began on 9 and 10 November in which Nazis in Germany and Austria conducted a nationwide pogrom against the Jewish people. By the morning of 10 November, scores of Jews were dead, hundreds bleeding, shops and homes in ruins, and synagogues defiled and debased. That was the night that began the Holocaust, the night that should have alerted the world to the gruesome design of the final solution.

By the summer of 1939 the Director of the Council for German Jewry (London), estimated the number of refugees in Belgium to be 12,000, in Switzerland 10,000 and in the Scandinavian countries 5,000. On 1 September 1939 the German military invasion of Poland had begun, with England and France declaring war on Germany two days later on 3 September.

The death toll caused by the Nazis and their collaborators during their twelve year reign was unprecedented in human history. The historian Omer Bartov comments on the centrality of the Holocaust in the 21st century as follows:

> '... the case of Nazism, and especially the Holocaust, is different. There are episodes in history whose centrality can only be recognized from a chronological distance. The

[31] Ibid., Document No. 414, pp. 933-939.
[32] L. Yahil, *supra* n. 18, pp. 109-110.

> mass of inexplicable, often horrifying details is endowed with sense and meaning only retrospectively, after it passed. Gradually such events come to cast a shadow over all that had previously seemed of greater significance, reaching backward and forward, until they finally touch our normal lives, reminding us with ever growing urgency that we are the survivors of cataclysms and catastrophes that we never experienced. The Holocaust is such an event.'[33]

The worlds reaction to the persecution and horrors of the Holocaust is imbued with the nature of law, as Michael Bazyler, professor of law at Chapman Law, points out in his lecture entitled: *The Holocaust, Genocide and the Law*.[34] Since 1933 legal decrees had taken away civil liberties from Jews shutting them out from public life and sustaining a livelihood, the Nuremberg Laws of 15 September 1935 being the most infamous. The persecution of the Jews through the instruments of law created an acceptable environment in which the non-Jewish German public participated in the large-scale deportations and murder of the Jews. Everything appeared quite normal making human death factories like Auschwitz possible. But this does not explain the indifference with which the world community responded.

When Rabbi Wise led a delegation of representatives of the most important Jewish organisations in the USA into a meeting with President Roosevelt on 8 December 1942 to urge the president to do everything in his power to stop the genocide, Roosevelt told him that he had already been informed of these events by American diplomats in neutral countries.[35] Roosevelt failed to mention, of course, that he did not consider the admission of German Jews to the USA a main concern, an attitude mirrored in US State Departments policies. Not without reason, FDR had made his old friend, Breckenridge Long, an anti-Semite and determined opponent of refugees, director of refugee policies.[36] Is this perhaps why, in 1944, the USA failed to bomb the rail link to Auschwitz? While a bombing might not have stopped the genocide, it might have sent a moral message, and possibly even more saved lives by interrupting, or at least delaying, the process of mass murder. The American explanation that these targets were not of vital importance for the course of the war sounds odd, given that efforts were made to save the famous Lipizzaner horses from falling into Russian hands and food parcels were dropped by parachute on Warsaw, although it was known that they might fall into German hands. The Roosevelt administration automatically rejected all requests to bomb the railways or roads to concentration camps because the fate of Jewish refugees was not a priority for the American president. In principle there was, however, no contradiction between the Allied victory and the rescuing of Jews. In 1944, Roosevelt, yield-

---

[33] O. Bartov, *Germanys War and the Holocaust. Disputed Histories* (Ithaca, NY, Cornell University Press 2003), p. 192.

[34] All materials are available at www.michaelbazyler.com/hgal.php.

[35] D. Wyman, *Das unerwünschte Volk. Amerika und die Vernichtung der europäischen Juden* [The Unwanted People, America and the Extermination of the European Jews] (Munich, Fischer 1986), p. 86.

[36] L. Davidson, 'The State Department & Zionism 1917-1945. A Reevaluation', in VII *Middle East Policy* (1999), p. 12.

ing to strong pressure exerted by the Congress, Jewish activists and Treasury Secretary, Henry Morgenthau Jr., took a step towards rescue by establishing the War Refugee Board. Although this commission had very little money or other support from the White House, it still played an important role in the rescue of over 200,000 refugees. Moreover, the commissions activities were not detrimental to the war effort. If it had been established earlier, many lives might have been saved.[37]

The defeat of Germany led the Allies to create an international legal tribunal at Nuremberg to try those responsible for the horrors of World War II. The legacy of Nuremberg permeates today the current rules of international criminal law, but why did not religious beliefs concerning the sanctity of life, or in secular accounts that emphasise the equality of persons, arouse a public outcry in the world about the duty to protect the vulnerable?[38]

Today, vulnerability-based humanitarian justifications are generally generous in the aftermath of major disasters involving human suffering such as earthquakes, floods or severe droughts by providing assistance to alleviate poverty and thus protect people from its related scourges of malnutrition, disease and the like similarly in seeking punishment for those that committed a war crime or crime against humanity. As to preventing a cataclysm like genocide, there is still procrastination to call the mass killings of people a genocide but rather an ethnic cleansing. This is due in part to a far from complete emerging global consensus about the fundamental nature of human rights, which is an important strand in the humanitarian account of cross-border duties. There is still considerable dispute about what rights are to be protected. Bodily integrity rights, not to be tortured, murdered, raped, imprisoned without due process, and the like, have gained acceptance but it has begun to be questioned by many since September 11 that at times of war voices and press can be silenced or modulated and citizens of a democratic country can be detained without charge or suspension of *habeas corpus* and others can be tortured by so-called enhanced interrogation. One is reminded of the Latin maxim, *inter arma silent leges*: In time of war, the laws are silent. 'More disputed are rights concerning moral, religious, and political choice, and whether there are attendant cross-border duties to promote and protect such rights,' says Peter G. Brown in his book on *Ethics, Economic and International Relations*. He remarks that 'consensus is weakest on the question of whether there are rights to subsistence (survival), and if there are, who has the corresponding duties. For the purpose of the argument in favor of universal trusteeship … [it] is an important ally … for the development of an international consensus on how to treat our fellow persons, and – suitably expanded – the rest of the commonwealth of life.'[39] We need to move away from the view of the state-based days of Westphalia beyond the international society of today to evolve

---

[37] The David Wyman Institute for Holocaust Studies, History Channel Distorted FDRs Response to the Holocaust. www.wymaninstitute.org

[38] R.E. Goodin, *Protecting the Vulnerable. A Reanalysis of Our Social Responsibilities* (Chicago, University of Chicago Press 1985).

[39] P.G. Brown, *Ethics, Economics and International Relations* (Edinburgh, Edinburgh University Press 2008), p. 134.

into a world community giving moral concern for each individual life predicated on the principle, under which individual states assume reciprocal obligations laying out standards to uphold regarding the concerns for each human within their borders so as to prevent abuses turning into horrific crimes infringing on the stability of other states around the world.. As Kant and his successors conjectured, the possibility of a new level of political community where the village has gone global in an Age of Globalisation based on moral and political concerns beyond the borders of a particular state. The international law of human rights has given legal basis for such concerns, setting out standards that states have committed to uphold. The modern international legal order must be predicated on a new principle, under which the individual states assume reciprocal obligations to contain transnational threats emerging from within their borders so as to prevent them from infringing on the peace and safety of fellow states around the world as well to assure the principles of self-determination, freedom of expression and the emergence of a normative entitlement to participate in electoral or other decision-making process. This moral cosmopolitanism rests on the idea that the flourishing well-being of human beings is a matter of concern to all. This applies to people whoever they are and it applies globally. Cosmopolitanism implies that citizens have a responsibility for institutions that destroy well-being elsewhere in the world. The world community has a moral cosmopolitan responsibility to prevent genocide in accordance with the Genocide Convention and not to be disbarred by laws as law disbarred the world community from intervening before the Holocaust. Laws must be applicable to prevent and deter the crime of crimes against humanity.

Part Two
Public Policy Considerations

GENOCIDE PREVENTION AND THE DYNAMICS OF CONFLICT

Ulrich Wagner and Thorsten Bonacker

From a social science perspective, genocide has many aspects of intergroup violence. Intergroup violence is defined as violent behaviour of members of one group against members of another group. Phenomenologically, it includes all kinds of violent behaviour. In the following, at first, we describe relevant aspects of group and intergroup behaviour. Then we will deliver a process model of intergroup violence and highlight the role of the media for both conflict escalation and peacebuilding. In the third part of this paper we use this model to derive implications for the prevention and treatment of intergroup violence and genocide.

I. Groups and intergroup processes

Experimental social psychological research has demonstrated repeatedly that group and intergroup behaviour can be evoked very easily. Tajfel, Billig, Bundy and Flament[1] were among the first who demonstrated this in the so-called minimal-group experiments. In these experiments, subjects are randomly assigned to a certain category, such as an artificial green or a blue group. In some experiments, the random character of assignment to the different categories was even clear to the subjects.[2] In the second phase of these experiments the subjects were asked to distribute material rewards to other people, such as small amounts of money. The subjects in the minimal-group experiments did not know who these other people were. They only are informed that one of the two persons belongs to the same group or category as the subject him- or herself, whereas the other person is a member of the other group. In addition, it is explicit that subjects do not assign rewards to themselves. Figure 1 (upper part) describes systematically how subjects in these minimal group experiments can decide: They can assign an amount of zero cents to the ingroup member and simultaneously assign 100 cents to the outgroup member, or they can assign 10 cents to the ingroup member, implying that then the outgroup

[1] H. Tajfel, et al., 'Social Categorization and Intergroup Behavior', in 1 *European Journal of Social Psychology* (1971), pp. 149-178.

[2] M. Billig & H. Tajfel, 'Social Categorization and Similarity in Intergroup Behaviour', in 3 *European Journal of Social Psychology* (1973), pp. 27-52.

C. Safferling and E. Conze (eds.), The Genocide Convention Sixty Years after its Adoption

member will receive 90, etc. Alternatively the subject can also decide to assign 100 cents to the ingroup member and nothing to the outgroup member (the choice at the right end of the scale).

The minimal group research paradigm

Ingroup member	0	10	20	30	40	50	60	70	80	90	100
Outgroup member	100	90	80	70	60	50	40	30	20	10	0
	O	O	O	O	O	O	⊗	O	O	O	O

Ingroup member	60	40
Outgroup member	50	10
	O	⊗

Figure 1

The minimal group experiments show, in different places of the world and with different participants, that subjects tend to prefer the ingroup member compared to the outgroup member. That is, they give a higher amount of money to the ingroup compared to the outgroup member by choosing, e.g., the 60 (for ingroup) to 40 (for outgroup) alternative. Other versions of the minimal group experiments forgo the zero-sum-matrixes. That means that subjects can for example decide between assigning 60 cents to the ingroup member and 50 cents to the outgroup member, as one option, or 40 cents to the ingroup member and 10 to the outgroup member (see Figure 1, lower part). These kinds of matrixes usually show that subjects in the minimal group experiments prefer the second option, that is, to maximise the difference between the ingroup and the outgroup, even if this goes at the expense of maximum ingroup profit.

Tajfel and Turner[3] took the results of the minimal group experiments as a basis for their social identity theory. According to them people adopt categories in order to attain or construct a self definition, their social identity. In addition, Tajfel and Turner assume that individuals try to maintain or enhance their self-esteem. It follows from these assumptions that a positive social identity can be achieved by devaluating the outgroup relative to the ingroup, i.e., by producing an ingroup bias. In other words, the ingroup bias demonstrated in the minimal group experiments is the result of the attempt to enhance group based social identity.

Intergroup behaviour depends on situational variations: People usually are members of different groups with which they identify: We all belong to different gender groups, different ethnic groups, different national groups, etc. These kinds of group memberships are not always relevant in all situations; whether one of the mentioned group memberships influences behaviour in a certain situation depends on

[3] H. Tajfel & J.C. Turner, 'An integrative theory of intergroup conflict', in W.G. Austin & S. Worchel (eds.), *The social psychology of intergroup relations* (Monterey, Brooks & Cole 1979), pp. 33-47.

situational cues. For example, nobody in a group of people recognises their possible differentiation according to gender up until someone tells a sexist joke which makes gender group membership immediately salient.

Social identity theory and related theories (as, for example, the self categorisation theory[3a]) make clear, that groups and group memberships are socially constructed. In accordance with that, a group can be defined as two or more individuals perceiving themselves to be members of the same social category.

II. Intergroup violence

A number of scholars from sociology and social psychology took the constructivist perspective described above as basis for developing a model for understanding and explaining intergroup violence and genocide. One of the prominent experts in this field is Erwin Staub.[4] Parts of his model are described in Figure 2, extended by some of our own considerations to the topic.

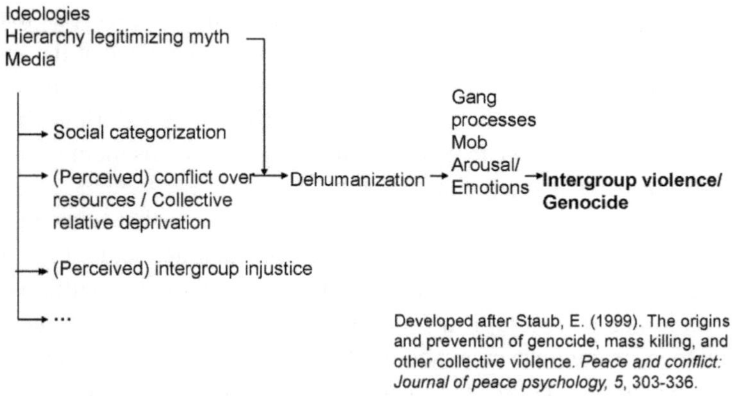

Figure 2

The model starts with social categorisation as described above. Social categorisation gives the basis for defining ingroup memberships and for defining outgroups. Intergroup conflict research shows that, in addition to the basic process described above, the ingroup bias evoked by simple ingroup-outgroup categorisation can be intensified by a number of factors. The most prominent is conflict between groups over scarce resources, may it really exist or be only perceived by the members of the different groups.[5] The more group members perceive their ingroup in a conflict

---

[3a] J.C. Turner, M.A. Hogg, P.J. Oaks, S.D. Reicher and M.S. Wetherell, 'Rediscovering the social group' (Oxford, Blackwell 1987).

[4] E. Staub, 'The Origins and Prevention of Genocide, Mass Killing, and other Collective Violence', in 5 *Peace and Conflict: Journal of Peace Psychology* (1999), pp. 303-336.

[5] H. Blumer, 'Racial Prejudice as a Sense of Group Position', in 23 *Pacific Sociological Review* (1958), pp. 3-7; M. Deutsch, 'A Theory of Co-operation and Competition', in 2 *Human Relations* (1949), pp. 129-152; M. Sherif, *In Common Predicament: Social Psychology of Intergroup Conflict and Cooperation* (Boston, Houghton Mifflin 1966).

over resources with an outgroup, as water, mineral resources, etc., the more group members accept outgroup devaluation, discrimination and violent behaviour against outgroup members. A further intensifying factor is intergroup injustice, either in the form of real or objective injustice between groups or only as perception of injustice.[6] Devaluative and hostile intergroup behaviour between, e.g., ethnic groups, will increase the more group members perceive their ingroup as being treated unjust, may it be in the allocation of resources or the way they can actively participate in the decision making process of their distribution. An example for the influence of procedural justice on the course of conflict is the dispute between ethnic groups about power sharing concerning their representation in constitutional assemblies and parliaments. One can easily think of further independent or moderating factors on intensifying intergroup violence and genocide.

In Staub's perspective, the three causal factors of intergroup violence and genocide, categorisation in in- and outgroup, conflict over resources, and intergroup injustice, can have the psychological consequence of dehumanisation. This is an extreme or strong kind of ingroup bias, in the process of which the outgroup and its members are no longer perceived as being humans. Other authors refer to that same process as infra-humanisation.[7] Dehumanisation can take place at the level of the single individual who is starting to behave violently against outgroup members.[8] More often, however, dehumanisation is a collective process during which societies make ideologies available that classify the outgroup and its members as infrahuman. Anti-Semitism has many facets of this.[9]

Figure 2 describes, in addition to Staub's model, two further relevant mediating processes for the emergence of intergroup violence and genocide: First, the emergence of gangs or mobs in the streets. Their appearance mediates between dehumanisation as an ideological process on the societal level and the real intergroup violence or conduct of genocide. Second, gang and mob violence can be assumed to be strongly connected to arousal and strong intergroup emotional processes in the coming perpetrators. These internal processes explain why the conduct of intergroup violence and genocide often takes forms that seem to be extremely brutal compared to 'normal' interpersonal violence.[10]

The question is why social categorisation, the perception of conflicts between groups and perceived intergroup injustice have this strong consequence of

---

[6] M. Deutsch, 'Justice and Conflict', in M. Deutsch & P.T. Coleman (eds.), *The Handbook of Conflict Resolution* (San Francisco, Jossey-Bass 2000), pp. 41-64.

[7] N. Haslam, 'Dehumanisation: An Integrative Review', in 10 *Personality and Social Psychology Review* (2006), pp. 252-264.

[8] R.D. Crelinsten & A.P. Schmid, *The Politics of Pain. Torturers and their Masters* (Leiden, COMT 1993).

[9] P. Glick, 'Sacrificial lambs dressed in wolves' clothing', in L.S. Newman & R. Erber (eds.), *Understanding Genocide: The Social Psychology of the Holocaust* (Oxford, Oxford University Press 2002), pp. 113-142.

[10] U. Wagner & O. Christ, 'Intergroup Aggression and Emotions: A Framework and First Data', in M. Gollwitzer & G. Steffgen (eds.), *Emotions and aggressive Behaviour* (Göttingen, Hogrefe & Huber 2007), pp. 133-148.

dehumanisation as a precondition of intergroup violence and genocide. We argue that this can only take place in societies where commonly shared ideologies or hierarchy legitimising myths[11] exist that produce collective and individual enemy images,[12] which legitimise the infra-humanisation of the outgroup in focus. An important factor transporting these kinds of ideologies as macro phenomena into the individual's head is the media (see Figure 2).

To discuss the role the media play in conflict escalation processes we turn to an international relations' theoretical perspective. The so-called Copenhagen School introduced the concept of securitisation to describe the escalation of intergroup conflicts. Genocide can only occur where outgroups are seen as an existential threat to the ingroup's identity, i.e., if the outgroup is perceived as a security risk. According to Wæver,[13] security *per se* does not exist in a vacuum, but is constructed through public communication.

Securitisation consists of three components, namely

1. claiming a threat to survival and demanding extraordinary measures,
2. adopting emergency action,
3. violating rules that otherwise bind.[14]

It is decisive to distinguish between a securitising move and securitisation. Asserting an existential threat and requesting extraordinary means constitute a securitising move. An issue becomes securitised only if an audience accepts the allegation that an existential threat exists and approves a response by emergency measures. Thus, securitisation is an inter-subjective practice, i.e., individuals agree in a shared discourse that an outgroup is a threat for their identity.

Security is neither something out there waiting to be found nor can it be defined objectively.[15] Rather, security is constituted in an inter-subjective practice between groups. The starting point of the securitisation concept is the speech act theory developed by John Austin[16] who demonstrated how we do things with words. The

---

[11] J.T. Jost, M.R. Banaji & B.A. Nosek, 'A Decade of System Justification Theory: Accumulated Evidence of conscious and unconscious Bolstering of the status quo', in 25 *Political Psychology* (2004), pp. 881-920; J. Sidanius & F. Pratto, *Social Dominance: An Intergroup Theory of social Hierarchy and Oppression* (New York, Cambridge University Press 1999).

[12] M.G. Alexander, M.B. Brewer & R.K. Herrmann, 'Images and Affect: A functional Analysis of out-group Stereotypes', in 77 *Journal of Personality and Social Psychology* (1999), pp. 78-93; A.J. Cuddy, S.T. Fiske & P. Glick, 'Warmth and Competence as universal Dimensions of social Perception: The stereotype content model and the BIAS map', in M.P. Zanna (ed.), *Advances in Experimental Social Psychology*, Vol. 40 (New York, Academic 2008), pp. 61-149.

[13] O. Wæver, 'Securitization and Desecuritization', in R.D. Lipschutz (ed.), *On Security* (New York, Columbia University Press 1995), pp. 46-86.

[14] B. Buzan, O. Wæver & J. de Wilde, *Security: A new framework for analysis* (Boulder, Lynne Rienner 1998), p. 25.

[15] O. Wæver, 'The EU as a security actor. Reflections from a pessimistic constructivist on post-sovereign security orders', in M. Kelstrup & M.C. Williams (eds.), *International relations theory and the politics of European integration* (London, Routledge 2000), pp. 250-294 at p. 251.

[16] J.L. Austin, *How to do things with words* (Oxford, Oxford University Press 1962).

utterance of 'security' means an action.[17] An issue may turn into a security issue once an actor – usually a group or a group member – presents it as an existential threat to a reference object. An existential threat endangers the self-determination and possibly even the mere existence of a group or a political unit, in terms of social identity theory, the social identity of the group members. Being about the question to be or not to be, a security problem can thus 'alter the premises for all other questions.'[18] As survival is at stake, the securitising ingroup claims that a threat cannot be adequately addressed by ordinary measure and must be responded by emergency means. Such use of all necessary means breaches the rules of normal politics and paves the way not only for collective violence, but for dehumanisation, mass homicide and – as a last consequence – genocide.[19] As securitisation is a matter of public communication usually located in the media we argue, that the media communication of existential threats identified with an outgroup is a necessary precondition for extreme intergroup violence and genocide. Prominent examples of such media campaigns preparing genocide are Rwanda and also Nazi-Germany.

III. Prevention and treatment of violence and genocide

Since the UN Genocide Convention came into effect in 1951, the international community has to react on 'acts committed with intent to destroy, in whole or in part, a national, ethnical, racial or religious group, as such' (Convention on the Prevention and Punishment of the Crime of Genocide, Art. 2). In international law, military interventions to prevent or to react on mass violence and genocide are legitimised by Chapter VII of the UN Charter, according to which coercive intervention in the affairs of a state is justified in case of a threat to international peace and security.[20] The term usually used for such situations is 'humanitarian intervention.' Humanitarian intervention means the use of force across borders by a state or groups of states or international organisations aimed at preventing or ending widespread and grave violations of core human rights of individuals other than its own citizens.[21] Obviously the international community has acted selectively on situations which can be described as genocide – like for instance Cambodia in the 1970s or Sudan today – by officially renaming them as mass violence to refuse international re-

---

[17] B. Buzan, O. Wæver & J. de Wilde, *supra* n. 14.

[18] *Idem.*

[19] B. Buzan & O. Wæver, *Regions and powers. The structure of international security* (Cambridge Cambridge University Press 2003); T. Gromes & T. Bonacker, 'The concept of securitisation as a tool for analysing the role of human-rights-related civil society in ethno-political conflicts', in *Working Paper SHUR* 5/07 (2007), at p. 2, retrieved from www.luiss.it/shur/wp-content/uploads/2008/10/shurwp05-07.pdf.

[20] J.N. Pieterse, 'Sociology of humanitarian intervention: Bosnia, Rwanda and Somalia compared', in 18 *International Political Science Review* (1997), pp. 71-93.

[21] J.L. Holzgrefe, 'The humanitarian intervention debate', in J.L. Holzgrefe & R.O. Keohane (eds.), *Humanitarian intervention. Ethical, legal and political dilemmas* (Cambridge, Cambridge University Press 2003), pp. 15-62.

sponsibility. Again media and public communication play an important role: 'Humanitarian intervention seems for the most part to be confined to cases in which there has been extensive television coverage, where there is some particular interest in intervention, and in which there is not likely to be dissent among powers or massive military opposition. In short, it may largely be confined to highly publicized situations of chaos and disintegration.'[22] Seybold[23] distinguishes four types of humanitarian military intervention according to different goals and strategies:

Type	*Strategy*	*Scenario*
Help deliver aid	Avoidance	Air drops Camp construction Direct assistance to population Transport Infrastructure repair
Protect aid operations	Deterrence and defence	Point protection Area protection
Save the victims	Deterrence, defence and compellence	Point protection, Area protection
Defeat the perpetrators	Compellence and offence	Military defeat Negotiated peace

Even if military humanitarian interventions are the most visible and controversial form of intervention, we also have to take other forms of intervention into account, e.g., civilian interventions carried out by NGOs, but also by states and international organisations in the context of development aid, or diplomatic pressure and sanctions. According to our model, the intervention and treatment of genocide can be perceived as the intervention of a third party which is based on international law to legitimise their intervention.

Interventions can take place very early in that they influence ideologies and thereby social categorisations, perceptions of conflicts and perceptions of intergroup justice. Third parties can also intervene in a way that they contribute to work against dehumanising ideologies. Third parties can work against the emergence of gangs and mob violence. If the mob already marauds against outgroup members, third parties can robustly act against this and thus interfere in an already ongoing act of intergroup violence. And finally, third party intervention can mean that third parties contribute to reconciliation and enduring peacebuilding in a post genocide period.

---

22 A. Roberts, 'The road to hell. A critique of humanitarian intervention', in 16 *Harvard International Review* (1993), pp. 10-14 at p. 12.

23 T. Seybolt, *Humanitarian military intervention. The conditions of success and failure* (Oxford, Oxford University Press 2007), p. 42.

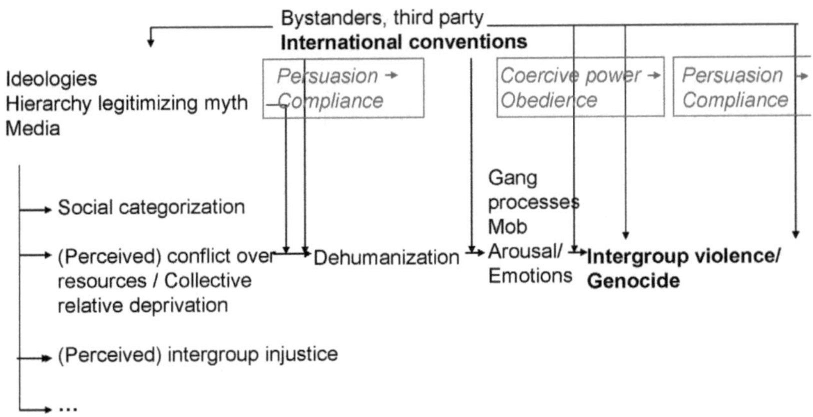

Figure 3

Two social psychological processes seem to be important to be considered in relation to the different opportunities for third party intervention: the use of coercive power and the degree to which the third party introduces itself as an outgroup.

At the beginning of intergroup conflicts, third party interventions usually imply non-military interventions. These kinds of interventions, as for example developmental support to reduce conflict over resources, really have the chance to focus on attitudes and value changes as well as changes in ideologies and stereotypes. Later interventions in an already bloody intergroup conflict often use coercive power in form of military intervention. As is known from social psychological research, coercive power is able to change behaviour by obedience; however, this behaviour change depends on surveillance.[24] As soon as a coercive power intervention by, e.g., the military comes to its end the induced behaviour changes tend to fall back into their old patterns. That is, coercive power interventions usually are not able to induce value and ideological changes and need continuous surveillance. Thus, any robust intervention against intergroup violence and genocide should be accompanied by soft, non-robust attempts to significantly change attitudes and ideologies. A real peacebuilding needs of course the restructuring of the intergroup situation according to distribution of resources and intergroup justice and the desecuritisation of the conflict, so that the outgroup is no longer perceived as an existential threat.

The second important influencing factor derived from our intergroup model is, how far the intervening third party presents itself to the antagonists in the genocide as an ingroup or an outgroup member. Internationally recognised norms such as the genocide convention play a crucial role here, because they symbolise a shared identity of different groups and states. If the intervening third party is perceived as a hostile outgroup, the third party's interventions and strategies are in danger to produce just the opposite outcome of the intended one: the opponents may show reluc-

---

[24] J.R.P. French & B.H. Raven, 'The bases of power', in D. Cartwright (ed.), *Studies in social power* (Ann Arbor, The University of Michigan Press 1959).

tance and boomerang effects may occur.[25] Thus, intervening third parties should summon common interests and achieve at least a partial group membership within the two conflicting groups, for example, in form of acting on behalf of a common world community symbolised by international law. Shared norms as a symbol of a collective identity could therefore contribute to avoid negative perceptions of the third party. This also presupposes that the intervening third party is legitimised by the international community and its representative, the United Nations.

The described theoretical considerations lead to a number of further implications. First, third parties should intervene as early as possible. Second, the attempt to avoid being perceived as an outgroup may imply to include local participants in the intervention process. This is widely discussed as a precondition for a successful peacebuilding process.[26] Third, taking into consideration that a third party's perspective of the conflict may not be identical with the conflict antagonists' views, the interventions should be configured according to the narratives and needs of victims and even perpetrators. The latter is important especially in post (civil) war times. Fourth, third parties should make their good deeds visible, that is they should use, among others, the media to make common interests clear. This also implies to make justice restoration processes, such as tribunals and truth commissions, accessible to the population. Fifth, third parties should adjust their contribution to restoration of justice to the (cultural) expectations of victims and perpetrators. Sixth, intervening third parties have to recognise the needs of victims for trust, reconciliation, and power and even the needs of the perpetrators.

---

[25] J.W. Brehm, *Responses to loss of freedom. A theory of psychological reactance* (Morristown, General Learning Press 1972).

[26] J. Prendergast & E. Plumb, 'Building local capacity: From implementation to peacebuilding', in S. Stedman, D. Rothchild & E.M. Cousens (eds.), *Ending Civil wars: The implementation of peace agreements* (Boulder, Lynne Rienner 2002), pp. 327-349.

WAR CRIMES, GENOCIDE TRIALS AND *VERGANGENHEITSPOLITIK* – THE GERMAN CASE

Annette Weinke

I. GERMANY AND INTERNATIONAL LAW AFTER 1945: A CASE OF 'POST-NUREMBERG REFLEX'?

The history of international criminal law since the Second World War is a story of multiple ironies and paradoxical twists, as a series of authors have remarked in recent years.[1] This is attributable to the conflicts and mutual blockades of the 'Cold War,' but also to course changes in US legal policy and the ambiguous actions of the American superpower. The United States provided the central concepts and organisational impetus for the London Agreement of 1945 and the Nuremberg war crimes program that followed, leading the way in building a 'normative architecture which repudiates genocide and crimes against humanity,'[2] but later American policy slowed down efforts to constitutionalise humanitarian international law.[3] The makers of US policy tended to back away from efforts to link international peace-keeping with the cause of human rights, though the idea was enshrined already in the April 1945 preamble to the United Nations Charter (a document very much in the spirit of Kant's universalist idea of 'eternal peace').[4] This reluctance is often

---

[1] See, e.g., R.M. Brown, 'The American Perspective on Nuremberg: A Case of Cascading Ironies', in H.R. Reginbogin & C.J.M. Safferling (eds.), *The Nuremberg Trials. International Criminal Law Since 1945/Die Nürnberger Prozesse. Völkerstrafrecht seit 1945* (München, Saur 2006), p. 21; J. Habermas, *Der gespaltene Westen* (Frankfurt a.M., Suhrkamp 2004), p. 158; P. Betts, 'Germany, International Justice and the 20th Century', 17 *History and Memory* (special issue on 20th Century Germany) (2005), pp. 45-86; H. Ahlbrecht, *Geschichte der völkerrechtlichen Strafgerichtsbarkeit im 20. Jahrhundert* (Baden-Baden, Nomos 1999).

[2] R.A. Falk, 'Remembering the Holocaust and the Geopolitical Persistence of Indifference', cited in R.M. Brown, *supra* n. 1, p. 21.

[3] Constitutionalisation refers to the substantive orientation of the norms toward protecting interests of the world community rather than interests of states, and introduction of elements of international public law enforcement going beyond simple co-ordination among sovereign states. C. Kreß, 'Jus conta bellum: Quo Vadis?', 155 *Kursbuch* (2004), pp. 62-80 at p. 72.

[4] While only a coincidence, at least based on current historical knowledge, it is perhaps paradigmatic in this regard that the IMT Statute was signed on the same day as the second atomic bomb was detonated above Nagasaki, on 8 August 1945; see N. Paech, 'Nürnberg und Nuklearfrage', in G. Hankel & G. Stuby (eds.), *Strafgerichte gegen Menschheitsverbrechen. Zum Völkerstrafrecht 50 Jahre nach den Nürnberger Prozessen* (Hamburg, Hamburger Edition 1995), p. 481.

C. Safferling and E. Conze (eds.), The Genocide Convention Sixty Years after its Adoption

seen in American reactions to the specifics of new international norms and laws: While relentless pressure from Eleanor Roosevelt and a variety of civil organisations moved the Truman Administration to finally join (with caveats) the UN Convention on Human Rights in December 1948,[5] less success awaited the concurrent efforts to achieve an international abolition of genocide as spearheaded by the Polish-Jewish legal scholar and emigrant Raphael Lemkin. It's true that the United States also joined the UN Genocide Convention in the same month, but another forty years passed before the Senate finally ratified the treaty in 1988. Political and ideological reservations and resistance to Lemkin's project came both from influential Southern-state senators and from certain former members of the Nuremberg prosecution team.[6] Yet the spirit and language of the 'Nuremberg Principles' did not recede into obscurity,[7] despite their general ineffectiveness in practical terms[8] under a bipolar world order. Again paradoxically, their continued vitality was largely due to American advocates of international law (not a few of whom were German and Austrian emigrants driven to the United States by the Nazi terror), as well as to American writers and peace activists, and former members of the American prosecution team at Nuremberg. Today, finally, the establishment and attempt to implement the International Criminal Court threatens to fizzle out because of continuing US resistance, despite many years of engagement by civil society groups and despite the large proportion of the American people and the great many US-based NGOs who do not share their own government's policy on macrocriminality.[9]

---

[5] See M.R. Ishay, *The History of Human Rights. From Ancient Times to the Globalization Era* (Berkeley and Los Angeles, University of California Press 2004), pp. 218-223; M. Mazower, 'The Strange Triumph of Human Rights, 1933-1950', in 47 *The Historical Journal* (2004), pp. 379-398; A. Weinke, 'Von Nürnberg nach Den Haag'? Das Internationale Militärtribunal in historischer Perspektive', in Justizministerium des Landes Nordrhein-Westfalen and Villa ten Hompel (eds.), *Vom Tribunal zum Weltgericht. Neue Fragestellungen zum Verhältnis von Menschenrechtsverbrechen und Völkerstrafrecht 60 Jahre nach dem Nürnberger Hauptkriegsverbrecherprozess* (Geldern, JVA Geldern 2008), p. 20.

[6] See J. Cooper, *Raphael Lemkin and the Struggle for the Genocide Convention* (Houndmills, Palgrave Macmillan 2008), pp. 189-208; Historian A. Rabinbach is of the opinion that the belated signing was a PR measure by the Reagan Administration to reduce the embarrassment of the Bitburg Affair; A. Rabinbach, 'The Challenge of the Unprecedented – Raphael Lemkin and the Concept of Genocide', 4 *Yearbook of the Simon-Dubnow-Institute* (2005), pp. 397-420.

[7] The literature still awaits a global history of 'Nuremberg' reception during the 'Cold War' that goes beyond the activities of the International Law Commission (ILC) of the UN to also cover the rise of a global-acting peace movement. A first overview from an international law perspective may be found in M. Koskenniemi, *The Gentle Civilizer of Nations. The Rise and Fall of International Law 1870-1960* (Cambridge, Cambridge University Press 2002); see also N. Paech, *supra* n. 4.

[8] One of the few exceptions is the 1961 trial of Adolf Eichmann in Israel, which also relied on the legal as well as evidentiary premises of Nuremberg; see G. Hausner, *Justice in Jerusalem* (New York, Harper & Row 1966); on the concept of 'Judeocide' as introduced in the Eichmann trial, see L. Douglas, *The Memory of Judgment. Making Law and History in the Trials of the Holocaust* (New Haven and London, Yale University Press 2001), pp. 117-119; a further example is the 1987 trial of Klaus Barbie in France; see G. Werle, Das Völkerstrafrecht im Jahrhundert der Weltkriege und der Zivilisationsverbrechen, in H. Schmid & J. Krzymianowska (eds.), *Politische Erinnerung. Geschichte und kollektive Identität* (Würzburg, Königshausen & Neumann 2007), p. 170 at p. 177.

[9] G. Hankel, 'Einleitung', in *idem* (ed.), *Die Macht und das Recht. Beiträge zum Völkerrecht und Völkerstrafrecht am Beginn des 21. Jahrhunderts* (Hamburg, Hamburger Edition 2008), p. 7 at p. 11.

During the same period, West Germany has gone in an opposite but perhaps equally paradoxical direction. Interpretations of the history will of course vary according to perspective. That the Federal Republic over the last sixty years evolved from an opponent to a supporter of an international criminal court can be viewed as the product of a democratic learning process. In this telling, the belated German acceptance of 'Nuremberg Principles' comes logically as part of a general democratisation and liberalisation process that has gradually transformed all aspects of the nation's social, political and economic life.[10] The German path from 'Nuremberg to The Hague' – as the title of a 2006 exhibition in Nuremberg partly sponsored by the FRG Foreign Ministry would have it[11] – expresses Germany's successful 'arrival in the West.'[12] One need not wonder why this narrative of transformation gets a warm welcome from Germany's intellectual elites. And there's no doubting that the society's attitudes to the Nazi past have changed recognisably since the late 1950s. This is indicated by the resumption at that time of criminal investigations, or the increased restitutions paid to Western countries.[13] The paradigm of gradual transformation is also so seductive because it imputes to Germany a global pioneer role in the prosecution of macrocriminality, and sets the country up as the model for other transitional justice processes.[14]

A critical question is whether this success story of a belated reconciliation with 'Nuremberg' obscures more than it explains. The actual history was nothing at all like a linear process of adaptation and acculturation; the 'Nuremberg Principles' were adopted only after decades of delay, and were in fact explicitly rejected as a matter of official policy until the late 1980s. The defensive stance against 'Nuremberg' hardened early in the FRG's history and persisted throughout. An eloquent example may be found in the history of international law written by Wilhelm Grewe,[15] with its clear influences from Carl Schmitt and Hans Morgenthau. Pro-

---

[10] See also A. Doering-Manteuffel, *Wie westlich sind die Deutschen? Amerikanisierung und Westernisierung im 20. Jahrhundert* (Göttingen, Vandenhoeck & Ruprecht 2002); N. Frei, *Vergangenheitspolitik. Die Anfänge der Bundesrepublik und die NS-Vergangenheit* (München, C.H. Beck 1996); P. Gassert, 'Die Bundesrepublik, Europa und der Westen. Zu Verwestlichung, Demokratisierung und einigen komparatischen Defiziten der zeithistorischen Forschung', in J. Baberowski, et al. (eds.), *Geschichte ist immer Gegenwart. Vier Thesen zur Zeitgeschichte* (Stuttgart and München, Deutsche Verlagsanstalt 2001), p. 67; U. Herbert (ed.), *Wandlungsprozesse in Westdeutschland. Belastung, Integration, Liberalisierung 1945-1980* (Göttingen, Wallstein 2002); K. Jarausch, *Die Umkehr. Deutsche Wandlungen 1945-1995* (München, Deutsche Verlagsanstalt 2004).

[11] www.menschenrechte.org/beitraege/straflosigkeit/strafgerichtshof.pdf.

[12] A. Schildt, *Ankunft im Westen. Ein Essay zur Erfolgsgeschichte der Bundesrepublik* (Frankfurt a.M., S. Fischer Verlag 1999); H.A. Winkler, *Der lange Weg nach Westen*, 2 Vols. (München, C.H. Beck 2000/01).

[13] See A. Weinke, *Eine Gesellschaft ermittelt gegen sich selbst. Die Geschichte der Zentralen Stelle Ludwigsburg 1958-2008* (Darmstadt, WBG 2008); C. Goschler, *Schuld und Schulden. Die Politik der Wiedergutmachung für NS-Verfolgte seit 1945* (Göttingen, Wallstein 2005).

[14] See also A. Weinke, 'Alliierter Angriff auf die nationale Souveränität? Die Strafverfolgung von Kriegs- und NS-Verbrechen in der Bundesrepublik, der DDR und Österreich', in N. Frei (ed.), *Transnationale Vergangenheitspolitik. Der Umgang mit deutschen Kriegsverbrechern in Europa nach dem Zweiten Weltkrieg* (Göttingen, Wallstein 2006), p. 37.

[15] W. Grewe, *Epochen der Völkerrechtsgeschichte* (Baden-Baden, Nomos 1984); see also H. Steiger, 'From the International Law of Christianity to the International Law of the World Citizen', 2(3) *Jour-*

ceeding from the postdoctoral habilitation thesis under the supervision of Ernst Forsthoff and first drafted during the war's final year, when Grewe still held an extraordinary professorship at the Berlin University Foreign Studies Faculty under the department chair of SD intellectual Franz Alfred Six,[16] the study was only published in 1984 in edited form with a postwar supplement including Nuremberg. An English translation appeared in 2000, shortly after the author's death, and also derives mainly from the text of 1944. Both editions combine harsh critique of 'Nuremberg' with the German apologia of *tu quoque* ('you too,' pointing to Allied hypocrisy), as was already common in the early occupation period. Without mentioning his role as a legal expert for the German defense team at Nuremberg,[17] Grewe describes the military tribunals of Nuremberg and Tokyo as 'occupation courts of victor powers' who themselves committed attacks and acts of war, both during the Second World War and afterward, 'that fell within the Nuremberg definitions of crimes against peace, war crimes and crimes against humanity.'[18] Very much bearing the style and content of the legalistic debating culture and the defensive nationalist character that prevailed during the early years of occupation and rebuilding, Grewe's argument exemplifies a common position in the old West German scholarship on constitutional and international law, which sees 'Nuremberg' as the end-point of a process of politicisation and moralisation in international law that began with 'Versailles,' strenuously omitting the German Reich's genocidal war as a central event in the emergence of humanitarian international criminal law.

Neither the 1961 trial of Eichmann in Jerusalem nor the start of the Auschwitz trials two years later caused fundamental changes in German attitudes toward 'Nuremberg' and the 'Nuremberg Principles.' Therefore we must ask what other factors influenced the German self-concept on this question over the long term. Did the attitude of persistent rejection reflect a 'post-Nuremberg reflex,' as the Cologne-based international law scholar Claus Kress more recently postulated?[19] Or

---

nal of the History of International Law (2001), pp. 180-193; M. Koskenniemi, 'Rezension zu Wilhelm Grewe, The Epochs of International Law, Berlin 2001', 35 *Kritische Justiz* (2002) , pp. 277-281; B. Fassbender, 'Stories of War and Peace. On Writing the History of International Law in the Third Reich and After', 13 *European Journal of International Law* (2002), pp. 479-512.

[16] On Grewe's relationship to Six see L. Hachmeister, *Der Gegnerforscher. Die Karriere des SS-Führers Franz Alfred Six* (München, C.H. Beck 1998), pp. 139-143.

[17] Together with Ernst Kaufmann and Ernst Rudolf Huber, Grewe supported the defence team for Ernst von Weizsäcker in Nuremberg follow-up trial No. 11 and provided assistance with legal arguments to bolster the postulate of a 'tragic collision of duties.'

[18] Grewe specifically cites the actions of the Soviet Union in Poland after the German invasion of 1939, as well as of the United States in the era after the European war, including the use of nuclear weapons in Japan as well as the war against the Viet Minh/NLF in Vietnam; W. Grewe, *supra* n. 15, p. 778; relevant passage in the English edition reads as follows: 'The tribunals were not true international courts, but rather victor's court in occupied territory. They asserted that those same victorious powers had committed acts of aggression and war in the course of or after the Second World War which, consistent with Nuremberg Principles, had to be regarded as crimes against the peace, war crimes and crimes against humanity'; *idem*, *The Epochs of International Law* (Berlin, De Gruyter 2000), p. 668.

[19] C. Kreß, 'Germany and International Criminal Law. Continuity or Change?', in H.R. Reginbogin & C.J.M. Safferling (eds.), *supra* n. 1, p. 235 at p. 237.

were other causes more decisive? Below I venture that German opposition to judicial requital for genocide can only be partly attributed to the reality that many West German legal and constitutional experts were themselves associated with National Socialism prior to 1945 and supported its ideology in whole or part. The relatively rapid change in the immediate postwar period from an initially cautious acceptance of 'Nuremberg' to a nearly unanimous rejection can only be understood if we consider the perceptions and reactions of a variety of social actors. We also must more closely examine the fabric of *Vergangenheitspolitik* ('policy regarding the past'), the evolving discourses in jurisprudence and scholarship and the early German legal rulings in Nazi crime cases. In the final section, I shall consider how the medium of the law changed understandings and behavior with regard to Nazi crimes over the long term.

II. 'Nuremberg' and its effects on German perceptions of genocide trials

Today it is widely acknowledged that the 'trial of the major war criminals' (Hermann Göring, et al.) was a watershed for international humanitarian law and the rise of a global human rights discourse. The American legal experts responsible for conceiving the ambitious project that became the International Military Tribunal (IMT) believed the purpose was to hold Germany's political and military leadership publicly accountable for the waging of aggressive war and for the persecution and murder of innumerable victims. The Americans clearly seem to have been fascinated with the idea that Germany's 'unconditional surrender' provided a unique historical opportunity to effect the older idea of 'outlawing' war. At the same time, they were deeply appalled at the unprecedented atrocities Germans had committed, both inside Germany and throughout occupied Europe. Already during the war, the fate of the Jews was at the center of international discussion about the legal problem of how to reach justice for the victims of Nazi crimes.[20] The Gordian knot between positivist and natural law concepts was eventually cut, mainly due to the theoretical expertise of European lawyers like Bohuslav Ecer, Hersch Lauterpacht and Raphael Lemkin, as well as the political initiative of Henry L. Stimson as US secretary of war.[21] The most important outcome of this Allied debate about German extreme human rights violations was Article 6c of the IMT charter, which defined

---

[20] See S. Aronson, 'Preparations for the Nuremberg Trial. The O.S.S., Charles Dwork, and the Holocaust', 19 *Holocaust and Genocide Studies* (1998), pp. 257-281; M. Marrus, 'A Jewish Lobby at Nuremberg: Jacob Robinson and the Institute of Jewish Affairs, 1945-46', in H.R. Reginbogin & C.J.M. Safferling (eds.), *supra* n. 1, p. 63.

[21] See A.J. Kochavi, *Prelude to Nuremberg. Allied War Crimes Policy and the Question of Punishment* (Chapel Hill N.C., University of North Carolina Press 1998); G.J. Bass, *Stay the Hand of Vengeance. The Politics of War Crimes Tribunals* (Princeton, Princeton University Press 2001); E. Borgwardt, *A New Deal for the World. America's Vision for Human Rights* (Cambridge, Harvard University Press 2005); G. Ginsburgs, *Moscow's Road to Nuremberg. The Soviet Background to the Trial* (The Hague and Boston, Brill 1996).

murder, extermination, enslavement and deportation on political, racial or religious grounds as 'crimes against humanity.' This signaled a clear and radical departure from the principles of state sovereignty and immunity, which until then had enjoyed almost uncontested legal sanctity in international relations – at least, on the level of Great Power politics. In practice, the IMT made limited use of the concept of 'crimes against humanity,' which largely derived from proposals drafted during the war by legal experts at UNWCC and the War Department,[22] and also in the main excluded Lemkin's development of the idea that the intentional destruction of a national, racial or religious group should be punished. These self-imposed limits reflected a tradition of legal conservatism, but also stemmed from the situation of Great Britain and France as colonial powers in decline. Two rulings clarified the IMT's limits: First, the Court recognised its own jurisdiction for crimes against humanity only in cases also linked to simultaneous crimes against peace and conspiracy to wage war; as a result, crimes against German, Polish and Austrian citizens before September 1939 did not fall under the Court's self-defined jurisdiction. Second, while Count 3 of the IMT indictment charges 'deliberate and systematic genocide,' particularly against 'Jews, Poles and Gypsies,' and although this charge was explored in British deputy prosecutor Sir David Maxwell-Fyfe's interrogation of former German foreign minister Constantin von Neurath, the count went completely unmentioned in the Court's final verdict of October 1946, much to Lemkin's disappointment. The judges instead attached paramount importance to 'crimes against peace,' arguing that 'to initiate a war of aggression is ... not only an international crime, it is the supreme crime, differing only from other war crimes in that it contains the accumulated evil of the whole.'[23] In what Lemkin would later call 'the blackest day of my life,' he wrote a harsh rebuke to the Court's narrow interpretation: 'It seems inconsistent with our concepts of civilization that selling a drug to an individual is a matter of worldly concern, while gassing millions of human beings might [merely] be a problem of internal concern.'[24]

In the course of 1946, the Americans and British abandoned their original plans for a second IMT.[25] From then on, war crimes trials against the middle and subordinate functionaries of the Nazi state were conducted separately in each of the four occupation zones. The Allies' solemn and unanimous promise to uniformly apply the new concepts of international law quickly proved impractical. Both Allied and German courts used Allied law in ways that bespoke individual political priorities, national legal traditions, and historical experiences with National Socialism. Even before the IMT verdict was delivered, each of the four victor powers established courts within their respective zones to try German soldiers and civilians accused of

---

[22] On the genesis of this concept see E. Borgwardt, *supra* n. 21, pp. 225-230; L. Douglas, *supra* n. 8, pp. 44-47.

[23] Cited in J. Cooper, *supra* n. 6, p. 73.

[24] R. Lemkin, Letter to the Editor, New York Times, 8 November 1948; cited in E. Borgwardt, *supra* n. 21, p. 230.

[25] See D. Bloxham, *Genocide on Trial. War Crimes Trials and the Formation of Holocaust History and Memory* (Oxford and New York, Oxford University Press 2001), at pp. 28-32.

crimes against Allied forces and civilians. The Allied powers' military courts were based mainly on national military codes, although a few of the IMT concepts were also used.[26] The Soviet military courts (SMTs) were especially controversial because of secret proceedings that imposed draconian sentences on 35,000 German nationals from 1945 to 1953; based on archival reviews, only a few thousand were actual Nazi perpetrators.[27]

With the enactment/adoption of Control Council Law No. 10 (CCL No. 10) in late 1945, the Allies established a basic set of rules under which the occupation authorities could proceed with further trials in their own zones. CCL No. 10 also empowered German courts to try cases of crimes committed against German nationals and stateless individuals before 1945.[28] Regardless of the occupation zone, the German courts mainly tried medical crimes and crimes of denunciation, although a few trials were for charges of violence against political opponents and Jews during the regime's early years. By comparison, German courts almost completely ignored[29] the deportations and systematic murder of Jews during the war itself (although these also affected about 60,000 German Jews from the original territory of the Reich and the Protectorate and thus could also be covered under older German law).[30] In contrast to the Soviet zone, German courts in the British and French zones were allowed to apply both German and Allied law – but the latter only at the request of the German authorities and with the requirement that the respective military government approved the application of Allied law.[31] By the late 1940s resistance grew to the use of this Allied 'foreign law' (as it was later called by the first chief justice of the *Bundesgerichtshof*, Hermann Weinkauff). Nevertheless, German courts in the Western zones delivered nearly 4,800 convictions on the basis of the Nuremberg legal guidelines and the old Reich penal code of 1871. Only a few of these trials were for homicide or its aiding and abetting, however.[32] Thus, with regard to Western-zone German courts during the occupation period I shall echo legal scholar Gerhard Werle's general conclusion about the West

---

[26] See F.M. Buscher, 'Bestrafen und erziehen. "Nürnberg" und das Kriegsverbrecherprogramm der USA', in N. Frei (ed.), *supra* n. 14, p. 94 at p. 100.

[27] See A. Hilger, 'Die Gerechtigkeit nehme ihren Lauf? Die Bestrafung deutscher Kriegs- und Gewaltverbrecher in der Sowjetunion und der SBZ/DDR', in N. Frei (ed.), *supra* n. 14, p. 180.

[28] See A. Weinke, *Die Verfolgung von NS-Tätern im geteilten Deutschland. Vergangenheitsbewältigungen 1949-1969 oder eine deutsch-deutsche Beziehungsgeschichte im Kalten Krieg* (Paderborn, Schöningh 2002).

[29] Only 13 cases with regard to deportation crimes were brought before West German courts until 1960, most of them ending with acquittals; see C.F. Rüter, 'Ost- und westdeutsche Strafverfahren gegen die Verantwortlichen für die Deportationen der Juden', in A. Klein & J. Wilhelm (eds.), *NS-Unrecht vor Kölner Gerichten nach 1945* (Köln, Greven Verlag 2005), p. 45.

[30] S. Friedländer, *Das Dritte Reich und die Juden. Verfolgung und Vernichtung* (Bonn, BpB 2006), p. 291.

[31] No authorisations to employ CCL No. 10 were granted in the American zone of occupation; see A. Eichmüller, 'Die Strafverfolgung von NS-Verbrechen durch westdeutsche Justizbehörden seit 1945. Eine Zahlenbilanz', 56 *Vierteljahreshefte für Zeitgeschichte* (2008), p. 621 at p. 633.

[32] A statistical overview is provided by A. Eichmüller, *supra* n. 31.

German judiciary after 1945: 'There are no systematic investigations to prosecute genocide.'[33]

This brings us to the question of how the German people reacted to the IMT and the various other Allied programs. The scholarly consensus today holds that Germans initially gave a fairly positive reception to the IMT. Opposition to Allied trials emerged later, in the context of the 'Cold War' and the increasingly unpopular de-Nazification screenings. A rough confirmation is provided by opinion polls conducted by the public relations branch of OMGUS during the IMT trial in 1945 and 1946. Almost 80 percent of surveyed Germans shared the impression that the trial of Hermann Göring, et al., had been generally 'fair,' while only 4 percent said it was 'unfair.' Four years later, however, the American survey-takers were confronted with the perplexing result that a third of Germans now said the IMT had treated the defendants in an 'unfair' manner, while the share of those still qualifying it as 'fair' had dropped to just 38 percent.[34] A few historians have noted that the shift in German perceptions must be viewed as part of a larger transformation that also manifested in anxiety about the 'collective guilt' of all Germans.[35] While the German fixation on a presumed Allied allegation of 'collective guilt' was partly a reaction to an over-ambitious educational initiative in the American zone, it was surely no coincidence that simmering protests against the war crimes trials turned vociferous just at the moment when Telford Taylor's prosecutorial team issued indictments to 200 leading members of Germany's military, legal, academic and diplomatic elites. Together with the so-called 'Dachau trials' (the US Army program), the twelve American follow-up trials from October 1946 to April 1949 prompted a heated German debate on 'Nuremberg' and its consequences.

The Catholic and Protestant (*Evangelische*) churches played a central role in the German discourse about Allied war crimes trials and the problem of justice for Nazi criminality. The churches' commitment to/involvement in these issues emerged partly from their promise to take over ethical and moral leadership in the context of social collapse at the end of the war. Their self-image as moral authorities was partly legitimated by the Nazis' temporary incarceration of a handful of church leaders for practicing passive dissent and even active opposition. At the same time, their anti-communist and nationalist attitudes and institutional involvement both in the Nazis' anti-Jewish policies and in the 'euthanasia' program (in which the churches' role can be described at best as that of a 'loyal opposition') caused postwar ambivalence about both de-Nazification and criminal prosecution. In their forceful critiques of 'Nuremberg,' church leaders conflated lamentations of the supposed general trend to secularisation with condemnations of the trials as 'cultural Bolshevism'

---

33 G. Werle, 'Der Holocaust als Gegenstand der bundesdeutschen Strafjustiz', 45 *Neue Juristische Wochenschrift* (1992), pp. 2529-2535 at p. 2531.

34 A.J. Merrit & R.L. Merrit (eds.), *Public Opinion in Semi-Sovereign Germany. The HICOG Surveys, 1949-1955* (Urbana, University of Illinois Press 1980), p. 11 and p. 101.

35 See N. Frei, 'Von deutscher Erfindungskraft. Oder: Die Kollektivschuldthese in der Nachkriegszeit', in *idem, 1945 und wir. Das Dritte Reich im Bewusstsein der Deutschen* (Munich, C.H. Beck 2005), p. 145; J. Friedemann & J. Später, 'Britische und deutsche Kollektivschuld-Debatte', in U. Herbert (ed.), *supra* n. 10, p. 53.

and 'instruments of revenge.'[36] Sociologist Jeffrey K. Olick points out that the churches' discourse on 'Nuremberg' – or more generally, on 'German guilt' – established a 'grammar of exculpation' shaping the way how Germans saw the present realities of Allied occupation and how they remembered the past of the war and Holocaust.[37]

Already in early 1946, the Protestant church umbrella organisation EKD issued a declaration that, on the one hand, recognised political vetting as a prerequisite for 'freeing the German people from the destructive influences of National Socialism,' but on the other discerned violations of the *nulla poena sine lege* principle, claiming the Allies were offending a natural sense of justice by charging Germans for crimes that were not illegal under the Third Reich.[38] Starting in December 1946 with the 'Doctors' trial' of former ranking functionaries in the Berlin-based 'euthanasia' program (the first of the American follow-up trials to IMT) the churches' own *Vergangenheitspolitik* adopted a fixed focus on the Allied proceedings.[39] In a two-prong approach, church dignitaries and functionaries (a few themselves victims of Nazi persecution) made court appearances as character witnesses for the defendants; meanwhile, church representatives drew up and ran a modern public relations campaign with the nominal aim of improving conditions for the prisoners. With time however the focus shifted to questioning the political and legal basis of the trials, which were portrayed as an obstacle to reconciliation in the 'christian spirit'.

As the Allied military governments yielded to civilian high commissioners and administrative restructuring, German criticisms of the treatment accorded to prisoners transformed into more fundamental challenges. Soon after the Federal Republic was founded in 1949, a group of influential legal scholars, judges and Nuremberg defence attorneys convened in Heidelberg with the aim of promoting a complete phase-out of Allied trials and an early release for all German prisoners. With the support of church leaders, the 'Heidelberg circle' sought in particular to persuade the American High Commission under John McCloy (former undersecretary of war and an initiator and staunch advocate of 'Nuremberg') that a greater regard for humanitarian concerns would signal 'good will' to the German people and make them more amenable to Western democratic ideals.[40] But even as

---

[36] Cited in J. Olick, *In the House of the Hangman. The Agonies of German Defeat, 1943- 1949* (Chicago, The University of Chicago Press 2005), p. 216 and p. 225.

[37] With 'grammar of exculpation' the author refers to 'ways of framing the problems of the German past so that they appear less burdening. Examples of this include not specifying what crimes one is talking about; avoidance of anti-Semitism as a causal factor; careful distinctions between 'us' and 'them' deployed with as much precision a variability; metaphorical language of demons, madmen, and villains; and, overwhelmingly in political rhetoric, passive and vague constructions – 'the crimes that were committed,' 'what happened in those years,' and many others; J. Olick, *supra* n. 36, p. 212.

[38] Cited in ibid., at p. 222.

[39] See P. Weindling, *Nazi medicine and the Nuremberg trials. from medical war crimes to informed consent* (New York, Palgrave Macmillan 2004); A. Weinke, *Die Nürnberger Prozesse* (München, C.H. Beck 2006), pp. 63-68.

[40] On the 'Heidelberg circle' see N. Frei, *supra* n. 10, pp. 163-166; G. Buchstab, 'Die Nürnberger Prozesse und der Heidelberger Kreis (1949-1955)', in P.R. Weilemann, et al. (eds.), *Macht und Zeitkritik. Festschrift für Hans Peter Schwarz* (Paderborn, Schöningh 1999), p. 61.

the Heidelberg circle and their allies argued the humanitarian and legal points to McCloy – for example by highlighting material and procedural deficits in some of the cases – they fell into conflict among themselves. The lawyers who defended leaders of the German industry in the business trials understood that their clients might soon be viewed as rehabilitated, given US policy changes and plans for economic reconstruction. They saw little cause to frighten the Americans with demands for a general amnesty that would connect their entrepreneurial clientele with ideological perpetrators from the ranks of the SS and SD. Former naval lawyer Otto Kranzbühler (who defended German steel magnate Alfred Krupp in trial No. 10) expressed his opinion that the *Einsatzgruppen* defendants accused of murdering hundreds of thousands of Baltic and Soviet Jews (trial No. 9) had in fact committed 'genocide,' and would have qualified as 'ordinary murderers' under the old German statutes.[41]

Kranzbühler's detractors within the Heidelberg circle argued that even *Einsatzgruppen* commanders like the infamous Otto Ohlendorf were drawn into the extermination actions on the Eastern Front out of idealistic notions, and in part against their own will. These '*Vergangenheitspolitik* extremists,' as historian Norbert Frei has called them, conveniently ignored that their claim was based solely on the word of the defendants themselves.[42] One of the most vocal was Hellmut Becker, legal defender of Ernst von Weizsäcker (former undersecretary at the Foreign Ministry and a defendant in trial No. 11). Becker declared that Ohlendorf was an 'educated' and 'quite unusual personality' who was unjustly depicted as the 'embodiment of the extermination program' by a 'not necessarily pleasant clique of generals' and their own defenders.[43] By Ohlendorf's own testimony, however, he was responsible as the commander of *Einsatzgruppe D* for the deaths of at least 90,000 Jewish civilians during operations in the Caucasus. The American judges sentenced him to death in April 1949 on the basis of CCL No. 10, rejecting his defence that he was forced to follow orders. Becker spent the next year and a half trying to move the American occupation authorities to commute Ohlendorf's sentence to a prison term. When Ohlendorf's lawyer Heinrich Malz (himself a former staff advisor to RSHA chief Ernst Kaltenbrunner) voiced his worries in summer 1949 that the general amnesty efforts might lose sight of his client's plight, Becker urged him to be patient. While lecturing on the Nuremberg trials in Professor Grewe's seminar at the Law Faculty of Freiburg University, Becker had formed the opinion that it was hard to elicit understanding for the 'tragedy of the Ohlendorf case,' as he now wrote to Malz. 'Nuremberg is a fortress that first must be slowly shelled until it is ready for the storming, and attacked at the points that are already the weakest ... You must view the Einsatzgruppen trials in connection with the larger happenings around Nuremberg, in much the same way that Hitler viewed the Polish question in 1938. The key in all these things lies in staying power, basically in not losing sight of the

[41] Heinrich Malz to Hellmut Becker, 2 August 1949; PAAA, Becker Papers, Vol. 13/2; Otto Kranzbühler to Gustav Schmoller, 15 August 1949; PAAA, Becker Papers, Vol. 14.

[42] N. Frei, *supra* n. 10, p. 217.

[43] Hellmut Becker to Herbert Blankenhorn, 23 December 1950; PAAA, Becker Papers, Vol. 16/1.

cause.'[44] But Becker was sorely mistaken, if his aim was to help Ohlendorf's case. Although McCloy responded to German pressure by reviewing all verdicts, in January 1951 he confirmed the death sentences against *Einsatzgruppen* commanders, even as he granted amnesty to Krupp and a dozen other industrialists, doctors and Nazi functionaries.[45] McCloy justified his decision to German President Heuss as follows: 'There are some crimes the extent and enormity of which belie the concept of decency ... I do not feel that the German people can possibly associate the interests of such criminals with their own.'[46]

We should note that Ohlendorf's most persistent lobbyists went on to remarkable careers. Malz made his way up to managing director of the German civil servants' union, while Becker – son of the once highly regarded Prussian Culture Minister Heinrich Becker – became one of the best-known reformers of the German educational system, serving as in-house counsel to the Frankfurt Institute for Social Research and, finally, as the director of the Max Planck Institute for Education Studies.

Most of the members of the Heidelberg circle agreed fundamentally that the use of international law against German defendants in itself constituted a serious violation of international law. Committed as they were to the larger political goal of a rapid termination of the war crimes trials,[47] the attorneys discovered that CCL No. 10 was a useful instrument in their effort to 'shell the fortress until it can be stormed.' Even before the campaign against Allied 'victor's justice' gained momentum in the late 1940s and early 1950s, their argument against the *ex-post-facto* character of CCL No. 10 became the dominant *leitmotif* in a German discourse that emphasised the sanctity of the 'German *Rechtsstaat*' ('rule of law') while ignoring the necessity of finding an effective legal response to the challenges of genocide, deportation and slave labor.[48] For observers without specific knowledge of legal matters, this debate among experts on the legality of CCL No. 10 must have created the impression that the German state and its national penal code were under grave threat, not from the continuation or revival of Nazi ideas, but above all from Allied law.[49] While Nuremberg law was rejected with the argument that it could not be harmonised with German legal tradition, it was also avowed that a number of the prisoners held by the Allies could and should be turned over to German courts. The underlying assumption, that the German justice system could handle prosecutions of Nazi crimes without need for international law, was based on two premises: First, there was the

---

44 Hellmut Becker to Malz, 5 August 1949; PAAA, Becker Papers, Vol. 13/2.

45 See S.J. Wiesen, *West German Industry and the Challenge of the Nazi Past, 1945-1955* (Chapel Hill N.C., University of North Carolina Press 2001), p. 202.

46 Cited in N. Frei, *supra* n. 10, p. 214.

47 See N. Frei, *supra* n. 10, p. 166.

48 See D.O. Pendas, '"Law, Not Vengeance." Human Rights, the Rule of Law, and the Claim of Memory in German Holocaust Trials', in M.P. Bradley & P. Petro (eds.), *Truth Claims. Representation and Human Rights* (Brunswick N.J., Rutgers University Press 2002), p. 23.

49 A resolution by the German Society for International Law led by former diplomat and international law scholar Paul Barandon claims the Allies violated the principles of the Geneva Convention by forcing German defendants to submit to special law.

belief that Nazi mass crimes would have been covered by the ordinary laws against homicide, even those considered to have applied under the Third Reich; this meant to judge criminal acts under the standards of law at the time of the acts, and also to consider extenuating circumstances (or aggravating circumstances) as specified under these laws. Second, there was the assumption that almost none of the many direct perpetrators had developed any form of personal initiative in carrying out the crimes, but that all had acted on the basis of an 'extermination order' issued by Hitler, Himmler and Heydrich.[50] At least implicitly, the demand to overturn CCL No. 10 was tied to a historical understanding of the Germans as *quasi* a 'people of abettors' who committed crimes in part because of outside pressure and in part because they had been unaware of the genocidal 'master plan.' Further, the widespread notion that the Germans themselves had suffered from Nazi rule more than anyone else was taken as a general extenuating circumstance with regard to the *mens rea* or mental element.

III. 'Coming to terms with the past' by means of criminal law?

The years immediately after the two German states were founded in 1949 were characterised by a 'let's get over it' attitude. After the first *Bundestag* elections were won resoundingly by the Christian Democrats under Konrad Adenauer, nearly all West German parliamentarians gave priority to the goal of eliminating the supposed excesses of what they called the 'Nuremberg System.' Only the Communists remained staunch advocates of 'Nuremberg,' in line with the Ulbricht regime in East Berlin. The Allies withdrew their authorisation for CCL No. 10 in 1951 at the request of the new German government. By then this was of little practical significance, since the newly-founded *Bundesgerichtshof* had in 1950 already ruled against application of CCL No. 10.[51] As government and bureaucracy reintegrated tens of thousands of de-nazified civil servants, including more than a few former members of the Gestapo and Waffen-SS,[52] and as more and more prisoners of the Allies were released, West German prosecutors felt little impulse to pursue further investigations against German suspects. The number of investigations and convictions in West Germany both sank steadily after 1949, dropping to almost none by the mid-1950s.

The unwinding of 'Nuremberg' essentially concluded in May 1958 with the early release of the last three *Einsatzgruppen* leaders; the same period, however, saw an increasing political and social involvement of the Federal Republic in international

---

[50] See G. Werle, *supra* n. 33, p. 2534.

[51] See U. Brochhagen, *Nach Nürnberg. Vergangenheitsbewältigung und Westintegration in der Ära Adenauer* (Hamburg, Junius Verlag 1994), pp. 166-168; G. Werle, 'Die Entwicklung des Völkerstrafrechts aus deutscher Perspektive', in G. Hankel (ed.), *supra* n. 9, p. 97 at p. 102.

[52] C. Garner, 'Public Service Personnel in West Germany in the 1950s. Controversial Policy Decision and Their Effects on Social Composition, Gender Structure, and the Role of Former Nazis', 29 *Journal of Social History* (1995), pp. 25-80.

affairs. In the early 1950s it had still been impossible to speak of German integration in the Western community, let alone moral rehabilitation, as the consequences of the catastrophic war of expansion and destruction were still visible everywhere in Europe. But the commitment to freedom as set forth in the German Basic Law, entry to the political and military alliances of the West and joining the European Convention on Human Rights (ECHR) seemed to assure the country's renewed conformity with universal standards of human and civil rights. That the German government was now also seeking to gain a foothold in the international discourse on human rights, however, did not really conform to the culture of impunity maintained in the treatment of Nazi crimes. The continuing defensive posture against 'Nuremberg' meant that the Federal Republic joined the ECHR under the curious stipulation that it was not actually required to apply the 'Nuremberg principles' insofar as these were included in the ECHR.[53] While any impressions of even implicit recognition of Nuremberg law were avoided to a positively embarrassing degree, West Germany in 1954 became one of the first states to follow Lemkin's appeal and transform the UN Genocide Convention into national law.

West Germany's entry to the Convention and definition of genocide as a crime under its law actually came at the initiative of the Heidelberg circle working in tandem with several *Bundestag* members and representatives of German refugee organisations. Their plan however was to initiate prosecutions of crimes related to the Soviet-ordered expulsion in 1945 of German populations from the easternmost territories of the pre-war German Reich and of ethnic Germans from Czechoslovakia and other areas. The Foreign Ministry, the Federal Justice Ministry and Adenauer's international law adviser, Professor Erich Kaufmann, all favored an unconditional adoption of the treaty. They thought thus to acknowledge that the National Socialist crimes were the reason for the criminalisation of genocide in the first place; but also to create a tool for possibly intervening against alleged crimes of genocide in the Communist countries of Eastern Europe, as the West German government held that such crimes had been committed or were still in progress there.[54] In the course of passing the legislation, the government formed close contacts with Lemkin, who was looking for additional states willing to ratify the Convention. Lemkin saw a potential alliance growing from the very fact that West Germany had put up a strong front *against* 'Nuremberg.' During a visit to the United States in the spring of 1954, Eugen Gerstenmaier (CDU), the chair of the *Bundestag*'s committee on foreign affairs, asked Lemkin to submit a memorandum on the Federal Justice Ministry's draft of the law. A few months earlier, Lemkin had alerted Adenauer and Federal Justice Minister Thomas Dehler (FDP) to the fact that the English original of the UN Genocide Convention had been given a faulty and imprecise translation into German. The original's 'destruction' was rendered in the German draft first as *Ausrottung* (extermination), then as *Vernichtung* (annihilation

[53] See G. Werle, *supra* n. 51, p. 103.

[54] Sanne to Mosler, 20 February 1952; Memorandum Schwarz-Liebermann v. Wahlendorf to Riesser, 21 April 1952; PAAA, B 80, Vol. 202.

or elimination), in place of the most literal German word, *Zerstörung*. This gave rise to two concers. He considered it dangerous for Germany to adopt terms that had played an 'outstanding role' in the IMT verdict, as this ran the risk of supporting Nuremberg jurists' plans to disseminate and generalise their principles. Furthermore, a narrowing of the legal text to 'physical harms' would depart from the spirit of the Convention and be counterproductive to German hopes of achieving culpability for 'psychological suffering,' such as that caused by the massive expulsions of German populations from areas of the Eastern bloc.[55] Lemkin reiterated his criticisms of the suspect terminology to the CDU parliamentary deputy Eduard Wahl, who was the formal head of the Heidelberg circle as well as a rapporteur to the *Bundestag* foreign affairs committee. Lemkin wrote:

> 'As the author of the Genocide Convention, I can assure you, Herr Professor, that I introduced the term "destruction" (without adjective) expressly for the purpose of emphasizing the disadvantagement of the sociological fabric of a group as such. In light of the history and sociology, the destruction of a national, religious, racial or ethnical group is possible even if the members of the group do not disappear. By contrast the terms of the "Nuremberg law" are of an exclusively physical nature, operating with "extermination and elimination." The four groups of the Genocide Convention are unknown to [the Nuremberg] Charter. This is why the Genocide Convention also contains terms that are independent of physical injuries, like "serious mental harm." Now I am very concerned that this exact term, which is illustrated by the suffering of 11 million expelled Germans, is missing from the German draft legislation.'

He appealed to Wahl to use his experiences in the 'fight for right' to block the efforts of a group of jurists 'known all too well' to him who wished to 'smuggle "Nuremberg Law" into "International Law" via the back door of the United Nations.'[56]

Although Lemkin's concerns were taken quite seriously in Bonn (he received the Federal Cross of Merit in 1955 for his service in the proscription of genocide), the German genocide paragraph achieved no practical meaning in the requital of macrocriminality. Because *ex-post-facto* punishment was ruled out by Article 103 of the Basic Law, the statute could not be applied either to Nazi crimes or to the Soviet-bloc expulsion of Germans in 1945. However, this did not put an end to the question of judicial punishment for Nazi crimes. After Adenauer's trip to Moscow in September 1955 had led to the release of almost 10,000 German POWs – among them a number of major Nazi perpetrators – the legacy resurfaced and became one of most controversial issues in public debate. The October 1958 foundation in Ludwigsburg of a national Central Office for co-ordinating Nazi crime investigations among the various state prosecutors was a turning point. As conceived by the state ministers of justice, Ludwigsburg was tasked with the systematic investigation of crimes that had been typical in the context of the Holocaust. Until the mid-1960s, prosecutors focused on crimes committed in concentration camps and the

---

55 Raphael Lemkin to Thomas Dehler, 4 May 1954; New York Public Library, Lemkin Papers, Reel 1.

56 Raphael Lemkin to Eduard Wahl, 4 May 1954; New York Public Library, Lemkin Papers, Reel 1.

so-called *Judenaktionen* in the German-occupied 'eastern territories.' Shortly after the creation of the agency, the number of investigations skyrocketed. Already in the first year of its existence, Ludwigsburg prosecutors opened 400 new cases. By the mid-1960s that number rose to more than 6,000 investigations.[57]

The period between 1960 and the late 1970s was shaped by a series of spectacular Nazi trials that gained national and international media attention. The fact that these trials could take place more than twenty years after the war was in itself remarkable, because it indicated increased awareness for the singularity of Holocaust crimes in contrast to 'normal' war crimes – a distinction Germans had still denied at the time of the Nuremberg trial. Nevertheless, the challenges of dealing legally with the specific character of state-sponsored crime remained enormous. One of the biggest obstacles was posed by the traditional German penal code. It not only predetermined the direction of the investigations, but also functioned as a threshold, preventing the opening of many court cases and limiting the number of convictions.[58] According to the doctrine of 'subjective participation' (*subjektive Teilnahmelehre*), which became the dominant interpretation in West German jurisdiction after the war, a majority of those actually convicted were qualified as accessories to murder on the basis of the 'aiding and abetting' paragraphs (§§ 44, 49 StGB). Even Nazi lawmakers and the executive planners of the genocide were able to exonerate themselves by arguing they had lacked 'base motives,' meaning an inner disposition to commit the crime, and had only 'executed orders' from above. Although most of the judges viewed racial hatred and anti-Semitism as a 'base motive,' they were reluctant to apply this attribute to anybody except the aforementioned three 'main perpetrators' of Hitler, Himmler and Heydrich. The paradoxical result of this judicial concept of Nazi criminality was that the legal standards of the Third Reich were to some extent perpetuated by the West German judiciary. Only those offenders who had actually transgressed the norms of the Nazi state in committing murder out of personal motives ('excessive perpetrators') received life sentences as murderers. Considering the reasoning of the courts and the arguments in legal academia, we may therefore rightly doubt that the second wave of Nazi trials really elicited a deeper understanding of state-sponsored mass murder.[59]

IV. Conclusion

In an international comparison, the Federal Republic and to a lesser extent the GDR were among the few states in which there was a systematic prosecution of crimes

---

[57] A. Rückerl, *Strafverfolgung von NS-Verbrechen 1945–1978. Eine Dokumentation* (Karlsruhe, C.F. Müller 1979), pp. 125-129; *idem*, *NS-Verbrechen vor Gericht. Versuch einer Vergangenheitsbewältigung* (Heidelberg, C.F. Müller 1984); E. Haberer, 'History and Justice. Paradigms of the Prosecution of Nazi Crimes', 19 *Holocaust and Genocide Studies* (2005), pp. 487-519; A. Weinke, *supra* n. 13.

[58] A. Weinke, *supra* n. 14.

[59] This is confirmed by the findings of Devin O. Pendas, who has analysed the media coverage on the Auschwitz trial; *The Auschwitz Trial, 1963-1965. Genocide, History, and the Limits of Law* (Cambridge, Cambridge University Press 2006).

from the Second World War era many years after the fact. It is logical to ask whether this 'exploration of conscience' by means of criminal law left a legacy in the collective memory, and whether this became the motivating force to any meaningful degree. Some time ago American legal scholar David Cohen advanced the thesis that Germany and Japan differed in their public recollection of Allied postwar trials. In Japanese society, Allied prosecutions remain present as an experience of national discrimination, while memory of the crimes themselves has largely fallen prey to amnesia. In Germany, Cohen argues, the reverse applies: 'Here the war crimes seem to remain in memory, while the thousands of trials to prosecute them by the Allies have been forgotten.'[60] This observation is true insofar as the increased willingness to deal with the German war of destruction and its ideological underpinnings really does seem to have been related to the decline of 'Nuremberg' as a rallying point for national self-definition and self-apologetics. It may have taken until the establishment of the Central Office in Ludwigsburg before the negative memory of the supposedly unjust Allied prosecutions and exaggerated perceptions of 're-education' measures gradually faded away. This went together with erosion of the mental barriers that had blocked a closer consideration of the mass crimes. Nevertheless the Central Office lacked the standing to mete out a just punishment to the majority of the leading perpetrators, and thus indirectly to make visible the human rights violations suffered by the victims; and this was also not its main objective. Its activities were still marked by the same social blind spots and pragmatic considerations that, to take a glaring example, continued to prevent binding convictions for the crimes of the German occupation in southern and southeastern Europe, down to the present day.

---

[60] D. Cohen, 'Öffentliche Erinnerung und Kriegsverbrecherprozesse in Asien und Europa', in C. Corneließen, et al. (eds.), *Erinnerungskulturen. Deutschland, Italien und Japan seit 1945 im Vergleich* (Frankfurt a.M., Fischer TB 2003), p. 51 at p. 52.

GENOCIDE AND THE GENOCIDE CONVENTION IN ISRAEL

Moshe Zimmermann

In Israel, the concept of genocide is quite problematic, not as much as a legal concept but rather when put in a general historical context. The following contribution is written by a historian, and deals with the reception of both the terminus technicus genocide and the Genocide Convention among the Israeli public, from a historical perspective.

The Holocaust, or Shoah – the most traumatic historical experience of the Jews in modern times and the pivot of collective Israeli memory – seems to be a most clear-cut case of genocide. By definition, the use of the term 'genocide' outside the context of the Shoah automatically calls up comparisons, among them, what makes the Shoah such a special case of genocide? For many, this question in itself raises suspicion: Is not the Shoah a singular historical event and the use of the term 'genocide' therefore nothing but an attempt to make relative this singular phenomenon? Will not the use of the term 'genocide' to describe mass-murder in Cambodia, the Sudan or Armenia ultimately lead to the use of the terms 'Holocaust' and 'Shoah' to describe these cases, too, thereby undermining the claim for the singularity of the genocide of the Jews during the Second World War? Indeed, calling mass-murders or cases of genocide a Shoah or Holocaust is no longer any rarity; a search for book-titles mentioning other Holocausts than the Jewish one, reveals references to the forgotten Holocaust of Nanjing, the Polish Holocaust or the Holocaust of the Assyrian Christians in Turkey, among others.[1] A most intriguing question then arises: Doesn't such an approach call for a discussion of the Israeli attitude toward what has happened to the Palestinians as genocide, even as a kind of Holocaust?

The aim of this contribution is not to clarify the notion of genocide objectively or legally in the Israeli context, but to shed some light on the relevant Israeli public discourse on genocide. It is a discussion about the instrumentalisation and the implications of the concept of genocide, including the very specific issue of the Genocide Convention, within the framework of internal Israeli debate. The important issue is not so much the law, the Convention, or the judicial system, but the norm for discussing the Holocaust and its reception among the Israeli public. This is very

[1] G. Yonan, *Ein vergessener Holocaust. Die Vernichtung der christlichen Assyrer in der Turkei* (Göttingen, Gesellschaft für Bedrohte Völker 1989); I. Chang, *The Rape of Nanking. The Forgotten Holocaust of WW II* (New York, Basic Books 1997); R.C. Lukas, *The Forgotten Holocaust: Poles under the German Occupation 1939-1944* (Lexington, Hippocrene Books 1986, 1997).

C. Safferling and E. Conze (eds.), The Genocide Convention Sixty Years after its Adoption

much like discussing Holocaust denial: A law may be introduced and even implemented – but the crucial question is that of attitudes toward it and its reception; what is decisive is what is in the minds and thoughts of people, not necessarily what they publicly admit in the shadow of the law, or the punishment specified by the law. What should interest us is the answer given to the following questions in Israel: Is genocide to be discussed as a phenomenon in which the Jewish role is solely – in the past as well as in the present and future – that of the victim? Or does Israel's signature to the Genocide Convention mean that a state of mind has been created that no longer automatically excludes a case in which Jews might become perpetrators? In other words, I intend to look at the Convention as a touchstone for the tension between relating to Jews as victims, and relating to them as perpetrators.

One of the most profound myths of Israeli society – and by Israeli society I mean the 80% Jewish majority, not the 20% Arab minority living in the State of Israel – is that of the eternal role of Jews as victims, including as victims of attempts at genocide. History is taught in schools and presented in the media as a sequence of persecutions against Jews, which culminated in attempted or successful genocides: The biblical Pharaoh wished to exterminate all Hebrews by killing new-born children; King Ahashueros and his minister Haman organised (according to the book of Esther) a big pogrom across the Persian empire; the Romans deported the Jews from Palestine after cruelly crushing their great mutiny – etc., etc. Whether or not these stories have a grain of truth in them is irrelevant: They became the founding myths of modern Israeli society, such that the story of the Chmelnitzki Pogroms of the 17th century and that of the Holocaust of 1941-1945 are merely additional elements in a long chain of persecutions and attempts at genocide of the Jews.

This was the perspective from which the Genocide Convention of December 1948 was signed by the State of Israel and ratified by Israel's parliament, the Knesset. This signature also led to the introduction of a law into the Israeli book of laws, passed by the Knesset on December 26, 1949: 'The Law Concerning the Prevention and Punishment of the Crime of Genocide' (in Hebrew *Hashmadat Am*, literally, 'destruction of a people'). This law was considered an enactment of the Convention within the Israeli legal system, and was thus presented to the Knesset by the Minister of Justice, who stated: 'One basic cause [for the introduction of the Convention] was the experience of the Second World War. It was the blood of millions of innocent civilians, killed during this war, that … moved all the delegations to the UN to acknowledge the feeling that the danger of this terrible crime is still looming.' He added, more specifically: 'The terrible Shoah of our people during and before the war served as a most salient example for the extent to which the crime of extermination of national groups may lead.'[2] Thus, from the point of view of Israel right after the creation of the State, the Jewish case was the absolute example of a general rule. It was also clear from the outset that in case of a repetition of such a crime, the Jews were expected to be the victims – never the perpetrators.

[2] Protocols of the Knesset 26 December 1949, p. 7 (in Hebrew). The Knesset passed the law on 29 March 1950.

Rabbi Nurok of the Religious Party, who lost his family in the Holocaust, declared explicitly during that same Knesset session that the only aim of the law was to protect Jews. This is why, in addition to entering the text of the Genocide Convention into Israeli law (concerning definition, punishment, interpretation), a special article was added to the law, which referred to the possibility of the crime of genocide being committed outside Israel: He who had committed this crime could be brought to justice in Israel, as if he had committed the crime on Israeli territory. This addition clearly contradicts Article 6 of the Genocide Convention, and can only be explained in light of the intention of the Israeli parliament to direct this law against past and future enemies of the Jews – solely. The retroactive intention of the law is obvious, too, in light of another, similar law, enacted in August 1, 1950, the 'Law for Prosecuting the Nazis and Their Accomplices,' which in principle relied on the Genocide Convention but dealt only with crimes committed between 1933 and 1945, and which invented a new category of crime, called 'crimes against the Jewish people.' The retroactive character of the Law for the Prevention of Genocide 1949 was so obvious, that the judge who issued the warrant for the arrest of Adolf Eichmann in 1960, 10 years after the law's enactment, relied on it explicitly. The same Minister of Justice who had presented the law before the Knesset in 1949 had to explain to the Knesset Committee for Constitutional and Legal Matters in May 1960 that the judge's decision was a mistake,[3] – as if he himself had not created the misleading interpretation of this very law.

The impression that the law introducing the Genocide Convention into the Israeli legal system had neither time nor space limitations was expressed in a very dramatic manner in the guidelines for civic education written by a well-known philosopher and teacher, Eliezer Schweid, 40 years after Israel was created:

> '... The law enacted in 1950 "concerning the prevention and punishment of the crime of genocide" implies that the State of Israel considers itself responsible for punishing and taking revenge on the Nazis and their helpers for the crime of the Shoah ... The state of Israel thus [!] becomes a living memory and testimony, representing the history of the Jewish people, with its singular fate and mission.'[4]

No wonder that the typical references made in Israel to the Genocide Convention or to the issue of genocide in general, even decades later, are based on the axiomatic assumption that Israel, as a representative of the Jewish people, can only be a potential victim of genocide, and that the only sense in adhering to the Convention is the notion of warding off this threat to Jews or acting as an instrument of punishment for past crimes against Jews.

The memory of the Shoah is a sacred pillar of Israeli collective identity and a central topic in the education system. In fact, because of the latter, educational

[3] H. Yablonka, *The State of Israel vs. Adolf Eichmann* (Tel Aviv, Schocken 2001) pp. 44, 299 (in Hebrew).

[4] The article originally appeared in *Ez Ha'Daat* 1987 and was quoted in the guidelines of the ministry of education, www.education.gov.il.

journeys to sites of the Shoah in present-day Poland have become popular, even trendy, since the late 1980s, when Eastern Europe gradually opened up to Israel. One of the institutions that has developed a special educational program that includes visits to concentration camps is the Israel Defense Forces (IDF). The pretentious name given to this program was, 'Witnesses in Uniform.' The guidelines for the program, written by high-ranking officers, use the term 'genocide' and warn against the repetition of genocide, but have in mind only the genocide of Jews. The intended lesson of the program is that the main task of the Israeli army is to prevent the next genocide of the Jewish people, i.e., the next Shoah. The idea of Israel as a potential perpetrator, especially against the background of its presence in the Palestinian occupied territories, seems totally irrelevant. After a ceremony at Auschwitz five years ago, when three Israeli fighter jets flew over the camp, the Commander-in-Chief of the Israeli Air Force commented: 'It is important to learn how a combination of ideology, ignorance and prejudices may originate a process of genocide. Important is the implication for the need of Israel and the Jewish people for military power [*sic*].'[5]

In order to prove this contention, Israeli politicians have interpreted not only post-war anti-Semitism, but also the policies of the regimes confronting Israel in the Middle East, as an attempt to practice genocide against Jews and Israel. The PLO was usually discussed as an organisation that aimed at a new genocide, a new Shoah. Iraq under Saddam Hussein was described in the same manner, and so is Iran under Ahmadinejad today. Arafat, Saddam Hussein and Ahmadinejad have all been referred to as new Hitlers, pursuant to which is the conviction that they planned or plan no less than a genocide against Israel. In the 1960s, a heated discussion in Israel concerning some German scientists serving the Egyptian ballistic rockets program convinced then-opposition leader Menahem Begin that a special clause should be added to the Genocide Convention (and not only to the Israeli law), abolishing the statute of limitations for the crime of genocide – just in order to be able to implement this Convention in the specific case of these scientists. When the Israeli parliament discussed the Iraqi challenge in 1990-1991, the notion of Israel being targeted for genocide was central. That German firms supplied Iraq with chemical weapons helped create the impression of continuity between the genocidal threat against Jews in Europe in the past and against Israel in the present. Iran's nuclear program, around which Israeli foreign policy theoretically revolves at present, is of course associated with the danger of the next genocide of Jews. More than three years ago, the Knesset discussed this eventuality in detail.[6] In reality, this discussion had started long before: As long as 15 years ago, in 1993, when the 'Cold War' was over, the Knesset not only discussed Iran's nuclear intentions, but also gave one of its members the opportunity to express his fear of genocide against Israel. The statement made by former Speaker of the Knesset Avrum Burg during that session, to the effect that there was no real danger of genocide of Jews or Israel and

[5] L. Papirblatt, 153 *Israeli Air Force Journal* (2003) (in Hebrew).
[6] Knesset Protocols 2 November 2005 (in Hebrew).

that therefore Israelis should develop a more universal approach to the threat of genocide, remains an exception.[7]

Public discussion in Israel of genocide or the Genocide Convention did not always touch upon a direct threat to Israel. In the 1970s it was Biafra, in the 1990s it was Kosovo, and today it is Darfur that sparks lively discussions of the question of genocide. Yet indirectly, the aim was and is solely to discuss Israel's situation. The debate about Kosovo boiled down to the question of whether the bombardment of Serbia was justified by the threat of genocide in Kosovo, because at the end of the day the relevant issue would be a comparison between the situation in Kosovo and that in Israel: If faced with the threat of genocide, shouldn't Israel react preemptively by sending its Air Force against its enemies? In 2001, during the conflict in Chechnya, right-wing MK Israel Katz went so far as to defend the Russian intervention against Moslem terrorists (the analogy was only too obvious), while Arab MK Kan'an (having the same analogy in mind) called the Russian move an act of genocide.

Kan'an's remarks were symptomatic of another approach, that which tends to refer to Israeli policies as genocidal – i.e., to relate to Israel as the potential or real perpetrator of a genocidal process. Very often this approach is nothing but a convenient propagandistic way to attack Israel's Achilles' heel: turning Israel (a representative of the Jewish people) from victim into perpetrator. But there have also been systematic efforts to show that Israel uses methods defined by the Convention (mainly in Arts. 2b and 2c) as genocidal: Professor Francis Boyle, no friend of Israel, legal advisor to the PLO, commented in 2000, the year of the second Intifada, that Israel had

> 'implemented a systematic and comprehensive military, political and economic campaign with the intent to destroy in substantial part the national, ethnical and racial group known as the Palestinian People … in violation of Genocide Convention Article II (a) … also caused serious bodily and mental harm … in violation … of Article II (b) [and] … II(c).'[8]

Calling Israel a 'serial human rights international law abuser' for violating various international conventions is no rarity. Not only the Israeli establishment, but also the Israeli public is always appalled by such accusations. During a parliamentary debate, the Israeli Minister of Science vehemently rejected a decision made by the UN in 1998, according to which Israeli occupation of Palestinian territories is an offence against the Convention. Yet the fact remains: The tool that in the past seemed to serve Israel as eternal victim, may in the future become an instrument in the campaign against Israel conceived as perpetrator.

Quoting the Genocide Convention in order to criticise official Israeli policy has not remained the exclusive habit of external critics. Within Israeli society, not only

[7] Knesset Protocols 27 January 2004 (in Hebrew).

[8] 'A proposal from 2000 by Francis Boyle, prof. of intnl law U of Illinois. legal advisor to the PLO.' See http://palestinethinktank.com/2009/10/10/.

Israeli Arabs but also Jews on the left have joined in this trend. Israeli occupation of Palestinian territories since the Six Day War in 1967 has prompted this criticism. On one occasion, in 1986, discussion revolved explicitly around the Genocide Convention. Because of the rising popularity of the idea of 'transfer' (i.e., expulsion) of Palestinian Arabs, two members of the Knesset, MK Mati Peled (a Jew) and MK Mohammed Miari (an Arab), proposed amending the Genocide Law of 1949 by adding the words 'discrimination and expropriation' as elements of a genocidal policy. Their intent was to prevent political parties in Israel from introducing racist and discriminatory slogans and measures into their platforms. The Knesset turned down this amendment without even having a real debate about it.[9] Only one year later, three months before the first Intifada broke out, Vice Defence Minister Michael Dekel went so far as to propose a 'transfer' of the Palestinians out of the occupied territories, thus causing a heated debate about the Convention once again. The same Mati Peled reminded the Vice Minister about the Convention. Abba Eban, former Minister of Foreign Affairs, made one of his last ironic speeches as a member of the Knesset, condemning the 'crazy idea,' while Rabbi Meir Kahane, the most radical racist in Israeli politics, conversely proposed a vote of no confidence against the government for not supporting Vice Minister Dekel's proposal. This debate signaled, more than 20 years ago, that the majority of Israelis do not grasp the full meaning of the term 'genocide' and do not really understand the wording of the Genocide Convention.

No wonder Israel's policy has been associated with genocide mainly by representatives of its Arab minority. This association has presented itself on many occasions: During the first Lebanon War in 1982; during the first Intifada in 1987; and at the beginning of the second Intifada in 2000, as well as during the second Lebanon War in 2006 and the Gaza War in 2009. The reaction to such rebukes, whose intention was to create the utmost provocation, was preordained: The Israeli majority automatically rejects associating Israeli political and military measures with the Shoah or with genocide. That genocide was mentioned by Arab Israelis made this rejection easier, of course.

Yet in principle there is no difference between Israel's majority and its minority, between left and right, or between Jews and Arabs for that matter; each group not only instrumentalises the notion of genocide and the memory of the Shoah for its specific purposes, but also is very much aware of the stunning effect this tactic creates in both the internal and the international arena.

---

[9] Knesset Protocols 2 July 1986 (in Hebrew).

Part Three
Interpretation of the Crime of Genocide

THE POLICY ELEMENT IN GENOCIDE: WHEN IS IT REQUIRED BY INTERNATIONAL RULES?

Antonio Cassese

One of the various obscure issues in determining whether the crime of genocide has been perpetrated relates to whether individual acts of genocide always need to be underpinned by a general genocidal policy. The problem is complicated by the fact that the Genocide Convention, taken literally, does not clarify the matter, for it does not explicitly provide for this requirement nor however does it exclude it. Two distinct and opposed schools of thought have taken shape on this issue.

According to one school, the annihilation of a 'protected group' in whole or part or even the killing of members of such group can only materialise when such prohibited acts are part and parcel of a general plan or policy. In other words, genocide may never consist of isolated acts directed against a specific protected group or members of the group: such acts, to qualify as genocide, need to be supported by or be predicated on a general action pursued by a government or a de facto state-like authority.

This view has been advanced by a number of scholars and has also been upheld in national legislation.

Let me first begin by mentioning national legislation. Most national laws implementing the international rules on genocide confine themselves to reproducing or incorporating those international rules into the national legal system. In some states, as for example Ethiopia and, in the past, Spain, the notion of 'protected group' has been broadened so as to also include political groups. Instead, in France, the recent law of 1992 (entered into force on 1st March 1994) that modified the Criminal Code in providing for genocide, markedly departs from international rules in at least two respects. First, it broadens the objective elements of genocide by also including among the protected groups 'any group determined by any other arbitrary standard' (*ou … un groupe déterminé à partir de tout autre critère arbitraire*); secondly, it replaces the subjective element of 'special intent' by the requirement that any act can qualify as genocide if it is performed to 'execute a concerted plan aiming at the partial or total destruction of a protected group' (*en execution d'un plan concerté tendant à la destruction totale ou partielle d'un groupe*). As explained in the governmental text designed to illustrate the whole set of new criminal provisions adopted for the new Code, the *Circulaire* of 14 May 1993, the French law-makers preferred to replace the subjective element of genocidal intent with the objective element of a

C. Safferling and E. Conze (eds.), The Genocide Convention Sixty Years after its Adoption

'concerted plan,' because 'this notion of a concerted plan offers the advantage of highlighting the planned and systematic nature of the criminal enterprise; furthermore, this notion appears in Article 6 of the Charter of the Nuremberg Tribunal and hence has already been tested in the case law.'[1]

Leaving aside the fact that nowhere can one find in the relevant provisions of Article 6 of the Nuremberg Charter any reference to a concerted plan,[2] it should be pointed out that in any event the French law does not discard altogether the subjective element from the notion of genocide; it simply shifts this element from a frame of mind of single individuals to an objective set of circumstances: it is required that genocidal aims be pursued by the policy-makers or plan-makers. Thus, the partial or total destruction of a protected group must no longer be the special intent of single perpetrators, acting singly or jointly; instead, that intent is required as part of the criminal planning by a group of persons (bent on genocide). As the genocidal intent remains as a basic legal ingredient of the crime, in this respect the French law does not depart from international rules too conspicuously.

Whether or not this construction of the French law is sound, it is plain that the other element required by this law, namely the objective existence of a 'concerted plan' amounts to a departure from, or at least a markedly unilateral interpretation of the Genocide Convention.

Let us now consider the views of the scholars who take the same stand. A number of criminal lawyers have propounded the opinion that genocide as a crime always requires a 'genocidal plan' or a 'genocidal campaign.' According to them only

---

[1] See the text of the *Circulaire* in *Code Pénal*, 94th edn. (Paris, Dalloz 1996-1997), p. 744.

[2] The introductory part of Art. 6 provides that 'The Tribunal established by the Agreement referred to in Article 1 hereof for the trial and punishment of the major war criminals of the European Axis countries shall have the power to try and punish persons who, acting in the interests of the European Axis countries, whether as individuals or as members of organizations, committed any of the following crimes.
The following acts, or any of them, are crimes coming within the jurisdiction of the Tribunal for which there shall be individual responsibility: ...'
The provision on crimes against humanity (which includes genocide) reads as follows:
'(c) CRIMES AGAINST HUMANITY: namely, murder, extermination, enslavement, deportation, and other inhumane acts committed against any civilian population, before or during the war, or persecutions on political, racial or religious grounds in execution of or in connection with any crime within the jurisdiction of the Tribunal, whether or not in violation of the domestic law of the country where perpetrated.'
The final provision stipulates that: 'Leaders, organizers, instigators and accomplices participating in the formulation or execution of a Common Plan or Conspiracy to commit any of the foregoing crimes are responsible for all acts performed by any persons in execution of such plan.'
Clearly, the reference to a 'common plan' in the last provision of the article is only intended to envisage a special category of criminality, namely 'conspiracy,' but does not require such 'conspiracy' for all the criminal acts provided for in paras. (a), (b) and (c). An allusion of a policy might be seen in the sentence in the introductory part of the article, where is it said that the Tribunal shall 'try and punish persons who, *acting in the interests of the European Axis countries,* whether as individuals or as members of organizations, committed any of the following crimes.' However, as German courts have repeatedly held in 1946-1950, a person can be responsible for a crime against humanity even if he does not identify with the genocidal policy of a dictatorship and does not act to pursue the interests of that dictatorship (for this case law see A. Cassese, *International Criminal Law*, 2nd edn. (Oxford, Oxford University Press 2008), pp. 114-116).

when this general policy element is present can one define acts performed by individuals falling under one of the five categories envisaged in the Genocide Convention (and the corresponding rules of international customary law) as genocide. This view[3] is not based on an interpretation of the Genocide Convention. It is rather grounded in a logical and I would say phenomenological construction of genocide as a historical event. The commentators under discussion start from the assumption or premise that this massive crime is collective in nature and cannot occur unless the action of single individuals is masterminded, guided, directed, or supported by a governmental authority or at any rate by a collective body or a multitude of organised persons. As Kress recently put it

> 'An individual perpetrator cannot realistically desire the destruction of a protected group to occur as a result of his or her individual genocidal conduct. The perpetrator's desire must rather be related to the result to be brought about by the collective activity to which he or she contributes.'[4]

The limitations of this ontological or phenomenological construction are evident: it is not based on the proper interpretation of the relevant international rules, but rather on the inherent features of what is considered to be genocide as a historical occurrence. I submit that the commentators under consideration move from an historical or sociological analysis of some major cases of genocide (say, that of the Jews in the 1940s or the genocide of Tutsis in 1994) and rightly infer from those events that a genocidal plan had been drawn up by the relevant authorities, a plan on the basis and in the execution of which thousands of individuals carried out genocidal acts against members of the target group. They *extrapolate* from these historical findings that a plan, or a concerted scheme or a conspiracy is always needed for genocide to occur.

It is notable that the same argument had already been put forward by some states during the drafting of the Convention. For instance, the Lebanon delegate to the Sixth Committee pointed out that the essential point was the 'particular motive of the perpetrator, namely racial, national or religious fanaticism.' He went on to note that

> 'Such a feeling could derive only from the attitude adopted by a collectivity and could be directed only against another collectivity. That fact – he concluded – was sufficient to transpose genocide from the category of individual crimes or massacres to a new legal category, that of collective crime.'[5]

---

[3] It would seem that this view is advocated by the American Greenawalt, the Spanish Gil Gil, the Canadian Schabas, the Swiss Vest and the German Kress: see A.K.A. Greenawalt, 'Rethinking Genocidal Intent: The Case for a Knowledge-Based Interpretation', 99 *Colum.L.R.* (1999), pp. 2259 et seq.; W.A. Schabas, *Genocide in International Law* (Cambridge, Cambridge University Press 2000), p. 208; A. Gil Gil, *Derecho Penal Internacional: Especial consideración del delito de genocidio* (Madrid, Editorial Tecnos 1999); H. Vest, *Genozid durch organisatorische Machtapparate* (Baden-Baden, Nomos Verlag 2002); C.Kress, 'The Darfur Report and Genocidal Intent', 3 *JICJ* (2005), pp. 562-578.

[4] C. Kress, ibid., p. 566 [italics in the original].

[5] UN Doc. A/C.6, p. 32.

It would not seem, however, that this argument had any follow-up at the normative level, or in other words that it was eventually reflected in one or another provision of the Genocide Convention.

The same view favourable to a 'policy' as a basic legal requirement of the notion of genocide has also been taken by international criminal tribunals, although without any supporting evidence or argument being provided. Thus, for instance, in 1997 an ICTY Trial Chamber stated in *Tadić* that a policy element is always required for crimes against humanity,[6] and cited many cases to support this view; it then went on to discuss whose policy was required, whether that of a state or also of other actors, correctly answered the question by broadening the policy-makers to non-state entities; in this connection it addressed in an *obiter* the different issue of genocide, noting that

> 'Similarly, the United States Court of Appeals for the Second Circuit recently recognized that "non-state actors" could be liable for committing genocide, the most egregious form of crimes against humanity, as well as war crimes.[7] Therefore, although a policy must exist to commit these acts, it need not be the policy of a State.'[8]

The contrary view holds that the policy element *is not required* by the relevant rules as a legal ingredient of the notion of genocide, although of course it frequently happens in practice that acts of genocide are accompanied by or are based on a plan or a sort of conspiratorial scheme. This view was first set out by an ICTR Trial Chamber in *Kayishema and Ruzindana* in 1999. The Chamber stated that:

> 'It is also the view of the Chamber that although a specific plan to destroy does not constitute an element of genocide, it would appear that it is not easy to carry out a genocide without such a plan, or organisation. Morris and Scharf note that "it is virtually impossible for the crime of genocide to be committed without some or indirect involvement on the part of the State given the magnitude of this crime." They suggested that "it is unnecessary for an individual to have knowledge of all details of the genocidal plan or policy." The Chamber concurs with this view.'[9]

The Chamber clinched the point later in the same judgment. It asked itself whether, based on its considerations on the applicable law, it could be said that a genocide had occurred in Rwanda in 1994; in this regard it pointed out that

> 'It is the opinion of the Trial Chamber that the existence of such a plan would be strong evidence of the specific intent requirement for the crime of genocide. To make a finding on whether this plan existed, the Trial Chamber examines evidence presented regarding the more important indicators of the plan.'[10]

---

[6] ICTY, *Prosecutor* v. *Tadić*, Case IT-94-1, Judgment of 7 May 1997, paras. 653-655.

[7] *Kadić* v. *Karadzić*, 70 F.3d 232 (2nd Cir. 1995), cert. denied, 64 *USLW* 3832 (18 Juni 1996).

[8] ICTY, *Prosecutor* v. *Tadić*, Case IT-94-1-T, Judgment of 7 May 1997, para. 655.

[9] ICTR, *Prosecutor* v. *Kayishema and Rudzindana*, Case ICTR-95-1-T, Judgment of 21 May 1999, para. 94.

[10] Ibid., para. 276.

A similar view was later expounded in 2001 by the ICTY Appeals Chamber in *Jelisić*. The Chamber held that

> 'the existence of a plan or policy is not a legal ingredient of the crime. However, in the context of proving specific intent, the existence of a plan or policy may become an important factor in most cases. The evidence may be consistent with the existence of a plan or policy, or may even show such existence, and the existence of a plan or policy may facilitate proof of the crime.'[11]

To support its proposition the Chamber cited an oral decision[12] by the Appeals Chamber for the ICTR in *Prosecutor* v. *Clément Kayishema and Obed Ruzindana*.

It is apparent from the above citations that, in holding that no policy element is required for genocide, the courts did not provide any legal justification supporting their view: they simply relied on either judicial precedents or some scholarly opinions.

In sum, both the opposing views summarised so far are not grounded in a proper analysis of the relevant international rules. They are rather predicated either on a historical or phenomenological survey of past genocides or on mere recitation of some judicial precedents that are not based on any compelling argument or interpretation. It would thus seem that there is room for a fresh start exclusively based on a careful construction of the relevant international rules. The aim of this analysis should be to establish whether a well-founded conclusion can be derived from a proper reading and interpretation of those rules.

If this approach is taken it is clear that both conflicting views mentioned above do not construe the existing law correctly. Arguably a *contextual element* is not required by customary and treaty rules on genocide for some instances of genocide, whilst it is needed for other categories. At least with regard to two categories of acts of genocide ((i) killing members of a protected group; (ii) causing serious bodily or mental harm to members of a protected group) one or more individuals may engage in the crime of genocide without any general policy or collective action being required for their being prosecuted and punished for that crime. One or more individuals can for example kill a number of members of a religious group with genocidal intent, even if no state authorities or other collectivity or *de facto* authority plans or engages in persecuting and destroying that group. After all, this is precisely what Jelisić did: according to the factual findings of the ICTY Trial Chamber that pronounced on the matter, he did not act on the basis or in the execution of a plan:

> 'The Trial Chamber considers that, in this case, the Prosecutor has not provided sufficient evidence allowing it to be established beyond all reasonable doubt that there existed a plan to destroy the Muslim group in Brčko or elsewhere within which the murders committed by the accused would allegedly fit.'[13]

---

[11] ICTY, *Prosecutor* v. *Jelisić*, Case IT-95-10-A, Judgment of the Appeals Chamber of 5 July 2001, para. 48.

[12] ICTR, *Prosecutor* v. *Clément Kayishema and Obed Ruzindana*, Case ICTR-95-1-A, Judgment of the Appeals Chamber of 1 June 2001.

[13] ICTY, *Prosecutor* v. *Jelisić*, Case IT-95-10-T, Judgment of 14 December 1999, para. 98.

Jelisić not only killed many Muslims but also proclaimed that he did so because he hated that ethnic and religious group and was bent on exterminating as many members of the group as possible.[14] Thus his action exhibited both the required elements of genocide: *actus reus* and special intent. This was the conclusion of the Appeals Chamber,[15] which thus rightly rectified the wrong legal findings of the Trial Chamber on this matter, according to which the 'words and attitude of Goran Jelisić as related by the witnesses essentially reveal a disturbed personality.'[16]

The same holds true for the other category of *actus reus*: causing serious bodily or mental harm to members of the group. One or more persons can engage in rape or torture or other forms of serious ill-treatment of members of an ethnic, religious, national or racial group with the intent of thereby destroying the group in whole or in part. If such acts occur within a state and the perpetrators are brought to trial, why should the courts of that state refuse to characterise those acts as genocide and instead downgrade them to common offences (torture, ill-treatment and so on) only because there is no evidence of a plan or concerted action by a state or state-like authority?

I therefore submit that for these two categories of genocide international rules do not require the existence of either a widespread or systematic practice or a plan as a legal ingredient of the crime of genocide.[17] It bears noting that this conclusion is also material at the procedural level, for it implies that the prosecutor in a national or international trial need not lead evidence on that practice or contextual element to prove that the acts in dispute amount to genocide.

Admittedly even genocidal acts belonging to one of the two categories at issue are hardly conceivable as isolated or sporadic events. Normally they are in fact part of a pattern of conduct tolerated, approved or condoned by governmental authorities. These circumstances remain nevertheless factual events, *not provided for or required* by the relevant treaty and customary rules.

Instead, the other three categories of genocide perforce not only presuppose, but rather take the shape of, some sort of collective or even organised action. I am referring to (i) deliberately inflicting on a protected group or members thereof conditions of life calculated to bring about its physical destruction in whole or in part; (ii) imposing measures intended to prevent births within a protected group; (iii) forcibly transferring children of a protected group to another group. Plainly, actions

---

14 Ibid., paras. 102-104.

15 ICTY, *Prosecutor* v. *Jelisić*, Case IT-95-10-A, Judgment of the Appeals Chamber of 5 July 2001, para. 48.

16 Ibid., para. 105.

17 The UN International Commission of Inquiry on Darfur held in its report that mass killing, large-scale rape as well as massive forcible expulsion of civilians from their homes, committed by or on behalf of the Sudanese authorities in Darfur did not amount to genocide, for lack of genocidal intent attributable to the Sudanese government. Nevertheless, in its view single individuals participating in such crimes might be found guilty of genocide by a court of law if such court were satisfied that the defendants had pursued a genocidal intent (UN Doc. S/2005/60, §§520-521). However, the Commission did not draw any distinction between mass murder and rape, on the one side, and forcible expulsion, on the other.

such as deliberate deprivation of resources indispensable for the survival of members of a protected group, e.g., food or medical supplies, or such action as systematic expulsion from home with a view to bringing about conditions of life leading to the destruction of the group, are necessarily carried out on a large scale and by a multitude of individuals in pursuance of a common plan, possibly with the support or at least the acquiescence of the authorities. Similarly, such measures designed to prevent births as prohibition of marriages, separation of the sexes, forced birth control, sterilisation, large-scale sexual mutilation, are all activities that only state organs or other official authorities may undertake, or authorise to undertake, or at least approve or condone.

In summary, close scrutiny of the international rules on genocide makes allowance for a nuanced or diversified interpretation of the requirement under discussion. This requirement is not a necessary and indispensable legal ingredient for two categories of genocidal conduct, although of course its existence is important at the evidentiary level to conclude that genocidal killings or serious harms have been undertaken. To hold otherwise is to confuse a requirement demanded by a legal rule with a factual occurrence in practice: one simply mixes up *quod plerumque accidit*, i.e., what in fact occurs very frequently in real life, with a specific and distinct ingredient required by legal rules for a conduct to be characterised as genocide.

Instead, with regard to the other three categories of genocidal conduct, the policy or plan is inherent in the very criminal conduct and therefore can be held to amount to a legal ingredient of the crime. However, the policy and plan does not constitute a discrete element of the offence, or in other words does not acquire the features of an element distinct from the conduct; rather, it is intrinsic to the nature of the conduct, or in other words coessential to that conduct.

THE TWO NOTIONS OF GENOCIDE: DISTINGUISHING MACRO PHENOMENA AND INDIVIDUAL MISCONDUCT

Stefan Kirsch

Both the 'ordinary' understanding of genocide, which covers mass killings of all kinds, as well as the legal concept of genocide relate to macro phenomena. While the former seems obvious, only a proper analysis of the intent requirement of the crime of genocide clearly reveals that genocide as a legal concept describes a systemic crime. Nevertheless, individual criminal responsibility for genocide cannot be determined by simply referring to the existence of a system of genocide or a genocidal campaign on its own.

I. THE 'SOCIAL' CONCEPT OF GENOCIDE

Although genocide has developed to become a legal notion[1] soon after the term had been coined by *Raphael Lemkin*,[2] most people do not refer to a legal definition when talking about genocide. Social scientists include in the victim groups all human groups as targeted by the perpetrators[3] or even depart entirely from the group element,[4] whereas the media as well as historians tend to use the term simply to describe the occurrence of mass killings or ethnic cleansing based on discriminatory motives.[5]

---

[1] Cf., Convention on the Prevention and Punishment of the Crime of Genocide as approved and proposed for signature and ratification or accession by UN GA Res. 260A(III) of 9 December 1948, 78 *UNTS* p. 277. The Convention entered into force on 12 January 1951.

[2] Cf., R. Lemkin, *Axis Rule in Occupied Europe: Laws of Occupation – Analysis of Government – Proposals for Redress* (Washington, Carnegie Endowment for International Peace, Division of International Law 1944).

[3] Cf., F. Chalk & K. Jonassohn, *The History and Sociology of Genocide: Analyses and Case Studies* (New Haven, Yale University Press 1990).

[4] Cf., L. van den Herik, 'The Schism between the Legal and the Social Concept of Genocide in Light of the Responsibility to Protect', in R. Henham & P. Behrens (eds.), *The Criminal Law of Genocide* (Aldershot, Ashgate 2007), p. 75: 'A discussion between lawyers and social scientists on genocide can have rather confusing results since each discipline employs its own definition. In other words: there is a schism between the legal and the social concept of genocide. Whereas the main characteristic of the legal concept of genocide is the specific intent to destroy a particular group in whole or in part, the social concept of genocide focuses more generally on the aspect of mass killing.'

[5] Cf., N. Jørgensen, 'Genocide as a Fact of Common Knowledge', 56 *ICLQ* (2007), p. 885 at p. 895.

C. Safferling and E. Conze (eds.), The Genocide Convention Sixty Years after its Adoption

Despite this rather loose notion, the term 'genocide' carries a powerful message and politicians and diplomats all over the world are aware of the stigma brought about by allegations that genocide has been committed. For that reason, it is troubling that even international criminal tribunals make use of such a broad 'social' concept of genocide instead of strictly limiting themselves to applying the legal definition of genocide relating to individual misconduct.

To illustrate this disquieting practise one might refer to the Trial Chamber's assessment in *Akayesu* that 'genocide was, indeed, committed in Rwanda in 1994 against the Tutsi as a group.'[6] Similarly the Trial Chamber in *Kayishema/Ruzindana* embarked on a mission to establish 'whether genocide took place in Rwanda in 1994.'[7] As to the relevance of such a finding, the judges set out that this question was 'so fundamental to the case against the accused that the Trial Chamber feels obliged to make a finding of fact on this issue.'[8] Eventually, the troubling use of a broad 'social' concept of genocide culminated in the 'landmark'[9] Appeals Chamber decision[10] recognising that genocide occurred in Rwanda as a fact of common knowledge.[11] As the Appeals Chamber set out:

> 'There is no reasonable basis for anyone to dispute that, during 1994, there was a campaign of mass killing intended to destroy, in whole or at least in very large part, Rwanda's Tutsi population, which (as judicially noticed by the Trial Chamber) was a protected group … During its early history, it was valuable for the purpose of the historical record for Trial Chambers to gather evidence documenting the overall course of the genocide and to enter findings of fact on the basis of that evidence. Trial and Appeal Judgements thereby produced (while varying as to the responsibility of particular accused) have unanimously and decisively confirmed the occurrence of genocide in Rwanda, which has also been documented by countless books, scholarly articles, media reports, U.N. reports and resolutions, national court decisions, and government and NGO reports. At this stage, the Tribunal need not demand further documentation. The fact of the Rwandan genocide is a part of world history, a fact as certain as any other, a classic instance of a "fact of common knowledge."'[12]

---

[6] ICTR, *Prosecutor* v. *Akayesu*, Case ICTR-96-4-T, Judgment, 2 September 1998, para. 126.

[7] ICTR, *Prosecutor* v. *Kayishema/Ruzindana,* Case ICTR-95-1-T, Judgment, 21 May 1999, para. 273.

[8] *Idem.*

[9] K.J. Heller, 'Prosecutor v. Karemera, Ngirumpatse, & Nzirorera', 101 *AJIL* (2007), p. 157 at p. 159. See also B. Heller, 'Noticing Genocide', 116 *YaleLJ* (2006), p. 98.

[10] ICTR, *Prosecutor* v. *Karemera, et al.*, Case ICTR-98-44-AR73(C), Decision on Prosecutor's Interlocutory Appeal of Decision on Judicial Notice, 16 June 2006, para. 35.

[11] Rule 94(A) of the Rules of Procedure and Evidence for the International Criminal Tribunal for Rwanda (RPE-ICTR) reads: 'A Trial Chamber shall not require proof of facts of common knowledge but shall take judicial notice thereof.' Cf., ICTR, *Prosecutor* v. *Semanza*, Case ICTR-97-20-A, Judgment of the Appeals Chamber, 20 May 2005, para. 194: 'The term "common knowledge" encompasses facts that are not reasonably subject to dispute: in other words, commonly accepted or universally known facts, such as general facts of history or geography, or the laws of nature. Such facts are not only widely known but also beyond reasonable dispute.'

[12] ICTR, *Prosecutor* v. *Karemera, et al.*, Case ICTR-98-44-AR73(C), Decision on Prosecutor's Interlocutory Appeal of Decision on Judicial Notice, 16 June 2006, para. 35 (footnotes omitted).

To be sure, it shall not be denied that mass killings and other horrendous crimes based on discriminatory motives occurred in Rwanda in 1994. Nevertheless, the benefit of such a finding in a verdict dealing with the criminal responsibility of one or more individuals might be outweighed by the potential prejudice caused by it. However, before turning to analyse the Appeals Chamber decision in more detail, we will first turn to explore the 'legal' concept of genocide more thoroughly.

II. The 'legal' concept of genocide

In contrast to the social concept of genocide, the legal concept of genocide is based on individual misconduct that satisfies certain requirements set out by criminal law.

Although these requirements slightly differ in national law, it might be fair to state that genocide is by far the most standardised criminal offence worldwide, because most of the provisions included in national law refer to or simply reproduce the wording of the Convention on the Prevention and Punishment of the Crime of Genocide. In addition, both Article 4(2) of the Statute of the International Criminal Tribunal for the former Yugoslavia and Article 2(2) of the Statute of the International Criminal Tribunal for Rwanda use a verbatim reproduction of Article 2 of the Genocide Convention[13] in order to define the offence of 'genocide,' and the same is true for Article 6 of the Rome Statute of the International Criminal Court.

Based on this wording, genocide requires neither successful destruction of a whole race or ethnicity nor even that crimes have occurred on a mass scale. From its language it rather appears that fulfilling the *actus reus* requirement simply calls for a serious attack on a member of a national, ethnical, racial or religious group. For that reason, much of the dispute with regard to the legal concept of genocide concerns the *mens rea* requirement, i.e., that the perpetrators act with a certain intent, namely to destroy, in whole or in part, a national, ethnical, racial or religious group, as such.

It is often said that what distinguishes genocide from all other crimes under international law is its *dolus specialis* or 'special intent' as an aggravated criminal intention, required in addition to the criminal intent accompanying the underlying offence.[14] Similarly, the International Criminal Tribunal for Rwanda as well as the

---

[13] According to Art. 2 of the Genocide Convention genocide means
'any of the following acts committed with intent to destroy, in whole or in part, a national, ethnical, racial or religious group, as such:
(a) Killing members of the group;
(b) Causing serious bodily or mental harm to members of the group;
(c) Deliberately inflicting on the group conditions of life calculated to bring about its physical destruction in whole or in part;
(d) Imposing measures intended to prevent births within the group;
(e) Forcibly transferring children of the group to another group.'

[14] Cf., A. Cassese, *International Criminal Law* (Oxford, Oxford University Press 2003), p. 103; J. Jones & S. Powles, *International Criminal Practice*, 3rd edn. (Ardsley, Transnational Publishers 2003), p. 154.

International Criminal Tribunal for the former Yugoslavia have on various occasions expressed their view that a perpetrator of the crime of genocide must act with the aim, goal, purpose or desire to destroy a part of the protected group: In *Akayesu*, the Trial Chamber set out that 'genocide is distinct from other crimes inasmuch as it embodies a special intent or *dolus specialis*. Special intent of a crime is the specific intention, required as a constitutive element of the crime, which demands that the perpetrator clearly seeks to produce the act charged.'[15] Even more graphic, the Trial Chamber in *Stakić* held that 'genocide is a unique crime where special emphasis is placed on the specific intent. The crime is, in fact, characterised and distinguished by a "surplus" of intent.'[16] It therefore follows that – as set out by the Trial Chamber in *Blagojević, et al.* – that it is 'not sufficient that the perpetrator simply knew that the underlying crime would inevitably or likely result in the destruction of the group. The group, in whole or in part, must be the aim of the underlying crime[s].'[17]

However, this interpretation, which may be called the *purpose*-based approach, has been challenged by the so-called *knowledge*-based approach.[18] According to the latter, the requirement of genocidal intent should be satisfied 'if the perpetrator acted in furtherance of a campaign targeting members of the protected group and knew that the goal or manifest effect of the campaign was the destruction of the group in whole or in part.'[19]

This paper does not aim to discuss the dispute between these two approaches regarding the *mens rea* requirement of genocide. Nevertheless, it is hardly acceptable that a subordinate, who – although clearly understanding that his acts contribute to the destruction of a protected group – carries out the tasks assigned to him simply to avoid discussion with his superiors and clearly without sharing their beliefs, might be seen as acting with the intent to destroy, in whole or in part, a protected group, as such. Of course, this concern might become troubling when it comes to determining the criminal responsibility of the superior,[20] but it is more than doubt-

---

15 ICTR, *Prosecutor* v. *Akayesu*, Case ICTR-96-4-T, Judgment, 2 September 1998, para. 498.

16 ICTY, *Prosecutor* v. *Stakić*, Case IT-97-24-T, Judgment, 31 July 2003, para. 520.

17 ICTY, *Prosecutor* v. *Blagojević, et al.*, Case IT-02-60-T, Judgment, 17 January 2005, para. 656.

18 Cf., C. Kreß, 'The Darfur Report and Genocidal Intent', 3 *JICJ* (2005), p. 562 at p. 566.

19 A.K.A. Greenawalt, 'Rethinking Genocidal Intent: The Case for a Knowledge-Based Interpretation', 99 *Colum. L. R.* (1999), p. 2259 at p. 2288. The text continues as follows: 'Drawing upon the Genocide Convention's core concern for the permanent losses to humanity that result from the annihilation of enumerated groups, this approach emphasizes the destructive result of genocidal acts instead of the specific reasons that move particular individuals to perform such acts. It addresses the related problems of subordinate actors and ambiguous goals by unhinging the question of genocidal liability from that of the perpetrator's particular motive or desires with regard to the group as a whole. And in the particular case of subordinate perpetrators, it does so without relying on an expansive liability framework that would attach liability for acts that are far beyond the direct responsibility of the particular perpetrator. In this way, it seeks to assert a more objective and principled standard of liability than that offered by the specific intent interpretation.'

20 Cf., C. Kreß, *supra* n. 18, at p. 574: 'Imagine that perpetrator A physically exterminates a preselected member of the targeted group with full knowledge of thereby contributing to a genocidal campaign but without the kind of individual desire required by the purpose-based approach. In such a

ful whether such a difficulty warrants equating mere indifference with intent, thereby diluting the concept of genocide as the most serious crime against humanity.

II.1 The 'systemic' nature of genocide

Despite these concerns, the *knowledge*-based approach is a useful means to demonstrate that the crime of genocide not only requires an attack on a member of a protected group – as the plain reading might suggest – but also the existence of an endeavour or plan that is capable of destroying the group at least in part.

Such an unwritten element of the crime of genocide has already been touched upon in *Jelisić*, when the International Criminal Tribunal for the former Yugoslavia was tasked to decide on what the Appeals Chamber later described as a 'one-man genocide'[21] mission.

Goran Jelisić was charged with genocide, multiple violations of the laws or customs of war and crimes against humanity. He was prosecuted for murdering thirteen persons, for inflicting bodily harm on four persons and for stealing money from the detainees in Luka camp. In addition the indictment set out that in May 1992 he systematically killed Muslim detainees at the Laser Bus Company, the Brčko police station and Luka camp.[22]

The accused, *Jelisić*, pleaded guilty to war crimes and crimes against humanity but not to genocide, which led to a trial focusing on the charge of genocide and sentencing only. The judges of the Trial Chamber reviewed the evidence presented by the prosecution and concluded that, without even needing to hear the arguments of the defence, the accused could not be found guilty of the crime of genocide.[23] Although the Trial Chamber established that Jelisić had killed numerous Muslim detainees at various detention sites, it considered that the prosecutor had not provided sufficient evidence for the existence of a plan to destroy the Muslim group within which the murders committed by *Goran Jelisić* would allegedly fit.

---

case, A fulfils the *actus reus* of killing a member of a group and acts with "the general intent underlying this offence." However, under the purpose-based approach, he cannot be convicted as a *principal* perpetrator of genocide, for want of an *intent* to destroy. Turning then to the question of *derivative* criminal responsibility, the problem arises in *which crime* A has participated. The only possible answer would be to say that A participated in the *collective* genocidal activity. Strictly speaking, however, this collective activity is no crime; it does not, as such, constitute one of the acts listed as forms of genocide *actus reus*. The problem of how to construe the individual criminal responsibility of perpetrator A triggers the arguably even more important problem of how to categorize superior B, who had instructed A to kill the victim. Because, if A has not committed a crime of genocide, it is at least questionable, whether B can be held responsible for having ordered or instigated a "crime" of genocide.'

[21] ICTY, *Prosecutor* v. *Jelisić*, Case IT-95-10-A, Judgment of the Appeals Chamber, 5 July 2001, para. 66.

[22] ICTY, *Prosecutor* v. *Jelisić*, Case IT-95-10-A, Judgment of the Appeals Chamber, 5 July 2001, para. 3.

[23] The Appeals Chamber, however, by majority (Judge Pocar dissenting) disagreed and allowed the prosecution's appeal. Nonetheless, the Appeals Chamber by majority (Judge Shahabuddeen and Judge Wald dissenting) considered, that in the circumstances of the case, it was not appropriate to order that the case be remitted for further proceedings, and declined to reverse the acquittal.

As a result the judges concluded that it was only as a single perpetrator that the accused could be declared guilty of genocide.[24] The Trial Chamber went on to state:

> '[100.] Such a case is theoretically possible. The murders committed by the accused are sufficient to establish the material element of the crime of genocide and it is a priori possible to conceive that the accused harboured the plan to exterminate an entire group without this intent having been supported by any organisation in which other individuals participated …
>
> [101.] The Trial Chamber observes, however, that it will be very difficult in practice to provide proof of the genocidal intent of an individual if the crimes committed are not widespread and if the crime charged is not backed by an organisation or a system.'[25]

In light of the finding that no plan or enterprise to destroy the Muslim group existed, the Trial Chamber did not elaborate on the features of an organisation or a system. Nonetheless, the Trial Chamber in *Jelisić* correctly identified the difficulty in assuming that somebody could be determined to destroy an entire group 'without this intent having been supported by any organisation in which other individuals participated.'[26]

It is indeed true that without any such support the intention to destroy a protected group turns into a vain wish or a mere attitude not capable to qualify an isolated attack as a crime of genocide, since a wrong mindset by itself is not suited to trigger criminal liability. At least according to modern criminal law doctrine, a wrong mindset by itself does not deserve punishment which is only triggered by acts that harm or violate 'legal goods' (*Rechtsgüter*).[27] And although it is well accepted that a mental element such as motive might not only be a determining factor as to the gravity of the offence within the sentencing stage but also serve to characterise a criminal offence and thereby distinguish it from other offences,[28]

---

[24] ICTY, *Prosecutor* v. *Jelisić*, Case IT-95-10-T, Judgment, 14 December 1999, para. 99.

[25] ICTY, *Prosecutor* v. *Jelisić*, Case IT-95-10-T, Judgment, 14 December 1999. Cf., also ICTY, *Prosecutor* v. *Jelisić*, Case IT-95-10-A, Judgment of the Appeals Chamber, 5 July 2001, para. 48: 'The Appeals Chamber is of the opinion that the existence of a plan or policy is not a legal ingredient of the crime. However, in the context of proving specific intent, the existence of a plan or policy may become an important factor in most cases. The evidence may be consistent with the existence of a plan or policy, or may even show such existence, and the existence of a plan or policy may facilitate proof of the crime.'

[26] ICTY, *Prosecutor* v. *Jelisić*, Case IT-95-10-T, Judgment, 14 December 1999, para. 100.

[27] Cf., M. Dubber, 'Theories of Crime and Punishment in German Criminal Law', 53 *AJCL* (2006), p. 679; M. Bohlander, *Principles of German Criminal Law* (Oxford, Hart Publishing 2009), p. 18. See also R. Hefendehl, et al. (eds.), *Die Rechtsgutstheorie: Legitimationsbasis des Strafrechts oder dogmatisches Glasperlenspiel?* (Baden-Baden, Nomos 2003).

[28] See, e.g., 'persecution' as a crime against humanity (as in Art. 7(1)(h) ICC Statute). Another example is 'Murder under specific aggravating circumstances' (*Mord*) under German criminal law: According to section 211(2) of the German Criminal Code (*Strafgesetzbuch*) 'A murderer under this provision is any person who kills a person for pleasure, for sexual gratification, out of greed or otherwise base motives …' A murderer shall be liable to imprisonment for life (sec. 211(1)), whereas 'whosoever kills a person without being a murderer under section 211 shall be convicted of murder ["Totschlag"] and be liable to imprisonment of not less than five years.'

genocide is not to be understood as attacking somebody 'on discriminatory grounds.' Therefore in the realm of criminal law an intention – i.e., the desire to achieve a certain goal – only gains relevance if the perpetrator truly believes[29] that he – or the criminal enterprise which he forms part of – possesses the means to achieve that goal.

However, it appears that the dominating *purpose*-based approach has clouded this insight and led to an understanding according to which convictions for genocide by international criminal tribunals were based on discriminatory motives rather than a detailed analysis on how the perpetrator's act fitted in an overall genocidal enterprise or plan.

Yet an individual perpetrator cannot realistically desire the destruction of a protected group to occur as a result of his or her individual conduct and therefore the perpetrator's desire instead must be related to the results to be brought about by a collective activity to which he or she contributes.[30] More specifically, the crime of genocide requires that the perpetrator knows for a fact that he is acting in furtherance of a – typically pre-planned and organised – attack which will lead to the destruction of a distinct group within the civilian population.

For all that, it is correct to point out that 'genocide, for all practical purposes, is a systemic crime' and 'a collective level of genocidal activity must normally be distinguished from the level of the individual genocidal conduct.'[31] Yet – as Claus Kreß pointed out correctly – the definition of the crime does not express this characteristic interplay between individual and collective act.[32] Nonetheless, in order to reconcile the typical interplay with the definition of the crime, he has also pointed out that genocidal intent must 'for all practical purposes have an overall genocidal campaign as an objective point of reference.'[33]

A phrasing that is much more adequate to this structure can be found in the French Criminal Law Code (*code penal*), which sets out that

> 'Genocide occurs where, in the *enforcement of a concerted plan* [emphasis added] aimed at the partial or total destruction of a national, ethnic, racial or religious group, or of a group determined by any other arbitrary criterion, one of the following actions are committed or caused to be committed against members of that group: ...'[34]

---

29 It is, of course, open to debate, how to judge a perpetrator who erroneously assumes that he – or the criminal enterprise which he forms part of – possesses the means to achieve that goal. One possible solution could be to treat such acts as attempted offence (*Versuch*), at least in situations where the error is not due to gross ignorance. Cf., section 23(3) of the German Criminal Code (*Strafgesetzbuch*): 'If the offender due to gross ignorance fails to realise that the attempt could under no circumstances have led to the completion of the offence due to the nature of its object or the means by which it was to be committed, the court may order a discharge, or mitigate the sentence as it sees fit ...' See also M. Bohlander, *supra* n. 27, at p. 144.

30 Cf., C. Kreß, *supra* n. 18, p. 566.

31 See C. Kreß, *supra* n. 18, p. 572. Cf., also C. Kreß, 'The Crime of Genocide under International Law', 6 *ICLR* (2006), p. 461 at p. 470.

32 C. Kreß, *supra* n. 31, p. 470.

33 Ibid., p. 472.

34 Art. 211-1 Code penal ('Constitue un génocide le fait, en exécution d'un plan concerté tendant à la destruction totale ou partielle d'un groupe national, ethnique, racial ou religieux, ou d'un groupe

Despite this shortcoming, it might not be realistic to expect that the wording of the Genocide Convention will be amended in the coming years. Nevertheless the French text could serve as a model to develop a better understanding of the provision as it stands.

II.2 **Individual misconduct**

Recognising a 'collective level of genocidal activity' within the legal concept of genocide, however, should not weaken the fundamental truth that genocide as a criminal offence requires a finding of individual misconduct and responsibility. Therefore, the major difficulty in prosecuting genocide is to identify individual misconduct that is similarly part of a joint plan or collective attack on a protected group and does not only occur in the background of such an attack.

Conduct that only occurs in the background of an attack against a protected group and is in no way related to the proper function of the genocidal enterprise cannot lead to criminal liability for genocide. Finding otherwise would be in clear violation of the fundamental criminal law principle that no criminal liability be imputed based on acts and conduct of third parties that are not related to the acts of the perpetrator. The notion of cumulation underlying this line of reasoning implies responsibility for the wrongdoing of third parties, which clearly conflicts with the principle of blameworthiness (*Schuldprinzip*).[35] For that reason even the requirement set out in the International Criminal Court's Elements of Crimes – namely that 'the conduct took place in the context of a manifest pattern of similar conduct directed against that group'[36] – is to be criticised for it neglects the necessity that the perpetrator's acts form part of a genocidal campaign rather than simply fitting into a pattern of similar but otherwise unrelated conduct.

Acknowledging the difficulties in forming practical examples that do not miss the complexity of the real world, I would nonetheless like to introduce the following situation in order to illustrate the position taken herein:

Let us assume that the armed forces of country C systematically raid villages in a region that is predominantly inhabited by a national minority in order to destroy this minority group. The military action is well planned and there is no doubt that it will be successful in reaching its reprehensible aim. Motivated by hatred against the national minority, Villager V, who has no relation whatsoever to the military campaign, kills one of his neighbours, who is a member of the minority group. Although V is fully aware of the ongoing military campaign, he knows that he is in no way related to the genocidal enterprise carried out by the military and that killing his neighbour for itself would not lead to the destruction of the national minority.

---

déterminé à partir de tout autre critère arbitraire, de commettre ou de faire commettre, à l'encontre de membres de ce groupe, l'un des actes suivants: …').

[35] Cf., M. Bohlander, *supra* n. 27, p. 20.

[36] E.g., Art. 6(b) Genocide by causing serious bodily or mental harm, Element No. 4.

In my view, it would be incorrect to conclude that V committed genocide. However, I recognise that we only need to add a nuance to the situation as I have described it to come nearer to this result.

Let us therefore amend the aforementioned example and assume that the national radio has repeatedly broadcasted speeches, in which the military leadership has encouraged the civilian population to join in attacking the minority group in order to speed up the operation or to avoid further casualties within the military.

I leave it open whether this modification necessarily leads to the conclusion that V has committed genocide, but I do hope that the amended example clearly shows the practical implications to identify genocidal conduct: The difficulty in identifying individual misconduct that is equally part of a collective attack on a protected group – and does not only occur in the background of such an attack – is that very often the conduct itself appears to be 'neutral' and only 'looking' into the perpetrator's mind allows one to establish whether the individual act was designed to fit into a collective level of genocidal activity.

For that reason, the major practical difficulty in prosecuting genocide lies in proving that the perpetrator intended the destruction of a protected group, which implies that the perpetrator was aware that his acts were an integral part of or at least fitted into a realistic plan to destroy a protected group. It can be shown, however, that the jurisprudence of the *ad hoc* tribunals falls short of this standard.

II.3 **Proving genocide**

In order to prove that an individual charged with genocide possessed the necessary *mens rea,* the *ad hoc* tribunals frequently rely on conclusions based on facts and circumstances. As set out by the Appeals Chamber in *Jelisić*:

> '[47.] … proof of specific intent … may, in the absence of direct explicit evidence, be inferred from a number of facts and circumstances, such as the general context, the perpetration of other culpable acts systematically directed against the same group, the scale of atrocities committed, the systematic targeting of victims on account of their membership of a particular group, or the repetition of destructive and discriminatory acts.'[37]

However, neither the 'general context' nor the 'the perpetration of other culpable acts' provide any clear hint as to whether the accused was aware that his acts were an integral part of or at least fitted into a realistic plan to destroy a protected group. Moreover, as pointed out by Behrens, the view expressed by some Trial Chambers that the 'scale of the atrocities' and the 'manner of killing' can allow an inference of genocidal intent is particularly unsatisfactory.[38]

---

[37] ICTY, *Prosecutor* v. *Jelisić*, Case IT-95-10-A, Judgment of the Appeals Chamber, 5 July 2001, para. 47. Cf., also ICTY, *Prosecutor* v. *Strugar*, Case IT-01-42-T, Judgment, 31 January 2005, para. 333.

[38] P. Behrens, 'A Moment of Kindness? – Consistency and Genocidal Intent', in R. Henham & P. Behrens, *supra* n. 4, p. 136.

Ultimately, the use of a fairly blurred standard of proof as to the *mens rea* requirement has reached its peak with the Appeals Chamber decision of 16 June 2006, which overturned an earlier Trial Chamber decision and determined that the fact that genocide occurred in Rwanda should have been recognised as a fact of common knowledge.[39]

The Appeals Chamber did not accept the Trial Chamber's arguments that whether genocide occurred was not relevant to the case that the prosecutor had to prove and that recognising it would improperly lighten the prosecution's burden of proof.[40]

As to the relevance, the Appeals Chamber set out two interrelated claims. First, that proof of a nationwide campaign is a 'necessary, although not sufficient, part'[41] of the prosecution's case, and second, that such proof 'provides the context for understanding the individual's actions.'[42] However, as set out by Kevin Jon Heller,[43] neither claim is persuasive.

The first claim, if taken literally, is simply incorrect, because regardless of whether a defendant is accused of genocide, conspiracy to commit genocide, or complicity in genocide, the occurrence of a nationwide genocidal campaign is not a necessary element of the crime. Moreover, the existence of a nationwide campaign of genocide does not tend to prove any of those elements.

> 'The fact that individuals were killed on a nationwide scale does not make it more likely that the defendant killed one of them. The fact that the victims of the nationwide killings were members of a protected group does not make it more likely that the defendant's alleged victims were also members of that group. And the fact that other unnamed individuals specifically intended to destroy a protected group does not make it more likely that the defendant harboured the same specific intent.'[44]

With regard to the systemic nature of the crime of genocide it should be added that even the existence of a genocidal plan or campaign does not make it more likely that the defendant played any particular role in such a campaign. In contrast, the prosecution must still identify the particular acts and conduct of the defendant that make him part of the genocidal campaign.

---

[39] ICTR, *Prosecutor* v. *Karemera, et al.*, Case ICTR-98-44-AR73(C), Decision on Prosecutor's Interlocutory Appeal of Decision on Judicial Notice, 16 June 2006.

[40] Cf., ICTR, *Prosecutor* v. *Karemera, et al.*, Case ICTR-98-44-R94, Decision on Prosecution Motion for Judicial Notice, 9 November 2005, para. 7.

[41] ICTR, *Prosecutor* v. *Karemera, et al.*, Case ICTR-98-44-AR73(C), Decision on Prosecutor's Interlocutory Appeal of Decision on Judicial Notice, 16 June 2006, para. 36.

[42] ICTR, *Prosecutor* v. *Karemera, et al.*, Case ICTR-98-44-AR73(C), Decision on Prosecutor's Interlocutory Appeal of Decision on Judicial Notice, 16 June 2006, para. 36. See also ICTR, *Prosecutor* v. *Kayishema/Ruzindana*, Case ICTR-95-1-T, Judgment, 21 May 1999, para. 274: 'The purpose of this Chapter is not to decide whether specific acts by particular individuals amounted to genocidal acts, that is, acts committed with the special intent to destroy the Tutsi group in whole or in part. Rather, this Chapter assesses whether the events in Rwanda as a whole, reveal the existence of the elements of the crime of genocide. Such a finding allows for a better understanding of the context within which perpetrators may have committed the crimes alleged in the Indictment.'

[43] K.J. Heller, *supra* n. 9, p. 157.

[44] Ibid., p. 159.

For that reason, the Appeals Chamber's second claim – that proof of a nationwide campaign of genocide 'provides the context for understanding the individual's actions' – must also fail. Even though genocide is a systemic crime and a collective level of genocidal activity must normally be distinguished from the level of the individual conduct, the existence of a nationwide genocidal campaign as such does not in any way help to identify the acts and conduct of the accused that make him part of such a campaign. Therefore, the Trial Chamber was right, when it initially determined:

> 'As a result, it does not matter whether genocide occurred in Rwanda or not, the Prosecutor must still prove the criminal responsibility of the Accused for the counts he has charged in the Indictment. Taking judicial notice of such a fact as common knowledge does not have any impact on the Prosecution's case against the Accused, because that is not a fact to be proved.'[45]

Leaving aside the Appeals Chamber decision and turning back to the critical issue of proof of the perpetrator's intent to destroy a protected group, attention should finally be drawn to the fact that the unsatisfactory practise of the *ad hoc* tribunals stands in contrast to the practise of the International Court of Justice, which has applied a much stricter standard of proof in the case concerning the application of the genocide convention. Dealing with the Applicant's contention that the very pattern of the atrocities committed over many communities, over a lengthy period, focused on Bosnian Muslims and also Croats, demonstrated the necessary genocidal intent, the Court acknowledged that it could not agree with such a 'broad proposition' and set out:

> 'The *dolus specialis*, the specific intent to destroy the group in whole or in part, has to be convincingly shown by reference to particular circumstances, unless a general plan to that end can be convincingly demonstrated to exist; and for a pattern of conduct to be accepted as evidence of its existence, it would have to be such that it could only point to the existence of such intent.'[46]

Hopefully, the correct standard applied by the International Court of Justice will find its way into the practise of the *ad hoc* tribunals as well as that of the International Criminal Court, since it properly distinguishes macro phenomena and individual misconduct.

---

[45] ICTR, *Prosecutor* v. *Karemera, et al.*, Case ICTR-98-44-R94, Decision on Prosecution Motion for Judicial Notice, 9 November 2005, para. 7.

[46] ICJ, *Bosnia and Herzegovina* v. *Serbia and Montenegro* ('Case concerning the application of the Convention on the Prevention and Punishment of the Crime of Genocide'), Judgment, 26 February 2007, para. 373.

III. Conclusion

The Trial Chamber in *Jelisić* correctly identified the difficulty in assuming that somebody could be determined to destroy an entire group without this intent having been supported by any organisation in which other individuals participated. Since an individual perpetrator cannot realistically desire the destruction of a protected group to occur as a result of his or her individual conduct, the perpetrator's desire must be related to the results to be brought about by a collective activity to which he or she contributes. More specifically, the crime of genocide requires that the perpetrator knows for a fact that he is acting in furtherance of a – typically pre-planned and organised – attack which will lead to the destruction of a distinct group within the civilian population.

Recognising a 'collective level of genocidal activity' within the legal concept of genocide, however, should not weaken the fundamental insight that genocide as a criminal offence requires a finding of individual misconduct and responsibility. Therefore, the major difficulty in prosecuting genocide is to identify individual misconduct that is equally part of a collective attack on a protected group and does not only occur in the background of such an attack.

DIFFERENT FORMS OF PARTICIPATION IN GENOCIDE

Henning Radtke

I. LEGAL BASIS FOR COMPLICITY IN INTERNATIONAL CRIMINAL LAW

Both in international and national criminal law, the punishability of natural persons requires the acting person's individual responsibility. Individual responsibility requires the attribution of individual behaviour to an event relating to criminal law. The attribution of a specific event to the action of a specific person within the macrocriminality of international criminal law, however, proves to be especially difficult. The relevant individual acts must always fit within a collective overall context depending on their nature.[1] This impedes the attribution of the individual act to the overall event which is important for complicity. This difficulty of participation in crimes of international criminal law also arises with regard to the crime of genocide. Here, the difficulty may be particularly severe, since the distinctive context of crimes against international criminal law is justified by a subjective characteristic: the intention to completely or partly destroy a specific group. In order to examine the different forms of punishable participation in the crime of genocide more closely, I will proceed in two steps. In the first step, I will address the different forms of participation in international criminal law in general. In doing so, I will particularly refer to the differentiation between the different forms of participation. In a second step, I will then examine specific problems of participating in genocide.

As far as I can see, international criminal law was, at first, shaped by a formal unitarian concept of perpetration. Everyone who has made an imputable contribution to the accomplishment of the elements of the offence is considered a perpetrator. The scope and the weight of his/her contribution are irrelevant.[2] According to the unitarian concept of perpetration, it is not necessary to differentiate between the perpetrator and the participant.[3] Later, differentiations were made between the differ-

[1] K. Ambos, *Der Allgemeine Teil des Völkerstrafrechts* [General Part of International Criminal Law] (Berlin, Duncker&Humblot 2004), pp. 518 et seq., with further references.

[2] A. Eser, P. Cramer & G. Heine, 'Vorbemerkungen zu §§ 25 ff.', in Schönke/Schröder (eds.), *Kommentar zum StGB* (Munich, C.H. Beck 2006), MN 11.

[3] J. Vogel, 'Individuelle Verantwortung im Völkerstrafrecht. Zugleich ein Beitrag zu den Regelungsmodellen der Beteiligung', 114 *ZStW* (2002), p. 403 at pp. 404 et seq.; cf., for German law: B. Schünemann, 'Vorbemerkungen zu §§ 25 ff.', in H.-W. Laufhütte, R. Rissing-van Saan & K. Tiedemann (eds.), *Leipziger Kommentar, StGB* [Commentary on Criminal Law], 12th edn. (Berlin, de Gruyter 2007), MNs 5 et seq.

C. Safferling and E. Conze (eds.), The Genocide Convention Sixty Years after its Adoption

ent forms of participation. The draft codes[4] already included a differentiation between perpetration and participation with the passage of 'complicity.' Article 25(3) ICC Statute[5] takes up this differentiation and distinguishes three forms of direct perpetration, as well as the different forms of participation. Article 25(3) lit. a ICC Statute refers to direct or immediate perpetration ('as an individual'), co-perpetration ('jointly with another') and perpetration by means ('through another person'). Perpetration by means may occur 'regardless of whether that other person is criminally responsible.' Accordingly, international criminal law also recognises perpetration by means, if the direct perpetrator is responsible for his own action ('the [indirect] perpetrator behind the [direct] perpetrator').[6] With respect to participation, Article 25(3) lit. b, c ICC Statute also refers to the forms of participation as 'ordering,' 'soliciting or inducing' and 'contributing in any other way,' as well as 'aiding and abetting'[7] which has already been elaborated upon by the jurisprudence of the *ad hoc* tribunals.

According to its wording, Article 25 ICC Statute does not effect any gradation between these different forms of participation, as is done in German criminal law using the so-called normative classification to define different levels between perpetration and other forms of participation. Some authors therefore claim that the differentiation of forms of participation only has a descriptive function in international criminal law, and is irrelevant with respect to conviction. The latter should focus solely on the responsibility of the person concerned, independent of the form of his/her participation in each specific, individual case.[8] The categorisation of Article 25 ICC Statute just mentioned however suggests a gradation of the different forms of participation with respect to their content of injustice.[9] The *ad hoc* tribunals also act on the assumption of a differentiation in terms of judgment between the forms of participation. They thereby refer to the respective form of participation as evidence of the individual's level of responsibility and consider it when fixing the sentence.[10]

---

[4] II(2) *ILC Yearbook* (1991); *ILC Yearbook* 1996.

[5] Text of the Rome Statute circulated as document A/CONF.183/9 of 17 July 1998 and corrected by procès-verbaux of 10 November 1998, 12 July 1999, 30 November 1999, 8 May 2000, 17 January 2001 and 16 January 2002. The statute entered into force on 1 July 2002.

[6] K. Ambos, in O. Triffterer (ed.), *Commentary on the Rome Statute of the International Criminal Court* (Munich, C.H. Beck 2008) Art. 25, MN 9.

[7] ICTY, *Prosecutor* v. *Furundzija*, Case IT-95-17/1, Judgment, 10 December 1999, paras. 190 et seq.

[8] A. Cassese, *International Criminal Law* (Oxford, Oxford University Press 2008), p. 188.

[9] G. Werle, *Völkerstrafrecht* [International Criminal Law] (Tübingen, Mohr Siebeck 2007), MN 411.

[10] G. Werle, *supra* n. 9; K. Ambos, *supra* n. 1, p. 543; H. Vest, *Genozid durch organisierte Machtapparate* [Genocide caused by organised Power Machinery] (Baden-Baden, Nomos 2002), p. 181; whereas an interpretation as an unitarian concept of perpetration is shown in C. Kreß, *Humanitäres Völkerrecht – Informationsschriften* [Journal of International Law of Peace and Armed Conflict] (1999), p. 4 at p. 9, and in K. Hamdorf, *Beteiligungsmodelle im Strafrecht* [Participation Concepts In Criminal Law] (Freiburg, edition iuscrim 2002), p. 396.

If the form of participation is significant when deciding the sentence, there is a need for regulations which clearly differentiate between the varied forms of participation in an offence of international criminal law. So far, the only generally accepted regulations to address this problem are on a small scale and differentiation of the forms of participation often proves difficult. Some of the problems of differentiation are touched upon in the following.

II. DIFFERENTIATION OF THE DIFFERENT FORMS OF PARTICIPATION

Perpetration by means causes particular problems in current international criminal law, with regard to the differentiation of perpetration and participation. In view of the extensive phrasing of the ICC Statute, difficult questions arise in relation to instigation when differentiating this form of participation. A case of perpetration by means, due to the dominance of the organisational structure, could turn out to be participation by 'ordering' or, in individual cases, also 'soliciting.'[11] Soliciting requires an existing factual superior-subordinate relationship.[12] Within this relationship, the superior person abuses his/her position to convince the subordinate that he/she should, or forces him/her[13] to commit a crime.[14] This would be defined as instigation. Perpetration by means could also be substantiated in these cases due to the hierarchical structure. If the form of participation in the offence of international criminal law in the jurisdiction of the *ad hoc* tribunals determines the extent of the sentence, the importance of the correct differentiation of the varied forms of participation is indicated very clearly. However, I do not see any criteria, any standard which enables the attribution of specific cases to perpetration by means on the one hand, or to ordering or soliciting on the other hand.

The classification of 'soliciting' is difficult in any case. Does it refer to perpetration or participation? The concept of 'soliciting' was intended to create a form of participation enabling the realisation of active (or direct) superior responsibility according to Article 28 ICC Statute.[15] This suggests drawing conclusions about the effect of superior responsibility on 'soliciting.' The question of whether superior responsibility is realised in customary international crimes through perpetration or participation is, however, largely unclear. The commission of a customary interna-

[11] See also H. Radtke, 'Mittelbare Täterschaft kraft Organisationsherrschaft im nationalen und internationalen Strafrecht', in C. Roxin, *Zur Strafbarkeit des untauglichen Versuchs* [On the Criminal Liability of the Futile Attempt] (Baden-Baden, Nomos 2006), p. 350 at p. 352.

[12] ICTY, *Prosecutor* v. *Blaškić*, Case IT-95-14-A, Judgment, 3 March 2000, para. 281; *Prosecutor* v. *Kordić/ Čerkez*, Case IT-95-14/2-T, Judgment, 26 February 2001, para. 388.

[13] K. Ambos, *supra* n. 6, Art. 25, MN 12.

[14] ICTR, *Prosecutor* v. *Akayesu*, Case ICTR-96-4-T, Judgment, 2 September 1998, para. 78; ICTY, *Prosecutor* v. *Krstić*, Case IT-98-33-A, Judgment of the Appeals Chamber, 19 April 2004, para. 60.

[15] K. Ambos, *supra* n. 1, p. 672 with further references. It becomes obvious that the dissociation between perpetration and participation could be done in a more extensive way than in German law, because in cases of indirect perpetration, dissociation between two forms of participation is sometimes insufficient.

tional crime by a subordinate[16] is a precondition of superior responsibility according to Article 28 ICC Statute. The superior is responsible for this offence, if he/she breaches his/her obligation of control towards the subordinate in an accusable way.[17] The form of participation can either be understood as an act of omission by the superior or as his/her participation in the offence committed by his/her subordinates.[18] A double character with elements of both would also be possible.[19] If superior responsibility was classified as committing an offence of omission, it would be logical to acknowledge its active counterpart, 'soliciting,' not as instigation, but as a form of perpetration by means. However, the jurisdiction of the International Tribunal for Rwanda (ICTR) militates against this assumption. The tribunal differentiates between the individual responsibilities in the sense of soliciting by superior responsibility in the following way: with respect to superior responsibility, the defendant must be in effective control of the persons, he/she must be able to stop them or to punish them after the offence. In the case of ordering, there is however only a necessity of an existing authority and direct influence of the ordering on the commission of the crime.[20] This crime would therefore be of a lesser order than that of (committing) superior responsibility. 'Ordering' according to Article 25(3) lit. c ICC Statute, would then be displayed as participating by means of instigation. A differentiation of the 'order' to superior responsibility would therefore be achieved. The differentiation between 'order' and perpetration by means would however remain indistinct – as referred to before.

My impression is that the differentiation between participation by instigation, and participation by aiding and abetting is similarly ambiguous. With respect to the term 'aiding and abetting,' in international criminal law 'aiding' refers to physical support and 'abetting' to psychological assistance by means of encouragement and advice.[21] The two types of assistance need not be cumulatively available according to Article 25(3) lit. c ICC Statute ('aids, abets or otherwise assists'); they can be available as alternatives.[22] International criminal law practice has, however, al-

---

[16] G. Werle, *supra* n. 9, MN 450.

[17] K. Ambos, *supra* n. 1, p. 667.

[18] G. Werle, *supra* n. 9, MN 467; H. Jung, in A. Eser (ed.), 'Einzelverantwortung und Mitverantwortung im Strafrecht' (Freiburg, edition iuscrim 1994), p. 175 at p. 182; J. Vogel, *supra* n. 3, p. 403 at p. 414; T. Weigend, 'Bemerkungen zur Vorgesetztenverantwortlichkeit im Völkerstrafrecht', 116 *ZStW* (2004), p. 999 at p. 1005; H. Radtke, 'Gedanken zur Vorgesetztenverantwortlichkeit im nationalen und internationalen Strafrecht', in *Festschrift für Egon Müller* (Baden-Baden, Nomos 2008), p. 577 at p. 591.

[19] K. Ambos, 'Superior Responsibility', in A. Cassese, P. Gaeta & J.R.W.D. Jones (eds.), *The Rome Statute of the International Criminal Court* (Oxford, Oxford University Press 2002), p. 824.

[20] ICTR, *Prosecutor* v. *Kamuhanda*, Case ICTR-99-54A-A, Judgment of the Appeals Chamber, 19 September 2005, para. 75. The order to 'start working' means, according to that, 'ordering' in the sense of Art. 25(3) lit. c ICC Statute and constitutes with it an individual responsibility (para. 76: 'the factual finding that the Appellant gave the order to start the massacre, and that this order was obeyed, was not unreasonable').

[21] ICTR, *Prosecutor* v. *Akayesu*, Case ICTR-96-4-T, Judgment, 2 September 1998, para. 78.

[22] K. Ambos, *Internationales Strafrecht* [International Criminal Law] (Munich, C.H. Beck 2008), para. 7, MN 42; J. Vogel, *supra* n. 3, p. 403 at p. 426; W.A. Schabas, *Genozid im Völkerrecht* [Genocide

ways evaluated this differently. For the ICC, the term aiding and abetting is already considered to mean the two types of assistance together.[23] This divergence between the text of the ICC Statute and the previous jurisdiction of the *ad hoc* tribunals alone demonstrates the shapelessness of aiding and abetting in international criminal law. This shapelessness is further intensified in the summary of the terms 'aiding' and 'abetting' in Article 25(3) lit. c ICC Statute by the addition of the phrase 'or otherwise assists.' Such wide field of application, also comprises the conception of the behaviour patterns ('orders, solicits or induces') described in Article 25(3) lit. b ICC Statute. In this way, instigation would be in danger of becoming a dependent part of aiding and abetting. The danger of 'breaking-up' instigation into aiding and abetting is reinforced by the common opinion in Anglo-American law that both forms of participation are broadly understood as factual accessory participation.[24] In my opinion, the danger has already been put into effect in the jurisdiction of the *ad hoc* tribunals. Each concurrent causative behaviour which does not necessarily initiate the offence is sufficient for the assumption of instigation.[25] This cannot be differentiated from mere support in the sense of 'aiding and abetting.' I consider this wrong, given that the offences of instigation and support are of different degrees of severity.

It would, however, be possible to reserve a specific narrow field of application for instigation, if the form of perpetration of incitement, regulated in Article 25(3) lit. d ICC Statute, in relation to genocide, was understood as instigation. The jurisdiction of the *ad hoc* tribunals however makes a clear distinction between instigation and incitement. Instigation means 'prompting another to commit an offence.'[26] It must refer to a limited circle of persons which the instigator has induced to commit the offence. However, with respect to incitement according to Article 25(3) lit. e ICC Statute, there must be a public appeal for people to commit a criminal offence, an individual crime of genocide. The appeal need not be explicit, but must be recognisable, and it may be propagated by the public media.[27] Thus the difference between instigation and incitement becomes apparent: instigation refers to encouraging, exciting or moving another specific person to commit a crime.[28] Incitement refers to animating an unmanaged group of people to commit a crime in a

---

in International Law] (Hamburg, Hamburger Edition 2003), p. 361, where 'abet' is understood to comprise these forms of participation which are mentioned in Art. 25(3) lit. b ICC Statute.

23 The adjudicational practise: G. Mettraux, *International Crimes and the Ad Hoc Tribunals* (Oxford, Oxford University Press 2005).

24 K. Ambos, *supra* n. 22, para. 7, MN 45; G.P. Fletcher, *Rethinking Criminal Law* (Oxford, Oxford University Press 1978), pp. 640 et seq. and p. 671; H.-H. Jescheck, 'Versuch und Rücktritt bei Beteiligung mehrerer Personen an der Straftat', 99 *ZStW* (1987), p. 112 at p. 127.

25 ICTY, *Prosecutor* v. *Blaškić*, Case IT-95-14-A, Judgment, 3 March 2000, para. 280; *Prosecutor* v. *Kordić/ Čerkez*, para. 387; *Prosecutor* v. *Galić*, Case IT-98-29-T, Judgment, 5 December 2003, para. 168; *Prosecutor* v. *Naletilić/Martinović,* Case No. IT-98-34-T, Judgment, 31 March 2003, para. 60.

26 ICTR, *Prosecutor* v. *Akayesu*, Case ICTR-96-4-T, Judgment, 2 September 1998, para. 482.

27 ICTR, *Prosecutor* v. *Akayesu*, Case ICTR-96-4-T, Judgment, 2 September 1998, para. 557; K. Ambos, *supra* n. 6, Art. 25, MN 32; W.A. Schabas, *supra* n. 22, p. 367.

28 The English Term 'to abet': B.A. Garner (ed.), *Black's Law Dictionary* (St. Paul, West Publishing 2007).

situation where there is no control of any kind over the progress of events.[29] In addition, the main perpetrator's attempt at or his/her accomplishment of genocide are not necessary with regard to incitement, in spite of the accessory principle which is usually applicable for the offences of complicity.[30] In fact, the mere act of causing others to commit genocide is sufficient. Incitement therefore becomes an independent offence of endangering large groups of people.[31] It is a different form of participation than instigation. Instigation is therefore at risk of being completely absorbed by aiding and abetting or rather by perpetration by means in cases with hierarchical structures. Some of the forms of criminal participation explicitly laid down in the ICC Statute would therefore simply be dispensable.

In addition to the differentiations presented above, the differentiation between (psychological) aiding and abetting, according to Article 25(3) lit. c ICC Statute, and superior responsibility, according to Article 28 ICC Statute, also presents problems. As pointed out, the attribution of superior responsibility to a form of perpetration is indistinct. Some authors classify the legal concept somewhere between the offences of omission and of complicity; others assign to it a twofold character comprising elements of both. The jurisdiction of the *ad hoc* tribunals intended to assign individual fields of application to aiding and abetting and superior responsibility. For punishment on the grounds of aiding and abetting, the person concerned must be aware of the fact that he/she is providing substantial assistance in the commission of an offence by his/her silence.[32] Then superior responsibility is only left with the case of the superior concerned, who either does not know or does not have a specific notion of the commission of a customary international crime committed by a subordinate.[33] Superior responsibility as a form of direct perpetration is therefore limited to a liability for offences the superior could have gained knowledge of. This liability due to slight unconscious negligence differs from the constitutional prin-

---

[29] ICTR, *Prosecutor* v. *Akayesu*, Case ICTR-96-4-T, Judgment, 2 September 1998, para. 562.

[30] Ibid., paras. 561-562.

[31] Ambos, *supra* n. 1, MN 627; *supra* n. 22, para. 7, MN 48. Its justification makes use of the concept of incitement, because public incitement causes and amplifies the danger of committing a large number of crimes against members of the selected group, cf., K. Ambos, *supra* n. 6, Art. 25, MN 34; G. Werle, *supra* n. 9, MN 725.

[32] O. Triffterer, 'Command Responsibility, Article 28 Rome Statute, an Extension of Individual Criminal Responsibility for Crimes within the Jurisdiction of the Court – Compatible with Article 22, nullum sine lege?', in T. Vogler, *Commemorative Publication* (Heidelberg, C.F. Müller 2004), p. 213 at p. 236; ICTR, *Prosecutor* v. *Ntangerura/Baganbiki/Imanishimwe*, Case ICTR-97-36, Judgment, 25 February 2004, paras. 375 et seq., 'The Appeals Chamber holds that the findings of the Trial Chamber do not permit it to be established Imanishimwe's omission was specifically aimed at giving the soldiers the possibility of going to perpetrate the massacre, or that he was aware of the assistance he was lending them ... The Appeals Chamber holds that the Prosecution failed to demonstrate that the Trial Chamber committed an error when it refused to conclude that Samuel Imanishimwe acted or omitted to act – for example, by not holding back his soldiers – in the knowledge that his act or omission would assist, encourage or lend moral support to the perpetration of crimes against the persons who had taken refuge at the Gashirabwoba football field.'

[33] T. Weigend, *supra* n. 18, p. 999 at p. 1008; K. Weltz, *Die Unterlassungshaftung im Völkerstrafrecht* [The Liability because of Omission in International Criminal Law] (Freiburg, edition iuscrim 2004), p. 261.

ciples of the appropriatness of delinquency and punishment and the idea of individual responsibiliy to such an extent that it can no longer be referred to as justifiable.[34]

I hope that in my previous remarks I have been able to clarify the difficulties which differentiation between the forms of participation implies in general in international criminal law. I would now like to refer to a more specific problem area, i.e., to the problems of participation in genocide.

III. Derivation of a limitation of participation from the criterion of intention in genocide

In outlining the offence of genocide, Article 6 ICC Statute requires the perpetrator's acts to be committed with the intent to destroy, in whole or in part, a national, ethnical, racial or religious group.[35] The intention must relate to the victim's membership of a certain group.[36] The requirement of intention of Article 30 ICC Statute according to which the perpetrator must know of the victim's group membership and must furthermore have a certain general attitude towards the relevant group, does not depend on the foregoing.[37] This, however, does not yet refer to the group member's subjective requirements. It would be possible to argue in the sense of a limited accessoriness,[38] meaning that only those who also display the special criterion of intention besides the fullfilment of the objective and subjective elements of the offence, can be participants. According to the statement of the ICTR, the specific intention of genocide must be present for all the participants who aid and abet in genocide or prepare, organise or accomplish it, besides the forms of participation stated in Article 2/4 lit. a-c ICTR/ICTY Statute.[39] In the other cases of complicity

---

34 Concerning to the discrepancy: O. Triffterer, 'Command Responsibility', in K. Lüderssen, *Commemorative Publication* (Baden-Baden, Nomos 2002), p. 437 at p. 452; O. Triffterer,'Causality, a Separate Element of the Doctrine of Superior Responsibility as Expressed in Article 28 Rome Statute?', in 15 *LeidenJIL* (2002), p. 179 at p. 187.

35 ICTR, *Prosecutor* v. *Ruggiu*, Case ICTR-97-32-T, Judgment, 1 June 2000, para. 14: 'must himself have the specific intent to commit genocide.'

36 R. Clark, 'Subjektive Merkmale im Völkerstrafrecht. Das Römische Statut des internationalen Strafgerichtshofs und die Verbrechenselemente', 114 *ZStW* (2002), p. 372 at p. 396.

37 *Idem*.

38 The validity of limited accessoriness' principles: ICTY, *Prosecutor* v. *Ordic,* Case IT-03-68-T, Judgment, 30 June 2006, para. 269: 'This requires a three-step test: (i) on the side of the principal perpetrator, there must be proof of the conduct which is punishable under the Statute, (ii) from the side of the participant the commission of the principal crime(s) must either be instigated or otherwise aided or abetted, and (iii) with regard to the participant's state of mind, the acts of participation must be performed with the awareness that they will assist the principal perpetrator in the commission of the crime'; speaking of a 'two-stage test': ICTR, *Prosecutor* v. *Kayishema,* Case ICTR-95-1-T, Judgment, 21 May 1999, para. 198; *Prosecutor* v. *Kayishema,* Case ICTR-95-1-A, Judgment of the Appeals Chamber, 1 June 2001, para.186.

39 ICTR, *Prosecutor* v. *Akayesu*, Case ICTR-96-4-T, Judgment, 2 September 1998, para. 546 f.: 'Consequently, where a person is accused of aiding and abetting, planning, preparing or executing genocide, it must be proven that such a person acted with specific genocidal intent, i.e. the intent to destroy, in whole or in part, a national, ethnical, racial or religious group, as such …'

according to Article 2/4(3) lit. e ICTR/ICTY Statute, personal intention is necessary.[40] In the case of participation according to Article 25(3) lit. c ICC Statute, meaning aiding and abetting, the intention of the respective perpetrator must be present correspondingly, however not in respect to Article 25(3) lit. b ICC Statute. In different decisions, the ICTR decided that, with respect to complicity in genocide, the accessory needs not have a personal intention of destruction, he/she only has to have reason to know of the main perpetrator's intention, meaning he/she should be acting with *dolus eventualis*.[41] Other participants only need a sure knowledge of the main perpetrator's genocide, and do not have to implement the intention of destruction in person.[42]

Ambos does not share this opinion.[43] It is a breach of the guilt principle of *dolus eventualis* being sufficient for the accessory's subjective elements of the offence with respect to the main perpetrator's intention of destruction. In cases of aiding and abetting, a sure knowledge of the intention of destruction is in fact necessary. With the special danger of these forms of participating in mind, the personal intention of destruction should be demanded with respect to the punishable nature of indirect perpetration, complicity, direct perpetration, incitement as well as conspiracy.

Only demanding *dolus eventualis* with regard to the main perpetrator's intention of destruction, however, causes less problems concerning the guilt principle than one would expect with respect to Ambos' remarks. The judges of the international criminal courts are obliged to adequately signify the complete criminal and individual responsibility in the penalty.[44] Insofar, the accessor's knowledge of the main perpetrator's intention of destruction, no matter of which nature, can and must be considered for the level of assessment of penalty. At this point it is possible to take the special circumstances of the individual case into account and to balance the differences in the content of injustice. For these reasons, it is not necessary to demand personal intention of destruction for the accessor. With respect to the corresponding element of the main perpetrator, *dolus eventualis* is sufficient.

---

[40] ICTR, *Prosecutor* v. *Akayesu*, Case ICTR-96-4-T, Judgment, 2 September 1998, para. 540: '... the Chamber is of the opinion that an accomplice to genocide need not necessarily possess the dolus specialis of genocide, namely the specific intent to destroy, in whole or in part, a national, ethnic, racial or religious group, as such.'

[41] ICTR, *Prosecutor* v. *Musema*, Case ICTR-96-13-A, Judgment, 27 January 2000, para. 182: 'However, if an accused knowingly aided and abetted in the commission of such a murder while he knew or had reason to know that the principal was acting with genocidal intent, the accused would be an accomplice to genocide, even though he did not share the murderer's intent to destroy the group.'

[42] ICTR, *Prosecutor* v. Musema, Case ICTR-96-13-A, Judgment, 27 January 2000, para. 183: 'In conclusion, the Chamber is of the opinion that an accused is liable for complicity in genocide if he knowingly and voluntarily aided or abetted or instigated one or more persons in the commission of genocide, while knowing that such a person or persons were committing genocide, even though the accused himself did not have the specific intent to destroy, in whole or in part, a national, ethnical, racial or religious group, as such.'

[43] K. Ambos, *supra* n. 6, Art. 25, MN 35; *supra* n. 1, MN 793.

[44] ICTY, *Prosecutor* v. *Delić*, Case IT-04-83, Judgment, 15 September 2008, para. 429 et seq.; ICTY, *Prosecutor* v. *Mucić, et al.*, Case IT-96-21-A, Judgment of the Appeals Chamber, 8 April 2003, para. 46.

IV. Result

It has therefore become clear that the categorisation of the forms of participation is basically provided by Article 25 ICC Statute and also implemented in the jurisdiction of the courts. However, an actual qualitative differentiation proves to be difficult. Within the present context, no complete solution for the problems touched upon can be provided. However, it seems clear to me that a differentiation is only possible by means of specific factual criteria. If, in the future, there might be an increased focus on the search for such criteria, my paper will have served its purpose.

THE SPECIAL INTENT REQUIREMENT IN THE CRIME OF GENOCIDE

Christoph Safferling

Applying an abstract phrase like a legal norm onto a specific case always is a debateable enterprise. Common language often differs from the legal language.[1] Take an example from a domestic environment: We would understand that a mother calls the person who caused the death of her only son a murderer. Yet in legal terms reckless driving might have caused the death, so that we would have to convict for reckless homicide, not for murder. The same is true for genocide. Politicians, historians might call a specific situation genocide whereas by legal terms it was not. When applying a legal norm a court must act in accordance with a commonly accepted methodology and cannot trust that it will eventually 'recognise' genocide, 'when it sees one.'[2] The ICTR Appeals Chamber in the *Karemera* case thus seems to be on slippery grounds, when it declares the fact that genocide occurred in Rwanda in 1994 as common knowledge.[3]

When applying criminal law, particular caution must be adopted. The outcome of a criminal trial is the conviction of an individual for his personal guilt. Motives, personal circumstances and personal capacities of the perpetrator must be taken into account in order to convict. When one aims to construct a collective responsibility, one does not need to analyse the mental circumstances, indeed I find it very questionable whether one can require *mens rea* so to speak of a collective entity. When prosecuting an individual for the crime of genocide aiming at a personal punishment, the culpability of this defendant must be established beyond reasonable doubt.

---

[1] Therefore it is methodically critical when courts rely extensively on an 'ordinary language' concept in the interpretation of certain elements of a norm. Two examples: *R.* v. *Adomato* [1994] 3 *All ER* 79; BGH, 60 *NJW* (2007), p. 524 at pp. 525 et seq.; E. Griew, 'Consistency, Communication and Codification: Reflections of Two Mens Rea Words', in P.R. Glazebrook (ed.), *Reshaping the Criminal Law* (London, Stevens & Sons 1978), p. 57; N. Lacey, 'A Clear Concept of Intention: Elusive or Illusory', 56 *MLR* (1993), p. 621 at p. 623.

[2] Alluding to Lord Lawton in *R.* v. *Bradbourn* (1985) *Cr. App. R.*, p. 181 at p. 183: 'Courts can recognise an elephant when they see one, but may not find it necessary to define them.' A polemic answer to this approach is given by A. Ashworth & A. von Hirsch, 'Recognising Elephants', [1997] *CrimLR*, p. 187.

[3] ICTR, *Prosecutor* v. *Karemera, et al.*, Case ICTR-98-44-AR73(C), Decision on Prosecutor's Interlocutory Appeal of Decision on Judicial Notice, 16 June 2006, para. 35.

C. Safferling and E. Conze (eds.), The Genocide Convention Sixty Years after its Adoption

Modern criminal law attributes responsibility for an act not only according to the naturalistic laws of causality; the commission of a crime always requires a specific subjective reference. An *actus reus* always calls for a *mens rea*, or in other words,[4] the material elements of the crime must be mirrored in its mental elements.[5] Generally speaking, a perpetrator must be aware of the material facts, circumstances and consequences, of his act and must have consciously decided against rightful behaviour. He must have acted knowingly and willingly.

The crime of genocide deviates from this general approach of reciprocity between objective and subjective requirements in that it states as a super-subjective requirement that the perpetrator must have acted with the 'intent to destroy in whole or in part, a national, ethnical, racial or religious group, as such.' In order to illustrate the specific difficulties in the interpretation of the mental elements of the crime of genocide, I want to give the following example:

Persons X and Y enter the house of family A and abduct their two children while the parents are asleep. Is this an act of genocide? The forcible transfer of children of one group to a different group indeed is a punishable act under Article II lit. (e) of the Genocide Convention. Imagine family A belongs to a certain religious group, which lives as a minority in state S, while X and Y belong to the majority in the said state and a different denomination. Is this an act of genocide? We do not know. And why? Because we have, with the information I have given you, no idea what the motives of X and Y were to abduct the two children. And we need to know the motives, because genocide requires that the perpetrator acts in order to destroy in whole or in part a national, ethnic, racial or religious group. As regards X and Y we would need to know whether by abducting the children of family A they intended to destroy the religious minority the family belonged to. From an objective point of view there is no way to differentiate an 'ordinary' child abduction, punishable according to the national laws of state S, from genocide, which would be punishable under international law. The crucial criterion, which separates genocide from other crimes, is a mental criterion. In this paper I will try to explore the scope of the mental side of the crime of genocide. I will argue that attempts to read the crime of genocide in a purely objective manner must fail and that one must carefully discriminate between mental requirements and the problem of proving them being fulfilled.

---

[4] This equals the common law terminology which is based on the phrase stemming from the Institutiones ch 1, Fo 10: 'actus non facit reum nisi mens sit rea'; it has been received into English law by the Leges Henrici Primi, c.5, 28b, which were compiled in 1128; see F. Liebermann, *Über das Englische Rechtsbuch Leges Henrici* [About the English Law Book Leges Henrici] (Halle 1901), pp. 53 et seq.; L.J. Downer, *Leges Henrici, Introduction* (Oxford, Oxford University Press 1972), pp. 1 et seq.; see also F. Pollock & F. Maitland, *History II*, 2nd edn. (Cambridge, Cambridge University Press 1911), p. 475.

[5] German law differentiates between *objektive und subjektive Tatbestandsmerkmale*; see C. Safferling, *Vorsatz und Schuld* [Intention and Culpability] (Tübingen, Mohr Siebeck 2008), pp. 1 et seq. Likewise the ICC Statute knows of material and mental elements of the crime, see, e.g., Art. 30(1) ICC.

I. THE BASIC STRUCTURE AND AIM OF THE CRIME OF GENOCIDE

I.1 Basic structure

When looking at the wording of the crime of genocide as contained in Article 6 ICC Statute (ICCSt) drafted in analogy to Article II of the Genocide Convention,[6] one can *prima facie* observe a clear threefold structure:

(1) There is a list of individual acts namely (a) Killing members of the group; (b) Causing serious bodily or mental harm to members of the group; (c) Deliberately inflicting on the group conditions of life calculated to bring about its physical destruction in whole or in part; (d) Imposing measures intended to prevent births within the group; (e) Forcibly transferring children of the group to another group.
(2) Any of these acts must have been directed against a member of a certain national, ethnical, racial or religious group. This element is often called the 'protected group' requirement.[7]
(3) These acts must have been committed with intent to destroy, in whole or in part, a national, ethnical, racial or religious group, as such.

The individual acts entailed in the list reproduced as (1) above are circumscribed in relative clarity.[8] Whereas killing (a) and the causing of serious harm (b) are terms which are well known to the national criminal law systems, birth prevention (d) and the transferral of children by force (e) are more specifically directed towards a group identity and as such bear a collective connotation.

The remaining alternative of inflicting life-endangering conditions on the group (c) takes in a way the position of a catch-all clause. Circumscribed as 'slow death measures',[9] this requirement embraces acts[10] like deprivation of nutrition or of medical care,[11] expulsion,[12] forced or slave labour.[13] None of these measures need

---

[6] Similarly Art. 4(2) ICTY Statute; Art. 2(2) ICTR Statute; § 6 German Code of Crimes Against International Law.

[7] See K. Ambos, *Internationales Strafrecht* [International Criminal Law], 2nd edn. (Munich, C.H. Beck 2008), § 7, MN 132.

[8] A more detailed analysis of these individual acts can be found in the paper of A. Cassese contained in this volume.

[9] G. Werle, *Völkerstrafrecht* [International Criminal Law], 2nd edn. (Tübingen, Mohr Siebeck 2007), MN 690; B. Lüders, *Die Strafbarkeit von Völkermord nach dem Römischen Statut* [Criminal Liability for Genocide according to the Rome Statute] (Berlin, Academic Publishing House 2004), p. 187; F. Selbmann, *Der Tatbestand des Genozids im Völkerstrafrecht* [Genocide in International Criminal Law] (Leipzig, Leipzig University Press 2003), p. 161.

[10] See also the Elements of Crime pertaining to Art. 6(2) lit. c.

[11] ICTR, *Prosecutor* v. *Akayesu*, ICTR-96-4-T, Judgment, 2 September 1998, para. 506; *Prosecutor* v. *Kayishema/Ruzindana*, ICTR-95-1-T, Judgment, 21 May 1999, paras. 115 et seq.; K. Ambos, *supra* n. 7, MN 139; C. Kreß, in W. Joecks, et al. (eds.), *Münchner Kommentar zum Strafgesesetzbuch* [Commentary on German Criminal Code] (Munich, C.H. Beck 2003), § 220a/§ 6 VStGB, MN 56.

[12] It is debatable whether any expulsion from home falls within the ambit of this provision. The interpretation depends on the view taken on the question of whether genocide requires the physical

have caused the death of a single member of the group; yet the infliction of the life-endangering conditions must be capable of destroying the group entirely or in part. The individual acts are objective criteria, i.e., material elements of the crime. It follows therefrom that terms as 'calculated' in (c) or 'intended' in (d) are not to be interpreted as subjective or mental elements. These terms express the need that the measures imposed are objectively capable of producing the wanted result, i.e., the destruction of the group or parts thereof.[14]

The second structural requirement, i.e., the definition of the 'protected group', is also objective in character. The interpretation of a national, ethnical, racial or religious group can thus not be derived from the point of view of the perpetrator.[15] A different view is taken by Ambos, who opines that genocide being a norm requiring a *special intent* allows for a subjective interpretation of the group constituting elements.[16] Although Ambos is right in stressing the intent requirement in genocide, a purely subjective approach would blur the ambit of the norm. The only reason for charging genocide would then lay in the fact that the perpetrator wanted to inflict harm for discriminatory reasons.[17] Relying on a more objective approach in this regard buttresses the structure of the norm and limits its scope to acts which are at least potentially dangerous to a specific group. Charging for attempted genocide can solve cases in which the perpetrator is mistaken on the 'protected group' requirement.[18]

The Genocide Convention aimes at the protection of certain 'stable' groups, while at the same time it excludes groups which are conceived as being rather 'mobile', like political, economic or social groups.[19] Setting apart the questions of

---

destruction of the group as a whole or in part, or whether the social dissolution of the group or parts thereof is seen as sufficient (see *infra* n. 71). In the case where an expulsion results in a situation where members of the group are left without shelter and nutrition it is commonly accepted that the 3rd alternative is fulfilled. ICTY, *Prosecutor* v. *Krstić*, IT-98-33-T, Judgment, 2 August 2001, para. 543 (653); see also C. Kreß, *supra* n. 11, MN 57.

[13] ICTR, *Prosecutor* v. *Akayesu*, ICTR-96-4-T, Judgment, 2 September 1998, para. 506; ICTR, *Prosecutor* v. *Kayishema/Ruzindana*, ICTR-95-1-T, Judgment, 21 May 1999, paras. 115 et seq.; K. Ambos, *supra* n. 7, MN 139; C. Kreß, *supra* n. 11, MN 56.

[14] See H. Vest, *Genozid durch organisatorische Machtapparate* [Genocide by Organised Groups] (Baden-Baden, Nomos 2002), pp. 124 et seq.; C. Kreß, *supra* n. 11, MN 54 as regards (c) and MN 61 as regards (d); similarly K. Ambos, *supra* n. 7, MNs 140 and 141; G. Werle, *supra* n. 9, MN 693; H. Satzger, *Internationales und Europäisches Strafrecht* [International and European Criminal Law], 3rd edn. (Baden-Baden, Nomos 2009), § 15, MN 21; probably also W.A. Schabas, *Genozid im Völkerrecht* [Genocide in Inernational Law: The Crime of Crimes] (Hamburg, Hamburger Editionen 2003), pp. 222 et seq.

[15] See C. Kreß, *supra* n. 11, MN 33.

[16] K. Ambos, *supra* n. 7, MN 133.

[17] C. Kreß, *supra* n. 11, MN 33; A. Zahar & G. Sluiter, *International Criminal Law. A Critical Restatement* (Oxford, Oxford University Press 2007), pp. 163 et seq.

[18] R. Arnold, 'The *mens rea* of Genocide under the statute of the ICC', 14 *CLF* (2003), pp. 127, 133 et seq.

[19] K. Ambos, *supra* n. 7, MN 132; H. Satzger, *supra* n. 14, MN 11; W.A. Schabas, in O. Triffterer (ed.), *Commentary on the Rome Statute*, 2nd edn. (Munich, C.H. Beck 2008), Art. 6, MN 12; A. Cassese, *International Criminal Law*, 2nd edn. (Oxford, Oxford University Press 2008), p. 130; in greater detail W.A. Schabas, *supra* n. 14, pp. 144 et seq.

whether this differentiation is a sensible one and whether the group-concept of 1948 can still be sustained today, international tribunals had severe difficulties in defining group parameters according to strict objective criteria.[20] The ICTR has thus introduced 'self-identification' of the group and 'identification by others' as relevant in defining an ethnic group.[21] This concept however must not be confused with the subjective approach discussed above. Even if the parameters of 'self-identification' and 'identification by others' allude to psychological processes, these are social and thus empirical circumstances, and in this sense constitute objective criteria.

It is only the third element which bears a special mental element of the crime: the intent to destroy the group as a whole or in parts.[22] It will be explored in the following in what way this specific criterion coins the crime of genocide in the context of national and international criminal law.

I.2 Aim of the norm

The reason for the centrality of the crime of genocide in the context of other core international crimes like crimes against humanity, war crimes and the crime of aggression does not lie in the enormous physical destruction, which as a matter of fact often goes hand in hand with genocide. The crucial point in the crime of genocide, as it has been crafted by Raphael Lemkin in the Genocide Convention, lies in the fact that the physical destruction – foreseen as material elements of the crime – is initiated by the perpetrator with the special purpose to destroy in whole or in part a national, ethnic, racial or religious group.

The international element in the crime of genocide is to be seen in the denial of the right to existence for a specifically defined protected group.[23] This right, however, is one of the backbones of public international law altogether. It comprises several aspects, which are of utmost importance for international law:

(1) The respect for the sovereignty of national states, which lays at the basis of the United Nations structure (Art. 2 No. 1 UN Charter);[24]
(2) The respect for the right to self-determination of peoples;[25]

---

[20] For an analysis of the jurisprudence at the ICTY and ICTR see the contributions of Judge Weinberg de Roca and M. Schuster in this volume. As concerns the Cambodian situation see the contribution of J. Assmann in this volume and S. Williams, 'Genocide: The Cambodian Experience', 5 *ICLR* (2005), p. 447.

[21] ICTR, *Prosecutor* v. *Kayishema/Ruzindana*, ICTR-95-1-T, Judgment, 21 May 1999, para. 98.

[22] F. Chalk & K. Jonassohn, *The History and Sociology of Genocide. Analyses and Case Studies* (New Haven and London, Yale University Press 1990), p. 26.

[23] G. Werle, *supra* n. 9, MN 661.

[24] K. Ipsen, *Völkerrecht* [Public International Law] (Munich, C.H. Beck 2008), § 26, MN 8; W. Graf Vitzthum, *Völkerrecht* [Public International Law] (Berlin, De Gruyter 2007), Chapter I, MN 45; A. Cassese, *International Law* (Oxford, Oxford University Press 2004), p. 48.

[25] Cf., Art. 1 International Covenant on Civil and Political Rights (ICCPR); M. Shaw, *International Law* (Cambridge, Cambridge University Press 2008), p. 251; W. Graf Vitzthum, *supra* n. 24, Chapter 3, MN 314.

(3) The respect for minority rights;[26] and
(4) The respect for the dignity of every human being who is a member of the protected group.[27] This goes hand in hand with the general aim of the UN to 'reaffirm faith in fundamental human rights, in the dignity and worth of the human person'.[28] The individual, however, is not *per se* protected by the Genocide Convention. It is the individual in its collective connectivity who is the possible victim of genocide.[29]

As the physical destruction of human life as such is not a matter for the international community but for national criminal law,[30] the international character of the crime of genocide is contained in the mental element that the perpetrator aims at the destruction of an entity which is protected by international law.[31]

II. Subjective requirements

In the following analysis of the different subjective criteria I will take general recourse to the Statute of the ICC. This document embraces not only the exact definition of the crime of genocide in Article 6 ICCSt, but contains a systematic enumeration of general principles of criminal law. Amongst these principles, we find in Article 30 ICCSt a norm which addresses the mental side of the crime in a general way. The question therefore is, whether this provision is applicable to the crime of genocide in Article 6 ICCSt. The Elements of Crimes take into account

---

[26] See Declaration on the Rights of Persons Belonging to National or Ethnic, Religious and Linguistic Minorities 46/153, 32 *International Legal Materials* (1993), pp. 912 et seq.; Art. 27 ICCPR; Art. 14 European Convention on Human Rights; ECtHR, *Belgian Linguistic* case, Application No. 1474/62, 1677/62, 1691/62, 1769/63, 1994/63, 2126/64, 23 July 1963; *Dudgeon* v. *UK*, No. 7525/76, 4 October 2007; A. Verdross & B. Simma, *Universelles Völkerrecht* [Universal Public International Law] (Berlin, Duncker & Humblodt 1984), §§ 1252 et seq.; W. Graf Vitzthum, *supra* n. 24, Chapter 3, MN 314.

[27] BGHSt 45, 64, 91; see also H. Gropengießer, 'The Criminal Law of Genocide – The German Perspective', 5 *ICLR* (2005), pp. 329, 334 et seq.

[28] UN Charter Preamble.

[29] ICTR, *Prosecutor* v. *Akayesu*, Case ICTR-96-4-T, Judgment, 2 September 1998, para. 521; C. Safferling, 'Das Opfer völkerrechtlicher Verbrechen', 115 *ZStW* (2003), pp. 352.

[30] On another level, international human rights law requires that the destruction of individual human life is being made an issue in national criminal law; see ECtHR, *Streletz, Kessler und Krenz* v. *Germany*, Case 34044/96, 35532/97, 44801/98, 2001-II, § 86; ECtHR, *Mastrometteo* v. *Italy*, Case 2002-VIII, § 89; see J. Meyer-Ladewig, *Hk-EMRK* [Commentary of the European Convention on Human Rights] (Baden-Baden, Nomos 2006), Art. 2, MNs 7-14; O. Lagodny, in J. Renzikowski (ed.), *Die EMRK im Privat-, Straf- und Öffentlichen Recht* [The ECHR in Civil, Criminal and Public Law] (Baden-Baden, Nomos 2004), p. 83; C. Grabenwarter, *Europäische Menschenrechtskonvention* [European Convention on Human Rights], 4th edn. (Munich, C.H. Beck 2009), § 20, MNs 16-19.

[31] A purely outcome oriented approach as formulated by Dadrian in 1975 cannot be reconciled with neither the wording of the convention nor the historic origins; this approach is described by H. Fein, 'Genocide: A Sociological Perspective', in 38 *Current Sociology* (1990), p. 19; see also M. Shaw, *What is Genocide?* (Cambridge and Malden, Polity Press 2007), p. 94.

that Article 30 ICCSt is applicable notwithstanding the special intent requirement. The 'intent to destroy' in Article 6 ICCSt is not a 'built-in' *mens rea* requirement,[32] but an additional mental element, which goes beyond what Article 30(1) understands as general intent. Therefore the subjective side of the crime of genocide is twofold: (1) the ordinary intent, and (2) the special intent.[33]

II.1 **Ordinary intent**

As regards the objective elements of the crime, the perpetrator must act with ordinary intent. According to Article 30 ICCSt it must be proven that the actor had knowledge of the circumstances, meant to engage in the conduct, and meant to cause the consequence or was aware of the fact that the consequence would occur in the ordinary course of events.[34]

The ordinary intent requirement embraces the question of whether the victim is a member of the protected group. The punishable act contained in the list of Article II(a)-(e) Genocide Convention must be directed against members of the group. This means that the individual victim must have been chosen because of the very membership in the relevant group. Arbitrary killings of several individuals do not suffice for genocide but can amount to crimes against humanity.[35] This is a logical consequence of the fact that the individual's life is not comprised by the scope of application of genocide. The group as a supra-individual, social entity, the group as such is protected by the prohibition of genocide.[36] The individual is only protected as a member of the group and not in its own, unique personality.

In the context of Article 30 ICCSt, the question of membership is a circumstance-element, so that by virtue of Article 30(3) ICCSt 'knowledge,' i.e., 'awareness' of the fact, has to be proven with the perpetrator. Should the actor be mistaken in that he is killing a person who in fact is not a member of the group, he is not responsible for genocide but only for attempt of genocide.[37] On the contrary, if the

---

32 See W.A. Schabas, *supra* n. 19, at p. 86.

33 K. Ambos, *supra* n. 7, MNs 131, 151; A. Paul, *Kritische Analyse* [Critical Analysis] (Berlin, Springer 2008), p. 137; G. Werle, *supra* n. 9, MN 707. For the ICTR: P. Akhavan, 'The Crime of Genocide in the ICTR Jurisprudence', 3 *JICJ* (2005), pp. 989, 991 et seq.; W.A. Schabas, *supra* n. 14, pp. 284 et seq.; H. Satzger, *supra* n. 14, MN 15.

34 G. Werle, *supra* n. 9, MN 707; H. Satzger, *supra* n. 14, MN 15; W.A. Schabas, *supra* n. 14, pp. 273 et seq.; A. Cassese, *supra* n. 19, pp. 60 et seq. In greater detail: A. Eser, in A. Cassese, P. Gaeta & J.R.W.D. Jones (eds.), *The Rome Statute – A Commentary* (Oxford, Oxford University Press 2002), pp. 904 et seq.; K. Piragoff & D. Robinson, in O. Triffterer (ed.), *Commentary on the Rome Statute*, 2nd edn. (Munich, C.H. Beck 2008), Art. 30, MNs 9 et seq.

35 ICTY, *Prosector* v. *Jelisić*, Case IT-95-10, Judgment of the Appeals Chamber, 5 July 2001, para. 108; G. Werle, *supra* n. 9, MN 715, who argues that for this reason the killings by the Khmer Rouge did not amout to genocide.

36 K. Ambos, *supra* n. 7, MN 166.

37 ICTR, *Prosecutor* v. *Akayesu*, Case ICTR-96-4-T, Judgment, 2 September 1998, para. 721; K. Ambos, *supra* n. 7, MN 154. This is a complicated and theoretical question of legal attribution of guilt. The attempt is successful in this regard that a person is dead. These cases are therefore not comparable to instances where the attempts to destroy a group did not result in person injury. These cases have indeed seldomly been made an issue, see M. Shaw, *supra* n. 31, p. 94.

perpetrator kills someone who is in fact a member of a protected group, which he does not know, he is guilty of a simple murder, but not of genocide.

As concerns the other material elements of the individual acts, ordinary intent has to be proven. The perpetrator must, e.g., know that he actually kills or harms a person; he must know that the conditions he imposes are indeed life threatening, that the measures imposed are capable of preventing births, or that he is transferring children by force. In this regard, the general rules apply.[38]

II.2 Special intent

The special intent requirement poses several questions. At first, it is questionable whether Article 30(2) ICCSt sets the standard for the interpretation not only for the general, but also for the special intent. Secondly, it must be determined what the conditions for the special intent are. Finally, the contents in relation to the destruction of the group must be addressed.

II.2.a *Applicability of Article 30 ICCSt*

In the search for a definition of the special intent requirement of genocide it is questionable whether Article 30(2) ICCSt is applicable. The wording would at first sight suggest such an interpretation, as Article 6 reads: 'with the intent to destroy'; German: *begangen in der Absicht, zu zerstören*; French: *commis dans l'intention de détruire*. Article 30(2)(b) ICCSt defines the term 'intent' in relation to a consequence, which could be the destruction of a group, that the perpetrator means to cause that consequence or is aware that this consequence will occur in the ordinary course of events.

Despite the alike wording both in Article 30 ICCSt and Article 6 ICCSt, the general definition of Article 30(2)(b) ICCSt is not applicable to the definition of specific intent in genocide.[39] The reason for this commonly accepted result lies in the fact that the crime of genocide does not presuppose a consequence, i.e., a result as regards the destruction of a protected group does not need to materialise, not during the committing of the crime, nor afterwards.[40] The group, which the perpetrator means to destroy, does not need to and hopefully will not be destroyed. The mental requirement of the 'intent to destroy' does not need to have a factual equivalent in the *actus reus* or in the words of the ICC Statute, the material elements, of the crime. Article 30, however, as the general definition of intent, is inapplicable, as it pertains to material elements, i.e., circumstances which are existing in the real world. The very fact that the special intent does not mirror a factual equivalent is expressed in German terminology with *überschießende Innentendenz*.[41]

---

[38] H. Satzger, *supra* n. 14, MN 15.
[39] A. Paul, *supra* n. 33, pp. 250 et seq.
[40] ICTR, *Prosecutor* v. *Akayesu*, ICTR-96-4-T, Judgment, 2 September 1998, para. 497.
[41] K. Ambos, *supra* n. 7, MN 151; C. Kreß, *supra* n. 11, MN 88.

II.2.b *Interpretation of the special intent*[42]

It follows from the aforesaid that an autonomous interpretation of the intent requirement in Article 6 ICCSt is necessary.[43] In order to find such an autonomous concept we can take a look at the Elements of Crimes. It is stated therein, that 'knowledge' of the circumstances is a basic requirement for the specific intent also as is clarified by the Elements of Crimes. What else is required 'will need to be decided by the Court on a case-by-case basis.'[44] It can be inferred from this statement that 'knowledge' is the bottom line for the 'special intent' as a necessary requisite. Whether it is at the same time a sufficient requisite is heavily disputed. Whereas some authors (II.2.b.1) opine that 'knowledge of destruction' should be enough to establish the special intent requirement ('knowledge-based interpretation'),[45] others (II.2.b.2) argue in favour of an interpretation which would require in addition a specific will to achieve the destruction of the group.[46]

II.2.b.1 Knowledge-based interpretation

The difficulty with any 'knowledge-based interpretation'[47] is the question of how to construct the point of reference. Knowledge can only pertain to in fact existing circumstances. This means that the perpetrator can have knowledge as regards the existence of the protected group, he can have knowledge as to the membership of the victim in the group. The destruction, however, does not need to have taken place; knowledge as regards 'destruction' can therefore only be constructed in two ways:

(a) The crime of genocide is understood as assuming an ongoing destruction of a protected group of which the perpetrator knows as an implicit requirement;[48] or

---

[42] In the jurisprudence of the UN tribunals as well as in legal writing, the terms special intent, specific intent, *dolus specialis* are used as synonyms. Critical in this regard, A. Paul, *supra* n. 33, p. 249.

[43] C. Kreß, *supra* n. 11, MN 83, who states that the special intent requirement in genocide is *interpretationsoffen*, open for free interpretation. H. Vest, *supra* n. 14, pp. 104 et seq. argues that preconcieved concepts of *mens rea* should not be transferred to the special intent requirement in genocide.

[44] Elements of Crimes Art. 6 Introduction.

[45] See, e.g., A.K.A. Greenawalt, 'Rethinking Genocidal Intent: The Case for a Knowledge-Based Interpretation', 99 *Colum. L. R.* (1999), p. 2259 at p. 2288; H. Vest, *supra* n. 14, p. 101; C. Kreß, *supra* n. 11, MN 86; A. Paul, *supra* n. 33, p. 255.

[46] K. Ambos, *Der Allgemeine Teil des Völkerstrafrechts* [General Part of International Criminal Law] (Berlin, Duncker & Humblodt 2002), p. 411; R. Clark, 'Subjektive Merkmale im Völkerstrafrecht: Das Römische Statut des Internationalen Strafgerichtshofs und die Verbrechenselemente', 114 *ZStW* (2002), pp. 372, 396; A. Gil Gil, 'Die Tatbestände der Verbrechen gegen die Menschlichkeit und des Völkermordes im Römischen Statut des Internationalen Strafgerichtshofs', 112 *ZStW* (2000), pp. 381, 393; G. Werle, *supra* n. 9, MN 72.

[47] K. Ambos, *supra* n. 7, MN 151.

[48] A. Gil Gil, *supra* n. 46, pp. 281, 295; A.K.A. Greenawalt, *supra* n. 45, pp. 2259, 2265 et seq.; W.A. Schabas, *supra* n. 32, p. 32; O. Triffterer, 'Kriminalpolitische und dogmatische Überlegungen zum Entwurf gleichlautender 'elements of crimes' für alle Tatbestände des Völkermordes' in B. Schünemann et al. (eds.), *Festschrift für Claus Roxin* (Berlin, De Gruyter 2001), p. 1422 at pp. 1438 et seq.

(b) The crime of genocide is understood as presupposing a collective (realistic) plan to destroy a protected group, of which the perpetrator knows.[49]

It should be clear that both ways encompass a prerequisite which goes beyond the wording of the norm. This is *per se* no detriment to the interpretation of a norm as long as the punishability is not broadened thereby. However I would be cautious in implementing an objective test like the two mentioned, for mainly three reasons.

(1) The problem with amending the norm by implementing further and unwritten objective requirements is that the basic structure of the norm is substantially modified. The basic ground for the criminal responsibility is moving away from the individual's motivation to act towards a participation in a collective enterprise. A person who is accused for genocide would in fact be accused of willingly participating in the collective attempt to destroy a certain protected group. This interpretation would modify 'genocide' from a 'hate crime' to a 'systematic crime.'[50]
(2) In many instances, such an objective test would indeed broaden the scope of the crime of genocide. Any guard in a concentration camp, established to humiliate and physically harm members of a protected group, would be guilty of genocide as long as he is aware of the fact that there is an overall plan to destroy the group in whole or in part, even if he acts only in order to fulfil his duty as a member of the armed forces and does not himself aim at the destruction of this group. In my eyes, such a person can only be held responsible for abetting in genocide.[51] This is without prejudice regarding the responsibility for crimes against humanity.
(3) If the knowledge-based approach is pertained to a destruction plan of a collective as is the case in (b) above, three further questions will arise: (1) what constitutes a community able to put forward a genocidal intent, (2) can a collective form an intent at all or is it not the case that the collective intent comes about by summing up the relevant wills of individuals, and (3) if the collective intent is not more than the sum of the individuals' wills, why does it suffice to know of the collective intent in order to commit genocide without being part of the collective will as such. This would result in a twofold system: there would be perpetrators who actually do have genocidal intent which would form the collective genocidal intent; at the same time there would be individuals who only know of the collective will to destroy, but do not aim at the destruction

---

[49] C. Kreß, *supra* n. 11, MN 86.

[50] The proposal for an amendment of the crime of genocide by A. Paul, *supra* n. 33, at p. 273, attempts to embrace both approaches: the perpetrator acts either with the goal to destroy or knowing that the certain result will be the destruction of a protected group. It is also punishable as genocide when the person acts in furtherance of a collective crime knowing that the goal or certain result to follow from collective crime will be the destruction of the protected group.

[51] See also K. Ambos, *supra* n. 7, MN 155; A. Bummel & F. Selbmann, 'Genozid – Eine Zwischenbilanz der Rechtsprechung des Internationalen Strafgerichtshofs für das ehemalige Jugoslawien', 1 *Journal of International Law of Peace and Armed Conflict* (2006), p. 60 at p. 67.

> themselves.[52] In my view, which is supported by the UN tribunals' jurisprudence, this equals the differentiation between perpetrator and abetter.[53] Consequently from his point of view of a knowledge-based interpretation, Kreß argues in favour of annihilating the difference between perpetrator and abetter as concerns the crime of genocide. Both the person who gives the order and the person who executes the order to commit genocide are meant to fall within the ambit of the crime of genocide as perpetrators.[54]

Perhaps such an objective test influences evidentiary problems in a positive way for the prosecution, and, not surprisingly, the ICTY prosecutor has argued in favour of the knowledge-based approach in the case against Jelisić.[55] But evidence problems cannot be answered by amending the elements of the crime and by lowering the mental requirements. To deflect the actor's goal from certain objective circumstances is not unusual regarding the question of mental elements of the crime.

II.2.b.2 Will-based interpretation

The jurisprudence has thus far desisted from applying an objective test to the special intent requirement.[56] The ICTR has stated:[57]

> 'Special intent of a crime is the specific intention, required as a constitutive element of the crime, which demands that the *perpetrator* clearly seeks to produce the act charged'[58] [emphasis added].

The ICTY follows this view when it stated: genocide is characterised by 'act committed with the goal of destroying all or part of a group.'[59] These interpretations aim at the individual's will and do not presuppose a collective genocidal intent.[60]

---

52 H. Vest, 'Humanitätsverbrechen – Herausforderung für das Individualstrafrecht?', 113 *ZStW* (2001), pp. 482 et seq.

53 ICTR, *Prosecutor* v. *Akayesu*, Case ICTR-96-4, Judgment, 2 September 1998, paras. 544-547; ICTY, *Prosecutor* v. *Jelisić*, Case IT-95-10-T, Judgment, 5 July 1999, para. 86; also K. Ambos, *supra* n. 7, MN 152; furthermore as regards German Law in general, H. Gropengießer, *supra* n. 27, p. 339.

54 C. Kreß, *supra* n. 11, MN 88 argues that the subjective differentiation between perpetrator (*Täter*) and abetter (*Teilnehmer*) has outlived itself and that the individual acts as in lit. (a), (b), (d) and (e) entail typical acts of an abetter.

55 ICTY, *Prosecutor* v. *Jelisić*, Case IT-95-10-T, Judgment, 5 July 1999, paras. 84 et seq., with reference to Prosecutor's pre-trial brief, 19 November 1998, para. 3.1, pp. 7-8.

56 G. Werle, *supra* n. 9, MN 712.

57 A summary of the ICTR jurisprudence in this regard can be found at A. Paul, *supra* n. 33, at pp. 242 et seq.

58 ICTR, *Prosecutor* v. *Akayesu*, Case ICTR-96-4-T, Judgment, 2 September 1998, paras. 497, 518. The wording of the judgment is misleading as it presupposes that the individual act has to be sought after, which is not the case.

59 ICTY, *Prosecutor* v. *Krstić*, Case IT-98-33, Judgment, 2 August 2001, para. 571. For a summary of the jurisprudence of the ICTY see A. Paul, *supra* n. 33, pp. 244 et seq.

60 C. Kreß, *supra* n. 11, MN 80 claims that it is not clear whether the point of reference lays in the individual or the collective.

Otherwise the ICTY could not have meditated the 'lone genocidal maniac',[61] as it has done in the *Jelisić* case:

> '[I]t is a priori possible to conceive that the accused [i.e., Jelisić] harboured the plan to exterminate an entire group without this intent having been supported by any organisation in which other individuals participated.'[62]

Also Kreß does not deny that there are cases in which one person alone could commit genocide on his own without being supported by a collective, be it the case that he is in possession of weapons of mass destruction, or that his single genocidal act triggers large scale atrocities.[63] The underlying concern of the knowledge-based approach is thus not the question of whether the crime of genocide presupposes a collective genocidal policy, but the question of how the individual will can be proven.[64]

> 'The Trial Chamber observes, however, that it will be very difficult in practice to provide proof of the genocidal intent of an individual if the crimes committed are not widespread and if the crime charged is not backed by an organisation or a system.'[65]

I will come back to this issue at the end of the paper.

II.2.c *Individual requirements*

Having set the general line for the interpretation of the specific intent in genocide it is now necessary to differentiate between the individual requirements which Article 6 ICCSt enumerates.

II.2.c.1 Destroy

The special intent must pertain to the destruction of a group. Whereas it is commonly accepted that the destruction must only be intended and not be achieved,[66] the question of whether the destruction must be physical or biological is heavily debated. The German *Bundesgerichtshof* (Federal Court of Justice)[67] and the Ger-

---

61 Rather polemic W.A. Schabas, 'The Jelisic Case and the Mens Rea of the Crime of Genocide', 14 *LeidenJIL* (2001), p. 125 at p. 138.

62 ICTY, *Prosecutor* v. *Jelisić*, Case IT-95-10-T, Judgment, 5 July 1999, para. 100 with reference to P.N. Drost, *The Crime of State, Vol II: Genocide* (Leiden, A.W. Sythoff 1959), p. 85.

63 C. Kreß, *supra* n. 11, MN 78; consenting A. Paul, *supra* n. 33, pp. 261 et seq.

64 See H.G. van der Wilt, 'Genocide, Complicity in Genocide and International v. Domestic Jurisdiction', 4 *JICJ* (2006), p. 239 at pp. 241 et seq.

65 ICTY, *Prosecutor* v. *Jelisić*, Case IT-95-10-T, Judgment, 5 July 1999, para. 101. Jelisić was not convicted for genocide by reason of benefit of doubt.

66 K. Ambos, *supra* n. 7, MN 156; G. Werle, *supra* n. 9, MN 712; C. Kreß, *supra* n. 11, MN 78 claims on the basis of a knowledge-based approach that there needs to be a realistic option that the destruction is achievable.

67 BGHSt 45, 64(80).

man *Bundesverfassungsgericht* (Federal Constitutional Court)[68] in particular has ruled that, in order to fulfil the requirements of genocidal intent, it suffices to attempt the destruction of the social existence of a group.[69] In contrast, the international tribunals adhere to a narrow interpretation.[70] The ICJ concurs, when stating:

> '[a] clear distinction must be drawn between physical destruction and mere dissolution of a group. The expulsion of a group or part of a group does not in itself suffice for genocide.'[71]

With due respect for the authority of the international jurisdiction and for the general need to narrow the ambit of the crime of genocide, I would suggest that the social destruction of a protected group can amount to genocide for mainly four reasons:

(a) A collective is a virtual reality independent from the life of the individual member. Therefore a group can only exist and be formed in a social context, i.e., it is defined and structured by a social context.[72] Any group is made to be a group by a constructed discrimination between one collective and another.[73] As Martin Shaw opines:

> 'Nigel Eltringham suggested, "from man's ever-present disposition, a taken-for granted assumption (or 'habit of the mind') that social distinctions are *a priori*, natural, self-evident, necessary and always present." If, however, we are to escape what René Lemarchand calls the "confinement of the apparently obvious," we must recognise that such classifications are made/invented by us.'[74]

---

68 BVerfG, 54 *NJW* (2001), p. 1848 at p. 1850.

69 See also K. Ambos & S. Wirth, in H. Fischer, C. Kreß & S. Lüder (eds.), *International and National Prosecution of Crimes under International Law* (Berlin, Berliner Wissenschaftsverlag 2001), p. 791; C. Safferling, 'Wider die Feinde der Humanität', 41 *JuS* (2001), p. 735 at p. 738. No violation of Art. 7 § 1 ECHR could be found, see ECtHR, *Jorgić* v. *Germany*, 12 July 2007, paras. 113 et seq.; see G. Werle, 'Deutsche Rechtsprechung zur Zerstörungsabsicht beim Völkermord und die Europäische Menschenrechtskonvention', in M. Hettinger, et al. (eds.), *Festschrift für Wilfried Küper* (Heidelberg, C.F. Müller 2007), pp. 675 et seq.

70 ICTY, *Prosecutor* v. *Krstić*, IT-98-33, Judgment, 2 August 2001, para. 580. For an overall analysis see A. Paul, *supra* n. 33, pp. 289-298 who finally agrees with the narrow interpretation; concurring C. Kreß, *supra* n. 11, MN 72.

71 ICJ, *Bosnia and Herzegovina* v. *Serbia and Montenegro* ('Case concerning the application of the Convention on the Prevention and Punishment of the Crime of Genocide'), 26 February 2007, para. 190; A. Gattini, 'Evidentiary Issues in the ICJ's Genocide Judgment', 5 *JICJ* (2007), p. 889; F. Meyer, 'Die Verantwortlichkeiten von Vertragsstaaten nach der Völkermordkonventionen', 8 *HRRS* (2007), p. 218.

72 A. Zick, in T. Bonacker (ed.), *Sozialwissenschaftliche Konflikttheorien. Eine Einführung* [Conflict Theories in Social Sciences. An Introduction], 4th edn. (Wiesbaden, VS Publishing House for Social Studies 2008), pp. 409 et seq.

73 D.D. Dutton, *The Psychology of Genocide, Massacres, and Extreme Violence. Why 'Normal' People Come to Commit Atrocities* (Westport, Praeger 2007), pp. 96 et seq.

74 M. Shaw, *supra* n. 31, p. 104.

In accepting criteria as 'self-identification' and 'identification by others' for the definition of a protected group, the UN tribunals have identified the social construction as relevant for the group-definition.[75]

(b) When looking at corporate law, we can draw an analogy: the liquidation of a company leaves the individual (former) member alive. Even if – for the sake of the argument – the parameter of what constitutes a group can be involuntary in nature, i.e., the individual does not have a choice as to which ethnical or racial group he or she belongs, this is, however, at least in a pluralistic society only partly true for the religious or national groups, which – in theory – leave a choice in 'membership.'[76]

(c) The individual acts as enumerated in Article II(a) to (e) Genocide Convention and Article 6 ICCSt, do in general presuppose the physical-biological destruction of the protected group. However the causing of serious bodily or mental harm lacks a clear link to the physical-biological destruction; in the contrary, the mental harm requirement points at a psychological context.[77]

(d) It is possible and necessary to differentiate between the individual act in its material and mental perspective as enumerated in Article II(a) to (e) Genocide Convention and the specific intent requirement. While the former needs to encompass the physical destruction, when, e.g., a member of the group is being killed as Article II(a) suggests, the latter does not necessarily need to be concerned with the same physical impact on the entire group.[78] In other words, it is possible to kill a member of the group aiming at the social destruction of the group.

(e) Finally, including the social existence of a group fulfils the aim of the Genocide Convention to protect minorities and preserve their survival for the international community.[79]

For these reasons it seems that the social dissolution of a protected group suffices in the context of the special intent requirement to constitute genocide.

II.2.c.2 In whole or in part

The critical point as regards the requirement that a partial destruction of the protected group is enough for establishing genocidal intent is the interpretation of the words 'in part.' The perpetrator does not need to aim at the destruction of the entire group, the definition of which is part of the material elements of the crime of genocide.[80]

---

75 See *supra* n. 21.
76 C. Kreß, *supra* n. 11, MN 47.
77 G. Werle, *supra* n. 9, MN 718.
78 K. Ambos, *supra* n. 7, MN 157.
79 See H. Vest, *supra* n. 14, p. 99; G. Werle, *supra* n. 9, MN 718.
80 See *supra* n. 15.

One could interpret the part of a group in a quantitative or a qualitative way, or in a combination of these two.[81] It should be clear from the wording, that as a general bottom line, the perpetrator's intent must always pertain to a group of substantial quantity. The murder of a single person, even if it is the charismatic leader of the group, will not amount to genocidal intent.[82] An exact number cannot be given in principle, but is depending on a case-by-case evaluation, as the ICTY has rightly pointed out in the *Krstić* case.[83] Such a decision is also required as to the exact definition and the size of the protected group.[84] Geographical borders might determine 'a part' of a group that the perpetrator aims to destruct, e.g., all Bosnian Muslims living in Srebrenica.[85] As long as the geographical scope is not zoomed down to villages and hamlets, this approach seems to be acceptable.[86] But is it feasible to construct further subgroups and identify a specific quality of the group, e.g., all male members, as a relevant entity? It has to be differentiated between the actually targeted group with regard to the individual act enumerated in Article 6(2) lit. (a)-(e) ICCSt and the *dolus specialis* requirement. Therefore it has to be shown that the perpetrator aims at destroying the entire or a substantial part of the group. The killing of all procreative male members of a group might indicate that the perpetrator indeed did intend the annihilation of the entire group.[87] If on the other hand, the killings were conducted in order to weaken the enemy's resistance, the perpetrator would lack genocidal intent, but would certainly be chargeable for crimes against humanity.

III. The proof of special intent

The main aim of a criminal trial is to establish whether the accused is guilty as charged. Evidence for the relevant elements, both material and mental, needs to be presented to an extent that proves the guilt beyond reasonable doubt. The mental elements of the crime are particularly critical in this regard. International criminal law, the crime of genocide in particular, is no exception to this general problem. It does not surprise that the ICTR states rather fatalistically:

---

81 C. Kreß, *supra* n. 11, MN 73.

82 Ibid., MN 76.

83 ICTY, *Prosecutor* v. *Krstić*, Case IT-98-33-A, Judgment of the Appeals Chamber, 19 April 2004, para. 14.

84 ICTY, *Prosecutor* v. *Krstić*, Case IT-98-33-A, Judgment of the Appeals Chamber, 19 April 2004, para. 13; K. Ambos, *supra* n. 7, MN 161; C. Kreß, *supra* n. 11, MN 76.

85 ICTY, *Prosecutor* v. *Jelisić*, Case IT-95-10, Judgment, 14 December 1999, para. 83; ICTY, *Prosecutor* v. *Krstić*, IT-98-33-T, 2 August 2001, Judgment, para. 590; BGHSt 45, 64(78); BGH, 54 *NJW* (2001), p. 2728.

86 Critical in this regard C. Kreß, *supra* n. 11, MN 77; K. Ambos, *supra* n. 7, MNs 163-65; A. Paul, *supra* n. 33, pp. 315-318.

87 ICTY, *Prosecutor* v. *Krstić*, Case IT-98-33-A, Judgment of the Appeals Chamber,19 April 2004, para. 19.

'Intent is a mental factor, which is difficult, even impossible, to determine.'[88]

But such fatalism is unnecessary. It is true that, unless there is a confession on the side of the accused,[89] the court will not know for sure what the accused knew or what he intended by his act. What courts do is that they operate on a high level of probability. This is achieved by looking at the factual circumstances of the case, the personality of the accused and the development of the act in question. It is against this yardstick that the court evaluates the probability that the accused did not want the result to come about or was not aware of a certain relevant circumstance. Therefore a court will convict a person for serious bodily harm who stabs another person with a butterfly-knife into the abdomen, as it is highly unlikely that the attacker did not want to harm the attacked person. In other words, he is convicted because due to the objective development of the act he must have intended to violate that person.

The same epistemological method – *dolus ex re*[90] – is applied when it comes to determine genocidal intent. Therefore, all available circumstantial evidence needs to be taken into account in order to suggest special intent to commit genocide.[91] This circumstantial evidence can be summarised in three groups: (1) evidence concerning *genocidal policy*, i.e., the existence of an overall destruction plan, a policy of persecution;[92] (2) evidence pertaining to the *conduct* itself, as the gravity of the crime, the systematic in the attack; and (3) evidence concerning the *person* of the accused, as his political role, his personality, his utterances both before and after the act in question, similar discriminating activity directed against the protected group.

The jurisprudence of the international tribunals suggests such an overall evaluation of circumstantial evidence.[93] Whereas policy-centered evidence (1) and conduct-centered evidence (2) will show whether there was a general genocidal intent, only person-centered evidence (3) will show whether the accused actually is to be blamed for genocidal intent himself. Should evidence as in group (3) determine that the accused knew of the overall genocidal policy but did not embrace the policy-goals himself, he can only be held responsible for aiding and abetting in genocide, but not for genocide itself.

The determination of the genocidal intent is a delicate issue. A careful evaluation is necessary on the basis of as much evidentiary material as possibly available. But

---

88 ICTR, *Prosecutor* v. *Akayesu*, ICTR-96-4-T, Judgment, 2 September 1998, para. 523.

89 A guilty plea will not help in this regard, as it has a completely different function in a procedural system; see C. Safferling, *Towards an International Criminal Procedure* (Oxford, Oxford University Press 2003), pp. 272-276.

90 K. Volk, '*dolus ex re*', in F. Haft, et al. (eds.), *Festschrift für Arthur Kaufmann* (Heidelberg, C.F. Müller 1993), p. 613 at p. 619.

91 See K. Ambos, *supra* n. 7, MN 153.

92 As regards the ICC situation in the DR Congo, see J.M. Kalere, 'Genocide in the African Great Lakes States', 5 *ICLR* (2005), p. 463 at p. 477.

93 As the evaluation of the evidence in the case ICTY, *Prosecutor* v. *Jelisić*, Case IT-95-10, paras. 102 et seq. suggests.

the legal method of how to produce a determination of special intent if direct evidence is unavailable is clear: *dolus* is to be inferred from the material elements of the crime and the political and personal circumstances of the act.

IV. Summary and future prospects

To summarise: I did not speak about the policy-implications within the crime of genocide. The little example was chosen in order to demonstrate mental element requirements. The crime of genocide presupposes a certain scale, isolated incidents will not be covered by the norm. But this was not my topic. My intention was to show two things: The genocidal intent is to be dealt with as a separate requirement. As we cannot look into people's brains, this intent must be inferred from objective facts. Yet it must be carefully observed that one does not overlook the personal side of the evidence. Without clear person-centered evidence indicating that the defendant did indeed embrace the goals of a genocidal policy, he cannot be convicted for the crime of genocide, which is reserved for the ultimate international criminal, aiming at the wiping out of a protected minority.

Part Four
Case Studies

THE CHALLENGES OF GENOCIDE TRIALS: 'THE CAMBODIAN SITUATION'

Jürgen Aßmann*

Justice in political matters is more tenuous than in any other field of jurisprudence, because it can so easily become a mere farce.[1]

After ten years' negotiation between multiple actors and numerous states, on July 1, 2006,[2] the newly created, but controversial, Extraordinary Chambers in the Courts of Cambodia ('ECCC' or 'Court') finally began to seek accountability for the crimes committed during the period of Democratic Kampuchea.[3] Although the subject of an international treaty between the United Nations and the Cambodian government concerning the prosecution of these crimes ('RGC-UN Agreement'),[4] the ECCC is nonetheless a Cambodian – and not an international – institution as a consequence of its establishment under domestic law.[5] As a hybrid tribunal, the ECCC is uniquely

* For many hours of fruitful discussions concerning the topic, I would like to thank my colleague and friend Mr. Alexander Bates, formerly Senior Assistant Prosecutor in the ECCC. Invaluable assistance in the research for this article has been given to me by Sonja Schiller, J.D., Washington University in St. Louis School of Law.

[1] O. Kirchheimer, *Political Justice: The Use of Legal Procedure for Political Ends* (Princeton, Princeton University Press 1961).

[2] Phuong Pham, et al., *So We Will Never Forget: A Population-Based Survey on Attitudes About Social Reconstruction and The Extraordinary Chambers in the Courts of Cambodia* (Berkeley, California, Human Rights Center, University of California, Berkeley 2009), p. 16. Proceedings before the ECCC started in June 2007, when core judicial personnel took their offices at the Court in Phnom Penh.

[3] Between 1975 and 1979, at least 1.7 million people perished during what is colloquially – rather than legally – known as the Cambodian genocide. Legal classification of the crimes committed in Cambodia remains problematic, but it is beyond the scope of this article to discuss. See W.A. Schabas, 'Problems of International Codification – Were the Atrocities in Cambodia and Kosovo Genocide?', 35 *New Eng. L. Rev.* (2001), p. 287. See also P. Wald, in *Justice Initiatives: The Extraordinary Chambers* (Open Society Institute, April 2006), p. 85. Nearly thirty years after the atrocities, in 1997, the United Nations Commission on Human Rights (UNCHR) finally called for the UN Secretary General to 'examine any request by Cambodia for assistance' concerning prosecution of past crimes committed by the Khmer Rouge. See *Situation of Human Rights in Cambodia*, UN Commission on Human Rights Resolution, 1997/49, at para. 12.

[4] See Agreement Between the United Nations and the Royal Government of Cambodia Concerning the Prosecution Under Cambodian Law of Crimes Committed During the Period of Democratic Kampuchea, entered into force on 29 April 2005, UN Doc. A/RES57/228B (Annex) (13 May 2003).

[5] G. Acquaviva, 'New Paths in International Criminal Justice? The Internal Rules of the Cambodian Extraordinary Chambers', 6 *JICJ* (2008), p. 130; see Law on Establishment of Extraordinary Chambers in the Courts of Cambodia for the Prosecution of Crimes Committed During the Period of Democratic Kampuchea (NS/RKM/1004/006), including amendments promulgated on 27 October 2004 (hereinafter, Law).

C. Safferling and E. Conze (eds.), The Genocide Convention Sixty Years after its Adoption

situated as a domestic court that applies domestic law, international law, and its own internal rules, and that exercises jurisdiction over grave breaches of the Geneva Conventions, genocide, crimes against humanity, and other enumerated crimes committed by the senior leaders of Democratic Kampuchea and those most responsible between 17 April 1975 and 6 January 1979.[6]

As a consequence of the many compromises made during the negotiations leading up to the RGC-UN Agreement, the Court's complex structure inhibits the institution from accomplishing its stated goals, using criminal prosecution as primary tool to achieve justice. Pervasive corruption and mismanagement allegations have marred the Court's reputation and have threatened its continued funding,[7] and complex legal, procedural, and evidentiary issues are challenging the Court. Victims enjoy unprecedented participation rights, which, however, are feared by some to impede the efficiency of the judicial process. In light of these challenges, the trials, themselves, may have limited potential as tools to achieve the ECCC's goals of justice and national reconciliation, implying that true justice may only be achieved outside of the courtroom through a more comprehensive process of national reconciliation and education.

I. The structure of the Extraordinary Chambers

Situated within the existing Cambodian justice system, the ECCC has no exact parallel amongst any of the world's other criminal tribunals specifically established to address accountability for mass atrocities. The Court's unique structure results from significant compromises between the negotiating parties, the United Nations and the Cambodian government. The ECCC is a domestic court, established pursuant to Cambodian law and operating within the pre-existing Cambodian judicial framework, but internationalised in composition. The majority of the ECCC's judicial and administrative personnel are Cambodian, and the Court uses Cambodian criminal procedure modelled on the civil law system, with prosecutions initiated by prosecutors but transferred to investigating judges who follow the inquisitive legal tradition. To accommodate the equal participation of Cambodian and international staff, the Court has one national and one international co-prosecutor and one national and one international co-investigating judge.[8] The co-investigating judges jointly share the responsibility of investigations, with the defence, the civil parties, and the prosecution holding the right to request investigative action. The ECCC's chambers consist of one Trial Chamber, comprised of three Cambodian and two foreign judges, and a Supreme Court Chamber, comprised of four Cambodian and

---

[6] See Law. To date, however, four of the five Charged Persons currently under investigation have been charged with genocide. The indictment against the Chairman of the most notorious former torture and execution center in Phnom Penh, S-21, charges him with crimes against humanity and war crimes.

[7] See most recently Open Society Justice Initiative, Recent Developments at the ECCC, March 2010 Update, www.justiceinitiative.org.

[8] See Law, Arts. 16 and 23.

three foreign judges.[9] Decisions can only be passed through the concurrence of at least one international judge: in the Pre-Trial and the Trial Chamber, decisions may be passed through a 'super-majority' of four judges; in the Supreme Court Chamber, a 'super-majority' of five judges is necessary.[10] The Pre-Trial Chamber hears appeals by the parties and regulates disputes between the co-prosecutors and the co-investigating judges. Significantly, the resolution of these intra-office conflicts is not bound by time constraints or by legal criteria.[11] The hybrid structure of the ECCC places it in a unique position in relation to the other criminal tribunals and at once ensures national lawyers' and judges' significant participation in the judicial process, while at the same time hindering the Court's efficiency and effectiveness.

The question of who will actually be prosecuted is currently under scrutiny by the Pre-Trial Chamber. The Court's jurisdiction limits prosecution to 'senior leaders of Democratic Kampuchea' or those 'most responsible [for serious crimes],' meaning that thousands of lower-ranking Khmer Rouge cadre will not face any form of criminal justice for crimes they may have committed. Furthermore, temporal jurisdiction is strictly limited to crimes committed between 17 April 1975 and 6 January 1979, effectively precluding any possible prosecution of non-Cambodian suspects.[12] Ultimately, the total number of accused persons will probably be only between five and one dozen. Jurisdictional restrictions on whom the Court may prosecute shapes what justice – according to the Court's mandate – could mean for Cambodia.

II. Challenges faced by the Extraordinary Chambers

II.1 Political challenges

Since the late 1990s, the interpretation of the personal jurisdiction of the ECCC has caused significant debate. Of particular concern in the Cambodian domestic theatre is that the Court might cast its net too far. Although scholars widely agree that no current members of the Cambodian government meet the jurisdictional criteria,[13] there is another group of former Khmer Rouge officials potentially responsible for atrocity crimes whom the current government is not interested in prosecuting. Pur-

---

[9] Law, Art. 9.

[10] Law, Art. 14; see also S. Worden, 'An Anatomy of the Extraordinary Chambers', in J. Ramji & B. van Schaak (eds.), *Bringing the Khmer Rouge to Justice: Prosecuting Mass Violence Before the Cambodian Courts* (Lewiston, The Edwin Mellen Press 2005).

[11] See Law, Art. 20; see also Internal Rules (Rev. 2), Rule 71, 5 September 2008 (hereinafter, Internal Rules).

[12] This will therefore prevent examination of the actions of the United States, China, or Thailand. See B. Kiernan, 'Conflict in Cambodia, 1945-2002', 34 *Critical Asian Studies* (2002), pp. 483-484; see also T. Fawthrop & H. Jarvis, *Getting Away with Genocide? Exclusive Justice and the Khmer Rouge Tribunal* (London, Pluto Press 2004), pp. 5-6.

[13] See S. Heder, 'The Defendants', in *Justice Initiatives: The Extraordinary Chambers* (Open Society Institute, April 2006), p. 56.

suant to Prime Minister Hun Sen's so-called 'win-win-strategy' in the late 1990s, which led to the final collapse of the Khmer Rouge-driven civil war, these officials are said to having been granted informal promises of non-prosecution. It is evident that these domestic issues cannot be decided in a vacuum by ECCC judges and prosecutors.

The Cambodian government's influence over the Court's judicial appointments, combined with pervasive allegation of corruption and mismanagement at the Court, threaten to undermine the Court's reputation and effectiveness and to dissuade international donors from further funding the Court's activities. Critics have long argued that the prosecution of the Khmer Rouge under the current structure of the Court jeopardises not only the requirement of a fair trial for the accused, but also the credibility of the international criminal legal system. By wielding significant control over the selection of judges (both Cambodian and foreign) and the appointment of local investigators who work for the investigating judges and prosecutors, the Cambodian government exerts political influence over the structure of the Court and is believed by many to continue to influence key judicial personnel, even after their appointment.[14] In spring 2009, government spokesman Khieu Kanharith has publicly declared that foreign judges at the Court are in Cambodia just for the money, and intend to stay as long as possible, using further prosecutions as a vehicle for this.[15] Since its inception, the Court has been confronted with allegations of corruption, particularly of kickbacks on salaries of national staff.[16] Within this context, the long impunity for crimes committed by the Khmer Rouge may be considered a result of reluctance to act by those with the power to intervene.

In response to continued allegations of corruption and mismanagement at the Court, the United Nations and the Cambodian government recently reaffirmed their commitment to combating corruption within the ECCC.[17] Past corruption allegations led some donors to freeze funding to the Court, and continued allegations threaten future donations that fund the Court's operation. To pre-empt potential elimination of funding, the United Nations and the Cambodian government agreed

---

[14] See cases of ECCC Co-Investigating Judge YOU Bunleng, who was appointed Appeals Court President, and of ECCC Deputy Co-Prosecutor YET Chakriya, who was recently named chief prosecutor at the Phnom Penh Municipal Court. Having core national staff concurrently serve the ECCC and domestic courts has significant negative effects on the Court's functioning. Similar influence probably persists among all judicial officers, who after the closure of the Court will have to continue their careers under the auspices of the ministry of justice. Amnesty International, in particular, has highlighted continuing concerns over Cambodian judges' capabilities and susceptibility to political influence. www.web.amnesty.org.

[15] See N. Pheaktra & G. Wilkins, 'Judges should focus on current KR suspects: Government', *The Phnom Penh Post*, 12 March 2009. The spokesman concluded that for this reason, his government position is that the Court should not go after more than the five current suspects.

[16] Open Society Justice Initiative, *Progress and Challenges at the Extraordinary Chambers in the Courts of Cambodia* (Phnom Penh, Cambodia: The Open Society Justice Initiative 2007).

[17] See K. Sothanarith, 'Tribunal to See Anti-Corruption Measure', *VOA Khmer* (24 February 2009), available at www.voanews.com. See also Joint Statement by Deputy Prime Minister HE Sok An and Assistant Secretary-General for Legal Affairs HE Peter Taksoe-Jensen, 23 February 2009, available at www.eccc.gov.kh.

to establish a basic system to fight corruption in the Court. Under this recent agreement, complaints from the Cambodian side of the Court will be referred to a national mechanism, and complaints from the international staff will be referred to the United Nations side. Complaints will then be forwarded to a joint session that will recommend action. As evident within these recent efforts, corruption continues to threaten the Court's effectiveness, however the ultimate impact of political influence and corruption upon the Court's continued funding and future proceedings remains to be observed.

Since the ECCC's inception, both domestic and international observers have closely scrutinised the Court's activities. Trial monitoring and training initiatives are to be applauded and encouraged as concrete examples of a developing and more independent civil society. Thus far, local and international media monitoring the Court have reasonably accounted for the difficulties plaguing the still-young institution and tried to paint a mostly favourable picture, despite the Court's weaknesses, and the majority of Cambodian civil society has adopted this view.

II.2 Legal and procedural challenges

In addition to its structural complexities, the Court faces a number of legal and procedural challenges that are aggravated by defects in the Cambodian judicial system. In Cambodia, the judicial system has long been criticised for its incompetence and lack of independence. The rule of law in Cambodia is perceived as 'an instrument to affirm the rightfulness of the power-holders.'[18] Accordingly, Cambodians 'trust the law but not the officers of the courts.'[19] As exacerbated by a culture of impunity, the legal and judicial system is considered one of the most corrupt institutions in Cambodia.[20] It is within this general perception of the judiciary that the ECCC has to establish its reputation.

A lack of resources, combined with a muddled legal framework, further diminishes the Cambodian judicial system's potential to enforce the law.[21] The ECCC Statute lists the crimes over which the Court has jurisdiction, including domestic crimes from the Cambodian Criminal Code of 1956, such as homicide, torture, and religious persecution. Additionally, the statute confers jurisdiction over crimes under international law, including genocide, crimes against humanity, war crimes (in the form of 'grave breaches'), destruction of cultural property in armed conflict, and crimes against internationally protected persons. However, the 1956 Criminal Code has not been applied since before the days of the Khmer Rouge, and only few Cambodian lawyers, whose legal qualifications have been publicly questioned even

---

[18] B. Rajagopal, 'The Pragmatics of Prosecuting the Khmer Rouge', 1 *YBIHL* (1998). Those in the Cambodian government have conventionally held a 'purely instrumental view of the law,' perceiving the law as a tool of legitimisation or a means of consolidating power. Ibid., p. 195.

[19] Phuong Pham, et al., *supra* n. 2, p. 15.

[20] Ibid., pp. 15-16. See also National Integrity Systems, Transparency International Country Study Report, *Cambodia 2006* (Berlin, Transparency International 2006), p. 16.

[21] Phuong Pham, et al., *supra* n. 2, p. 15.

by state officials,[22] are conversant with the principles of international criminal law. A major task for them, in conjunction with the international judges, will be to determine the state of customary international law in 1975; to examine how various modes of responsibility can be applied to senior leaders of the Khmer Rouge; and, with respect to the crime of genocide, to analyse the evidentiary question of whether specific genocidal intent can be established[23] and whether the victims belonged to one of the four protected groups specified under Article 4 of the ECCC law. Whether the Court's lawyers and judges achieve a thorough understanding of how to marry domestic and international law before the ECCC will determine the limits of the Court's effectiveness.

Although the ECCC Statute declares domestic criminal procedure laws applicable, ECCC judges have followed other war crimes tribunals' practice of adopting a set of Internal Rules to specifically govern the Court's proceedings. One of the goals of the creation of the Internal Rules had been to fill gaps in Cambodian procedure, which is mainly based on the French inquisitory tradition. This system, which favours two investigative institutions (the Office of the co-prosecutors and the Office of the co-investigating judges) instead of one, has hardly been used before in the prosecution of mass atrocities. Its application, unfamiliar to many of the Court's common law jurists with experience at the International Criminal Tribunal for the Former Yugoslavia, the International Criminal Tribunal for Rwanda, and the Special Court for Sierra Leone, gives rise to a significant number of legal uncertainties. One of these issues is how the trial judges will interpret their supposedly active role during the trial process, especially given the fact the Trial Chamber President is a Cambodian judge. In their August 2008 Decision on Nuon Chea's Appeal Against Order Refusing Request for Annulment,[24] the Pre-Trial Chamber pronounced that the Internal Rules supersede Cambodian and international procedure, and that Cambodian Criminal Procedure applies only when a question unaddressed by the Internal Rules arises.[25] However, it is highly debated whether judges in a civil system are entitled to approve regulations that, although admittedly created in good faith, violate conventional legal interpretation.[26]

In theory, victims' procedural rights before the ECCC permit them to participate in the truth-finding process in many ways, with a view to assist the prosecution.[27]

---

[22] See Y. Samean, 'Blasting Courts, CPP Senator Says Judiciary Needs Training', *The Cambodia Daily*, 26 November 2008, p. 29.

[23] The elements of the crime of genocide have been imported directly from the Genocide Convention of 1948, however, the modes of participation are more restricted: 'direct and public incitement,' for example, does not form part of the applicable law in the ECCC.

[24] Nuon Chea's Appeal Against Order Refusing Request for Annulment, 26 August 2008, available at www.eccc.gov.kh.

[25] Some mixed tribunals apply domestic procedure; others formulate their own internal rules to stipulate procedure. For example, the Special Court for Sierra Leone drafted its own Rules of Procedure. See J. Lee & K. Yookyung Choi, *Introduction to the Khmer Rouge Tribunal* (DC-Cam Legal Training Project 2005), available at www.genocidewatch.org.

[26] See S. Studzinsky, 'Nebenklage vor den Extraordinary Chambers of the Courts of Cambodia (ECCC) – Herausforderung und Chance oder mission impossible?', *ZIS* (2009), p. 45.

[27] See Internal Rules, Rule 23(1) (stating that the purpose of civil party action before the ECCC is to permit victims to 'participate in criminal proceedings against those responsible for crimes within the jurisdiction of the ECCC by supporting the prosecution').

For example, civil parties may request experts,[28] summons witnesses,[29] enforce reparations,[30] and request that the co-investigating judges take an investigative action[31] or interview witnesses.[32] Many victims seek reparations, others intend to contribute to truth-telling. Civil parties' participation rights will certainly bring a new integrity and purpose to the trials, as well as restore voice and power to the Khmer Rouge victims and their families. Furthermore, in a hybrid tribunal that has consistently upheld the involvement of domestic judges and lawyers and the application of domestic substantive and procedural law, promoting the parallel – though indirect – participation of Khmer Rouge victims additionally ensures the involvement and the integration of the Cambodian people. As with every new feature that is unfamiliar to the judicial decision-makers, however, the Court is still striving to meaningfully define victims' roles in the judicial process and to channel it in a way to benefit both the Court and civil society.

The ECCC Internal Rules grant victims unprecedented rights to participate as full parties to criminal proceedings, exceeding victims' participation rights before the International Criminal Court. Victims are permitted both to testify as witnesses and to participate in court proceedings as civil parties after submitting Victim Participation forms. The co-prosecutors assess the complaints, while the co-investigating judges or the Trial Chamber consider civil party applications. To join the case as a civil party, the victim must have been harmed as direct result of crimes covered by the Court's jurisdiction and the co-investigating judges or the Trial Chamber must be seized with the case.[33] A complainant must either have witnessed, have knowledge of, or have been a victim of crimes under the Court's jurisdiction. The complaint may be broad and may relate to any crime under the ECCC's jurisdiction. Those who can provide information relating to the claims brought under the complaint may be designated as witnesses, and the Witness Expert Support Unit provides witness protection at all stages of the proceedings and emotional and psychological support services.[34]

How the variety of interests of the various civil parties can be reconciled with the desire of the judicial officers to have 'smooth' proceedings remains a challenge. Various Pre-Trial Chamber decisions have demonstrated a general climate of fear that civil party participation will become too unwieldy at the Court.[35] The Internal Rules have limited the period during which civil parties may join the case.[36] Addi-

---

[28] Internal Rules, Rule 31(1).

[29] Ibid., Rule 80(2).

[30] Ibid., Rule 113(1).

[31] Ibid., Rule 55(10).

[32] Ibid., Rule 59(5).

[33] See Public Directions on Unrepresented Civil Parties' Rights to Address the Pre-Trial Chamber in Person, Criminal Case File #002/19-09-2007-ECCC/OCIJ(PTC03), Cambodia: Extraordinary Chambers in the Courts of Cambodia, available at www.eccc.gov.kh; Phuong Pham, et al., *supra* n. 2, p. 18.

[34] Phuong Pham, et al., *supra* n. 2, pp. 17-18.

[35] See S. Studzinsky, *supra* n. 26.

[36] Under the revised Internal Rules, 'civil party applications must be filed within the Victims Unit at least 10 (ten) working days before the initial hearing.' See Internal Rules, Rule 23, available at www.eccc.gov.kh.

tionally, unrepresented civil parties may only address the Court through their lawyers or with the Court's permission.[37] Still, the broad possibilities of victim participation remain as much an asset, as a challenge, to the ECCC.

II.3 Evidentiary challenges

As a consequence of the time passed since the commission of the charged crimes and of the complexity of the charges against leaders of a regime, the ECCC faces considerable evidentiary challenges, including poor memories, lost documents, uncertain identification, and reluctant, frightened, and confused witnesses. Neither trials of crimes that were committed decades earlier nor trials of crimes attributed to the leaders of an entire regime[38] are uncommon in domestic or international tribunals. However, the combined factors of antiquity and complexity that characterise evidentiary issues before the ECCC would seriously challenge even the most experienced and diligent tribunal. Passage of time threatens to erode the probative value of the evidence, increasing the need to test the reliability of documents that inculpate the Accused and scrutinise the credibility of witnesses' and victims' testimony of life under the Khmer Rouge.

The majority of evidence before the Court was collected by non-governmental organisations, rather than by police officers, posing an additional evidentiary challenge before the Court. Before the establishment of the Court, significant efforts were made by the Documentation Centre of Cambodia ('DC-Cam')[39] to preserve hundreds of thousands of pages of documents and to record 'histories' from victims and their families, which now form a considerable part of the evidence on file. Because DC-Cam staff members are not police officers, however, it would be unrealistic to expect the same degree of rigor in questioning, and consequently their work is expected to be the subject of considerable legal argument before the ECCC.

The lack of a functioning witness protection procedure in Cambodia poses an additional significant problem that the ECCC must overcome. Local authorities, with whom the Court is working, have no prior knowledge or experience related to witness support and protection. Additionally, the neutrality and professionalism of these officers, as well as their ability to keep witness matters private and confidential, remains uncertain. Whether the conducted witness protection trainings have adequately prepared the police to ensure the safety and security of witnesses remains to be tested in practice. Because witnesses may be reluctant to testify in the absence of a functional witness protection program, ensuring the existence and functioning of such program is fundamental to the Court's effectiveness.

---

[37] See Public Directions on Unrepresented Civil Parties' Rights to Address the Pre-Trial Chamber in Person, Criminal Case File #002/19-09/2007-ECCC/OCIJ(PTC03).

[38] Most notably of Jean Kambanda in the ICTR and Slobodan Milošević in the ICTY.

[39] Initially a field office of Yale University's Cambodian Genocide Program, DC-Cam became an independent research institute in 1997. See www.dccam.org.

II.4 Practical challenges

To mention under-funding and under-staffing of an institution in a developing country like Cambodia as a problem might appear vulgar. However, despite an annual budget which amounts to almost 3% of the entire state budget, the ECCC Administration has had considerable difficulty in securing the long-term operation of the Court. With donors contributing in a two-step procedure (first, approving the Court budget, and second, separately deciding the individual pledge amounts), financing urgently needed staff salary increases remains precarious. Certain offices of the Court therefore rely heavily on interns to cope with everyday workload, and their heavy turnover has negative consequences for the necessary institutional knowledge of the ECCC.

A second major practical obstacle to smooth proceedings is the language issue, which is particularly pressing in the Cambodian context where evidence is predominantly found in Khmer script documents. The setting up of a fully operational court management section responsible for this has taken a long time. As of the time of writing, this section is now able to provide the Court filings in all the three working languages of the ECCC (Khmer, English, and French) in a timely manner. However, the translation of these filings into three languages is time-consuming and binds resources that are missing elsewhere for the translations of the evidence. Until proper translations have been produced, foreign staff cannot have access to these sources. For possible 'hybrid tribunals' in the future, two lessons learned from the ECCC should be to allow not more than two working languages and to require that all domestic staff must, as a key requirement, have a working knowledge of English.

III. Challenges confronted by Cambodian Society

In Cambodia, the absence of a strong legal tradition has produced a weak rule of law, challenging the assessment of when or whether the Court's stated goals of reconciliation and justice will have been met. Surveys have concluded that ordinary Cambodians are broadly in favour of prosecutions, provided the trials are fair. Emerging from these surveys is an underlying insistence that the trials be conducted according to international standards or with some form of international participation.[40] This insistence is likely more indicative of a distrust of domestic governmental interference,[41] rather than a respect for the rights of the suspects or other principles of fair trials.[42] Particularly in a country plagued with a corrupt, non-transparent

40 Phuong Pham, et al., *supra* n. 2, p. 18.

41 The Cambodian criminal justice system has historically been governed by political rather than judicial power, and the concepts of the presumption of innocence and other defendants' rights have not been well-practiced. S. Marks, 'Forgetting – The Policies and Practices of the Past: Impunity in Cambodia', 18 *Fletcher Forum for World Affairs* (1994), p. 17.

42 Many of the victims and their families, particularly those outside educated communities, and local NGOs, have publicly already expressed their difficulty understanding the irony that former Khmer

judicial system, average Cambodians have difficulty comprehending the concept of trying anyone – much less former Khmer Rouge senior officials – under an impartial judiciary. When reminded of the Khmer Rouge's absolute denial of due process and legal representation to their victims, even those Cambodians who understand the importance of the uniform application of due process might struggle to comprehend the rationale behind extending these same rights to those who so arbitrarily denied any form of justice to their innocent victims.

Defences pled at trial could impede the trials' capacity to achieve justice and national reconciliation by threatening to remove or displace criminal responsibility. In defence of the accused, ECCC defence lawyers will likely argue that their clients were not aware of the individual acts of slaughter in the fields, however numerous, and that lower-ranking cadre's crimes cannot be linked to the Accused.[43] However, within Cambodian society, the prevailing view holds that the highest-ranking members of the Khmer Rouge ordered and directed the summary execution, forced labour and deliberate starvation of the Cambodian people between 1975 and 1979, and that the responsibility for the atrocities therefore starts and ends with this small group of suspects. Should the defence's 'bottom-up' rather than 'top-down' model of criminal responsibility emerge during trial, Cambodians could struggle to ascertain an accurate understanding of their history and to achieve a sense of reconciliation.[44] Consequently, many observers have demanded comprehensive educational programs to disseminate the Court's objectives, principles, and methods in advance of the forthcoming trials. As reinforced by the lack of a strong legal tradition, raising awareness – and not simply expectations – of the trials among Cambodians has proven difficult.

Without any prior systematic effort to develop a truth-seeking process or another method of addressing past crimes, the ECCC offers the first – and arguably the last – means of achieving any formal recognition or acknowledgment of Cambodians' suffering during and since the Khmer Rouge period.[45] Achieving 'justice' and 'reconciliation' – two of the stated goals of the establishment of the ECCC – becomes more difficult without any concise definition of these terms. The presence of conflicting cultural definitions of reconciliation further hampers the Court's ability to achieve justice and national reconciliation. When viewed in light of Cambodia's legal history, criminal prosecution of the Khmer Rouge may not have the same meaning to – or achieve justice for – Cambodians as it does for the international community.[46] Leading monks have expressed a scepticism of the international di-

Rouge leaders are allowed to defend themselves in fair trials when the regime itself so horribly failed to deliver any form of justice.

[43] Another option which some suspects have preferred so far is the exercise of their right to remain silent.

[44] S. Heder, 'Reassessing the Role of Senior Leaders and Local Officials in Democratic Kampuchea Crimes: Cambodian Accountability in Comparative Perspective', in J. Ramji & B. van Schaak, *supra* n. 10.

[45] Phuong Pham, et al., *supra* n. 2, p. 8.

[46] B. Rajagopal, *supra* n. 18, p. 195.

mension to the trials, a desire to ground accountability in Buddhist principles, and an urge to seek reconciliation rather than retribution, providing an alternative perspective on the ECCC.[47] Commentators have consequently picked up on this theme, urging a refocusing on a culture of peace, justice and truthfulness, rather than on values of victimhood and vengeance.[48] The concept of reconciliation can seem to directly conflict with the tradition of prosecuting crimes of mass atrocity, but where prosecutions are to be as limited as they are in Cambodia, the vast wealth of indigenous cultural and religious practice might offer an extremely useful means of achieving society-wide understanding. Despite leading NGOs' efforts to assist the ECCC in exploring these possibilities, Cambodia's largely rural demography and the slow pace that has thus far characterised outreach activities and victims' participation require additional efforts to be undertaken. If defined by these more domestic standards, reconciliation could mean offering acknowledgment and forgiveness, rather than supplanting international conceptions of guilt and accountability onto Cambodian cultural values. Because of the Court's hybrid composition, its jurisdiction over domestic and international crimes, and funding by Cambodian and non-Cambodian donors, both the Cambodian and international community arguably share a voice in defining what justice and reconciliation might mean. Ultimately, these same, hybrid standards and values will be used to adjudge the success or failure of the judicial process and its results.

IV. Conclusion

Three decades of domestic and international inaction in addressing the crimes committed during Democratic Kampuchea have produced a culture of impunity and have resulted in high – possibly unattainable – expectations that the Court will achieve complete reconciliation and justice, establish a complete historical record of Democratic Kampuchea, and reform and improve the Cambodian judiciary.[49] However, as stated by a prominent Cambodia rights advocate, Cambodian judges can learn from the international process – from [the ECCC's] international judges and their codes of conduct. People may have the opportunity to watch a fair trial and compare it with the trials they have seen in the past, and in the future. If there is a good strategy as to how to introduce the lessons from the Court into the Cambodian judiciary, it is to record it, to transcribe it, and to have Cambodian judges and lawyers review this process and examine the record, to train them.[50]

---

[47] I. Harris, '"Onslaught on Beings:" A Theraveda Buddhist Perspective on Accountability for Crimes Committed in the Democratic Kampuchea Period', in J. Ramji & B. van Schaak, *supra* n. 10.

[48] A. Rigby, '"Forgiving the Past?" Pathways Towards a Culture of Reconciliation', *The Stockholm International Forum for Truth, Justice and Reconciliation* (2002).

[49] Phuong Pham, et al., *supra* n. 2, p. 7.

[50] Thun Saray, 'No Perfect Justice', in *Justice Initiatives: The Extraordinary Chambers* (Open Society Institute, April 2006), p. 111.

The international human rights community and a number of Cambodians are invested in bringing the Khmer Rouge to justice to ensure international accountability and to rebuild a society based on the rule of law and respect for human life.[51]

The major political, legal, and procedural challenges faced by the Court should mask neither the ultimate moral obligation for accountability nor the powerful symbolic effect of the entire judicial process. Although the ECCC may be far from being a perfect mechanism to achieve accountability, the Court still has the potential to herald a symbolic new beginning in Cambodia's history in which a process of education and reflection may lead to the hoped-for reconciliation. Undue political influence and lack of procedural fairness would derail the judicial process, impairing efforts to achieve accountability and to improve the Cambodian judiciary.[52] That would terribly deceive both the Cambodian people and the international community, who both seek accountability for crimes of international concern. After more than two years of operation, the Court still faces a considerable task ahead. Only through adherence to the international and domestic legal framework, however, will the Court promote the rule of law for Cambodia and succeed in its endeavour to bring accountability, reconciliation, and justice to the Cambodian people.

---

[51] B. Rajagopal, *supra* n. 18, p. 197.

[52] Phuong Pham, et al., *supra* n. 2, p. 7; Open Society Justice Initiative, Recent Developments at the ECCC, March 2010 update, www.justiceinitiative.org.

THE INTERNATIONAL CRIMINAL COURT AND THE CRIME OF GENOCIDE

Hans-Peter Kaul

I. INTRODUCTION

The crime of genocide holds the first and thus a particularly prominent place in the list of crimes enshrined in Article 5(1) of the Rome Statute[1] (hereinafter, the Statute) which sets out the crimes within the jurisdiction of the International Criminal Court (hereinafter, the ICC). The first sentence of Article 5(1) of the Statute clarifies that the jurisdiction of the Court shall be limited to the most serious crimes of concern to the international community as a whole. The fact that Article 5 of the Statute then lists the crime of genocide along with crimes against humanity, war crimes and the crime of aggression confirms that also the crime of genocide is indeed a crime of such concern. As is well known, none of the crimes listed in Article 5 of the Statute were 'invented' by the drafters of the Statute. Rather, they all have strong foundations in international law and international humanitarian law, which often go back more than 50 years. This is true in particular with regard to the crime of genocide which was recognised in the Convention on the Prevention and Punishment of the Crime of Genocide[2] (hereinafter, the Genocide Convention) of 1948.

The definition of the crime of genocide which was provided for in the Genocide Convention is literally the same as the one we can now find in Article 6 of the Statute. However, the General Assembly resolution which approved the conventional text had already called on the International Law Commission to 'study the desirability and possibility of establishing an international judicial organ for the trial of persons charged with genocide or other crimes over which jurisdiction will be conferred upon that organ by international conventions.'[3] This suggestion was echoed in Article VI of the Genocide Convention, which states that '[p]ersons charged

---

[1] Rome Statute of the International Criminal Court, text circulated as document A/CONF.183/9 of 17 July 1998 and corrected by procès-verbaux of 10 November 1998, 12 July 1999, 30 November 1999, 8 May 2000, 17 January 2001 and 16 January 2002, 2187 *UNTS* p. 90. The Statute entered into force on 1 July 2002.

[2] Convention on the Prevention and Punishment of the Crime of Genocide, 9 December 1948, 78 *UNTS* p. 277. The Convention entered into force on 12 January 1951.

[3] General Assembly, UN Doc. A/RES/3/260 (9 December 1948).

C. Safferling and E. Conze (eds.), The Genocide Convention Sixty Years after its Adoption

with genocide … shall be tried by a competent [national tribunal], or by such international penal tribunal as may have jurisdiction with respect to those Contracting Parties which shall have accepted its jurisdiction.' With the establishment of the ICC in 2003, this 'international penal tribunal' is now finally in existence.

On 14 July 2008, Mr Luis Moreno-Ocampo, the Prosecutor of the ICC (hereinafter, the Prosecutor), submitted an application for a warrant of arrest against Mr Omar Hassan Ahmad Al Bashir (hereinafter, Omar Al Bashir), the current President of the Republic of the Sudan. The same day, the Prosecutor issued a public summary[4] of his application showing that the application contained three counts of genocide. On 4 March 2009, Pre-Trial Chamber I (hereinafter, the Chamber), composed of Judge Kuenyehia from Ghana, Judge Steiner from Brazil and Judge Ušacka from Latvia, issued a warrant of arrest[5] against Omar Al Bashir for crimes against humanity and war crimes. Yet, the Majority of the Chamber, Judge Ušacka dissenting, (hereinafter, the Majority) found that the materials provided by the Prosecutor in support of the application failed to establish reasonable grounds to believe that the government of Sudan (hereinafter, the GoS) acted with *dolus specialis* (specific intent) to destroy in whole or in part the Fur, Masalit and Zaghawa groups. Consequently, the counts concerning the crime of genocide are not included in the warrant of arrest against Omar Al Bashir. On 6 July, the Prosecutor submitted an appeal[6] against the decision of 4 March 2009 in which he seeks to reverse the decision of the Chamber not to confirm the counts concerning the crime of genocide in the warrant of arrest against Omar Al Bashir. This appeal is still pending (see post scriptum at p. 211 *infra*). To date, these are the first instances in which the crime of genocide has become relevant in concrete judicial proceedings and decisions of the ICC.

It is against this background that this contribution will, in its first part, recall once again the origin and essential content of Article 6 of the Statute. Likewise, as the crime of genocide was dealt with and elaborated further in the Elements of Crimes pursuant to Article 9 of the Statute, it seems appropriate to include in this first part some observations pertaining to these Elements of Crimes. In the second part of this article, it will be outlined how the situation in Darfur, the Sudan, was referred to the Prosecutor of the ICC by Security Council Resolution 1593 in 2005.[7] This will then lead to a summary of the applications submitted by the Prosecutor and the Chamber's decision of 4 March 2009 in the concrete case against Omar Al Bashir. Thirdly and finally, it seems appropriate to conclude this article with some observations on the general significance of the inclusion of the crime of genocide in the Statute and jurisdiction of the ICC.

---

[4] ICC, *Public Summary of Prosecutor's Application under Article 58*, ICC-02/05-152, 14 July 2008.

[5] ICC, *Warrant of Arrest for Omar Hassan Ahmad Al Bashi*, ICC-02/05-01/09-1, 4 March 2009.

[6] ICC, *Prosecution Document in Support of Appeal against the 'Decision on the Prosecution's Application for a Warrant of Arrest against Omar Hassan Ahmad Al Bashir'*, ICC-02/05-01/09-25, 6 July 2009.

[7] Security Council, UN Doc. S/RES/1593, 31 March 2005.

II. The crime of genocide as defined in the ICC's legal framework

II.1 The concept of genocide – from Lemkin to Article 6 of the Rome Statute

The term 'genocide' (Greek *genos* for race and Latin *caedere* for killing)[8] was first coined by Raphael Lemkin, an American lawyer of Polish origin, during World War II to describe the crimes committed against the Jews by the Nazis.[9]

However, at that time, genocide was recognised in international law as a mere 'sub-class of crimes against humanity' and it was only with the adoption of the Genocide Convention that genocide became a category of crimes of its own, endowed with its own specific *actus reus* (material element) and *mens rea* (mental element).[10]

About half a century later, Article 6 of the Statute, which grants the ICC jurisdiction *ratione materiae* over the crime of genocide, then reproduced word for word the text of Article 2 of the Genocide Convention. This verbatim inclusion suggests that the drafters of the Statute considered this article as constituting 'an almost sacred document of international law that must not be touched in any form whatsoever.'[11]

Yet, it should be noted that this faithful reproduction of the Genocide Convention's terms turned the conventional definition, which is generally also recognised as a definition under customary international law,[12] in a genuine statutory norm of modern international criminal law establishing individual criminal responsibility.

Genocide under the Statute requires the commission of one of the five acts specified in Article 6(a) to (e) of the Statute. In addition to the acts of killing of or causing serious bodily or mental harm to the members of a group, this article also includes acts against the physical or psychological integrity of members of a group or its existence or biological continuity as well as the act of forcibly transferring children of one group to another.

The material element of the crime strictly speaking does not require that the individual act be part of a systematic or widespread attack on a group as required for crimes against humanity pursuant to Article 7 of the Statute. Nonetheless, experience shows that the genocidal acts in question will quite regularly or typically be

---

[8] R. Lemkin, *Axis Rule in Occupied Europe: laws of occupation, analysis of government, proposals for redress*, 2nd edn. (Lawbook Exchange 2008), p. 79.

[9] G. Werle, *Principles of International Criminal Law* (Cambridge, Cambridge University Press 2005), p. 190.

[10] A. Cassese, 'Genocide', in A. Cassese, et al. (eds.), *The Rome Statute of the International Criminal Court* (Oxford, Oxford University Press 2002), p. 335 at p. 339.

[11] C. Kreß, 'The Crime of Genocide under International Law', in 6 *ICLR* (2006), p. 461 at p. 499.

[12] See ICJ, *Application of the Convention on the Prevention and Punishment of the Crime of Genocide, Provisional Measures*, Order of 8 April 1993, ICJ Rep. 1993, p. 3.

also crimes against humanity and thereby *ipso facto* contain this contextual element.[13]

As Article 6 demonstrates, the mental element of genocide requires 'intent to destroy.' Furthermore, the material elements of the crime must be committed with 'intent and knowledge' as referred to in Article 30 of the Statute. This article reads as follows:

> '1. Unless otherwise provided, a person shall be criminally responsible and liable for punishment for a crime within the jurisdiction of the Court only if the material elements are committed with intent and knowledge.
> 2. For the purposes of this article, a person has intent where:
> (a) In relation to conduct, that person means to engage in the conduct;
> (b) In relation to a consequence, that person means to cause that consequence or is aware that it will occur in the ordinary course of events.
> 3. For the purposes of this article, "knowledge" means awareness that a circumstance exists or a consequence will occur in the ordinary course of events. "Know" and "knowingly" shall be construed accordingly.'

Yet, it is important to stress that this intent has been formulated in a specific manner in the Elements of Crimes which will be discussed below.

Finally, it has to be emphasised that deliberate acts taken with the intent of preventing members of a group from using their language, practicing their religion or carrying out the group's cultural activities, sometimes referred to as 'cultural genocide,' do not fall as such within the Article 6 definition of genocide, unless the acts were also one of the five prohibited acts committed with the required intent. In this respect, it has been suggested that the act of forcibly transferring children of one group to another, enshrined in Article 6(e) of the Statute, is 'situated at the border line with so-called cultural genocide.'[14]

Likewise, acts committed with the intention to disrupt or destroy the ecosystem in a particular area by attacks upon the environment, sometimes called 'ecocide,' have not been included in the definition, and would not constitute genocide, unless the attacks involved one of the five prohibited acts committed with the necessary intent.[15]

The first part of this article shall conclude by explaining the nature and role of the Elements of Crimes pursuant to Article 9 of the Statute, in particular those regarding genocide.

---

[13] With regard to the relation of genocide and crimes against humanity see A. Cassese, et al., *The Rome Statute of the International Criminal Court: A Commentary*, Vol. 1 (New York, Oxford University Press 2002), p. 339; O. Triffterer, *Commentary on the Rome Statute of the International Criminal Court – Observers' Notes, Article by Article*, 2nd edn. (Munich, C.H.Beck 2008), p. 156.

[14] C. Kreß, *supra* n. 11, at p. 484.

[15] W.A. Schabas, 'Genozid im Völkerrecht' [Genocide in International Law] (Hamburg, Hamburger Edition 2003), pp. 266-267.

II.2 The concept of genocide as specified in the Elements of Crimes

The concept of Elements of Crimes was foreign to most legal systems prior to the Rome Conference. They were included on the strong demand of the United States and a small number of other states which apply this particular concept, albeit in a binding form. According to Article 9 of the Statute, however, the Elements of Crimes are not as such binding upon the judges. Rather, as the wording of Article 9(1) of the Statute indicates, the Elements of Crimes 'shall assist the International Criminal Court in the interpretation and application of Articles 6, 7 and 8 [of the Statute].'

The Elements of Crimes nevertheless perform a useful role, insofar as they specify and narrowly define the individual elements of the offences of genocide, crimes against humanity and war crimes under Articles 6 to 8 of the Statute. This is done in full harmony with the general definitions and their international criminal law content. In other words, like the definitions of the crimes in the Statute itself, the Elements of Crimes were elaborated to be in full conformity with customary international law. Whether that quality makes them binding in their specific wording is a question which will have to be decided by the judges of the ICC. Indeed, the ultimate value of the Elements of Crimes can only be proven by the actual practice of the ICC judges.[16]

In this respect, the hope is that the Elements of Crimes will contribute to legal certainty and thereby to an increased fairness of the trials before the ICC.

With regard to genocide, the Elements of Crimes require three fundamental components in order to define a specific act as amounting to an act of genocide. These elements include the existence of a victimised group, the perpetrator's intent to destroy in whole or in part the targeted group and finally a prohibited conduct having taken place 'in the context of a manifest pattern of similar conduct directed against that group [or a] conduct that could itself effect such destruction.'[17]

The victimised group requirement entails that the act has to be committed against an identifiable group, commonly referred to as 'protected group,'[18] namely a national, ethnic, racial or religious group. This list is exhaustive and the drafters of the Statute clearly rejected attempts to enlarge the scope of the list. In this regard, it is interesting to note that political, economic and social groups were deliberately excluded as potential targets of the crime of genocide.[19] The protected groups therefore share the common aspect that group membership is 'determined by birth and of a permanent and stable nature.'[20] This common element might help to explain

---

[16] See H.Y. Hebel, 'The Making of the Elements of Crimes', in R.S. Lee & H. Friman, *The International Criminal Court – Elements of Crimes and Rules of Procedure and Evidence* (Ardsley, New York, Transnational Publishers 2001), p. 3.

[17] ICC, *Elements of Crimes*, Arts. 6(a)(4), 6(b)(4), 6(c)(5), 6(d)(5), 6(e)(7), *Dokumentenbezeichnung*.

[18] See for example W.A. Schabas, 'Article 6 – Genocide', in O. Triffterer (ed.), *Commentary on the Rome Statute of the International Criminal Court – Observers' Notes, Article by Article*, 2nd edn. (Munich, C.H.Beck 2008), p. 143 at p. 149.

[19] Ibid., p. 149.

[20] G. Werle, *Principles of International Criminal Law* (Cambridge, Cambridge University Press 2005), p. 194.

the limitation of the scope of genocide insofar as these groups' members are in greatest need of protection since, at least in the case of national, racial or ethnic groups, they cannot 'separate themselves from the group by merely distancing them from the group.'[21] Thus, as one author puts it, 'the fate of the individual is indissolubly linked with the fate of the group.'[22]

The definition is furthermore narrowed down by the requirement that the acts be targeted at the group 'as such.' Indeed, this formula means that the victim of the crime of genocide is the group itself and not the individual.

The second fundamental component relates to the specific intent or *dolus specialis* which needs to be proven in order to qualify an act as genocide.

Indeed, in addition to the Article 30 'general intent requirement,' *dolus specialis* has to be proven, showing that the crimes were planned with that specific intention of destroying a particular group, as such.

The Elements of Crimes list the specific intent requirement as the third component under each category of genocide and they consistently define the specific intent as follows: 'The perpetrator intended to destroy, in whole or in part, that national, ethnical, racial or religious group, as such.'[23]

With regard to this 'specific intent requirement,' it has been proposed in the literature that this concept be envisaged according to either a knowledge-based or a purpose-based approach.[24] The difference between the two is said to reside in the fact that the purpose-based approach, by contrast to the knowledge-based approach, requires the individual intent to mirror the collective goal in the form of a personal desire, aim, goal or purpose. However, the purpose-based approach has been considered to be flawed inasmuch as it requires 'a combination of an *actus reus* formulated from the perspective of the subordinate level with what is typically a leadership standard of *mens rea*.'[25]

The third common element, often referred to as 'the contextual element,' is defined in the Elements of Crimes as the requirement that '[t]he conduct took place in the context of a manifest pattern of similar conduct directed against that group or was conduct that could itself effect such destruction.'[26] However, as will be demonstrated below, this element has not yet been clarified by established jurisprudence and there is no unanimity regarding the question of whether or not it should be recognised.

---

[21] Ibid., p. 198.

[22] *Idem.*

[23] See ICC, *Elements of Crimes*, Art. 6(a)(3); Art. 6(b)(3.); Art. 6(c)(3); Art. 6(d)(3); Art. 6(e)(3).

[24] For a more detailed elaboration of this concept see C. Kreß, *supra* n. 11, at pp. 496-497.

[25] Ibid., pp. 496-497.

[26] See ICC, *Elements of Crimes*, Art. 6 (a)(4); Art. 6(b)(4); Art. 6(c)(5); Art. 6(d)(5); Art. 6(e)(7).

III. The crime of genocide as applied in the ICC's recent practice

III.1 Procedural and historical background

On 14 July 2008, the Prosecutor of the ICC submitted an application for a warrant of arrest against Omar Al Bashir.[27]

As regards the background of this application, it should be recalled that already in September 2004, international attention regarding the situation in Darfur had heightened as a consequence of a statement[28] by the United States' (hereinafter, the US) Secretary of State Colin Powell to the Senate Foreign Relations Committee, affirming that genocide was occurring in Darfur and that the GoS and the Janjaweed bore responsibility. This assertion was based on data collected from a field investigation in 2004, the 'Darfur Atrocities Documentation Project,'[29] which was sponsored by the US State Department.

In September 2004, the United Nations Security Council (hereinafter, the UNSC) passed Resolution 1564,[30] which called for an 'international commission of inquiry on Darfur' to assess the Sudanese conflict. This resolution specifically directed the commission, which was to be chaired by Professor Antonio Cassese, to 'determine … whether or not acts of genocide have occurred.'[31]

In January 2005, the United Nations (hereinafter, the UN) released the commission's report which stated that, while there were mass murders and rapes, they could not label this conduct as genocide because 'the crucial element of genocidal intent appear[ed] to be missing.'[32]

In this report, the commission further recommended that the UNSC should refer the situation in Darfur to the ICC, pursuant to Article 13(b) of the Statute.[33]

Indeed, it was stated that the crimes committed in Darfur fell within the jurisdiction of the Court.[34] Furthermore, the commission emphasised that the Sudanese justice system had demonstrated its inability and unwillingness to investigate and prosecute the perpetrators of these crimes,[35] a statement which quite obviously constituted a reference to the complementarity principle enshrined in Article 17 of the Statute.

---

[27] See ICC, *Public Redacted Version of Prosecution's Application under Article 58 filed on 14 July 2008*, ICC-02/05-157, 12 September 2008.

[28] Voice of America. Text of Colin Powell Testimony to Senate Foreign Relations Committee (September 2009) available at www.voanews.com.

[29] S. Totten, 'The Darfur Atrocities Documentation Project', in 68 *Social Education* (2004).

[30] Security Council, UN Doc. S/RES/1564 (18 September 2004).

[31] Ibid., para. 12.

[32] Report of the International Commission of Inquiry on Darfur to the Secretary-General – Pursuant to Security Council Resolution of 18 September 2004, UN Doc. S/2005/60 (1 February 2005), para. 640.

[33] Ibid., para. 584.

[34] Ibid., paras. 583-616.

[35] Ibid., para. 640.

In March 2005, the UNSC followed suit and referred, with Resolution 1593,[36] the situation in the Sudan, Darfur, to the Prosecutor.

In July 2008, the Prosecutor submitted an application for a warrant of arrest against Omar Al Bashir, which included three counts of genocide, specified in paragraph 62 of the 'Public Summary of Prosecutor's Application.'[37] These three counts respectively referred to Article 6(a), (b) and (c) of the Statute, i.e., '[g]enocide by killing members of each target group,' '[g]enocide by causing serious bodily or mental harm to members of each target group,' as well as '[g]enocide by deliberately inflicting on each target group conditions of life calculated to bring about the group's physical destruction.'[38]

For each individual count, it was alleged that Omar Al Bashir had committed the respective crimes 'through other persons … against the Fur, Masalit and Zaghawa ethnic groups in Darfur, the Sudan, by using the state apparatus, the Armed Forces and Militia/Janjaweed to commit acts … with intent to destroy the groups as such, in part, in violation of Arts. 6(a) and 25(3)(a) of the Rome Statute.'[39]

In December 2008, the Chamber requested the Prosecutor to provide additional information and supporting materials pursuant to Regulation 28(1) of the Regulations of the Court.[40]

On 4 March 2009, the Chamber issued a warrant of arrest against Omar Al Bashir for war crimes and crimes against humanity.[41] However, in its 'Decision on the Prosecutor's Application for a Warrant of Arrest against Omar Al Bashir'[42] (hereinafter, the Decision), the Majority, Judge Ušacka dissenting, declined to include the counts concerning the crime of genocide in the warrant of arrest. This outcome was based on the Majority's finding that the materials provided by the Prosecutor in support of his application failed to provide 'reasonable grounds to believe' that the GoS had acted with specific intent (*dolus specialis*) to destroy in whole or in part the Fur, Masalit and Zaghawa groups.

In spite of this outcome, the Decision provides a first important illustration of the Chamber's actual application of the ICC's legal framework relating to the crime of genocide.

III.2 The majority's decision not to include the charges of genocide in the warrant of arrest

The Majority first undertook an interpretation of the Elements of Crimes concerning genocide. For that purpose, it distinguished between the contextual element of the crime of genocide on the one side and specific elements on the other.

---

[36] Security Council, UN Doc. S/RES/1593 (31 March 2005).

[37] ICC, *supra* n. 5, ICC-02/05-152, at para. 62.

[38] Ibid., para. 62.

[39] *Idem.*

[40] ICC, *Decision Requesting Additional Information and Supporting Materials,* ICC-02/05-166 (9 December 2008).

[41] ICC, *supra* n. 5, ICC-02/05-01/09-1.

[42] ICC, *Decision on the Prosecution's Application for a Warrant of Arrest against Omar Hassan Ahmad Al Bashir*, ICC-02/05-01/09-3 (4 March 2009).

III.2.a *The contextual element*

As outlined above, the Elements of Crimes require a contextual element in order to qualify an act as amounting to genocide. Yet, the Majority pointed to the existing difference of view concerning the question of whether or not such a contextual element should be recognised.

Indeed, the Majority observed that the definition of the crime of genocide in the Genocide Convention does not expressly require any contextual element. Moreover, it acknowledged that the Genocide Convention definition had been interpreted in the case-law of the International Criminal Tribunal for the former Yougoslavia (hereinafter, the ICTY) and the International Criminal Tribunal for Rwanda (hereinafter, the ICTR) as excluding any type of contextual element, such as a genocidal policy or plan. Thus, the *ad hoc* tribunals' jurisprudence emphasised that the protection offered to the targeted groups was dependent on the existence of an intent to destroy, in whole or in part, the targeted group. As soon as such intent exists and materialises in an isolated act against a single individual, the protection is triggered, regardless of whether the latent threat to the existence of the targeted group posed by the said intent has turned into a concrete threat to the existence of the group in whole or in part.

Yet, the Elements of Crimes require a so-called contextual element which was interpreted by the Majority as implying that the crime of genocide was only completed when the relevant conduct presented a concrete threat to the existence of the targeted group, or part thereof.

Regarding the question of whether or not this additional element should be recognised, the Majority considered that the Elements of Crimes must be applied 'unless the competent Chamber finds an irreconcilable contradiction between these documents on the one hand and the Statute on the other hand.'[43] Only such an irreconcilable contradiction would require the provisions contained in the Statute to prevail.

In the present case, the Majority did not observe any irreconcilable contradiction between the definition of the crime of genocide provided for in Article 6 of the Statute and the contextual element provided for in the Elements of Crimes.

It considered, on the contrary, that

> 'the definition of the crime of genocide, so as to require for its completion an actual threat to the targeted group, or a part thereof, [was] (i) not *per se* contrary to article 6 of the Statute; (ii) fully respect[ed] the requirements of article 22(2) of the Statute that the definition of the crimes "shall be strictly construed and shall not be extended by analogy" and [that] "[i]n case of ambiguity, the definition sh[ould] be interpreted in favor of the person being investigated, prosecuted or convicted"; and (iii) [was] fully consistent with the traditional consideration of the crime of genocide as the "crime of the crimes."'[44]

---

43 ICC, *supra* n. 42, ICC-02/05-01/09-3, at para. 128.

44 Ibid., paras. 117-132.

Therefore, the Majority considered that the Elements of Crimes should be applied.

III.2.b *The specific elements*

Having recognised the applicability of the contextual element, the Majority proceeded by elaborating upon the two specific elements, i.e., the existence of a protected group and the presence of a specific intent.

III.2.b.1 Existence of a protected group

Regarding the requirement of the existence of a protected group, the Majority was of the opinion that there must be a positive definition of the targeted group while a negative definition would not suffice for the purpose of Article 6 of the Statute.

It was held that there were no *reasonable grounds to believe* that distinct national, racial or religious groups had been targeted but that there were *reasonable grounds to believe* in the existence of three distinct ethnic groups as a target. Indeed, it was considered that each of the three ethnic groups – the Fur, the Masalit and the Zaghawa – had its own language, its own tribal customs and its own traditional links to its lands.[45]

III.2.b.2 The specific intent requirement

The second specific element relates to the specific intent or *dolus specialis* which needs to be proven in order to qualify an act as amounting to genocide.

Indeed, as outlined above, the Elements of Crimes for genocide endow each of the five categories of genocidal act with a third element that consistently defines the specific intent as follows: 'The perpetrator intended to destroy, in whole or in part, that national, ethnical, racial or religious group, as such.'[46]

The Majority deduced from these provisions that the crime of genocide included two subjective elements:

> 'a general subjective element that must cover any genocidal act provided for in article 6(a) to (e) of the Statute, and which consists of article 30 intent and knowledge requirement [and] an additional subjective element, normally referred to as "*dolus specialis*" or specific intent, according to which any genocidal acts must be carried out with the "intent to destroy in whole or in part" the targeted group.'[47]

The Majority went on in applying the law on the proof by inference to the Article 58 evidentiary standard in relation to the alleged GoS's genocidal intent.

First, it noted that the Prosecutor admitted that he relied exclusively on proof by inference to substantiate his allegations concerning Omar Al Bashir's reported responsibility for genocide.

---

45 Ibid., paras. 135-137.

46 See ICC, *Elements of Crimes*, Art. 6(a)(3); Art. 6(b)(3); Art. 6(c)(3); Art. 6(d)(3); Art. 6(e)(3).

47 ICC, *supra* n. 42, ICC-02/05-01/09-3, at para. 139.

Before engaging in the actual evaluation of evidence, the Majority pointed out that it seemed appropriate to refer to 'the GoS's genocidal intent' as opposed to 'Omar Al Bashir's genocidal intent.'

It was underscored that, according to the Prosecutor, Omar Al Bashir was in full control of the 'apparatus' of the State of Sudan which he used to carry out a genocidal campaign against the Fur, Masalit and Zaghawa groups.

Consequently, the Majority considered that, if the materials provided by the Prosecutor supported his allegations in this regard, the existence of reasonable grounds to believe that Omar Al Bashir had a genocidal intent would automatically lead to the conclusion that there were also reasonable grounds to believe that a genocidal campaign against the Fur, Masalit and Zaghawa groups was a core component of the GoS's counter-insurgency campaign.

However, it was emphasised that the situation would be different if the materials provided by the Prosecutor showed reasonable grounds to believe that Omar Al Bashir shared the control over the 'apparatus' of the State of Sudan with other high-ranking Sudanese political and military leaders. In this situation, the Majority was of the view that the existence of reasonable grounds to believe that one of the core components of the GoS's counter-insurgency campaign was a genocidal campaign against the Fur, Masalit and Zaghawa groups would be dependent upon the existence of reasonable grounds to believe that those who shared the control of the 'apparatus' of the State of Sudan with Omar Al Bashir agreed that the GoS's counter-insurgency campaign would, *inter alia*, aim at the destruction, in whole or in part, of the Fur, Masalit and Zaghawa groups.[48]

In applying the law on the proof by inference to the Article 58 evidentiary standard in relation to the existence of a GoS's genocidal intent, the Majority agreed with the Prosecutor in that such a standard would be met only if the materials provided showed that the *only* reasonable conclusion to be drawn was the existence of reasonable grounds to believe in the existence of a GoS's specific intent to destroy in whole or in part the Fur, Masalit and Zaghawa groups.[49]

The Prosecutor listed nine different factors from which to infer the existence of a GoS's genocidal intent. These factors were classified by the Majority into three different categories, namely the alleged existence of a GoS strategy to deny and conceal the crimes allegedly committed in the Darfur region against the members of the Fur, Masalit and Zaghawa groups; some official statements and public documents, which, according to the Prosecutor, provided reasonable grounds to believe in the (pre) existence of a GoS genocidal policy; as well as the nature and extent of the acts of violence committed by GoS forces against the Fur, Masalit, and Zaghawa civilian population.[50]

After having analysed the materials provided by the Prosecutor, the Majority concluded that the existence of *reasonable grounds to believe* that the GoS acted

48 Ibid., paras. 148-151.
49 Ibid., para. 158.
50 Ibid., para. 164.

with a specific intent to destroy in whole or in part the Fur, Masalit and Zaghawa groups was not the only reasonable conclusion that could be drawn.[51]

However, the Majority emphasised that, 'if, as a result of the ongoing Prosecutor investigation into the crimes allegedly committed by President Al Bashir, additional evidence on the existence of a GoS's genocidal intent [was] gathered, the Majority's opinion in this decision would not prevent the Prosecutor from requesting, pursuant to Article 58(6) of the Rome Statute, an amendment to the Warrant of Arrest against Omar Al Bashir in order to include the crime of genocide.'[52]

III.3 Judge Ušacka's 'Separate and Partly Dissenting Opinion'

Judge Ušacka agreed with the Majority as to the outcome of the decision, i.e., the issuance of the warrant of arrest, but she expressed a 'Separate and Partly Dissenting Opinion'[53] pertaining to the crime of genocide, particularly inasmuch as the alleged genocidal intent and the alleged criminal responsibility of Omar Al Bashir were concerned. Indeed, by contrast to the Majority, she was of the opinion that there were 'reasonable grounds to believe' that Omar Al Bashir had committed the crime of genocide.

This conclusion resulted mainly from a different construction of the standard of proof required to establish the existence of 'reasonable grounds to belief.' Indeed, Judge Ušacka had a different opinion regarding the issue of whether or not the Prosecutor must demonstrate at this stage of the proceedings that the *only* reasonable inference from the evidence was that of genocidal intent.

Judge Ušacka highlighted that the evidentiary threshold increases at each stage of the proceedings, i.e., the warrant of arrest/summons to appear stage, the confirmation of charges stage and finally the conviction stage. In her view, the evidentiary threshold at the warrant of arrest stage had the lowest level in comparison to the other stages. On this basis, Judge Ušacka examined the evidence provided by the Prosecutor in regard to the three counts of genocide.

She first analysed the three common elements of the different counts. She considered that the contextual element was met, regardless of whether or not it should be applied.[54] In this regard, she disagreed with the Majority's view that a concrete threat was required to satisfy the contextual elements.

Inasmuch as the protected group was concerned, she disagreed with the Majority's findings leading to the recognition of three separate groups and defined the victimised group as constituting a 'single ethnic African group of the African tribes, which consists of smaller groups, namely the Fur, Masalit and Zaghawa.'[55]

As regards the contentious element of the specific intent, Judge Ušacka's analysis of the evidence led her to the conclusion that the possession of genocidal intent

---

[51] Ibid., para. 205.

[52] Ibid., para. 207.

[53] ICC, *supra* n. 42, *Separate and Partly Dissenting Opinion of Judge Ušacka*, ICC-02/05-01/09-3.

[54] Ibid., para. 20.

[55] Ibid., para. 26.

was one of the reasonable inferences which could be drawn from the available evidence.

In her view, this inference did not need to be the only reasonable inference at this stage of the proceedings.[56] Although she admitted that a different conclusion could be reached under a stricter evidentiary threshold, she clarified that this could not be considered at the warrant of arrest stage.[57]

In addition, Judge Ušacka argued that the Prosecutor presented no evidence which would conclusively exclude the reasonable inference of a genocidal intent.[58]

While the Majority noted that during the attacks most of the members of the targeted group had been neither killed nor injured, Judge Ušacka stated that the means of the genocidal destruction 'need not be the most efficient.'[59]

As a conclusion, Judge Ušacka was satisfied that there were *reasonable grounds to believe* that Omar Al Bashir possessed genocidal intent.[60]

Judge Ušacka went on to assess the evidence provided with regard to the three counts of genocide and came to the conclusion that there were reasonable grounds to believe that each had been committed.[61]

Finally, she disagreed with the Majority on the question of the mode of liability. Failing to find any evidence which would address the issue of the 'locus of control,' she was unable to decide whether such control rested fully with Omar Al Bashir, or whether it was shared by others. As a result, she did not find any reasonable grounds to believe that Omar Al Bashir was responsible through co-perpetration and she would thus have based the warrant of arrest only on the mode of indirect perpetration.[62]

III.4 The Prosecutor's application for leave to appeal pursuant to Article 82(1)(d) of the Statute

On 10 March 2009, the Prosecutor submitted a public redacted version of his application for leave to appeal the Chamber's decision.[63]

In this application, he sought leave to appeal three issues. First, he requested the Appeals Chamber to clarify whether the correct standard of proof in the context of Article 58 of the Statute required that the *only* reasonable conclusion to be drawn from the evidence was the existence of *reasonable grounds to believe* that the person had committed a crime within the jurisdiction of the Court. The second issue related to the question whether the Majority had considered specific extraneous

---

56 Ibid., para. 32.
57 Ibid., para. 85.
58 Ibid., para. 83.
59 Ibid., para. 78.
60 Ibid., para. 86.
61 Ibid., paras. 91-102.
62 Ibid., paras. 103-104.
63 ICC, *Prosecution's Application for Leave to Appeal the 'Decision on the Prosecution's Application for a Warrant of Arrest against Omar Hassan Ahmad Al Bashir'*, ICC-02/05-01/09-12 (10 March 2009).

factors in assessing the existence of reasonable grounds to establish genocidal intent. Finally, he asked whether the Majority had failed to consider both separately and collectively specific critical factors in assessing the existence of reasonable grounds to establish genocidal intent.[64]

The Chamber, in its decision,[65] only granted the Prosecutor's application in relation to the first issue and rejected the application in relation to the two other issues. It was stated that the first issue met the two cumulative criteria provided for in Article 82(1)(d) of the Statute, i.e., the existence of a decision that involves an issue that would significantly affect the fair and expedious conduct of the proceedings on the outcome of the trial and the criterion that an immediate resolution by the Appeals Chamber may materially advance the proceedings.

By contrast, the second and third issues were considered as consisting of a mere disagreement with the Majority's assessment of the evidence submitted by the Prosecutor to support his genocide-related allegations and were therefore not issues as defined by Article 82(1)(d) of the Statute.[66]

Pursuant to this decision, on 6 July 2009, the Prosecutor submitted the public version of the 'Prosecution Document in Support of Appeal against the "Decision on the Prosecution's Application for a Warrant of Arrest against Omar Hassan Ahmad Al Bashir"'[67] which contains the Prosecutor's statements regarding the above-mentioned first issue.

As ground of appeal, the prosecutor submits that 'the Majority applied the wrong legal standard for drawing inferences for the purposes of Article 58'[68] and thereby imposed on the prosecutor an evidentiary burden that is inappropriate for the procedural stage at hand.

The Prosecutor's submission concerns the argument used by the Majority that, in order to establish 'reasonable grounds to believe' and to issue a warrant of arrest on genocide charges, the inference of specific genocidal intent must be the only reasonable inference available on the evidence.

The Prosecutor states that, by doing so, the Majority applied an erroneous evidentiary test, 'effectively equal to that of "beyond reasonable doubts" which is required at the trial stage for the conviction of the Accused.'[69]

According to the Prosecutor, this standard is not applicable at the warrant of arrest stage. At this early stage, it is sufficient if the inference of genocidal intent drawn from the evidence is reasonable and there is no requirement that the inference be the only one available.

---

[64] Ibid., para. 13.

[65] ICC, *Decision on 'Prosecution's Application for Leave to Appeal the "Decision on the Prosecution's Application for a Warrant of Arrest against Omar Hassan Ahmad Al Bashir"'*, ICC-02/05-01/09-21 (24 June 2009).

[66] Ibid., pp. 8-9.

[67] ICC, *Prosecution Document in Support of Appeal against the 'Decision on the Prosecution's Application for a Warrant of Arrest against Omar Hassan Ahmad Al Bashir'*, ICC-02/05-01/09-25 (6 July 2009).

[68] Ibid., para. 19.

[69] Ibid., para. 3.

The Prosecutor contends that the requirement of the 'only reasonable inference available on the evidence' is not contained in Article 58 of the Statute. Furthermore, this requirement cannot be considered as a consequence of the Prosecutor's reliance on indirect evidence since the Statute provides no basis for creating or applying different standards of proof for direct evidence and indirect evidence.[70]

According to the Prosecutor, the lower standard at the warrant of arrest stage is also consistent with the prior jurisprudence of international tribunals such as the ICC, the ICTY, the ICTR and the European Court on Human Rights as well as with the practice in national legal systems.[71]

Finally, it is affirmed that requiring such a high standard at the warrant of arrest stage, 'when the suspect is still at large and when their detention may be required "to ensure that the person does not obstruct or endanger the investigation," could well endanger the lives of prospective witnesses.'[72]

In light of these considerations, the Prosecutor requests the Appeals Chamber to

> 'overturn the Decision to the extent that it held the Prosecution had not established "reasonable grounds to believe" that President Omar Al Bashir had genocidal intent; set out the correct standard for drawing inferences under Article 58 of the Statute; and apply that correct standard to the facts found by the Pre-Trial Chamber, entering a finding that there are reasonable grounds to believe that President Omar Al Bashir is criminally responsible for genocide under Articles 6(a), (b) and (c) of the Statute, and direct the Pre-Trial Chamber to issue a warrant of arrest on those counts; or in the alternative, remand the matter to the Pre-Trial Chamber to decide on whether there are reasonable grounds to believe that President Omar Al Bashir is criminally responsible for genocide under Articles 6(a), (b) and (c) of the Statute, applying the correct standard.'[73]

It remains to be seen whether and to which extent the Appeals Chamber will accept these submissions. It is likely that the Appeals Chamber will see these appeal proceedings as an opportunity to clarify some of the issues raised by the Prosecutor's appeal.

IV. Conclusion

The fundamental importance of the crime of genocide pursuant to Articles 5(1)(a) and 6 of the Statute and the Court's recent judicial proceedings regarding the crime of genocide may lead, in a quite natural way, to a number of questions:

What are some of the main implications and consequences of the inclusion of the crime of genocide in the Rome Statute? What is the significance of this evolu-

[70] Ibid., para. 38.
[71] Ibid., paras. 43-50.
[72] Ibid., para. 46.
[73] Ibid., para. 65.

tion of the prohibition of genocide, as stipulated in the Genocide Convention of 1948?

Obviously, these are questions of some complexity and importance to which an appropriate or even full answer is, at this stage, hardly possible. On the other hand, there are a number of elements and observations which merit a recapitulation in order to better understand and appreciate this recent legal development.

It is worth recalling as a first observation that during the codification process of the Statute, before and during the Rome Conference in 1998, the proposal to include the crime of genocide in the list of core crimes never met any opposition. Quite to the contrary, this proposal seemed so obvious to the international community that it enjoyed full support of the participating states. Furthermore, there was almost consensus that not only the concept as such but the wording of the Genocide Convention and the five forms of genocide as set out in this convention should as such be transferred to the future Rome Statute. This demonstrates that the prohibition of genocide was generally regarded, already at the end of the last century, as universally accepted customary international law and even as *jus cogens*. Also those states which later did not become States Parties to the Rome Statute never questioned the inclusion of this core crime in the future jurisdiction *ratione materiae* of the Court. Thus, current Article 6 of the Statute concerning the crime of genocide seems to be based on the free and unanimous consent of the international community. Article 6 of the Statute may, therefore, be regarded as a recent and strong reaffirmation of the prohibition of this international crime.

In the same manner, attention must again be drawn to the fact that, through Article 6 of the Statute, the existing obligation for States Parties of the Genocide Convention to prevent genocide and to punish the perpetrators – a matter of state responsibility – was turned into and consolidated in a genuine and general norm of international criminal law establishing individual criminal responsibility of perpetrators of this crime. As this is the case with general norms of criminal law, the previously existing general prohibition of genocide is through Articles 6 and 77(1) of the Statute now strengthened and 'armed' with an appropriate sanction. Article 77(1)(b) of the Statute provides that genocide may be punished with a penalty of up to a term of life imprisonment. Obviously, this amounts to a considerable strengthening of this prohibition.

Thirdly, many believe that the Elements of Crimes regarding genocide have, to some extent, clarified the five forms of genocide set out in Article 6 of the Statute. It is also safe to assume that the common and consensual elaboration of the Elements of Crimes regarding genocide in the ICC Preparatory Commission (1999-2001) probably has fostered a better understanding of the crime of genocide. Thus, the subsequent elaboration of the Elements of Crimes regarding genocide after the adoption of the Statute on 17 July 1998 may be regarded as a further consolidation and clarification of this crime. As the Elements of Crimes shall assist the Court in the interpretation of the core crimes, one may expect that also the Elements of Crimes regarding genocide will increase the chance for a better practical manageability of and more consistent solutions to the difficult issues related to genocide.

Finally, the inclusion of the crime of genocide in the Statute has acted as a catalyst for the introduction of national criminal law regarding genocide in quite a number of countries. This has had the far-reaching consequence that many States Parties have in their implementing legislation for the first time transferred the prohibition of genocide in their national criminal law.[74] While a small number of states had already before the adoption of the Statute national criminal norms regarding genocide,[75] the increasing adoption of such national criminal law, in the framework of implementing legislation, is obviously another avenue to strengthen this prohibition and the related awareness of this prohibition both internationally and nationally.

In sum, there is little doubt that the inclusion of the crime of genocide in the Statute adopted in 1998 has opened a new chapter. It has considerably strengthened this prohibition; it has also increased international awareness and universal rejection of and abhorrence regarding this crime as well as the commitment to investigate and prosecute crimes of genocide.

Needless to say, especially for a judge of the International Criminal Court, we all must hope that there is in the future no necessity to investigate or prosecute this crime.

Post Scriptum

After the submission of the manuscript, some important developments arose in the case against Al Bashir. The Appeals Chamber has ruled on 3 February 2010 on the appeal referred to on p. 196 and requested Pre-Trial Chamber I to review its decision of 4 March 2009. Pre-Trial Chamber I, following the direction provided by the Appeals Chamber, issued a second warrant of arrest against Omar Hassan Ahmad Al Bashir on 12 July 2010 for three counts of genocide committed against the Fur, Masalit and Zaghawa ethnic groups. See ICC, *Judgment on the appeal of the Prosecutor against the "Decision on the Prosecution's Application for a Warrant of Arrest against Omar Hassan Ahmad Al Bashir"*, ICC-02/05-01/09-OA, 3 February 2010 and ICC, *Second Warrant of Arrest for Omar Hassan Ahmad al Bashir*, ICC-02/05-01/09, 12 July 2010".

---

[74] See for example Art. 6 *Völkerstrafgesetzbuch* [German Code of Crimes against International Law (CCAIL)], BGBl. 2002 I, p. 2144, which contains a *quasi verbatim* translation of Art. 6 of the Rome Statute; *Australian Implementation of the Rome Statute of the International Criminal Court Act* 27 of 18 July 2002.

[75] See for example the United Kingdom's Genocide Act passed in 1969, Art. 211-1 *Code pénal* [French criminal code] of 1994, Arts. 1 to 7 Lei N° 2.889 de 1° de outoubro de 1965 [Brazilian Law No. 2.889 of 1 October 1965], Art. 281 of the Penal Code of the Empire of Ethiopia of 23 July 1957.

THE CRIME OF GENOCIDE APPLIED IN PRACTICE – SELECTED ASPECTS OF THE JURISPRUDENCE OF THE *AD HOC* TRIBUNALS' APPEALS CHAMBERS

Matthias Schuster*

I. Introduction

In 1993, the United Nations Security Council, expressing 'its grave alarm at continuing reports of widespread and flagrant violations of international humanitarian law occurring within the territories of the former Yugoslavia,' established the International Criminal Tribunal for the former Yugoslavia (ICTY).[1] This was followed in 1994 by the establishment of the International Criminal Tribunal for Rwanda (ICTR), which was triggered by the Security Council's 'grave concern at the reports indicating that genocide and other systematic, widespread and flagrant violations of international humanitarian law have been committed in Rwanda.'[2]

The statutes of the tribunals – annexed to the respective resolutions of the Security Council – enumerate a number of crimes falling under the tribunals' jurisdiction. While there are slight differences in relation to war crimes and crimes against humanity, both statutes contain identical provisions as regards the crime of genocide.[3] These provisions in turn were taken verbatim from the Genocide Convention of 1948.[4]

As it happened, the *ad hoc* tribunals were the first courts – both on a domestic and an international level – to find an accused guilty of genocide under the wording of the Genocide Convention.[5] Consequently, this article will focus on some of the

* The views expressed in this article are those of the author alone and do not necessarily reflect the views of the ICTY or the United Nations in general.

[1] International Tribunal for the Prosecution of Persons Responsible for Serious Violations of International Humanitarian Law Committed in the Territory of the Former Yugoslavia since 1991, established by UNSC Res. 827 (25 May 1993) UN Doc. S/RES/827.

[2] International Criminal Tribunal for the Prosecution of Persons Responsible for Genocide and Other Serious Violations of International Humanitarian Law Committed in the Territory of Rwanda and Rwandan Citizens responsible for genocide and other such violations committed in the territory of neighbouring states, between 1 January 1994 and 31 December 1994, established by UNSC Res. 955 (8 November 1994) UN Doc. S/RES/955.

[3] See Art. 4 of the ICTY Statute and Art. 2 of the ICTR Statute.

[4] See Arts. 2 and 3 of the Convention on the Prevention and Punishment of the Crime of Genocide of 9 December 1948, 78 *UNTS* p. 277.

[5] Adolf Eichmann and John Demjanjuk were prosecuted and convicted by Israeli courts for 'a crime against the Jewish people.' While this crime is modeled on Art. 2 of the Genocide Convention,

C. Safferling and E. Conze (eds.), The Genocide Convention Sixty Years after its Adoption

legal difficulties that the ICTY and ICTR have been encountering in the past 15 years when interpreting the law on genocide and applying it to the facts in evidence before them. Special attention will be paid to the jurisprudence on appeal. The reason for this is simple: The Appeals Chambers of the tribunals, which are distinct but are nevertheless comprised of the same judges,[6] are the final arbiters of any legal disputes arising out of appeals against decisions of the Trial Chambers.[7] Indeed, the *ratio decidendi* of the Appeals Chamber's decisions is binding on the respective tribunal's Trial Chambers.[8]

Before introducing and analysing some of the relevant jurisprudence, it is useful to recall the text of the genocide provision in the tribunals' statutes:

> '1. The International Tribunal shall have the power to prosecute persons committing genocide as defined in paragraph 2 of this Article or of committing any of the other acts enumerated in paragraph 3 of this Article.
>
> 2. Genocide means any of the following acts committed with intent to destroy, in whole or in part, a national, ethnical, racial or religious group, as such:
> (a) Killing members of the group;
> (b) Causing serious bodily or mental harm to members of the group;
> (c) Deliberately inflicting on the group conditions of life calculated to bring about its physical destruction in whole or in part;
> (d) Imposing measures intended to prevent births within the group;
> (e) Forcibly transferring children of the group to another group.
>
> 3. The following acts shall be punishable:
> (a) Genocide;
> (b) Conspiracy to commit genocide;
> (c) Direct and public incitement to commit genocide;
> (d) Attempt to commit genocide;
> (e) Complicity in genocide.'[9]

It is perceptible from this wording that genocide holds a special place among international crimes. There are certain genocidal acts, listed in para. 2(a)-(e), which

---

it is contained in Israel's 'Nazis and Nazi Collaborators (Punishment) Law 5710-1950' and is limited to genocidal acts committed against Jews by the Nazis between 30 January 1933 and 8 May 1945. The full text of the law can be found at www.mfa.gov.il. See for further information W.A. Schabas, *Genocide in International Law* (Cambridge, Cambridge University Press 2000), pp. 360-361 and 386 et seq.

[6] See Arts. 12(3) and 14(2-4) of the ICTY Statute and Arts. 11(3) and 15(3-4) of the ICTR Statute. The idea behind this approach was to obtain a uniform jurisprudence from the tribunals' appellate bodies. See also 'Report of the Secretary-General Pursuant to Paragraph 5 of Security Council Resolution 955 (1994)', UN Doc. S/1995/134, 13 February 1995, para. 9. See in more detail: M.A. Drumbl & K.S. Gallant, 'Appeals in the *Ad Hoc* International Criminal Tribunals: Structure, Procedure, and Recent Cases', 3 *The Journal of Appellate Practice and Process* (2001), p. 589 at pp. 606-609.

[7] In practice, almost every judgment rendered by a Trial Chamber has been appealed by either the prosecution or the defence.

[8] See ICTY, *Prosecutor* v. *Aleksovski*, Case IT-95-14/1-A, Judgment of the Appeals Chamber, 24 March 2000, para. 113. See also X. Tracol, 'The Precedent of Appeals Chambers Decisions in the International Criminal Tribunals', 17 *LeidenJIL* (2004), pp. 67-102.

[9] Art. 7 of the ICTY Statute. The only difference in Art. 2 of the ICTR Statute is that the words 'International Tribunal' are replaced with 'International Tribunal for Rwanda.'

form the *actus reus* of the crime. The *mens rea* of genocide is bifurcated: Unlike the sometimes looser requirements for other crimes under the statutes, a perpetrator must perform the genocidal acts intentionally.[10] In addition, and this is what distinguishes genocide from other crimes, the genocidal acts must be carried out with the specific intent (*dolus specialis*) to destroy – in whole or in part – a protected group as such. What makes matters more complicated is the fact that the tribunals' provisions on genocide also contain, in paragraph 3, certain modes of liability (e.g., complicity), which seem to conflict with the statutes' general provisions that set out the modes of liability for all crimes under the *ad hoc* tribunals' jurisdiction (e.g., committing, aiding and abetting).

Leaving aside the *actus reus* of the crime[11] and questions pertaining to its modes of liability,[12] this article will discuss the ICTY's and ICTR's jurisprudence on the crime of genocide in relation to its most important facet, that is, the specific intent requirement. With that purpose in mind, the text will progressively explore how the tribunals have interpreted the 'intent to destroy, in whole or in part, a national, ethnical, racial or religious group, as such.'

II. THE PROTECTED GROUP

Given the current proliferation of the term 'genocide' in relation to almost each and every atrocity committed around the world,[13] it is necessary to remember that the

---

[10] However, there is no requirement of premeditation, see ICTY, *Prosecutor* v. *Stakić*, Case IT-07-24-T, Judgment, 31 July 2003, para. 515; ICTR, *Prosecutor* v. *Semanza*, Case ICTR-97-20-T, Judgment, 15 May 2003, para. 319. See also ICTR, *Prosecutor* v. *Kayishema and Ruzindana*, Case ICTR-95-1-A, Judgment of the Appeals Chamber, 1 June 2001, para. 151. For the genocidal act of 'killings,' compare in this context the jurisprudence of the *ad hoc* tribunals in relation to 'murder' as a crime against humanity, which lets it suffice that the perpetrator's act was committed in the knowledge that death was its probable consequence (see ICTY, *Prosecutor* v. *Martić*, Case IT-95-11-T, Judgment, 12 June 2007, para. 58 and ICTR, *Prosecutor* v. *Zigiranyirazo*, Case ICTR-01-73-T, Judgment, 18 December 2008, para. 442; contra *Semanza* Judgment, *op. cit.*, para. 339: The Appeals Chamber has not yet clarified the divergent jurisprudence on this point. But see ICTY, *Prosecutor* v. *Kordić and Čerkez*, Case IT-95-14/2-A, Judgment of the Appeals Chamber, 17 December 2004, para. 113: 'The elements of murder as a crime against humanity are undisputed.' To explain the difference, an ICTR Trial Chamber has argued – albeit without further reasoning – that 'by their very nature, [genocidal] acts are conscious, intentional, volitional acts that an individual cannot commit by accident or as a result of mere negligence.' ICTR, *Prosecutor* v. *Bagilishema*, Case ICTR-95-1A-T, Judgment, 7 June 2001, para. 58.

[11] For an in-depth analysis, see G. Boas, et al., *Elements of Crimes Under International Law*, International Criminal Law Practitioner Library Series, Vol. 2 (Cambridge, Cambridge University Press 2008), pp. 176-188. See also G. Werle, *Principles of International Criminal Law* (Asser Press, The Hague 2005), pp. 199-203.

[12] Very comprehensive on the tribunals' jurisprudence on this issue: G. Dawson & R. Boynton, 'Reconciling Complicity in Genocide and Aiding and Abetting Genocide in the Jurisprudence of the United Nations *Ad Hoc* Tribunals', 21 *Harv. HRLJ* (2008), pp. 241-279; and G. Boas, et al., *Forms of Responsibility in International Criminal Law*, International Criminal Law Practitioner Library Series, Vol. 1 (Cambridge, Cambridge University Press 2007), pp. 278-342.

[13] This could be explained by the fact that '[g]enocide has taken on a life of its own in the popular mind; victims of almost all massacres feel cheated when a court or commission finds that their perpe-

drafters of the Genocide Convention deliberately limited the scope of the treaty to four protected groups, namely, national, ethnic, racial, or religious groups.[14] This enumeration is exclusive and exhaustive.[15] Therefore, 'political' groups do not enjoy protection under the Genocide Convention.[16]

At first glance, it seems possible to provide objective and precise definitions of the terms 'national,' 'ethnic,' 'racial,' and 'religious.' In fact the earliest trial judgment of the ICTR in the *Akayesu* case did just that.[17] For instance, the Trial Chamber held that '[a]n ethnic group is generally defined as a group whose members share a common language or culture.'[18] However, the Chamber ran immediately into conceptual trouble with this purely objective approach. As it was, the situation in Rwanda could not be easily categorised. According to the Trial Chamber's own findings, the three groups living in Rwanda – the Tutsi, Hutu, and Twa – spoke the same language and essentially shared the same culture.[19] On the other hand, there were certain 'objective indicators' of a distinct ethnic identity, such as the fact that each Rwandan carried an identity card specifying the ethnicity of its bearer: Tutsi, Hutu, or Twa. Moreover, the Chamber also noted that it was 'patrilineal lines of heredity' that determined ethnicity. Finally, the Chamber recalled that the witnesses who had testified before it 'identified themselves by ethnic group and generally knew the ethnic group to which their friends and neighbours belonged.'[20] However, the Trial Chamber in the end apparently was not convinced that from an objective point of view the Tutsi constituted an ethnic group – in what observers have described as 'remarkable'[21] and a 'surprise,'[22] the Chamber declined to find that the Tutsi were an ethnic group under the statutory definition but rather 'in any case ... a stable and permanent group,'[23] which according to the Trial Chamber's interpretation of the *travaux préparatoires* of the Genocide Convention was also protected.[24] In other words, the Trial Chamber expanded the notion of the protected

---

trators have only committed a crime against humanity not a genocide', P. Wald, 'Genocide and Crimes Against Humanity', 6 *Washington University Global Studies Law Review* (2007), p. 621 at p. 633.

[14] The rationale being that these groups are stable, homogenous and that membership is involuntary. See G. Werle, *supra* n. 11, p. 194, fn. 39 with further references. See also ICTR, *Prosecutor* v. *Akayesu*, Case ICTR-96-4-T, Judgment, 2 September 1998, para. 511.

[15] ICTY, *Prosecutor* v. *Krstić*, Case IT-98-33-T, Judgment, 2 August 2001, para. 554. Contra *Akayesu* Judgment, *supra* n. 14, para. 701: 'any stable and permanent group.'

[16] See ICTY, *Prosecutor* v. *Jelisić*, Case IT-95-10-T, Judgment, 14 December 1999, para. 69. For an overview of the Genocide Convention's drafting history, see G. Boas, et al., *supra* n. 11, pp. 147-149.

[17] *Akayesu* Judgment, *supra* n. 14, paras. 512-515, unfortunately providing few sources for its views. For a critical assessment of the judgment and the methodology employed therein, see A. Zahar & G. Sluiter, *International Criminal Law* (Oxford, Oxford University Press 2008), pp. 157-172.

[18] *Akayesu* Judgment, *supra* n. 14, para. 513.

[19] Ibid., para. 170: 'The Trial Chamber notes that the Tutsi population does not have its own language or a distinct culture from the rest of the Rwandan population.'

[20] Ibid., para. 171. See also para. 702.

[21] G. Werle, *supra* n. 11, p. 194.

[22] A. Zahar & G. Sluiter, *supra* n. 17, p. 160.

[23] *Akayesu* Judgment, *supra* n. 14, para. 702.

[24] Ibid., para. 701. See also ICTR, *Prosecutor* v. *Rutaganda*, Case ICTR-96-3-T, Judgment and Sentence, 6 December 1999, para. 57.

group under the genocide definition to any stable and permanent group, as apparently it was otherwise unable to characterise the Tutsi as an ethnic group.

The *Akayesu* Trial Chamber's approach seems questionable for two reasons: first, it conflicts with the notion of *nullum crimen sine lege* as a principle recognised under international customary law;[25] and second, it is derived from an unnecessarily rigid assumption, namely, that the protected group must be determined according to strictly objective criteria. Consequently, it received much criticism,[26] and later decisions by Trial Chambers of the ICTR and the ICTY have attempted to move away from the *Akayesu* Judgment's purely objective methodology. In fact, the very next judgment of the ICTR in the *Kayishema and Ruzindana* case – rendered by a different Trial Chamber – introduced subjective criteria into the definition of an ethnic group and held that such a group

> 'is one whose members share a common language and culture; *or a group which distinguishes itself, as such (self-identification); or a group identified as such by others, including perpetrators of the crimes (identification by others).*'[27]

The Trial Chamber's factual finding that the Tutsi were an ethnic group was primarily based on the fact that all citizens of Rwanda were required to carry identification cards specifying their ethnicity as Hutu, Tutsi, or Twa.[28] It thus focused on the idea that membership in the group can be socially ascribed.

The next judgment of the ICTR – rendered by the same bench of judges who decided *Akayesu* – also seemed to tilt somewhat towards a subjective solution:

> 'Moreover, the Chamber notes that for the purposes of applying the Genocide Convention, membership of a group is in essence, a subjective, rather than an objective concept. The victim is perceived by the perpetrator of genocide as belonging to a group slated for destruction. In some instances, the victim may perceive himself/herself as belonging to the said group.'[29]

However, the Trial Chamber quickly qualified its statement:

> 'Nevertheless, the Chamber is of the view that a subjective definition alone is not enough to determine victims groups …'[30]

---

[25] See G. Werle, *supra* n. 11, p. 32 with further references. See also 'Report of the Secretary-General Pursuant to Paragraph 2 of Security Council Resolution 808 (1993)', UN Doc. S/25704, 3 May 1994, para. 29: 'It should be pointed out that, in assigning to the International Tribunal the task of prosecuting persons responsible for serious violations of international humanitarian law, the Security Council would not be creating or purporting to "legislate" that law. Rather, the International Tribunal would have the task of applying existing international humanitarian law.'

[26] See for instance W.A. Schabas, *supra* n. 5, pp. 132-133.

[27] ICTR, *Prosecutor* v. *Kayishema and Ruzindana*, Case ICTR-95-1-T, Judgment, 21 May 1999, para. 98 [emphasis added].

[28] Ibid., paras. 523-524.

[29] *Rutaganda* Judgment, *supra* n. 24, para. 56.

[30] Ibid., para. 57.

Later judgments of the ICTR have either veered in a more subjective direction[31] or simply withdrawn to a formulation that left the issue open.[32] Exemplary for this approach is the holding of the *Semanza* Trial Chamber that 'the determination of a protected group is to be made on a case-by-case basis, consulting both objective and subjective criteria.'[33]

In *Jelisić*, the first case of the ICTY that addressed the question of a protected group, the Trial Chamber went even further than *Kayishema and Ruzindana* and interpreted the protected group in an entirely subjective manner:

> 'Although the objective determination of a religious group still remains possible, to attempt to define a national, ethnical or racial group today using objective and scientifically irreproachable criteria would be a perilous exercise whose result would not necessarily correspond to the perception of the persons concerned by such categorisation. Therefore, it is more appropriate to evaluate the status of a national, ethnical or racial group from the point of view of those persons who wish to single that group out from the rest of the community. The Trial Chamber consequently elects to evaluate membership in a national, ethnical or racial group using a subjective criterion. It is the stigmatisation of a group as a distinct national, ethnical or racial unit by the community which allows it to be determined whether a targeted population constitutes a national, ethnical or racial group in the eyes of the alleged perpetrators.'[34]

This was to a large extent followed in *Krstić* and *Blagojević and Jokić*, the only cases before the ICTY so far where accused have been convicted for genocide (in relation to the massacres committed at Srebrenica):

> 'A group's cultural, religious, ethnical or national characteristics must be identified within the socio-historic context which it inhabits … [T]he Chamber identifies the relevant group by using as a criterion the stigmatization of the group, notably by the perpetrators of the crime, on the basis of its perceived national, ethnical, racial or religious characteristics.'[35] … 'Originally viewed as a religious group, the Bosnian Muslims were recognized as a "nation" by the Yugoslav Constitution of 1963. The evidence tendered at the trial also shows very clearly that the highest Bosnian Serb political authorities and the Bosnian Serb forces operation in Srebrenica in July 1995 viewed the Bosnian Muslims as a specific national group.'[36]

---

[31] See for instance ICTR, *Prosecutor* v. *Ndindabahizi*, Case ICTR-2001-71-I, Judgment and Sentence, 15 July 2004, para. 468: 'In assessing whether [the victim] was a member of a protected group, in this case of the Tutsi ethnicity, the subjective intentions of the perpetrators are of primary importance.' See also para. 469: 'In light of these factors, the Chamber infers that [the victim] was targeted because he was understood to be, at least in part, Tutsi.' See also *Bagilishema* Judgment, *supra* n. 10, para. 65.

[32] See for an overview: G. Boas, et al., *supra* n. 11, pp. 173-176 with further references.

[33] *Semanza* Judgment, *supra* n. 10, para. 317.

[34] *Jelisić* Judgment, *supra* n. 16, para. 70.

[35] *Krstić* Judgment, *supra* n. 15, para. 557.

[36] Ibid., para. 559. See also ICTY, *Prosecutor* v. *Blagojević and Jokić*, Case IT-02-60-T, Judgment, 17 January 2005, para. 667. However, it is notable, and somewhat contradictory, that the *Blagojevic and Jokić* Trial Chamber also repeated the *Semanza* Trial Chamber's statement as regards the determination of a protected group on a case-by-case basis, using both objective and subjective criteria. *Idem.*

Interestingly enough, the *ad hoc* tribunals' Appeals Chambers have never decided on the interpretation of the term 'protected group.' However, there is some scattered jurisprudence. In *Stakić*, the ICTY Appeals Chamber appears to have hinted that a purely subjective approach in determining what constitutes a protected group would not be supported by the Genocide Convention,[37] stating that neither the *Rutaganda* nor the *Krstić* Trial Chambers had actually excluded objective criteria and that other Trial Chambers of the ICTR had 'also concluded that target groups cannot be only subjectively defined.'[38]

In *Nahimana, et al.*, the ICTR Appeals Chamber – composed of the same judges as in *Stakić* – assessed whether the Trial Chamber had erred when, in the section of the trial judgment dealing with genocide, it had also made reference to Hutu individuals who were killed because they supported the Tutsi ethnic group. Touching upon the issue of whether subjective criteria were permitted when deciding on the status of a group, the Appeals Chamber stated that

> '[i]n the instant case, only the Tutsi ethnic group may be regarded as a protected group under Article 2 of the Statute and Article 2 of the Convention on the Prevention and Punishment of the Crime of Genocide, since the group of "Hutu political opponents" or the group of "Tutsi individuals and Hutu political opponents" does not constitute a "national, ethnical, racial or religious group" under these provisions. Furthermore, although the jurisprudence of the *ad hoc* Tribunals acknowledges that the perception of the perpetrators of the crimes may in some circumstances be taken into account for purposes of determining membership of a protected group, in this instance neither the Trial Chamber nor the Prosecutor cited any evidence to suggest that the Appellants or the perpetrators of the crimes perceived Hutu political opponents as Tutsi. In other words, in the present case Hutu political opponents were acknowledged as such and were not "perceived" as Tutsi. Even if the perpetrators of the genocide believed that eliminating Hutu political opponents was necessary for the successful execution of their genocidal project against the Tutsi population, the killing of Hutu political opponents cannot constitute acts of genocide.'[39]

Thus, it appears that the Appeals Chambers have accepted a mixed subjective-objective assessment when it comes to the determination of the protected group under the genocide provisions of the ICTR and ICTY Statutes, and in particular, that the perception of the perpetrators *vis-à-vis* the victims can play a certain role in this assessment.

Of course, as some observers have mentioned, the issue has now become somewhat 'academic'[40] in relation to the *ad hoc* tribunals, considering the body of case-

---

[37] ICTY, *Prosecutor* v. *Stakić*, Case IT-97-24-A, Judgment of the Appeals Chamber, 22 March 2006, para. 25.

[38] *Idem.* However, this re-interprets the holding of the *Krstić* Trial Judgment, does not account for the clear language used in the *Jelisić* Trial Judgment and makes no reference to the above-cited ICTR trial judgments (see *supra* n. 31).

[39] ICTR, *Prosecutor* v. *Nahimana, et al.*, Case ICTR-99-52-A, Judgment of the Appeals Chamber, 28 November 2007, para. 496 (footnotes omitted).

[40] G. Boas, et al., *supra* n. 11, p. 176.

law addressing the genocides in Rwanda and in Srebrenica. Moreover, the ICTR Appeals Chamber has even taken judicial notice of the fact that '[b]etween 6 April 1994 and 17 July 1994, there was a genocide in Rwanda against the Tutsi ethnic group,'[41] i.e., the Appeals Chamber accepted as common knowledge – without further proof necessary – the existence of the Tutsi group as a protected group.[42] Nevertheless, it would have been certainly desirable if the appellate bodies of the *ad hoc* tribunals had clarified the law on such a central element of the definition of the crime of genocide. On the other hand, the Appeals Chambers are not alone in their reluctance as both the International Court of Justice[43] and the International Criminal Court[44] have shied away from pronouncing on the issue when they had the opportunity to do so.

Having said that, the ICTY Appeals Chamber did settle two questions pertaining to what constitutes a protected group and who belongs to it. The first issue had been decided differently by various Trial Chambers and concerned the question of whether a protected group could be defined negatively. The *Jelisić* Trial Chamber, probably as a consequence of its subjective 'stigmatisation' approach, held that

> '[a] group may be stigmatised … by way of positive or negative criteria. A "positive approach" would consist of the perpetrators of the crime distinguishing a group by the characteristics which they deem to be particular to a national, ethnical, racial or religious group. A "negative approach" would consist of identifying individuals as not being part of the group to which the perpetrators of the crime consider that they themselves belong and which to them displays specific national, ethnical, racial or religious characteristics. Thereby, all individuals thus rejected would, by exclusion, make up a distinct group.'[45]

---

[41] ICTR, *Prosecutor* v. *Karemera, et al.*, Case ICTR-98-44-AR73(C), Decision on Prosecutor's Interlocutory Appeal of Decision on Judicial Notice, 16 June 2006, paras. 33-38. See also ICTR, *Prosecutor* v. *Semanza*, Case ICTR-97-20-A, Judgment of the Appeals Chamber, 20 May 2005, para. 192.

[42] Given that the *ratio decidendi* of Appeals Chamber decisions is binding on Trial Chambers, there has been no need for Trial Chambers in subsequent judgments to prove each time that the Tutsi constituted an ethnic group, protected under the Genocide Convention. See for instance ICTR, *Prosecutor* v. *Bagosora, et al.*, Case ICTR-98-41-T, Judgment, 18 December 2008, para. 2117.

[43] ICJ, Case Concerning the Application of the Convention on the Prevention and Punishment of the Crime of Genocide *Bosnia and Herzegovina* v. *Serbia and Montenegro*, Judgment, 26 February 2007, para. 191: 'The Parties essentially agree that international jurisprudence accepts a combined subjective-objective approach. The issue is not in any event significant on the facts of this case and the Court takes it no further.'

[44] ICC, *Prosecutor* v. *Al Bashir*, Case ICC-02/05-01/09, ICC Pre-Trial Chamber, Decision on the Prosecution's Application for a Warrant of Arrest against Omar Hassan Ahmad Al Bashir, 4 March 2009, para. 137, fn. 152: 'The Majority notes that neither the Statute nor the rules provide for a definition of "ethnic group." The Majority also observes that international case law has not provided either a clear definition of what an "ethnic group" is. In this regard, the Majority observes that the ICJ, in its recent Judgment on Genocide, did not rule on whether a wholly objective (based on anthropological considerations), a wholly subjective (based only upon the perception of the perpetrators), or a combined objective/subjective approach to the definition of the relevant group should be adopted … However, the Majority considers that, for the purpose of the present decision, it is unnecessary to further explore this issue.' But see Separate and Partly Dissenting Opinion of Judge Anita Ušacka, para. 23.

[45] *Jelisić* Judgment, *supra* n. 16, para. 71.

Thus, an example in the context of the conflict in Bosnia and Herzegovina would be the description of the protected group as encompassing all 'non-Serbs.' The *Stakić* Trial Chamber on the other hand did not agree with this 'negative approach' and stressed that 'a target group may be distinguishable on more than basis and the elements of genocide must be considered in relation to each group separately, e.g., Bosnian Muslims and Bosnian Croats.'[46] Even though this issue seems rather theoretical, it could have practical consequences in a situation where the prosecution faces difficulties in proving its case in relation to one of the (positively defined) targeted groups, which in turn is a component of the larger (negatively defined) group.[47] However, when the prosecution appealed, the *Stakić* Appeals Chamber confirmed the interpretation of the Trial Chamber. It held that support for the view that a group targeted for genocide must be positively defined could be found in the etymology of the term 'genocide,' the drafting history of the Genocide Convention, subsequent discussion by experts and the wording of the ICTY Statute's genocide provision.[48] The Appeals Chamber emphasised that 'genocide was originally conceived of as the destruction of a race, tribe, nation, or other group with a particular positive identity – not as the destruction of various people lacking a distinct identity'[49] and that 'given that negatively defined groups lack specific characteristics, defining groups by reference to a negative would run counter to the intent of the Genocide Convention's drafters.'[50] Therefore, the prosecution is required to prove in relation to each specific group, e.g., Bosnian Croats or Bosnian Muslims, that it was a protected group under the genocide definition. Consequently, the elements of the crime must be considered separately in relation to different protected groups.[51]

The second issue that was clarified by the ICTY Appeals Chamber is also of practical relevance as it concerns the question of whether the intent of a perpetrator

---

46 *Stakić* Judgment, *supra* n. 10, para. 512. See also ICTY, *Prosecutor* v. *Brđanin*, Case IT-99-36-T, Judgment, 1 September 2004, paras. 685-686.

47 See *Stakić* Appeal Judgment, *supra* n. 37, Partly Dissenting Opinion of Judge Shahabuddeen, para. 16: 'If the prosecution were required to proceed against each component group separately, it would fail to prove its case if it did not prove a required ingredient in the case of a component group (for example, that those destroyed formed a significant element of the component group or part of the component group). Yet the same deficiency would not prove crucial if the prosecution were allowed to collect component groups in one compendious group and to proceed against the latter as the relevant group. This is so because, if the compendious group answers to the prescribed criteria of what is a group, the ingredients of the crime would have to be proved in relation to the compendious group as the relevant group, and not in relation to each component group separately considered. Therefore, what may be a deficiency in a prosecution concerning a component group may not necessarily be a deficiency in a prosecution concerning the compendious group.'

48 *Stakić* Appeal Judgment, *supra* n. 37, paras. 20-24.

49 Ibid., para. 21. However, see Partly Dissenting Opinion of Judge Shahabuddeen, para. 12: 'I cannot think of anything which necessarily prevents several different victim groups from being defined as collectively belonging to a "group" *other than that* of the perpetrator' [emphasis in the original].

50 Ibid., para. 22.

51 See in support of the *Stakić* Appeal Judgment: *Bosnia and Herzegovina* v. *Serbia and Montenegro*, *supra* n. 43, paras. 194-196.

of genocide must be directed at the destruction of the civilian component of a group only. The Appeals Chamber held that

> '[p]rovided the part intended to be destroyed is substantial, and provided that the perpetrator intends to destroy that part as such, there is nothing in the definition of genocide prohibiting, for example, a conviction where the perpetrator killed detained military personnel belonging to a protected group because of their membership in that group. It may be that, in practice, the perpetrator's genocidal intent will almost invariably encompass civilians, but that is not a legal requirement of the offence of genocide.'[52]

In sum, the question of how to best define the term 'protected group' as provided in the Genocide Convention and the *ad hoc* tribunals' statutes has been a recurrent theme in the jurisprudence of both the ICTR and ICTY. What looks like fairly straightforward wording has been the subject of countless debates, both in judgments of the Chambers and also in the academic world.[53] Of course, one should not forget that the tribunals were established to deal with very specific situations, and some of the problems encountered – such as the problem of whether the Tutsi in Rwanda are an ethnic group in the meaning of the Genocide Convention – were inherent to these special circumstances. Nevertheless, future courts and tribunals will have to address the same legal questions. Fortunately, they will operate with the advantage of finding guidance in the case-law of the *ad hoc* tribunals.

III. The destruction of the group

Another issue that was addressed by the *ad hoc* tribunals concerned the interpretation of a perpetrator's intent to *destroy* a protected group. In particular, the question arose whether the intended destruction must be physical in nature or whether it suffices that the perpetrator aims at destroying the protected group's social identity. Again, this issue is not purely theoretical. Unlike in the Rwandan context, where – as the evidence in the cases before the ICTR showed – the perpetrators clearly intended the physical destruction of the Tutsi group, a great number of the crimes in the former Yugoslavia were committed during general campaigns of 'ethnic cleansing,' which had the aim of expelling certain ethnic groups out of their homelands in order to change the overall ethnic composition of the region. Many people were forcibly transferred, killed or otherwise mistreated in the course of these events. Could then for example the killing of people, with the mere intent to expel from a certain area the remainder of the ethnic group to which they belong, constitute genocide?

---

[52] ICTY, *Prosecutor* v. *Krstić*, Case IT-98-33-A, Judgment of the Appeals Chamber, 19 April 2004, para. 226.

[53] In addition to the above-mentioned sources, see also A. Cassese, *International Criminal Law*, 2nd edn. (Oxford, Oxford University Press 2008), p. 138.

Most of the judgments of the ICTR[54] and ICTY[55] have interpreted the 'intent to destroy' in a narrow manner, explaining that the perpetrator must intend the actual physical or biological destruction of the group. With the term 'physical' referring to the immediate and/or direct deaths of the victims, and the term 'biological' denoting the eventual disappearance of the group,[56] there is no room for concepts such as 'cultural' genocide, which merely affect the social identity of the group. Indeed, the ICTY Trial Chamber in the *Krstić* case rejected the expansionist interpretation by the United Nations General Assembly[57] and German courts:[58]

> '[C]ustomary international law limits the definition of genocide to those acts seeking the physical or biological destruction of all or part of the group. Hence, an enterprise attacking only the cultural or sociological characteristics of a human group in order to annihilate these elements which give to that group its own identity distinct from the rest of the community would not fall under the definition of genocide.'[59]

The Appeals Chamber in the same case explicitly affirmed that the Trial Chamber had correctly identified the governing legal principle: 'The Genocide Convention, and customary international law in general, prohibit only the physical or biological destruction of the group.'[60]

It was thus somewhat surprising that in the *Blagojević and Jokić* case, the ICTY Trial Chamber held that 'the term "destroy" in the genocide definition can encompass the forcible transfer of a population.'[61] It further expounded as follows:

> 'The Trial Chamber finds in this respect that the physical or biological destruction of a group is not necessarily the death of the group members. While killing large numbers of a group may be the most direct means of destroying a group, other acts or series of acts, can also lead to the destruction of the group. A group is comprised of its individuals, but also of its history, traditions, the relationship between its members, the relationship with other groups, the relationship with the land. The Trial Chamber finds that the physical or biological destruction of the group is the likely outcome of a forc-

---

54 See for instance *Semanza* Judgment, *supra* n. 10, para. 315.

55 See for instance *Stakić* Judgment, *supra* n. 10, para. 519.

56 G. Boas, et al., *supra* n. 11, p. 164.

57 UNGA Res. 47/121 (18 December 1992) UN Doc. A/Res/47/121, p. 2, declaring that 'ethnic cleansing' is a form of genocide.

58 See for instance the decision of the Federal Constitutional Court of Germany, Case 2 BvR 1290/99, 12 December 2000, para. 22, arguing that the 'social existence' of a group is also protected. The European Court of Human Rights rejected a complaint directed against this jurisprudence, stating that 'the national courts' [broader] interpretation of the crime of genocide could reasonably be regarded as consistent with the essence of that offence and could reasonably be foreseen by the applicant at the material time.' *Jorgić* v. *Germany*, Application No. 74613/01, Judgment, 12 July 2007, para. 114.

59 *Krstić* Judgment, *supra* n. 15, para. 580.

60 *Krstić* Appeal Judgment, *supra* n. 52, para. 25. But see Partial Dissenting Opinion of Judge Shahabuddeen, para. 49: 'It is not apparent why an intent to destroy a group in a non-physical or non-biological way should be outside the ordinary reach of the Convention on which the Statute is based, provided that that intent attached to a listed act, this being of a physical or biological nature.'

61 *Blagojević and Jokić* Judgment, *supra* n. 36, para. 665.

ible transfer of the population when this transfer is conducted in such a way that the group can no longer reconstitute itself – particularly when it involves the separation of its members. In such cases the Trial Chamber finds that the forcible transfer of individuals could lead to the material destruction of the group, since the group ceases to exist as a group, or at least as the group it was. The Trial Chamber emphasises that its reasoning and conclusion are not an argument for the recognition of cultural genocide, but rather an attempt to clarify the meaning of physical or biological destruction.'[62]

As the Trial Chamber did not find that Blagojević had known of the mass killings in Srebrenica, it consequently inferred genocidal intent, *inter alia*, from his knowledge of the transfer of parts of the Bosnian Muslim population of Srebrenica:

> 'The forcible transfer of the women, children and elderly is a manifestation of the specific intent to rid the Srebrenica enclave of its Muslim population.'

The Appeals Chamber rejected this reasoning:

> '[T]he Appeals Chamber accepts that the forcible transfer operation, the separations, and the mistreatment and murders in Bratunac town are relevant considerations in assessing whether the principal perpetrators had genocidal intent. However, the Appeals Chamber is not convinced by the Trial Chamber's reasoning that the forcible transfer operation alone or coupled with the murders and mistreatment in Bratunac town would suffice to demonstrate the principal perpetrators' intent to 'destroy' the protected group. The *Krstić* Appeal Judgement clearly held that 'forcible transfer does not constitute in and of itself a genocidal act', and it is simply a relevant consideration as part of the overall factual assessment.'[63]

In this context it is noteworthy that the International Court of Justice also follows the narrow interpretation of the *ad hoc* tribunals:

> 'Neither the intent, as a matter of policy, to render an area "ethnically homogeneous," nor the operations that may be carried out to implement such policy, can *as such* be designated as genocide: the intent that characterizes genocide is "to destroy, in whole or in part" a particular group, and deportation or displacement of the members of a group, even if effected by force, is not necessarily equivalent to destruction of that group, nor is such destruction an automatic consequence of the displacement.'[64]

It remains to be seen whether other courts in the future subscribe to the strict interpretation of the term 'destroy' as applied by the *ad hoc* tribunals or whether they will also take into account the emerging jurisprudence of national courts, such as

---

[62] Ibid., para. 666.

[63] ICTY, *Prosecutor* v. *Blagojević and Jokić*, Case IT-02-60-A, Judgment of the Appeals Chamber, 9 May 2007, para. 123 (footnotes omitted). See *infra* (V.) for a more detailed discussion on how to infer genocidal intent.

[64] *Bosnia and Herzegovina* v. *Serbia and Montenegro, supra* n. 43, para. 190 [emphasis in the original].

those in Germany, which are based on a much broader understanding of a perpetrator's intent to destroy.[65] It should be noted that while the majority of legal commentators have spoken out against expanding the notion of 'destroy,'[66] there are also observers who argue in favor of a broader concept.[67]

IV. 'In whole or in part ... as such'

It is clear from the wording of the genocide definition that there is no need for the perpetrator to intend the destruction of the whole group in its entirety. The intent to destroy part of the protected group suffices. Indeed, the International Law Commission, in its 1996 Draft Code of Crimes Against the Peace and Security of Mankind pointed out that '[i]t is not necessary to intend to achieve the complete annihilation of a group from every corner of the globe.'[68] This sentiment was echoed by the ICTY Appeals Chamber in the *Krstić* case:

> 'Nazi Germany may have intended only to eliminate Jews within Europe alone; that ambition probably did not extend, even at the height of its power, to an undertaking of that enterprise on a global scale. Similarly, the perpetrators of genocide in Rwanda did not seriously contemplate the elimination of the Tutsi population beyond the country's borders. The intent to destroy formed by a perpetrator of genocide will always be limited by the opportunity presented to him.'[69]

However, the question remains what is meant by 'part' of the protected group. Does this term connote a quantitative pre-condition, such as the intended number of victims or could it also refer to a qualitative criterion, such as the intended elimination of the leadership of the group? Can there be genocide in a geographically limited area?

The ICTR Trial Chamber in *Kayishema and Ruzindana* was the first to pronounce on the issue when it held that '"in part" requires the intention to destroy a considerable number of individuals.'[70] In *Bagilishema*, the ICTR Trial Chamber 'consider[ed] that the intention to destroy must target at least a substantial part of

---

[65] See in this regard *Al Bashir* Decision, *supra* n. 44, Separate and Partly Dissenting Opinion of Judge Anita Ušacka, para. 62, adopting the more expansive approach outlined by Judge Shahabuddeen in his Partial Dissenting Opinion appended to the *Krstić* Appeal Judgment (see *supra* n. 60).

[66] See for instance C. Kreß, 'The Crime of Genocide Under International Law', 6 *ICLR* (2006), p. 461 at pp. 486 et seq., arguing that 'a broad construction of the term "destroy" in reliance on the social concept of the term may seem politically attractive, but it is difficult to see how such an approach could be portrayed as remaining within the confines of an existing customary rule of international *criminal* law' (at p. 489 [emphasis in the original]).

[67] See G. Werle, *supra* n. 11, pp. 192-193, arguing that '[t]he idea that physical existence alone is protected by the criminalization of genocide is ... too narrow' (at p. 193).

[68] 'Report of the International Law Commission on the Work of its Forty-Eighth Session (1996)', UN Doc. A/51/10(Supp.), 1 January 1996, p. 89.

[69] *Krstić* Appeal Judgment, *supra* n. 52, para. 13 (footnote omitted).

[70] *Kayishema and Ruzindana* Judgment, *supra* n. 27, para. 96.

the group.'[71] However, at the ICTR, Chambers did not explore the question further. This is not surprising, given the factual context of the Rwandan genocide with its overwhelming 'campaign of mass killing intended to destroy, in whole, or at least in very large part, Rwanda's Tutsi population.'[72]

However, the situation was not as clear-cut in the cases prosecuted at the ICTY. In *Jelisić*, the Trial Chamber raised the question of 'what proportion of the group is marked for destruction and beyond what threshold could the crime be qualified as genocide?'[73] It proceeded to state that

> 'Genocidal intent may ... be manifest in two forms. It may consist of desiring the extermination of a very large number of the members of the group, in which case it would constitute an intention to destroy a group en masse. However, it may also consist of the desired destruction of a more limited number of persons selected for the impact that their disappearance would have upon the survival of the group as such. This would then constitute an intention to destroy the group "selectively."'

The Trial Chamber thus did not only follow the numerical approach but also took up the prosecution's argument that it is sufficient for the genocidal intent to be directed against a representative fraction of the protected group, such as its leaders. It quoted with approval from the Report of the Commission of Experts,[74] which had stated that

> '[i]f essentially the total leadership of a group is targeted, it could also amount to genocide. Such leadership includes political and administrative leaders, religious leaders, academics and intellectuals, business leaders and others – the totality per se may be a strong indication of genocide regardless of the actual numbers killed.'[75]

In addition, the Chamber held that

> '[i]n view of the object and goal of the [Genocide] Convention and the subsequent interpretation thereof ... international custom admits the characterisation of genocide even when the exterminatory intent only extends to a limited geographic zone.'

The Trial Chamber did not explain further what it understood by 'limited geographic zone.' Hence, the *Stakić* Trial Chamber only

---

[71] *Bagilishema* Judgment, *supra* n. 10, para. 64. See also *Semanza* Judgment, *supra* n. 10, para. 316; *Bagosora, et al.*, Judgment, *supra* n. 42, para. 2115 and ICTR, *Prosecutor* v. *Gacumbitsi*, Case ICTR-2001-64-A, Judgment of the Appeals Chamber, 7 July 2006, para. 44.

[72] *Karemera, et al.*, Appeal Decision, *supra* n. 41, para. 35.

[73] *Jelisić* Judgment, *supra* n. 16, para. 80.

[74] Established by the UN Secretary-General in 1992 to examine and analyse information in relation to violations of international humanitarian law in the former Yugoslavia. See UNSC Res. 780 (6 October 1992) UN Doc. S/RES/780.

[75] 'Final Report of the Commission of Experts Established Pursuant to Security Council Resolution 780 (1992)', UN Doc. S/1994/674, 27 May 1994, para. 94.

> 'with some hesitancy follows the jurisprudence ... which permits a characterisation of genocide even when the specific intent extends only to a limited geographical area, such as a municipality. The Trial Chamber is aware that this approach might distort the definition of genocide if it is not applied with caution.'[76]

However, legal principles were truly tested for the first time in the *Krstić* trial, which addressed the events at Srebrenica. For an ease of understanding, it is useful to briefly recall the factual circumstances of that case. Srebrenica, a town in Eastern Bosnia and Herzegovina, and the surrounding area were of strategic importance to both the Bosnian Muslims and the Bosnian Serbs. In the summer of 1995, Bosnian Serb forces overran the enclave and by July had occupied it. They proceeded to separate the Bosnian Muslim women, children and the elderly from the men. While the women and children were removed from Srebrenica, 7,000 to 8,000 Bosnian Muslim men were captured and subsequently killed in mass executions by the Bosnian Serb forces. General Krstić, who had been a commander in the Bosnian Serb army, was charged by the prosecution with genocide in relation to these crimes. After finding that Krstić was one of those responsible for the killings – a genocidal act – the Trial Chamber had to satisfy itself that he had also acted with the necessary genocidal intent. The Trial Chamber concluded that

> 'the protected group, within the meaning of Article 4 of the Statute, must be defined, in the present case, as the Bosnian Muslims. The Bosnian Muslims of Srebrenica or the Bosnian Muslims of Eastern Bosnia constitute a part of the protected group under Article 4.'[77]

The Trial Chamber had thus identified the Bosnian Muslims of Srebrenica as the part of the group that was targeted by the perpetrators. However, in another part of its judgment, the Chamber also held that

> 'the military aged Bosnian Muslim men of Srebrenica do in fact constitute a substantial part of the Bosnian Muslim group, because the killing of these men inevitably and fundamentally would result in the annihilation of the entire Bosnian Muslim community. In this respect, the intent to kill the men amounted to an intent to destroy a substantial part of the Bosnian Muslim group.'[78]

At first glance, it is not clear what the Trial Chamber had in mind. Did it regard the Bosnian Muslims in Srebrenica as the relevant part of the group of the Bosnian Muslims or rather the military aged Bosnian Muslim men of Srebrenica? The following diagrams help illustrate the problem:

---

76 *Stakić* Judgment, *supra* n. 10, para. 523.
77 *Krstić* Judgment, *supra* n. 15, para. 560.
78 Ibid., para. 634. See also para. 581.

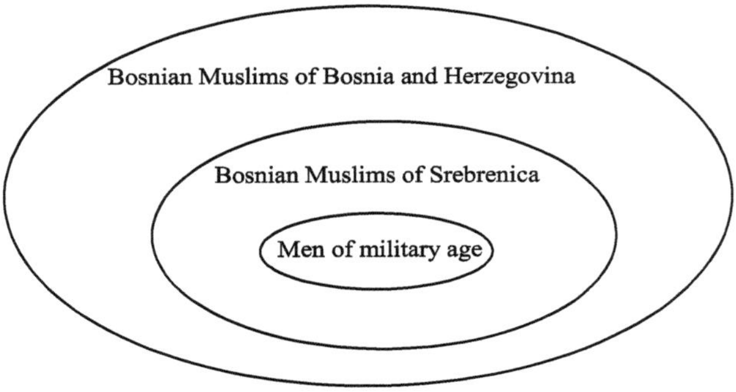

or

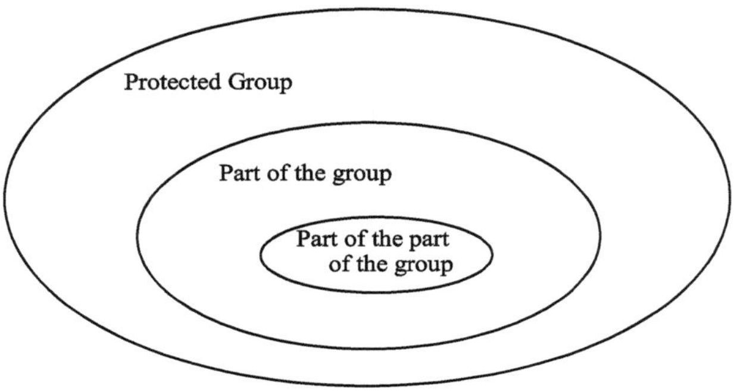

Hence, when the Trial Chamber ultimately convicted Krstić for genocide, one of the complaints brought by the defence in their appeal challenging the verdict was that

> '[t]he Trial Chamber ... measured the killing of military age men against the Bosnian Muslim community at Srebrenica and found it to be substantial. But in doing so, it incorrectly diluted the genocide formula by measuring a part (military age men) against another part (of Srebrenica) and finding it substantial. The Trial Chamber never employed the correct formula of measuring the part intended to be destroyed (military age men of Srebrenica) against the group (Bosnian Muslims).'[79]

The Appeals Chamber rejected this argument. Even though it noted that in parts of the Trial Judgment, the Trial Chamber had 'used imprecise language which lends support to the defence's argument,'[80] it held that

> '[t]he Defence misunderstands the Trial Chamber's analysis. The Trial Chamber stated that the part of the group Radislav Krstić intended to destroy was the Bosnian Muslim population of Srebrenica. The men of military age, who formed a further part of that group, were not viewed by the Trial Chamber as a separate, smaller part within the meaning of Article 4 [of the ICTY Statute]. Rather, the Trial Chamber treated the killing of the

[79] *Prosecutor* v. *Krstić*, Case IT-98-33-A, Defence Appeal Brief (Public Version), 10 January 2002, para. 40.

[80] *Krstić* Appeal Judgment, *supra* n. 52, para. 22.

men of military age as evidence from which to infer that Radislav Krstić and some members of the VRS Main Staff had the requisite intent to destroy all the Bosnian Muslims of Srebrenica, the only part of the protected group relevant to the Article 4 analysis.'[81]

The Appeals Chamber also clarified that

> '[t]he intent requirement of genocide under Article 4 of the Statute is ... satisfied where evidence shows that the alleged perpetrator intended to destroy at least a substantial part of the protected group. The determination of when the targeted part is substantial enough to meet this requirement may involve a number of considerations. The numeric size of the targeted part of the group is the necessary and important starting point, though not in all cases the ending point of the inquiry. The number of individuals targeted should be evaluated not only in absolute terms, but also in relation to the overall size of the entire group. In addition to the numeric size of the targeted portion, its prominence within the group can be a useful consideration. If a specific part of the group is emblematic of the overall group, or is essential to its survival, that may support a finding that the part qualifies as substantial within the meaning of Article 4.'[82]

Even though the number of the targeted people at Srebrenica – approximately 3% of the Bosnian Muslim population in Bosnia and Herzegovina – was not significant enough in quantitative terms, the Appeals Chamber stressed that Srebrenica nevertheless was

> 'important due to its prominence in the eyes of both the Bosnian Muslims and the international community. The town of Srebrenica was the most visible of the "safe areas" established by the UN Security Council in Bosnia. By 1995 it had received significant attention in the international media ... The elimination of the Muslim population of Srebrenica, despite the assurances given by the international community, would serve as a potent example to all Bosnian Muslims of their vulnerability and defenselessness in the face of Serb military forces. The fate of the Bosnian Muslims of Srebrenica would be emblematic of that of all Bosnian Muslims.'[83]

The defence further alleged that the Trial Chamber had 'equat[ed] an intent to destroy a group with an intent to displace a group from a particular territory'[84] when it made reference to the 'physical disappearance of the Bosnian Muslim population at Srebrenica.'[85] This argument was also linked to the fact that the Bosnian Serb forces had transferred the women and children out of Srebrenica while limiting the killings to the men. In particular, the defence argued that

> '[t]he fact that the Bosnian Serb Army went to great trouble to round up buses from throughout the country and transport the women and children to safety, rather than

---

81 Ibid., para. 19 (footnote omitted).
82 Ibid., para. 12 (footnote omitted).
83 *Krstić* Appeal Judgment, *supra* n. 52, para. 16.
84 *Krstić* Defence Appeal Brief, *supra* n. 79, para. 47.
85 *Krstić* Judgment, *supra* n. 15, para. 595.

> killing them while they were in their custody, or even letting them starve in Potočari, demonstrates that there was no intent to destroy the Bosnian Muslims as an ethnic group.'[86]

The Appeals Chamber rejected these claims:

> 'The Trial Chamber was also entitled to consider the long-term impact that the elimination of seven to eight thousand men from Srebrenica would have on the survival of that community. In examining these consequences, the Trial Chamber properly focused on the likelihood of the community's physical survival. As the Trial Chamber found, the massacred men amounted to about one fifth of the overall Srebrenica community. The Trial Chamber found that, given the patriarchal character of the Bosnian Muslim society in Srebrenica, the destruction of such a sizeable number of men would "inevitably result in the physical disappearance of the Bosnian Muslim population at Srebrenica." Evidence introduced at trial supported this finding, by showing that, with the majority of the men killed officially listed as missing, their spouses are unable to remarry and, consequently, to have new children. The physical destruction of the men therefore had severe procreative implications for the Srebrenica Muslim community, potentially consigning the community to extinction.'[87]

In other words, because of the impact that the killing of the men had on the group of the Bosnian Muslims of Srebrenica (as a substantial part of the group of the Bosnian Muslims in Bosnia and Herzegovina), potentially leading to its destruction, it was irrelevant that not all members of the group were targeted for physical destruction.[88] Indeed, the Appeals Chamber held that the events in Srebrenica signified 'the type of physical destruction the Genocide Convention is designed to prevent.'[89]

It should be mentioned that while this reasoning was accepted in a subsequent judgment concerning an accused who was charged with genocide in Srebrenica,[90] some observers have voiced doubts both in relation to the status of the Bosnian Muslims in Srebrenica as a substantial part of the Bosnian Muslim population in general and in relation to the genocidal intent that was directed at it in particular.[91] In any case, the Srebrenica situation shows that it is not always easy for a criminal court to establish that genocide has occurred. This holds especially true in circum-

---

86 *Krstić* Defence Appeal Brief, *supra* n. 79, para. 56.

87 *Krstić* Appeal Judgment, *supra* n. 52, para. 28, referring to paras. 93 and 592-595 of the *Krstić* Judgment (footnotes omitted).

88 The Appeals Chamber also pointed out that '[t]he decision not to kill the women or children may be explained by the Bosnian Serbs' sensitivity to public opinion' (*Krstić* Appeal Judgment, *supra* n. 52, para. 31), and that in any event 'the offence of genocide does not require proof that the perpetrator chose the most efficient method to accomplish his objective of destroying the targeted part' (ibid., para. 32).

89 *Krstić* Appeal Judgment, *supra* n. 52, para. 29.

90 See *Blagojević and Jokić* Judgment, *supra* n. 36, paras. 673-677.

91 See for instance C. Kreß, *supra* n. 66, pp. 491-492. See also W.A. Schabas, 'Darfur and the "Odious Scourge": The Commission of Inquiry's Findings on Genocide', 18 *LeidenJIL* (2005), p. 871 at pp. 874 and 881.

stances where only a relatively small part of a group was targeted or was even within reach of the perpetrators.

Much has been written about what is meant by the perpetrator's intent to target a group 'as such.'[92] There have been only a few references in the jurisprudence of the *ad hoc* tribunals. In the *Niyitegeka* case, the ICTR Appeals Chamber elaborated on the meaning of the term:

> 'The words "as such," however, constitute an important element of genocide, the "crime of crimes." It was deliberately included by the authors of the Genocide Convention in order to reconcile the two diverging approaches in favour of and against including a motivational component as an additional element of the crime. The term "as such" has the *effet utile* of drawing a clear distinction between mass murder and crimes in which the perpetrator targets a specific group because of its nationality, race, ethnicity or religion. In other words, the term "as such" clarifies the specific intent requirement. It does not prohibit a conviction for genocide in a case in which the perpetrator was also driven by other motivations that are legally irrelevant in this context. Thus the Trial Chamber was correct in interpreting "as such" to mean that the proscribed acts were committed against the victims *because of* their membership in the protected group, but not *solely* because of such membership.'[93]

In *Ntakirutimana and Ntakirutimana*, the ICTR Appeals Chamber explained further that it

> 'need not consider whether the Trial Chamber erred in finding that the refugees were targeted "solely" for their Tutsi ethnicity because the definition of the crime of genocide does not contain such a requirement. It is immaterial, as a matter of law, whether the refugees were targeted solely on the basis of their ethnicity or whether they were targeted for their ethnicity in addition to other reasons.'[94]

Therefore, it is simply irrelevant whether a perpetrator has personal motives, such as the wish for economic benefits or revenge. In the words of the *Jelisić* Appeal Judgment, which referred to the 'inscrutability of motives in criminal law,'[95] there is therefore a 'necessity to distinguish specific intent from motive.'[96]

---

[92] See A. Zahar & G. Sluiter, *supra* n. 17, pp. 179-181 with further references.

[93] ICTR, *Prosecutor* v. *Niyitegeka*, Case ICTR-96-14-A, Judgment of the Appeals Chamber, 9 July 2004, para. 53 (footnotes omitted), rejecting the defence appeal based on the allegation that Niyitegeka had targeted Tutsi because he perceived them to be the enemy or supporters of the enemy. See also *Stakić* Appeal Judgment, *supra* n. 37, para. 20: 'The term "as such" has great significance, for it shows that the offence requires intent to destroy a collection of people who have a particular group identity.'

[94] ICTR, *Prosecutor* v. *Ntakirutimana and Ntakirutimana*, Cases ICTR-96-10-A and ICTR-96-17-A, Judgment of the Appeals Chamber, 13 December 2004, para. 304.

[95] ICTY, *Prosecutor* v. *Tadić*, Case IT-95-1-A, Judgment of the Appeals Chamber, 15 July 1999, para. 269.

[96] ICTY, *Prosecutor* v. *Jelisić*, Case IT-95-10-A, Judgment of the Appeals Chamber, 5 July 2001, para. 49.

V. Proving genocidal intent

Before concluding, it is necessary to point out one more practical problem in the prosecution of genocide. As explained before, genocide is a crime that requires a specific intent. However, there will be few cases where that intent is emphatically expressed by the perpetrator: '[E]xplicit manifestations of criminal intent are, for obvious reasons, often rare in the context of criminal trials.'[97] The *ad hoc* tribunals have therefore permitted that the intent be determined based on inferences drawn from the evidence at hand. 'In order to prevent perpetrators from escaping convictions simply because such manifestations are absent, the requisite intent may normally be inferred from relevant facts and circumstances.'[98] In the *Jelisić* case, the ICTY Appeals Chamber explained what those facts and circumstances could be, namely,

> 'the general context, the perpetration of other culpable acts systematically directed against the same group, the scale of atrocities committed, the systematic targeting of victims on account of their membership of a particular group, or the repetition of destructive and discriminatory acts.'[99]

However, the ICTR Appeals Chamber emphasised that

> 'the inferential approach does not relieve the Prosecution of its burden to prove each element of its case, including genocidal intent, beyond reasonable doubt. Rather, it is simply a different means of satisfying that burden.'[100]

For example, in the *Seromba* case, the ICTR Appeals Chamber established the genocidal intent of the accused, a priest, because he had known 'that there were approximately 1,500 Tutsis in the church and that the destruction of the church [for which Seromba, together with others, was found responsible] would necessarily cause their death,'[101] because of the fact that 'he had turned away Tutsi refugees from the presbytery, whereupon two of them were killed';[102] and because of utterances by Seromba who had referred to killed Tutsi as *saleté* (dirt) and stated: 'Destroy the church. We, the Hutu, are many in number and, furthermore, in the house of God. Demons have gotten in there.'[103]

---

97 *Kayishema and Ruzindana* Appeal Judgment, *supra* n. 10, para. 159.

98 *Idem*. See also ICTR, *Prosecutor* v. *Seromba*, Case ICTR-01-66-A, Judgment of the Appeals Chamber, 12 March 2008, para. 176 with further references.

99 *Jelisić* Appeal Judgment, *supra* n. 96, para. 47. The Appeals Chamber in this context rejected the Trial Chamber's assertion that the existence of a plan or policy is a legal ingredient of the crime. However, it also recognised that the existence of a plan or policy may facilitate proof of the crime. Ibid., para. 48.

100 *Gacumbitsi* Appeal Judgment, *supra* n. 71, para. 41.

101 *Seromba* Appeal Judgment, *supra* n. 98, para. 177.

102 Ibid., para. 178.

103 Ibid., para. 180.

One may ask to what extent, if any, the above-cited decision of the ICTR Appeals Chamber in the *Karemera, et al.* case, in which it accepted as a fact of common knowledge that genocide had occurred in Rwanda, has an impact of the burden of proof borne by the prosecution in subsequent cases before the ICTR.[104] Indeed, one could argue that if the genocidal intent of a perpetrator can be inferred from the general context of the events, a prior general finding that genocide occurred could be prejudicial to the defence. However, the Appeals Chamber was quick to refute any such claims:

> '[A]llowing judicial notice of a fact of common knowledge ... does not lessen the Prosecution's burden of proof or violate the procedural rights of the Accused. Rather, it provides an alternative way that that burden can be satisfied, obviating the necessity to introduce evidence documenting what is already common knowledge. The Prosecution must, of course, still introduce evidence demonstrating that the specific events alleged in the Indictment constituted genocide and that the conduct and mental state of the Accused specifically make them culpable for genocide.'[105]

Considering recent ICTR judgments, the *Karemera, et al.* Appeal Decision does not seem to have any impact on the fact-finding process carried out by the Trial Chambers. They still satisfy themselves in relation to each and every charged incident whether the perpetrator had genocidal intent, independent of the general assessment that 'there was a genocide in Rwanda against the Tutsi ethnic group.'[106]

VI. Conclusion

This paper has focused on only one, yet admittedly very significant, part of the genocide definition, i.e., a perpetrator's 'intent to destroy, in whole or in part, a national, ethnical, racial or religious group, as such.' It is this specific intent that makes genocide special – however, the meaning of each of the terms in the definition is fraught with controversy. The ICTY and the ICTR have been the first international courts to address some of these issues in the course of their work. Their respective Appeals Chambers have aimed to establish uniformity in the emerging jurisprudence of the Trial Chambers. As it turned out, the application of the genocide provisions in practice – as opposed to their discussion in an academic vacuum – is not always without its problems. While there are extreme cases, such as the situation in Rwanda, which make the qualification of mass crimes as genocide relatively easy, there are other situations which are not as obvious. In the end, future

[104] See ICTR, *Prosecutor* v. *Karemera, et al.*, Case ICTR-98-44-T, Decision on Prosecution Motion for Judicial Notice, 9 November 2005, para. 7.

[105] *Karemera, et al.*, Appeal Decision, *supra* n. 41, para. 37.

[106] Ibid., para. 33. See for instance ICTR, *Prosecutor* v. *Karera*, Case ICTR-01-74-T, Judgment, 7 December 2007, paras. 536-540. See also *Bagosora, et al.*, Judgment, *supra* n. 42, paras. 1998 and 2084 et seq. and ICTR, *Prosecutor* v. *Rukundo*, Case ICTR-2001-70-T, Judgment, 27 February 2009, paras. 48 and 566 et seq.

international and domestic courts will have the advantage of being able to draw upon the experience of the *ad hoc* tribunals. The wealth of existing case-law will thus facilitate the future development of the law on genocide.

INTERNATIONAL GENOCIDE TRIALS: THREE CASE STUDIES

Inés Mónica Weinberg de Roca and Margaret Patten Knowlan

I. Introduction

The Security Council of the United Nations created the International Criminal Tribunal for Rwanda (the 'Tribunal' or 'ICTR') to prosecute those most responsible for genocide and other serious violations of international humanitarian law committed in 1994 in Rwanda and in neighboring states. One might expect 'those most responsible' to only include senior government and military officials. However, those convicted by the ICTR as *genocidaires* have also included those with professions one might not expect, such as doctors and religious leaders. In my tenure as a judge with the Tribunal from 2003 to 2008, I was struck by the professions and ordinariness of the accused. While the nature of the crimes were ghastly and horrendous, even more horrifying was the fact that the convicted perpetrators were ordinary, even formerly exemplary people who at a given time and place were capable of committing extraordinary crimes of genocide and crimes against humanity.

This paper will discuss three cases from the ICTR involving convictions for genocide, *Ntakirutimana*,[1] *Zigiranyirazo*,[2] and *Bikindi*.[3] I have chosen these cases as I was on the bench for all three, and was intrigued by the backgrounds of these convicted *genocidaires*. Each case also raised an interesting legal issue. In *Ntakirutimana*, the Accused were a pastor and a doctor, and the Appeals Chamber clarified the elements of extermination as a crime against humanity. In *Zigiranyirazo*, the Accused was a businessman, convicted for participating in joint criminal enterprise ('JCE') to kill Tutsi. In *Bikindi*, the Accused was a popular entertainer, and the Trial Chamber considered whether song could constitute incitement to commit genocide.

II. Ntakirutimana

Elizaphan Ntakirutimana was a 70 year-old pastor of the Seventh Day Adventist Church at the time of the genocide. His son, Gérard Ntakirutimana, was a doctor

[1] ICTR, *Prosecutor* v. *Elizaphan Ntakirutimana & Gérard Ntakirutimana,* Cases ICTR-96-10-T & ICTR-96-17-T, Judgment, 21 February 2003; Judgment, 13 December 2004.

[2] ICTR, *Prosecutor* v. *Protais Zigiranyirazo*, Case ICTR-01-73-T, Judgment, 18 December 2008.

[3] ICTR, *Prosecutor* v. *Simon Bikindi*, Case ICTR-01-72-T, Judgment, 2 December 2008.

C. Safferling and E. Conze (eds.), The Genocide Convention Sixty Years after its Adoption

who had trained abroad and returned home to practice medicine in Rwanda. At the time of the genocide they both worked at the Mugonero Complex (the "Complex"), which contained a chapel, a nursing school and a hospital. Elizaphan and Gérard were implicated in the attacks on the refugees at the Complex, many of whom were their colleagues. The defence argued that it was unthinkable that these persons could have committed the crimes with which they are charged. Trial Chamber I of the ICTR found otherwise, and recalled a statement by one of the defence witnesses, that thousands of religious persons committed crimes during the events in Rwanda in 1994.

The prosecution alleged that Elizaphan, the pastor, had advised Tutsi to take shelter at the Complex, which had swelled in numbers to an estimated 2,000 to 6,000 a week after the genocide began. On the morning of 15 April 1994, six pastors and another prominent Tutsi among the group wrote a letter to Elizaphan, as he held the most senior position in the region within the Seventh Day Adventist Church. In this letter they informed the Accused that they had heard that 'tomorrow we shall die with our families' and requested Elizaphan to intervene by contacting the *bourgmestre* as soon as possible.[4] The prosecution alleged that Elizaphan did not intervene, and that the Complex was the site of a massacre in which hundreds were killed. The prosecution also alleged that Elizaphan conveyed attackers to various locations and was involved in the attack on the nearby Murambi Church.

The prosecution alleged that Gérard, Elizaphan's son the doctor, separated Tutsi from Hutu at the Complex, denied medicine to Tutsi at the hospital, cut off utility supplies to the Complex including water and electricity, procured gendarmes and ammunition for the attack on Tutsi at the Complex, participated in the attack, and took stock of the bodies that evening.

The Trial Chamber accepted that Elizaphan visited the *bourgmestre* the morning after the letter was written. Although the Chamber was unable to determine what was said at that meeting, it found that Elizaphan sent a message on the morning of the massacre through *gendarmes* that he could not help them. The Chamber also found that Elizaphan conveyed attackers to Murambi Church and ordered the removal of the church roof so that it could no longer be used as a shelter for Tutsi, and that in so doing, he facilitated the hunting down and the killing of the Tutsi refugees. The Chamber also found that Elizaphan transported armed attackers to various locations to pursue and kill Tutsi, and that he participated in vehicle convoys carrying armed attackers to various locations in the Bisesero area. For these crimes, Elizaphan was convicted of genocide.

The Chamber found that Gérard transported attackers to various locations where he himself shot at refugees, and that during an attack at a primary school, he shot and killed a Tutsi civilian. For these crimes, Gérard was convicted of both genocide and murder as a crime against humanity.

---

4 This incident inspired Philip Gourevich, a writer with The New Yorker magazine, to write a non-fiction book titled *We wish to inform you that tomorrow we will be killed with our families. Stories from Rwanda* (New York, USA, Picador 1999).

Elizaphan's position as a pastor in the Church was considered to be both a mitigating circumstance, considering the life he had led before 1994, and an aggravating circumstance, considering the abuse of the trust his congregation had placed in him. The Chamber accepted the evidence that until 1994 the pastor lived an exemplary life as a church leader: a highly religious and tolerant person, who showed no ethnic bias, including in times of unrest and ethnic tension, for over half a century. However, the Chamber also considered that as a highly respected personality and a man wielding certain authority within the Seventh Day Adventist Church, he abused the trust placed in him. The letter, written to him by the pastors was a symbol of his perceived authority. Many of the refugees at the Complex were faithful Seventh Day Adventists. The Chamber found that he distanced himself from his Tutsi pastors and his flock in their hour of need, and that his presence at the scenes of attack could only be construed by attackers as an approval of their actions. Elizaphan was sentenced to ten years imprisonment.

The Chamber found Gérard's background to be only an aggravating circumstance in sentencing. The Chamber noted that he was a prominent personality, one of the few individuals in his area of origin to have achieved a higher education. As a medical doctor, he took lives instead of saving them, abusing the trust placed in him. Gérard was sentenced to twenty-five years imprisonment.

Both Accused and the prosecution appealed. The Appeals Chamber of the ICTR affirmed Elizaphan's conviction for genocide, and reversed his acquittal for extermination as a crime against humanity, entering a conviction for this crime. The Appeals Chamber affirmed Gérard's convictions, quashed a conviction for murder as a crime against humanity and entered a new conviction for aiding and abetting genocide and two convictions for aiding and abetting extermination as a crime against humanity. Both Accused' sentences were affirmed.

Of particular interest, the Appeals Chamber reversed the acquittals for extermination as a crime against humanity. The Trial Chamber had acquitted Elizaphan of extermination because it was not convinced that he had personally killed anyone, and Gérard because it was not convinced that he had killed more than three victims.

However, the Appeals Chamber found that the Trial Chamber had failed to consider whether the acts of aiding and abetting which had supported the conviction for genocide could also support a conviction for aiding and abetting the crime of extermination. Specifically, the Appeals Chamber found that in carrying out the acts of participation, such as transporting attackers to kill survivors and requesting that the roof of a church be removed so that the Tutsi could not shelter there, Elizaphan was making a substantial contribution to the acts of mass killing. The Appeals Chamber also found that he had knowledge of the perpetrators' intent as the extermination of the Tutsi refugees, and that he therefore had the required *mens rea* for aiding and abetting the extermination of Tutsi as a crime against humanity. Likewise, Gérard was found guilty of the same crime for his participation in a number of attacks and for his procurement of *gendarmes* and ammunition for the attackers. He also knew the intent of the attackers and he made a substantial contribution to the acts of mass killing. The Appeals Chamber further held that the Trial Chamber erred when it held that an element of the crime of extermination is that the victims must be named or described persons. Therefore, Elizaphan's and Gérard's acquittals for extermination as crimes against humanity were reversed and convictions on these counts were entered.

III. Zigiranyirazo

Upon the death of President Habyarimana on 6 April 1994, Protais Zigiranyirazo was alleged to have been the most important influential male family member of the presidential family. He had no formal governmental or military position, his influence within Rwanda was based on his status as the late President's brother-in-law. While Zigiranyirazo had been involved in Rwandan politics from 1969 to 1989, as a Member of Parliament and *préfet,* he was a businessman at the time of the genocide.

According to the prosecution, Zigiranyirazo met with government, military and family authorities in the *préfectures* of Kigali-*ville* and Gisenyi, both preceding and following the death of President Habyarimana, to plan, prepare and facilitate attacks on Tutsi during 1994 with the intent to destroy, in whole or in part, the Tutsi ethnic group. In furtherance of this plan, several roadblocks were established in April 1994, in direct proximity of Zigiranyirazo's three homes. The prosecution further alleged that Zigiranyirazo participated in the killings of approximately 2000 Tutsi at Kesho and Rurunga Hills, as well as the murders of three *gendarmes* and a moderate Hutu named Stanislas Sinibagiwe.

Trial Chamber III of the ICTR acquitted Zigiranyirazo of most of the crimes alleged, but found him guilty of participating in a JCE to commit genocide and extermination as a crime against humanity for his role at Kesho Hill. The Chamber also convicted Zigiranyirazo of aiding and abetting genocide for his actions at a roadblock near one of his homes.

The prosecution argued that Zigiranyirazo's position as a trusted and influential person in his community, as evidenced in part by his status as the brother-in-law of the former President, should be considered an aggravating factor in sentencing. The Chamber found however that the influence Zigiranyirazo derived from this status was not significant enough to amount to an aggravating factor. For his convictions for genocide and extermination as a crime against humanity resulting from his actions at Kesho Hill, Zigiranyirzo was sentenced to 20 years imprisonment for each crime, to be served concurrently. For his conviction for genocide resulting from his actions at the roadblock, Zigiranyirzo was sentenced to 15 years imprisonment, also to be served concurrently. Both Parties appealed the Judgment, but at the time of writing, the Appeals Chamber had not yet issued an Appeals Judgment.

What was interesting about this case from a legal perspective was that it was one of the few convictions at the ICTR based on a JCE.[5] The Trial Chamber found that Zigiranyirazo had participated in a JCE with other officials and assailants to kill Tutsi on Kesho Hill on 8 April 1994. Specifically, the Chamber found that following a first unsuccessful attack on hundreds and possibly more than a thousand Tutsi civilians seeking refuge on Kesho Hill, the Accused arrived as part of a convoy which included officials, Presidential Guards, soldiers, *Interahamwe* and civilians. Upon arrival, the Accused and two other officials addressed the assailants. The Chamber did not make a finding on the precise words spoken by the Accused, or whether any of the three ordered the attack. However, the Chamber found that the crowd of assailants applauded the Accused's speech, and immediately after the speeches, commenced the attack using guns, grenades and traditional weapons, on the Tutsi civilians who had sought refuge on the hill. The Chamber found that between 800 and 1500 Tutsi were killed that day.

Given the ethnicity of the victims, the scale of the killings, and the context of a genocide within which they took place, the Chamber found that the only reasonable conclusion was that the physical perpetrators of the killings possessed the intent to destroy in whole or in part the Tutsi ethnic group. Accordingly, the Chamber found that acts of genocide occurred on Kesho Hill on 8 April 1994.

Regarding whether Zigiranyirazo was criminally responsible for this attack through the participation in a JCE, the Chamber recalled that there were a plurality of people who were involved in the attack on Kesho Hill, whether through physically perpetrating the attack themselves, or through speaking to the assailants immediately before the attack. These people included Presidential Guard, soldiers, *Interahamwe*, and civilians, as well as the Accused and the officials accompanying him.

Regarding the common plan, design or purpose, the Chamber found that there were at least hundreds, if not over a thousand assailants who arrived, many of whom were armed with a range of weapons. They arrived together as part of a convoy, and participated in a meeting where the Accused and other officials delivered speeches. The attack could only be described as a coordinated operation backed by Presidential Guards, soldiers, *Interahamwe*, and civilians, armed with guns, grenades and traditional weapons, with organisational support from prominent personalities, such as the Accused. The Chamber considered that prior planning and coordination was the only reasonable explanation for the manner in which the perpetrators conducted the attack. This finding was supported further as it appeared that prior planning and coordination, resulting in a large number of well-armed assailants and the presence of officials to provide encouragement, distinguished this attack from the prior unsuccessful attack. Accordingly, the Chamber found that the only reasonable inference from the evidence was that a common criminal purpose existed to kill Tutsi on Kesho Hill.

---

[5] ICTR, *Prosecutor* v. *Aloys Simba*, Case ICTR-01-76-T, Judgment, 13 December 2005; Judgment, 27 November 2007.

With respect to whether Zigiranyirazo shared the common purpose of killing Tutsi, the Chamber recalled that he arrived at the massacre site with the assailants. He and the other officials addressed the assailants who then applauded and immediately commenced their attack. The assailants' applause indicated to the Chamber that Zigiranyirazo and other officials' speeches were received well by the assailants. Furthermore, the Accused did not leave the massacre site until after the attack had commenced. The Chamber therefore considered that the Accused, the other officials, and the assailants shared the common purpose of killing Tutsi, thus being members of the basic form of JCE. The Chamber also found that the assailants who physically perpetrated the killings possessed the genocidal intent, and that given the scale of the killings and their context, this genocidal intent was shared by all participants in the JCE, including the Accused.

Finally, given the influence which Zigiranyirazo's position of authority yielded, the Chamber considered that his arrival at the site with the assailants, his speech to the assailants, and his presence when the attack commenced, demonstrated support for the attack, and thus amounted to a form of encouragement to the assailants. Indeed, the applause that followed the Accused's speech, and the immediate commencement of the attack after the speeches, demonstrated the significant effect which the Accused, and the other speakers, had on the assailants' conduct. Accordingly, the Chamber found that the Accused significantly contributed to the execution of the joint criminal purpose to kill Tutsi at Kesho Hill by encouraging assailants to attack.

IV. Bikindi

Simon Bikindi was a famous singer and performer in Rwanda, and was essentially a celebrity on trial. He was an educated man, having completed a Bachelor's degree, and had worked for the Ministry of Youth and Association Movements. At the time of the genocide, Bikindi had written 40-60 songs and was the leader of the *Irindiro* ballet, which performed for social and cultural events, as well as political gatherings. The *Irindiro* Ballet was a group of some renown both within Rwanda and abroad, having toured Europe, Asia and North America.

The prosecution alleged that Bikindi participated in a campaign of violence against Tutsi and moderate Hutu during the genocide in Rwanda through his musical compositions and through the speeches he made at public gatherings. He was alleged to have collaborated with leading figures in the *Mouvement républicain national pour la démocratie et le développement* (MRND), the *Coalition pour la défense de la République* (CDR), the *Interahamwe* and the *Radio Télévision Libre des Mille Collines* (RTLM) to disseminate anti-Tutsi ideology and encourage the genocide. The prosecution further alleged that he participated in the military training of *Interahamwe*, encouraged the militias to attack the Tutsi population, and was responsible for a number of specific attacks and killings.

Trial Chamber III of the ICTR acquitted Bikindi of all allegations except for his use of a public address system attached to a vehicle on the road between Kivumu and Kayove *communes* in late June 1994. The Chamber found that he spoke over the public address system, stating that the Hutu should rise up and exterminate the Tutsi minority, and asking if people had been killing Tutsi. For these acts, he was found guilty of direct and public incitement to commit genocide.

The defence argued that Bikindi's exceptional musical talent should be considered a mitigating factor in sentencing due to his contribution to Rwandan cultural society. The Chamber found this to be an aggravating factor, in that, 'to the contrary, [these factors] evidence Bikindi's stature in Rwanda in 1994, which he abused by adding his voice to the anti-Tutsi campaign.'[6] The Chamber found that the influence Bikindi derived from his status as a well-known and popular artist made it likely that others would follow his exhortations, and considered that he abused his stature by using his influence to incite genocide. For these acts, Bikindi was sentenced to fifteen years imprisonment. Both Parties appealed the Judgment, but at the time of writing, the Appeals Chamber had not yet issued an Appeals Judgment.

What made this case unique were the allegations related to his music. This was the first trial in international criminal law in which a person was accused of inciting genocide through song. There were three songs in particular that the prosecution alleged incited violence against Tutsi: *Twasezerye* (translated to 'We Said Goodbye to the Monarchy'); *Nanga Abahutu* ('I Hate These Hutus'); and *Bene Sebahinzi* ('The Sons of the Father of the Cultivators'). The Chamber found that these three songs referred to relations between Hutu and Tutsi, painting Tutsi in a negative light. The Chamber found that *Twasezerye* documented a past of monarchical and colonial domination along ethnic lines, *Nanga Abahutu* discussed various types of people to be hated, and *Bene Sebahinzi* warned of the dangers of a cunning external infiltrator. The Chamber further found that these three songs were deployed in a propaganda campaign in 1994 in Rwanda to incite people to attack and kill Tutsi.

Despite this interpretation, however, the Chamber did not find Bikindi criminally responsible for the effect his music had during the genocide. The Chamber found that there was insufficient evidence that Bikindi intended these songs to incite attacks and killings. Although the Chamber found that Bikindi composed *Nanga Abahutu* and *Bene Sebahinzi* with the specific intention to disseminate pro-Hutu ideology and anti-Tutsi propoganda, and thus to encourage ethnic hatred, this fell short of intending to incite genocide.

Even if the Chamber had found Bikindi had possessed the requisite intent, a conviction would not have followed for a number of reasons. First, as the jurisdiction of the ICTR is limited to acts that occurred in 1994 only, and Bikindi wrote his songs before 1994, he could not be found criminally responsible for their composition. Secondly, while it was accepted that Bikindi's songs were broadcast repeat-

---

[6] ICTR, *Prosecutor* v. *Simon Bikindi*, Case ICTR-01-72-T, Judgment, 2 December 2008, para. 455.

edly on RTLM radio station in an effort to put the Hutu on notice to unite and be vigilant against the Tutsi, it was not established that Bikindi had any control or influence over the broadcasts. Thirdly, while there was evidence that Bikindi and his *Irindiro* troupe had performed at political rallies in the 1990s, the prosecution proved that he had attended only one rally in 1994, and only his attendance, not his participation through speech or song.

In conclusion, while the Chamber indicated a willingness to convict for incitement to commit genocide on the basis of song, the evidence was lacking in this case.

V. Conclusion

The three cases discussed above illustrate a number of interesting points. First, it was not just senior military and political officials who were implicated in the Rwandan genocide. In these cases, a pastor, a doctor, an influential businessman of the late President's family, and an entertainer were convicted of crimes against humanity and genocide. Genocide occurs within a society and the perpetrators are ordinary people who live within this society. At a given time and place events can trigger human reactions which transform ordinary humans into horrendous criminals. Secondly, the cases demonstrate the evolution of international criminal law. The ICTR is but one of many international criminal tribunals, all participating in the creation of a growing body of jurisprudence. These tribunals and their evolving jurisprudence are a strong stand against the impunity of those who violate international criminal and humanitarian law, which sadly happens over and over again.

Part Five
Genocide and the International Court of Justice

THE ICJ JUDGMENT IN THE *BOSNIAN GENOCIDE* CASE AND BEYOND: A NEED TO RECONCEPTUALISE?

Anja Seibert-Fohr

I. INTRODUCTION

Not long before the Convention's 60th Anniversary, the International Court of Justice (ICJ) in February 2007 rendered its first substantive judgment under the Genocide Convention. It concerned a case brought by Bosnia and Herzegovina against the Federal Republic of Yugoslavia (FRY) (then Serbia and Montenegro) with respect to the armed conflict in the 1990s.[1] This was the first time a case in which a violation of the Convention was pleaded reached the merits stage at the ICJ. Previously there had only been an advisory opinion in 1951 which had dealt with the general question whether reservations were admissible under the Genocide Convention.[2] It took over 40 years more until the question whether a state had violated the Convention was brought to the ICJ in a concrete case. By the time the Bosnian Case was finally decided, the International Criminal Tribunal for the Former Yugoslavia (hereafter, ICTY) and the International Criminal Tribunal for Rwanda (hereafter, ICTR) had already by and large settled their jurisprudence on the crime of genocide.[3] So the question arose whether the ICJ was competent to decide the case or whether it was the exclusive competence of criminal tribunals to consider the commission of genocide. When the Court affirmed its jurisdiction and rendered its decision on commission and complicity in genocide it attracted repeated criticism for interfering with criminal matters.[4]

---

[1] ICJ, *Application of the Convention on the Prevention and Punishment of the Crime of Genocide (Bosnia and Herzegovina* v. *Serbia and Montenegro)*, (hereinafter, *Bosnian Genocide* case), Judgment of 26 February 2007, para. 170, ICJ Reports 2007, pp. 40ff. Accessible at www.icj-cij.org/docket/files/91/13685.pdf, last visited 20 February 2009.

[2] ICJ, *Reservations to the Convention on the Prevention and Punishment of the Crime of Genocide*, Advisory Opinion, ICJ Rep. 1951, p. 23.

[3] See, e.g., ICTR, *Prosecutor* v. *Jean-Paul Akayesu*, Case ICTR-96-4-T, Judgment, 2 September 1998, para. 731, *Alfred Musema* v. *Prosecutor*, Case ICTR-96-13-A, Judgment of the Appeals Chamber, 16 November 2001; ICTY, *Prosecutor* v. *Radislav Krstic*, Case IT-98-33-A, Judgment of the Appeals Chamber, 19 April 2004.

[4] See, e.g., A. Cassese, 'On the Use of Criminal Law Notions in Determining State Responsibility', 5 *JICJ* (2007), p. 875; P. Gaeta, 'On What Conditions Can a State Be Held Responsible for Genocide?', 18 *EJIL* (2007), pp. 631; R.J. Goldstoneand & R.J. Hamilton, 'Bosnia v. Serbia, Lessons from

C. Safferling and E. Conze (eds.), The Genocide Convention Sixty Years after its Adoption

This paper considers the different positions on the competence of the ICJ and critically examines the 2007 judgment. The jurisdiction of the Court is closely related to the question whether states incur responsibility for genocide under the Genocide Convention. The paper tries to respond to those authors challenging the concept of state responsibility for genocide by offering a compromise formula which may guide the future conceptualisation of the Convention. The analysis of the Convention affirms that despite its strong criminal law focus, it also provides for obligations beyond criminalisation and punishment which are indeed relevant for inter-state disputes. But though the ICJ was competent to decide the case, there are flaws in its legal reasoning which unfortunately might have long-term implications beyond the case. As an alternative, this paper advocates a human rights analysis of the Convention and thereby offers a perspective which, so far, has been largely neglected but may become relevant in future cases.

II. History of proceedings

The *Bosnian Genocide* case should be considered in the context of other cases related to the Genocide Convention. An important step for the interpretation of the Convention was the ICJ's Advisory Opinion on *Reservations to the Convention on the Prevention and Punishment of the Crime of Genocide.* The Court stressed here that the Convention had been adopted for a 'humanitarian and civilizing purpose.'[5] It allowed minor reservations to the Convention but excluded reservations affecting this object and purpose.[6] The basic consideration of the nature and object of the Convention has significantly influenced the Court's later interpretation of the Convention. It became again relevant in the 1990s when several cases challenged violations of the Genocide Convention.[7] Most relevant are the Yugoslavian cases brought to the Court by Bosnia and Herzegovina and later by Croatia,[8] and the cases brought by the Democratic Republic of Congo against Rwanda, Uganda and Burundi.

---

the Encounter of the International Court of Justice with the International Criminal Tribunal for the Former Yugoslavia', 20 *LeidenJIL* (2008), p. 95.

[5] ICJ, *Reservations to the Convention on the Prevention and Punishment of the Crime of Genocide*, Advisory Opinion, ICJ Rep. 1951, p. 23.

[6] Ibid., pp. 22 et seq.

[7] The first case concerning a breach of the Convention was already brought to the ICJ in 1973 by Pakistan. This case against India, however, did not concern the question whether India was responsible for genocide, but only the question whether the transfer of alleged perpetrators to Bangladesh for trial was in violation of the Genocide Convention. The case was later settled. *Trial of Pakistani Prisoners of War* (*Pakistan* v. *India*), Pleading, Oral Arguments, Documents. For this dispute see also W.A. Schabas, *Genocide in International Law* (Cambridge, Cambridge University Press 2000), pp. 425-427.

[8] Apart from the *Bosnian Genocide* case brought in 1993, Croatia brought suit against Serbia and Montenegro in 1999 and Yugoslavia challenged several NATO members for their conduct during the bombing campaign concerning Kosovo. The application for provisional measures in the latter case was rejected by the ICJ in the absence of an arguable case for violation of the Genocide Convention. *Legality of Use of Force* case (*Yugoslavia* v. *Belgium, et al.*), Request for the Indication of Provisional Measures, Order, 2 June 1999.

In the proceedings concerning the *Bosnian Genocide* case which were initiated already in 1993, the Court rendered several decisions concerning admissibility and jurisdictional issues, before it could finally decide on the merits of the case. Already in its Judgment of 1996 on Preliminary Objections, the Court recognised that the rights and obligations enshrined by the Convention are rights and obligations *erga omnes*.[9] In its decision of 2006 in the case of *Armed Activities on the Territory of the Congo (Democratic Republic of the Congo* v. *Rwanda)*, the Court confirmed that the prohibition of genocide is a preemptory norm of international law (*jus cogens*).[10] But it did not further elaborate on this *obiter dictum*, since the decision was concerned with jurisdictional and admissibility issues which led the Court to conclude that it did not have jurisdiction to decide the case.[11] The consideration of the universal and fundamental importance of the prohibition of genocide, however, paved the path for the Court's 2007 judgment on the merits of the *Bosnian Genocide* case which specified the scope of state responsibility under the Convention.

III. Subject-matter jurisdiction of the ICJ in genocide cases

Before the Court was able to elaborate on substantive issues, it had to deal with the question of its jurisdiction.[12] Article IX of the Genocide Convention provides that disputes between state parties relating to *the interpretation, application or fulfillment of the Genocide Convention* shall be submitted to the ICJ.[13] What is meant by fulfillment was controversial among the parties to the dispute. Serbia and Montenegro had argued that the Convention only obliged state parties to criminalise, punish and extradite those guilty. Apart from this there was no responsibility of state for acts of genocide as such. The commission of genocide according to the Respondent was a matter of individual criminal responsibility.[14] It was therefore not possible to argue that a state party itself had violated the Convention by committing genocide.

But the Court rejected this argument. It held that Article I which requires state parties to prevent and punish genocide also prohibits state from committing geno-

---

[9] ICJ, *Application of the Convention on the Prevention and Punishment of the Crime of Genocide (Bosnia and Herzegovina* v. *Yugoslavia (Serbia and Montenegro))*, Judgment (Preliminary Objections), 11 July 1996, ICJ Rep. 1996 (II), at p. 616, para. 31.

[10] ICJ, *Armed Activities on the Territory of the Congo* (*Democratic Republic of the Congo* v. *Rwanda* New Application: 2002), Judgment, 3 February 2006, ICJ Rep. 2006, para. 64.

[11] The Court held that Rwanda's reservation to the compromissory clause of Art. IX was not incompatible with the object and purpose of the Convention. Therefore the Court did not have jurisdiction to decide the case. Ibid., para. 126.

[12] ICJ, *Bosnian Genocide* case, *supra* n. 1, paras. 80-141.

[13] It reads: 'Disputes between the Contracting Parties relating to the interpretation, application or fulfilment of the present Convention, including those relating to the responsibility of a state for genocide or for any of the other acts enumerated in article III, shall be submitted to the International Court of Justice at the request of any of the parties to the dispute.' Convention on the Prevention and Punishment of the Crime of Genocide, 9 December 1948, 78 *UNTS* 227 (hereinafter, Genocide Convention). The jurisdiction of the ICJ needs to be distinguished from criminal jurisdiction. *Persons* charged with genocide shall be tried by a competent domestic or international penal tribunal. (Art. VI.)

[14] ICJ, *Bosnian Genocide* case, *supra* n. 1, para. 156.

cide through its authorities.[15] According to the Court the obligation to prevent genocide necessarily implies the prohibition to commit genocide. It extended the prohibition to conspiracy, incitement, attempt and complicity in genocide.[16] The term 'commission' and the reference to other forms of participation in the context of state responsibility were misleading and therefore unfortunate. Such criminal law notions might suggest that what was at issue was the commission of a crime by a state. The ICJ, however, stressed that it was concerned with international responsibility, not with criminal responsibility. It pointed out that international responsibility was 'quite different in nature from criminal responsibility.'[17] It would have helped if the Court had referred to the simple notion of state responsibility for violating the Genocide Convention and had specified the obligation to prevent genocide in non-criminal terms.

III.1 The scope of primary obligations under the Genocide Convention

In order to understand the notion of international responsibility it is necessary to consider the term 'prevent' in Article 1 Genocide Convention in more detail. This expression plays a significant role for the protection of international human rights and has been interpreted comprehensively in the context of other international treaties. One example is the Convention against Torture and Other Cruel, Inhuman or Degrading Treatment or Punishment. It exhibits some parallels to the Genocide Convention and therefore warrants a similar interpretation with respect to state obligations.[18]

A comparison of the two instruments shows that the argument that the Genocide Convention is merely about individual criminal responsibility and the duty to criminalize genocide, does not persuade. Like the Genocide Convention, the Torture Convention initially defines the abuse.[19] Genocide and torture both constitute serious human rights violations. They are characterised by a physical act and a mental element. Torture needs to be inflicted intentionally with a specified aim, such as for example to obtain a confession.[20] Genocide requires the intent to de-

---

[15] Ibid., para. 166.

[16] Ibid., para. 167.

[17] *Idem.*

[18] Convention against Torture and Other Cruel, Inhuman or Degrading Treatment or Punishment, opened for signature by GA Res. 39/46, UN GAOR, 39th Sess., Supp. No. 51, UN Doc. A/39/51, at p.197, 4 February 1985, and entered into force 26 June 1987, reprinted in 23 ILM 1027 (1984) (hereinafter, Torture Convention).

[19] Pursuant to Art. 1(1) Torture Convention torture 'means any act by which severe pain or suffering, whether physical or mental, is intentionally inflicted on a person for such purposes as obtaining from him or a third person information or a confession, punishing him for an act he or a third person has committed or is suspected of having committed, or intimidating or coercing him or a third person, or for any reason based on discrimination of any kind, when such pain or suffering is inflicted by or at the instigation of or with the consent or acquiescence of a public official or other person acting in an official capacity. It does not include pain or suffering arising only from, inherent in or incidental to lawful sanctions.'

[20] Art. 1(1) defines as torture: 'Act by which severe pain or suffering, whether physical or mental, is intentionally inflicted on a person for such purposes as obtaining from him or a third person informa-

stroy a protected group as such or part thereof. The fact that both require a specific state of mind – in criminal terms *mens rea* – does not mean that they are only matters of criminal law. Though human rights violations usually do not require such a specific mental element, there are indeed exceptions with respect to some particularly serious violations. This does not negate the human rights character of their prohibition in the respective Conventions.

With respect to state obligations, the Torture Convention shows that the prohibition of torture does not only become relevant in criminal matters. It is also a matter of general human rights protection which requires measures of protection beyond criminalisation and prosecution. The second article of the Torture Convention makes this plain. It obliges state parties to *prevent* acts of torture.[21] Subsequent provisions then similar to the Genocide Convention[22] deal with the obligation to criminalise,[23] the establishment of criminal jurisdiction,[24] prosecution and extradition of offenders.[25] Both Conventions thus exhibit a similar structure which distinguishes between criminal and other measures of implementation.

The term prevention in the Torture Convention is broad. It does not only mean that states should intervene when ill-treatment takes place. It *primarily* obliges state parties to refrain from committing torture. No state party to the Convention has ever argued that it is not responsible for acts of torture committed by its authorities because the Convention only obliges to prevent torture. The duty to prevent means that state authorities must not be involved in any conduct constituting torture.[26] Why then should the term prevention in the Genocide Convention be interpreted narrowly in the sense that it only requires criminalisation and punishment? Or why should it be limited to a duty to intervene into third party abuses? An effective protection against genocide by state requires above all that state authorities are not involved in genocide.

There are thus good arguments for interpreting the duty to prevent in the Genocide Convention similar to its counterpart in the Torture Convention. The Genocide Convention is not only a criminal law treaty but should also be understood as a more comprehensive human rights instrument. Both, international criminal law and human rights law are two sides of one coin – the prohibition of genocide. They complement each other as measures to render the prohibition of genocide effective.

The collective notion of genocide does not negate its human rights character. After all, there are also other areas of human rights law, such as minority rights,

tion or a confession, punishing him for an act he or a third person has committed or is suspected of having committed, or intimidating or coercing him or a third person, or for any reason based on discrimination of any kind, when such pain or suffering is inflicted by or at the instigation of or with the consent or acquiescence of a public official or other person acting in an official capacity.'

[21] Art. 2(1) Torture Convention reads: 'Each state Party shall take effective legislative, administrative, judicial or other measures to prevent acts of torture in any territory under its jurisdiction.'

[22] See Arts. V and VI Genocide Convention.

[23] Art. 4 Torture Convention.

[24] Art. 5 Torture Convention.

[25] Arts. 6-8 Torture Convention. Arts. 10-11 specify non-criminal measures of prevention.

[26] In fact, torture can only be committed if there has been some kind of involvement of state authorities. See Art. 1 Torture Convention (note 20).

which seek to protect collectives. That the prohibition of genocide is motivated by human rights protection was already implicitly acknowledged by the ICJ in its 1951 Advisory Opinion when it referred to the 'humanitarian and civilizing purpose' of the Convention.[27] Its purpose is to effectuate the prohibition of genocide. This does not only require the adoption of criminal measures but a comprehensive approach which also includes other state obligations. Just like a state can breach a human rights convention by *committing* a human rights violation, it can also violate the Genocide Convention if its authorities are involved in genocide. A violation of the Torture Convention could be challenged by another state party in an inter-state complaint before the Torture Committee.[28] Under the Genocide Convention the competent organ to hear such inter-state complaints pursuant to Article IX is the ICJ.

III.2 The applicability of the concept of state responsibility

Those authors who advocate a narrow reading of the Genocide Convention regularly refer to the drafting history in order to underline that it was exclusively intended as a criminal law instrument.[29] However, the negotiations leading to the adoption of the Convention are not this unambiguous. The question of state responsibility was discussed controversially in the Sixth Committee of the General Assembly. Only a few states advocated a narrow conception of the Convention so that it would exclusively deal with individual criminal responsibility.[30] Others, such as the United Kingdom and Belgium, objected and asked for a provision on state responsibility.

The rejection of a proposed amendment by the United Kingdom is regularly cited as evidence for the denial of state responsibility.[31] But the amendment specifically dealt with state *criminal* responsibility. It read as follows:

> 'Criminal responsibility for any act of genocide as specified in articles II and IV shall extend not only to all private persons or associations, but also to state, governments, or organs or authorities of the state or government. Such acts committed by or on behalf of state or governments constitute a breach of the present Convention.'[32]

---

[27] ICJ, *Reservations to the Convention on the Prevention and Punishment of the Crime of Genocide*, Advisory Opinion, ICJ Rep. 1951, p. 23. See also *Bosnian Genocide* case, *supra* n. 1, para. 162.

[28] Art. 21 Torture Convention sets out a procedure for the relevant committee to consider complaints from one State Party which considers that another State Party is not giving effect to the provisions of the Convention. This procedure applies only to States Parties who have made a declaration accepting the competence of the committee in this regard.

[29] See, e.g., P. Gaeta, 'On What Conditions Can a State Be Held Responsible for Genocide?', 18 *EJIL* (2007), p. 631 at pp. 633-635.

[30] UN Doc. A/C.6/SR.95 (Chaumont, France; Maktos, United States).

[31] UN Doc. A/C.6/SR.96, p. 355.

[32] Official Records of the General Assembly, Third Session, *Part I, Sixth Committee, Annexes,* UN Doc. A/C.6/236 and Corr.1. For the underlying intention of the United Kingdom, see UN Doc. A/C.6/SR. 69 and A/C.6/SR.92 (Fitzmaurice, UK). For the drafting history, see also Summary of the discussions in various United Nations organs and the resulting decisions: Working paper prepared by the Secretariat, UN Doc. A/CN.4/165 and Corr.1 (1964).

It was not the concept of state responsibility in general which attracted opposition by other delegations, but the notion of state crimes which was heavily contested.[33]

The ordinary concept of state responsibility indeed found entry into the Convention when Article IX was adopted.[34] This provision explicitly refers to 'the responsibility of a state for genocide.' While the earlier amendment had not found the requisite approval, this text was adopted[35] because it clarified that it envisaged a form of state responsibility which was not criminal in nature.[36] The drafting history thus shows that the traditional concept of state responsibility for the failure to comply with the Convention was indeed reflected in 1948. When the International Court of Justice almost 60 years later affirmed the applicability of these rules in the *Bosnian Genocide* case it did not read a novel theory into the Genocide Convention but just elaborated on a concept already contemplated.

IV. The Court's criminal law analysis

The above analysis of the Convention shows that the Court's interpretation of Article 1 as an autonomous obligation of state and the application of the rules of state responsibility was fully warranted. The Court was right when it recognised a duty to abstain from acts constituting genocide. If one considers the term 'committing genocide' from a human rights perspective, not as a criminal law notion, there was nothing wrong with the ICJ's point of departure. But unfortunately the methodology applied by the ICJ in the subsequent examination of state responsibility exhibits some flaws. Its legal analysis heavily relied on criminal terms and thus did not fully grasp the concept of state responsibility.[37] In order to understand one needs to consider the line of its analysis step by step.

IV.1 The Court's line of reasoning

The problematic part of the judgment starts with the following consideration of the Court:

---

[33] UN Doc. A/C.6/SR.95 (France; Panama); UN Doc. A/C.6/SR.96.

[34] For this interpretation see also ICJ, *Bosnian Genocide* case (note 1), paras. 176-178. But see N. Robinson, *The Genocide Convention. Its Origins and Interpretation* (New York, Institue for Jewish Affairs 1949), pp. 42-43; see also Judges Shi and Vereshchetin, ICJ, *Application of the Convention on the Prevention and Punishment of the Crime of Genocide (Bosnia and Herzegovina* v. *Yugoslavia (Serbia and Montenegro)), Preliminary Objections,* Joint Declaration of Judge Shi and Judge Vereshchetin, ICJ Rep. 1995, p. 595.

[35] UN Doc. A/C.6/SR. 105.

[36] UN Doc. A/C.6/SR.103 (Fitzmaurice, UK; Chaumont, France). But see ibid. (Ingles, Philippines). For the United States opposition to the notion of damages for injuries suffered by a state's own nationals, see UN Doc. A/C.6/SR. 133 (Gross, US).

[37] For this issue see A. Seibert-Fohr, 'State Responsibility for Genocide under the Genocide Convention', in P. Gaeta (ed.), *The UN Genocide Convention: A Commentary* (2009, p. 349).

'[T]he Contracting Parties are bound by the obligation under the Convention not to commit, through their organs or persons or groups whose conduct is attributable to them, genocide and the other acts enumerated in Article III.'[38]

In other words, the starting point of its examination was factually a criminal analysis. The Court evaluated whether the crime of genocide had been *committed* by the *principal perpetrators* and then asked whether it could be attributed to the Respondent. In this part it heavily relied on the jurisprudence of the ICTY.[39] In fact, crucial questions, as for example whether the crimes had been committed with genocidal intent, were answered in just one paragraph with hardly any reference and consideration of factual evidence.[40] The ICJ contented itself with the assertion that it had carefully examined the ICTY's criminal proceedings and observed that none of those convicted were found to have acted with genocidal intent.[41] Only the massacre at Srebrenica in July 1995 had been committed with an intent to destroy in part the group of Muslims of Bosnia and Herzegovina and thus amounted to genocide.[42] The Court's main focus was clearly on the conduct of the immediate perpetrators. It heavily relied on evidence considered by the ICTY without engaging in a comprehensive independent consideration of evidence.[43] While this part covers almost 140 paragraphs, only 6 paragraphs deal with the FRY's conduct and intentions. The Court formulated a high threshold for special intent, requiring a convincing demonstration of intent.[44] A pattern of conduct did not suffice.[45]

Having concluded that only the massacre in Srebrenica constituted genocide, the Court analysed whether the conduct by the Bosnian Serbs could be attributed to the Federal Republic of Yugoslavia. But the Court denied responsibility of the FRY for the massacre because it could not be attributed to it: Neither had there been a participation of the Federal Republic of Yugoslavia in the massacre, nor could the Bosnian Serbs be characterised as its *de jure* or *de facto* organs.[46] Moreover, their conduct was neither directed nor controlled by the FRY. The ICJ reaffirmed its Nicaragua jurisprudence that attribution of third party conduct requires 'effective control' of the operation. It distinguished the question of state responsibility from the characterisation of a conflict as an international armed conflict which had been at issue in the ICTY's *Tadić* case. Absent such effective control over Bosnian Serb forces, the Court concluded that the FRY had not committed genocide. Neither could it be held responsible for conspiracy, incitement or complicity because it had not been established that Serbian authorities were clearly aware that genocide was about to take place when it supplied aid to the Bosnian Serbs.

---

[38] ICJ, *Bosnian Genocide* case, *supra* n. 1, para. 179.

[39] See ibid., e.g., para. 374.

[40] See ibid., e.g., paras. 277, 319, 328, 334, 354, 361, 367.

[41] Ibid., para. 277.

[42] Ibid., para. 297.

[43] Ibid., e.g., paras. 361, 367.

[44] For the standard of proof see A. Gattini, 'Evidentiary Issues in the ICJ's Genocide Judgment', 5 *JICJ* (2007), p. 889.

[45] ICJ, *Bosnian Genocide* case, *supra* n. 1, para. 373.

[46] Ibid., para. 395.

While the first part of the judgment had been concerned with the duty not to commit or to participate in genocide, the second part was on the duty to take active measures to prevent others from committing genocide. It was about third party intervention.[47] Here the standards for state responsibility were lower than for commission and participation.[48] Instead of requiring conclusive evidence of a state's positive knowledge that genocide was about to take place,[49] it was sufficient that FRY's authorities had been put on notice and must had been aware that there was a serious risk of genocide in Srebrenica.[50] By not intervening, it had failed to prevent genocide and therefore violated its obligation under the Genocide Convention. Finally the respondent was also held responsible for failing to cooperate with the ICTY in violation of Article VI.[51]

IV.2 **The need to reconceptualise**

A major problem lay in the Court's method of analysis. It was focused on the perpetration of the crime of genocide by the principle perpetrators and thus strictly accessory.[52] The whole situation in Bosnia was picked into pieces in order to find whether the alleged perpetrators had committed the crime of genocide in any of these incidents.[53] This is adequate for criminal cases, but the question in the *Bosnian Genocide* case was different. It concerned the general question of responsibility of the Federal Republic of Yugoslavia. The focus on each single incident risked loosing the overall picture. In order to determine state responsibility which in its nature is quite different from individual criminal responsibility, it is not enough to analyse the conduct of the immediate perpetrator and then ask whether it can be attributed to a state. Such analysis is too narrow. It would have been preferable to first outline comprehensively the primary duties of the Respondent and then to consider whether and how it had failed to abide by theses obligations. I will elaborate on this below.[54]

---

47 According to the Court States Parties are obliged 'to employ all means reasonable(y) available to them, so as to prevent genocide so far as possible.' Ibid., para. 430.

48 It requires the capacity to influence the action of persons likely to commit or committing genocide. Ibid., para. 430.

49 The Court required that the organ 'acted knowingly' for commission and conspiracy. Ibid., paras. 421-422.

50 Ibid., para. 438. The cognitive element was described as awareness of the danger that genocide would be committed, para. 432.

51 Art. VI Genocide Convention reads: 'Persons charged with genocide or any of the other acts enumerated in article III shall be tried by a competent tribunal of the state in the territory of which the act was committed, or by such international penal tribunal as may have jurisdiction with respect to those Contracting Parties which shall have accepted its jurisdiction.'

52 For this approach see para. 431 where the Court held that 'if neither genocide nor any of the other acts listed in Art. III of the Convention are ultimately carried out, then a state that omitted to act when it could have done so cannot be held responsible a posteriori, since the event did not happen which, under the rule set out above, must occur for there to be a violation of the obligation to prevent.'

53 See, e.g., ICJ, *Bosnian Genocide* case, *supra* n. 1, para. 376.

54 See *infra* sec. V.

The fact that the ICJ's legal analysis in the main part of its judgment largely paralleled criminal law analysis, led to unequivocal criticism in legal literature.[55] The ICJ seemed to have obliterated the distinction between individual criminal responsibility and state responsibility. But the Court explicitly rejected the notion of state criminal responsibility. What the majority of judges presumably had in mind was a form of aggravated state responsibility which is not criminal in nature but only requires a similarly high threshold to establish.

The reason for the ensuing controversy is probably that the ICJ was not precise enough in its interpretation of Article I. It could have been more specific with respect to the duty to prevent by outlining the exact scope of this primary obligation by state under the Genocide Convention. Instead of examining the commission of genocide by individual perpetrators and questions of attribution the Court right from the beginning on should have focused on the question which obligations *States Parties* undertake under the Convention. The real issue of the case was less about attribution than about the scope of primary obligations. With this point of departure it would have been easier to set the record straight and to verify that the Court effectively did not deal with criminal matters. Considering the Convention from a human rights point of view would have helped to clarify that what was at issue was the *duty to refrain* from any kind of involvement in genocide (as part of the obligation to prevent). The Court could have avoided much criticism if it had applied such a human rights analysis rather than an analysis heavily penetrated by criminal law notions, such as the concept of commission, incitement and conspiracy.

V. The missing piece

The focus on commission and conspiracy had a very practical drawback. It led the Court to a narrow analysis of the case. There is a missing piece in the evaluation of the FRY's responsibility which lies exactly between the commission of genocide and the prevention of such crimes being committed by third parties. The duty to refrain does not only rule out criminal categories of commission and participation in a crime. It prohibits any kind of contribution even if it does not amount to complicity pursuant to the high standards of criminal law. A consideration of international human rights law again helps to understand this. All comprehensive human rights conventions provide that the contracting parties are obliged to ensure human rights protection.[56] The competent Courts and human rights treaty bodies agree

---

[55] A. Cassese, 'On the Use of Criminal Law Notions in Determining State Responsibility', 5 *JICJ* (2007), pp. 875.

[56] The International Covenant on Civil and Political Rights uses the term 'respect and ensure.' Art. 2(1) ICCPR reads: 'Each state Party to the present Covenant undertakes to respect and to ensure to all individuals within its territory and subject to its jurisdiction the rights recognized in the present Covenant, without distinction of any kind, such as race, colour, sex, language, religion, political or other opinion, national or social origin, property, birth or other status.' International Covenant on Civil and Political Rights, 16 December 1966, 999 *UNTS* 171, 6 ILM 368 (1967) (hereinafter, ICCPR or Cov-

that this does not only mean that state authorities shall not commit violations. It also obliges state to refrain from any conduct contributing even less directly to a human rights abuse. Therefore human rights law does not only become relevant if state officials are the immediate perpetrators or if the abuser can be attributed to the state.

The obligations under the human rights conventions are much broader than the actual crimes. For example, a state can be responsible for a violation of the right to life even if the state official who is the immediate perpetrator is not criminally responsible for murder. A judgment of the European Court of Human Rights illustrates this. The well-known *McCann* case of 1995 concerned an erroneous shooting of alleged terrorists.[57] The United Kingdom had been informed that the IRA was planning a car bomb attack in Gibraltar. British soldiers shot the suspects because they thought that the suspects were trying to detonate the bomb. The Court held that the soldiers had reasonably believed that it was necessary to shoot the suspect to prevent the attack.[58] But even though the soldiers as the immediate perpetrators could not be held criminally responsible, the United Kingdom was held responsible for breaching the Convention because of the defective planning of the operation as a contributing factor to the taking of life.[59] According to the court, the duty to respect the right of life went beyond the prohibition of criminal conduct and thus required a higher standard of protection. Any kind of contribution to the taking of life was considered a violation of the Convention. The state was therefore required to exercise the 'greatest of care' in its activities.[60]

Considering the 'humanitarian and civilizing purpose' of the Genocide Convention,[61] it is adequate to frame the primary obligations undertaken by its States Parties accordingly. There is a duty of each State Party not to contribute to genocide. This does not only prevent authorities from actually committing acts of genocide,

---

enant). The European Human Rights Convention refers to the term 'secure.' Art. 1 reads: 'The High Contracting Parties shall secure to everyone within their jurisdiction the rights and freedoms defined in Section I of this Convention.' (ETS No. 5), 213 *UNTS* 222, entered into force 3 September 1953, as amended by Protocols Nos. 3, 5, 8, and 11 which entered into force on 21 September 1970, 20 December 1971, 1 January 1990, and 1 November 1998 respectively.

[57] ECHR, *McCann and Others* v. *the United Kingdom*, Judgment of 27 September 1995, Series A, No. 324, Application No. 18984/91(1995).

[58] According to the Court they had acted on an honest belief which was perceived by them, for good reasons, to be valid at the time but subsequently turned out to be mistaken. Ibid., para. 200.

[59] The authorities had failed to take appropriate care in the operation. Ibid., para. 212. The Court considered the decision by British authorities not to prevent the suspects from travelling into Gibraltar and the failure of the authorities to make sufficient allowances for the possibility that their intelligence assessments might, in some respects at least, be erroneous. They also criticised the automatic recourse to lethal force when the soldiers opened fire. Therefore the Court was not persuaded that the killing of the three terrorists constituted a use of force which was no more than absolutely necessary in defence of persons from unlawful violence within the meaning of Art. 2 ECHR.

[60] The Court held that 'the authorities were bound by their obligation to respect the right to life of the suspects to exercise the greatest of care in evaluating the information at their disposal before transmitting it to soldiers whose use of firearms automatically involved shooting to kill.' Ibid., para. 211.

[61] Ibid., para. 162. See also ICJ, *Reservations to the Convention on the Prevention and Punishment of the Crime of Genocide*, Advisory Opinion, ICJ Rep. 1951, p. 23.

but also to refrain from any kind of involvement even beyond complicity in genocide.[62] The analysis of the ICJ in the *Bosnian Genocide* case does not adequately grasp active conduct below the level of complicity. By focusing on crimes and attribution, the Court missed an important aspect of the state's primary obligations under the Convention.[63]

Instead, it relied on the duty to prevent third parties from committing genocide. But there is a qualitative difference between responsibility for *active* involvement and responsibility for the failure to intervene when third parties commit a crime. After all, the Court itself held that there had been substantial political, military and financial aid by the Federal Republic of Yugoslavia to Bosnian Serbs which continued even during the massacre in Srebrenica.[64] It acknowledged that the atrocities in Srebrenica were committed *with these resources*.[65] So why shouldn't the Federal Republic be held responsible for this active aid and assistance?

By focusing on the commission of genocide as an aggravated form of state responsibility, the Court unnecessarily complicated its analysis and foreclosed the option for a more flexible examination which is genuine to the rules of state responsibility. The traditional concept does not distinguish between different categories of severity; it would have enabled the Court to adequately address the contribution by the FRY without raising it to a higher level of responsibility.

The drawback of the Court's approach is illustrated by the high standard of proof the Court required for the establishment of the FRY's responsibility. It applied a standard of beyond reasonable doubt which obviously draws from international criminal law.[66] It would have been more adequate to consider state responsibility on the basis of a standard of carelessness which is common in the context of human rights obligations.[67] Since the high threshold which the Court set for responsibility for genocide could not be established in this case, it had to resort to the duty to prevent others from committing genocide to hold the FRY responsible.

The whole line of reasoning was probably the result of a compromise between those judges advocating the concept of state responsibility for genocide and those more hesitant. It ultimately led to a standard of aggravated state responsibility and

---

62 In other words, a state is not only responsible for violating the Genocide Convention if it exercises effective control over the perpetrators. Its primary obligation is more comprehensive. It also obliges state to refrain from any kind of influence on abuses. Any kind of knowing contribution is impermissible.

63 Primary obligations in human rights law are broader, not limited to commission, incitement, and conspiracy. A state is responsible for a human rights violation even if the offense itself has not been carried out by its authorities. Since primary obligations do not only oblige state not to commit a violation but also to refrain from any kind of contribution it is irrelevant whether the principle perpetrator can be attributed to the state. The crucial question, therefore, is not about attribution but about the scope of primary obligations.

64 See ICJ, *Bosnian Genocide* case, *supra* n. 1, para. 422.

65 Ibid., para. 422. The reason for not holding the FRY responsible for this aid and assistance was that it had not been 'clearly aware that genocide was about to take place or was under way.'

66 See ICJ, *Bosnian Genocide* case, *supra* n. 1, paras. 421-422.

67 See *supra* n. 57.

a more lenient standard for the failure to prevent genocide by others. But this was a flawed compromise because it left out the FRY's active involvement in Bosnia.[68]

VI. Conclusion and Suggestions for the Future Conceptualisation

Despite its flaws, the significance of the 2007 judgment in the *Bosnian Genocide* case should not be underestimated. It was an important landmark in the recognition of state responsibility for genocide under the Genocide Convention. The judgment occasionally has been criticised as contributing to the fragmentation of law. But the recognition of state responsibility for genocide was unproblematic in this respect. The evolution of different forms of responsibility is not a matter of fragmentation but symptomatic for the sophistication of international law. Criminal responsibility of individual perpetrators and the responsibility of states for their involvement in genocide are different in nature and therefore require a different line of analysis. Ironically, the effort by the International Court of Justice to realign the standards for state responsibility for genocide with the standards for individual criminal responsibility gave rise to irritation and arguably rendered things more difficult than necessary.

Considering the difference between individual criminal responsibility and state responsibility, the role of the International Court of Justice and the role of international criminal courts are not competing but complementary. Both seek to enforce the prohibition of genocide by different means. Any rivalry among these different jurisdictions would be unwarranted and inappropriate. While the ICTY's task is to consider individual criminal responsibility, the ICJ was asked to render a decision whether the FRY had violated its obligations under the Genocide Convention. After the death of Milošević, the judgment was awaited with high expectations. The hope that the case before the ICJ would bring light into the involvement of the FRY in the Bosnian massacres illustrates the significance of the ICJ's jurisdiction in genocide cases. Such proceedings offer a macro-perspective which cannot be reached by international criminal tribunals. The task of the latter is qualitatively different because they have to deal with individual guilt.

Unfortunately, the International Court of Justice developed such a high threshold for state responsibility that it has been considered a pyrrhic victory.[69] It only covers the most serious acts of state responsibility and requires a very high standard of proof.[70] The Court limited itself to an analysis which heavily drew from interna-

---

[68] Perhaps the compromise also goes back to unanimity among the judges as to whether Serbia and Montenegro at all could be held responsible for the FRY's activities.

[69] R.J. Goldstone & R.J. Hamilton, 'Bosnia v. Serbia, Lessons from the Encounter of the International Court of Justice with the International Criminal Tribunal for the Former Yugoslavia', 20 *LeidenJIL* (2008), p. 95.

[70] For the Court a pattern of conduct did not suffice to establish genocidal intent, see ICJ, *Bosnian Genocide* case, *supra* n. 1, para. 373.

tional criminal law when it considered the violation of the Convention. It dealt with state responsibility, not with criminal responsibility, but factually applied criminal law standards and thereby missed part of the obligation under the Convention. The focus on the qualification of the conduct by the immediate perpetrators was fateful. In the realm of international human rights there is room for state responsibility even if the immediate perpetrator cannot be held criminally accountable.

It would have been preferable if the Court had further elaborated on the specific obligations undertaken by states under the Genocide Convention. There is an obligation under the Genocide Convention which goes beyond crimes and attribution. In order to understand what states are obliged to do pursuant to the Convention, a human rights perspective leads us beyond the demanding concept of crimes. The prohibition for state authorities to commit genocide is structurally the same as the prohibition of committing serious human rights violations, which follows from the respect and ensure provisions of the comprehensive human rights conventions and the duty to prevent torture under the Torture Convention. States Parties are obliged to refrain from any kind of involvement in genocide. The contracting parties have to exercise greatest care to avoid any contribution. In this respect human rights obligations are broader than criminal responsibility. This is not to question the validity of the concepts of participation in international criminal law, but to adequately grasp the protective obligations undertaken by the contracting states under the Genocide Convention.

The *Bosnian Genocide* case was just the first time the ICJ rendered a comprehensive substantive decision on genocide. With the 2008 admissibility decision in the *Croatian Genocide* case, we are expecting another decision on the merits.[71] The court thus will have the occasion to refine its approach and to go beyond its decision in the *Bosnian Genocide* case by considering the Convention from a human rights perspective.

---

[71] See ICJ, *Application of the Convention on the Prevention and Punishment of the Crime of Genocide (Croatia* v. *Serbia)*, Judgment of 18 November 2008, not yet published. Accessible at www.icj-cij.org, last visited 20 February 2009.

GENOCIDE AND THE INTERNATIONAL COURT OF JUSTICE

Bruno Simma

I. INTRODUCTION

Most of the previous chapters have dealt in some way or another with the sanctioning of genocide, or with international law under the influence of the Genocide Convention. However, I would still like to address the specific contribution of the Hague Court to the fulfilment of the great promises proclaimed on 9 December 1948, in its judgment of 26 February 2007 in the *Bosnian Genocide* case.[1]

In 1961, a man stood trial for genocide in Jerusalem. Adolf Eichmann's trial before the District Court of Jerusalem was a seminal moment in 20th century history. In her famous book, *Eichmann in Jerusalem,* Hannah Arendt described this trial in vivid language, recounting its pomp and ceremony in the hallowed Beth Ha'am, the House of the People; the judges in black robes, and masses of documents piled everywhere. According to her, it was a masterpiece of legal drama: on trial stood a man accused of having committed the crime of crimes. As the world watched the proceedings unfold, there was a sense that much more was going on than the mere handling of a criminal case. Indeed, an entire system was on trial, and although the Israeli court did not have the power to adjudge a state responsible for genocide, the relationship between individual and state was very much in question.

Fast-forwarding a few decades, the world witnessed another trial for genocide, this time in The Hague. Again, a hallowed room, the Great Hall of Justice, was the centre of activity. Again, there were judges in black robes and masses of documents; pomp and circumstance were in abundance throughout. This time, however, the forum was the International Court of Justice, the principal judicial organ of the United Nations, and the accused, this time called the Respondent, not an individual, but the Republic of Serbia. It was a very different trial, this time conducted squarely against a state. The case, which was under deliberation for the longest period in the history of the Court, led also to one of the longest judgments ever rendered by it,

[1] ICJ, *Case concerning the Application of the Convention on the Prevention and Punishment of the Crime of Genocide* (*Bosnia and Herzegovina* v. *Serbia and Montenegro*) (hereinafter, *Bosnian Genocide* case), Judgment of 26 February 2007, ICJ Reports 2007, pp. 40ff.

C. Safferling and E. Conze (eds.), The Genocide Convention Sixty Years after its Adoption

comprising no less than 200 printed pages and 471 paragraphs. It turned out to be also one of the most controversial.

These legal processes, much as they are about reconciliation, a search for truth and a desire to do justice, raise serious questions. How can we as lawyers debate the technicalities of whether genocide merely brings about (something similar to 'civil') responsibility of a state *versus* the comparatively greater declaration of individual or collective criminal responsibility? Are we in presence here of a technicalisation of something that should be kept outside the realm of legal scholarship altogether? Or rather, are we falling right into the trap which Hannah Arendt warned us against so often, of trying to rationalise punishment and delve out guilt for crimes so monstrous and severe that they 'explode the limits of the law'? These remain questions to consider when discussing the 'crime of crimes,' but this paper is written by a judge of a court which had to grapple with some of these very questions, but from the very particular perspective of a court designed to deal with inter-state disputes, thus a court with parties before it, a court constrained by its own peculiar institutional structure, and facing a respondent state which used every means at its disposal to demonstrate that the Court did not have jurisdiction in the case. It is from that vantage point that I wish to explore the judgment's contribution to our understanding of the international law on genocide, its prevention, and the delicate, difficult, but necessary task of attempting to rebuild order after its commission. I would never suggest that the Court's Judgment – or the Judgment of any court – can help erase the past and correct injustice when an act of the magnitude of genocide has occurred. Such is not the power given to judges; nor is it the province of law. But law can play an important role in re-constructing the narrative of what happened; in attempting to untangle history and fact from accusation and distortion; and perhaps, by so doing, contributing to a future where genocide will not happen again. It is from that point of view that I will analyse the Court's judgment. Without taking a position as regards the merits of that case, or the reasons for which the Court arrived at its decision, I wish to discuss the Court's various findings and what they represent for international law.

Although the Court's judgment may have been controversial, it has certainly resonated for the parties and for the Balkan region more generally. In the case I am going to discuss, the Court had decided in 1996 that it did possess jurisdiction, that is, eleven years before it could render its judgement on the merits. This was not the Court's fault: during that period, Serbia's international legal 'self-understanding' had turned around 180 degrees, and this had also led to a great many difficulties for the Court. The Court finally managed to maintain its jurisdiction in the case by what I would call a robust recourse to the principle of *res judicata*. By the way, recently the Court found that it had jurisdiction in a similar case, this time pitting Croatia against Serbia, and will thus proceed to the merits of the case in due course. Serbia reacted by indicating through the press that it would either file a counterclaim or a separate proceeding altogether against Croatia for, on its part, having committed genocide on Serbian territory. Apparently, Serbia is willing to invest substantial sums and resources to bring such a claim forward, despite the lack of indictments in the ICTY for that crime in either Croatian or Serbian territory. This is perhaps demonstrative of the purpose of adjudication being far more than simply 'winning a case' as argued between parties. The importance of judicial proceedings within international law goes much further than that.

II. On the duty to prevent genocide

I think it is now opportune to turn straight to the Court's 2007 judgment, beginning with the Court's finding that Serbia had violated its duty to prevent genocide – the finding most heavily discussed in the aftermath of the Court's judgment, and this for a variety of reasons.

A preliminary comment is in order. First, an international legal obligation to prevent is nothing new, existing as it does, be it in express terms or implicitly, in human rights conventions (in particular, the recent order on provisional measures in the case between Georgia and Russia, in which the Court confirms that such an obligation arises from CERD)[2] and in many other conventions regarding the suppression of certain crimes, such as corruption or the hijacking of airplanes. The Court's comments on the duty to prevent genocide were not of a general nature designed to apply in all cases where there exists an obligation to prevent a certain act. The Court said so itself, when it refused 'to find whether, apart from the texts applicable to specific fields, there is a general obligation on States to prevent the commission by other persons or entities of acts contrary to certain norms of general international law,' and 'confine[d] itself to determining the specific scope of the duty to prevent in the Genocide Convention.'[3]

In so doing, the Court adopted a strict approach to the definition of genocide which is broadly consonant with its limited jurisdiction under Article IX of the Convention. Bosnia-Herzegovina had argued that the totality of all crimes committed on its territory by the Republika Srpska during the three years from Bosnia-Herzegovina's declaration of independence in April 1992 to the Dayton Peace Negotiations in the fall of 1995 constituted a single, continuous act of genocide. The Court expressly recognised that it

> 'did not have the power to rule on alleged breaches of other obligations under international law, not amounting to genocide, particularly those protecting human rights in armed conflict. That is so even if the alleged breaches are of obligations under peremptory norms, or of obligations which protect essential humanitarian values, and which may be owed *erga omnes*.'[4]

---

[2] See, ICJ, *Application of the International Convention on the Elimination of All Forms of Racial Discrimination (Georgia* v. *Russian Federation)*, Order of 15 October 2008, unpublished. Accessible at www.icj-cij.org.

[3] ICJ, *Bosnian Genocide* case, *supra* n. 1, Judgment, p. 220, para. 429.

[4] Ibid., p. 104, para. 147.

Thus, whether heinous and despicable acts which might constitute crimes against humanity or whether war crimes may or may not have occurred was immaterial for the purposes of the case; the Court simply did not have the power to establish whether this happened as a matter of fact.

The duty to prevent genocide cannot be seen so broadly as a duty to prevent a genocide happening anywhere in the world. The Court dealt carefully with that point when it listed the 'various parameters'[5] which operate in the assessment of whether a state has duly discharged its obligations. The first of those parameters is the 'capacity to influence effectively the action of persons likely to commit, or already committing, genocide.' That capacity rests upon factors such as geographical distance and political ties to the state concerned or to the main actors in the events. An interesting element in this reasoning is thus that a state's positive obligation to prevent genocide is not limited territorially, but may extend outside its own borders. This is a significant new development. It is in line with a recent trend in the jurisprudence of international human rights courts and treaty bodies. In our specific context, what the Court has said goes far beyond that, however. One might even speak of the emergence of a new concept, that of the 'capacity to influence.' As the Court itself stated, the obligation to prevent genocide is 'both normative and compelling' on all States Parties to the Convention.[6]

Furthermore, there is no threshold criterion of application, such as state jurisdiction, mentioned in the text of either the Genocide Convention or the judgment of the Court. This is significant – the duty to prevent can be scaled and evaluated carefully on the basis of a state's actual ability and influence over the relevant players. This might be criticised as creating a 'differentiated' standard for states, but it is consistent with international law in which, for instance, the interpretation of economic and social rights as well as of environmental regulation has often to take into account the resources and abilities of a state. In other words, the more a state *can* do, the more is expected from a state. However, one cannot take this so far as to say that powerful states have an obligation to prevent every and all genocide, nor that they have the obligation – or freedom! – to resort to force in order to prevent genocide. In this regard, the Court itself says that states 'may only act within the limits permitted by international law.'[7]

We should also note that the obligation to prevent was not found by the Court to be one of result, but rather, one of objective 'due diligence' and conduct. In the words of the Court itself, a state is not under an obligation to succeed in preventing genocide at all costs, but it must employ all reasonable means available to it to do so.[8] An assessment *in concreto* of the various facts at hand, such as geographical distance and the political links of a state to the relevant actors, is an important element for evaluating a state's potential breach of its duty to prevent. Again, this

---

[5] Ibid., p. 221, para. 430.
[6] Ibid., p. 220, para. 427.
[7] Ibid., p. 222, para. 431.
[8] Ibid., p. 221, para. 430.

duty is circumscribed by the limits of international law itself – states are not free to use every means at their disposal, especially if their connection to a situation of possible genocide is tenuous.

III. Distinguishing between a failure to prevent genocide and complicity in its commission

Although a failure to prevent genocide can only be adjudged once genocide has actually been committed, the Court made another interesting statement, namely, that 'a State's obligation to prevent, and the corresponding duty to act, arise at the instant that the State learns of, or should normally have learned of, the existence of a serious risk that genocide will be committed.'[9] It is here that one can identify the difference between complicity in committing genocide and the failure to prevent it: failure to prevent can result merely from the state's awareness of a serious risk that genocide will be committed, and need not result from a positive act on its part. This distinction is delicate and the Court certainly faced a challenge in arriving at its conclusions on this point. The Court relied upon Article 14, paragraph 3, of the ILC Articles on State Responsibility,[10] which expressly links a breach of a duty to prevent a wrongful act to the commission of that wrongful act. The Court also pointed to two specific differences: the fact that Article III of the Genocide Convention places the state under a negative obligation, namely not to directly or indirectly support the commission of genocide, whereas the duty to prevent involves positive obligations. Further, the *mens rea* necessary for a finding of complicity requires that the accomplice both had full knowledge of the facts and did give support to the actors involved notwithstanding such knowledge. This is a higher test than that articulated for the breach of the duty to prevent, where it suffices that a state 'was aware, or should normally have been aware, of the serious danger that acts of genocide would be committed.'[11]

It is this argumentation which led to the Court's reasoning regarding the question of what kind of reparation was due to Bosnia-Herzegovina because of Serbia's failure to prevent the genocide in Srebenica. As the Court explained:

> 'The question is whether there is a sufficiently direct and certain causal nexus between the wrongful act, the Respondent's breach of the obligation to prevent genocide, and the injury suffered by the Applicant, consisting of all damage of any type, material or moral, caused by the acts of genocide. Such a nexus could be considered established only if the Court were able to conclude from the case as a whole and with a sufficient

---

[9] Ibid., p. 221, para. 431.

[10] International Law Commission, 'Report on the work of its fifty-third session', Official Records of the General Assembly, 56th Sess., Supp. No. 10 and corrigendum (A/56/10 and Corr.1), annexed to GA Res. 56/83, UN Doc. A/RES/56/83 (85th plenary meeting, 12 December 2001) (hereinafter, ILC Articles on State Responsibility).

[11] ICJ, *Bosnian Genocide* case, *supra* n. 1, Judgment, p. 223, para. 432.

degree of certainty that the genocide at Srebenica would in fact have been averted if the Respondent had acted in compliance with its legal obligations.'[12]

IV. The 'reinforcing' effect of provisional measures orders on Serbia's obligations

Another aspect of the Court's judgment on the prevention of genocide that should also be emphasised is that the Court was able to rely on two provisional measures orders which it had issued against the Federal Republic of Yugoslavia, on 8 April and 13 September 1993. In both of these Orders, the Court had made clear that the FRY had due diligence obligations to 'ensure that any military, paramilitary or irregular armed units which may be supported by it' did not commit genocide or participate in any conspiracy to commit genocide. One could argue that this created a reinforced obligation to prevent on the part of Serbia, due to the fact that Serbia had been reminded repeatedly of its obligation to prevent the commission of genocide. However, the effect of the provisional measures orders should not be understood as creating special obligations on the part of Serbia, but rather, reducing the evidentiary burden placed on Bosnia-Herzegovina to establish that Serbia was or should have been aware of the great likelihood that genocide might occur.

Let me conclude what I had to say about the obligation to prevent genocide by expressing my conviction that the Court's findings in this regard will remain the most important part of the 2007 judgment. Judicial decisions are looking backwards by their very nature, but what the Court spelled out on prevention is also, and in the first place, designed for the future and, if I may say so, it ought to make foreign offices worldwide somewhat concerned. I would call it my court's specific contribution to the development (and continued vitality) of the 'responsibility to protect.'

V. Can a state commit genocide?

One of the more interesting questions finally put to rest in the 2007 judgment concerned whether States Parties to the Convention are themselves under an obligation not to commit genocide. The Court's answer is a clear 'yes.' The relevant conclusion is found in paragraph 166 of the judgment, and was not in reply to any argument advanced by the Parties to the case. Here is the Court's reasoning:

> '[The prohibition follows, *inter alia*] from the expressly stated obligation to prevent the commission of acts of genocide. That obligation requires the States parties, *inter alia*, to employ the means at their disposal, in circumstances to be described more specifically later in this Judgment, to prevent persons or groups not directly under their authority from committing an act of genocide or any of the other acts mentioned in

[12] Ibid., pp. 233-4, paras. 461-462.

> Article III. It would be paradoxical if States were thus under an obligation to prevent, so far as within their power, commission of genocide by persons over whom they have a certain influence, but were not forbidden to commit such acts through their own organs, or persons over whom they have such firm control that their conduct is attributable to the State concerned under international law. In short, the obligation to prevent genocide necessarily implies the prohibition of the commission of genocide.'[13]

It would be strange indeed to think that there is in the Convention no direct obligation on states not to commit genocide, but oddly enough, its text does not contain any express statement to that effect. In that sense, the Court's clarification of the scope of the obligations contained in Article III of the Convention was a welcome statement of the law on the matter, since there should be no doubt as to whether states themselves are also under a treaty obligation to refrain from committing genocide.

But do not get this wrong: a breach of this obligation does not make a state criminally responsible. There is no such thing as a 'crime of the state' in the sense of criminal law. The responsibility incurred will be state responsibility in the ordinary sense, albeit of a particularly grave kind. And such responsibility will have to be established by attributing to the state acts of individuals functioning as its organs or agents. Thus, looked at from a purely formal angle, it is perhaps true that there is no need for a prohibition against genocide addressed at states as such. There need not be a prohibition on states to commit genocide in order for there to be state responsibility for genocide when it is attributable to them. That said, if one looks carefully at the genesis of the Genocide Convention, arising as it did out of the ashes of the Second World War, it is clear that the Contracting Parties to the Convention anticipated the importance of a state apparatus in the commission of a widespread and systematic crime such as genocide. Can an entity ultimately guided and controlled by individuals, one which holds the monopoly of force within a territory and which has the capacity to control every aspect of – and extinguish – human existence, not be subject to the same obligations as those very individuals themselves? Whether or not it is necessary for a state to be under the obligation to not commit genocide because the act *eventually* may be attributable to that state is immaterial: as the Court explained, the state is also under that obligation, and nothing in the regime of state responsibility prevents this conclusion.

VI. Attribution of responsibility for genocide

The theoretical question of whether a state or its organs can commit genocide set aside for a moment, another important question is the determination of the precise instant when an individual act also becomes attributable to a state. The Court made a substantial contribution to the development of international law in this regard, as its analysis carefully considered the method whereby it can be assessed whether

[13] Ibid., p. 113, para. 166.

genocide may have been committed. The Court's analysis is also instructive in general matters of state responsibility and the attribution of internationally wrongful acts to a state which were committed by persons or groups which are not organs of that state. Perhaps not since the 1920s Mexico-United States Mixed Arbitrations, and perhaps the contributions of the Iran-United States Claims Tribunal, has there been such a substantial advance in this particular field. Thus, the Court's pronouncements in this respect deserve careful attention.

First comes the question of the automatic attribution to a state of a genocide committed by one of its organs. The question whether a state can commit genocide deserves to be looked at from a somewhat different angle than that applicable to the question whether a state may be held responsible for a genocide committed by one of its organs. This is because an instance of what I would call a 'top-down' genocide, where the intention to commit genocide was shared by various organs of the state and controlled from the highest levels of the state apparatus, is very different from a case of, so to speak, 'bottom-up' attribution of genocide, that is, when a state is responsible for the acts of a military or government official who abuses his or her authority or directly contravenes orders. The first alternative appears to have been the basis of the submission of Bosnia to the effect that the entirety of the Serbian State apparatus was responsible for the commission of one comprehensive genocide extending throughout the entire course of the war on Bosnian territory – a submission squarely rejected by the Court. The second alternative, to arrive at a finding of genocide by considering Serb behaviour 'from the bottom up' was considered, but equally rejected by the Court when it held that no Serbian state organs, whether *de jure* or *de facto*, were involved in the commission of atrocities in a manner which could be attributed to Belgrade. Instead, Serbia was found responsible for having failed in its duty to prevent genocide. Let us first turn to what we can discern from the Court's reasoning regarding the various ways in which the commission of genocide may also incur the responsibility of a state.

State responsibility for genocide may only come about if there exists a 'duality of responsibility' under international law.[14] By duality of responsibility, what the Court means is that there might well exist individual criminal responsibility as well as state responsibility for the very same acts. One does not preclude the other. As I have emphasised before, the Court does not consider that any eventual responsibility of the state in this regard could be of a 'criminal nature.'[15] As the Court explained, the obligations imposed on individuals and states might be distinct, but certain acts may well violate both categories of obligations and thus create the situation of a 'duality of responsibility.' The key question, as with most internationally wrongful acts, remains the question of *attributing* the acts in question to a state. That was the principal problem grappled with by the Court, and it was handled through recourse to the traditional solutions favoured in the doctrines relating to attribution of state responsibility. The Court found that, according to the principle

---

[14] Ibid., p. 116, para. 173.
[15] Ibid., p. 115, para. 170.

embodied in Article 4 of the ILC Articles on State Responsibility – a codification of customary international law – genocide committed by an organ of the state was considered to have been committed by that state.[16] As the Court explained,

> 'The rules for attributing alleged internationally wrongful conduct to a State do not vary with the nature of the wrongful act in question in the absence of a clearly expressed *lex specialis*. Genocide will be considered as attributable to a State if and to the extent that the physical acts constitutive of genocide that have been committed by organs or persons other than the State's own agents were carried out, wholly or in part, on the instructions or directions of the State, or under its effective control.'[17]

These criteria for attributing state responsibility for genocide are admittedly strict and rather formal. Critics have even suggested that this 'banalises' the crime of genocide: by relying so strongly on the quality of state organ in matters of attribution, the state might even be held in certain cases to be 'innocent' of having committed genocide, yet if a state organ were involved, the state would automatically and forever wear the stigma which attaches to the crime of genocide,[18] and without the state being able to argue that the organ had acted *ultra vires* or against specific instructions – an important exception in the law of state responsibility which was not explained by the Court. But I do not believe that it is necessary to delve this far, in the light of the Court's jurisprudence. First, we can turn to the *Armed Activities* case, pitting the Democratic Republic of the Congo against Uganda, where the Court recognised Article 7 of the ILC Articles on State Responsibility, which makes precisely this point on the question of attribution, as a codification of customary international law.[19] Secondly, Serbia never claimed that any other regime in matters of attribution should have applied, whether in its written or oral submissions, and in fact conceded in its Rejoinder of 22 February 1999 that the standard regime should apply.[20] Thirdly, Bosnia-Herzegovina itself claimed strongly that the standard regime as regards the rules of attribution of state responsibility should apply with equal force to allegations of state responsibility for genocide.

There is therefore no reason to suggest that any different criterion of attribution should have applied in the case of genocide. In fact, any deliberate weakening of the test codified by the ILC, such as adding a component where genocidal intent on the part of the state would have to be established by an applicant state *alongside* the genocidal intent already demonstrated by a state official or state organ, would have made it much more difficult to attribute state responsibility for genocide. How could the 'intention' of a state be discerned? Which organs of state should one examine to

---

[16] Ibid., p. 202, para. 385.

[17] Ibid., pp. 208-9, para. 401.

[18] ICTY, *Prosecutor* v. *Krstić*, Case IT-98-33-A, Judgment of the Appeals Chamber, 19 April 2004, para. 37.

[19] See ICJ, *Case concerning Armed Activities on the Territory of the Congo (Democratic Republic of the Congo* v. *Uganda)*, Judgment of 19 December 2005, ICJ Rep. 2005, p. 168.

[20] ICJ, *Bosnian Genocide* case, *supra* n. 1, Rejoinder of the Federal Republic of Yugoslavia, 22 February 1999, not yet published. Accessible at www.icj-cij.org, p. 644.

determine a specific *dolus specialis*? These are difficult questions to articulate, and they might be setting evidentiary burdens which would be extremely difficult to reconcile with the Court's role as a forum for the resolution of state-to-state disputes. Thus, the Court's focus on formal criteria in articulating its test for attribution of state responsibility for genocide is consonant with its function within the international legal order, and should accordingly be understood in that context.

VII. What is an 'organ of state'?

Furthermore, the discussion on 'automatic attribution' brings us to the next question raised in the Bosnia-Serbia judgment which merits discussion. This is a question which I am sure has bedevilled many a participant in an international law moot court competition such as Jessup, Telders, or Rousseau. That question concerns the definition of what exactly *is* an organ of state? In our case the Court concluded that the genocide committed in Srebenica could not be attributed to the FRY (now Serbia), and thus it could not be said that Serbia itself was responsible for it. This was so despite the substantial links which connected the Republika Srpska and its army, the VRS, to the FRY, and the decision has been subject to criticism for this reason. I have even heard that a request for revision of our judgment might eventually reach the Court should the ICTY one day conclude that organs of the FRY had participated in the massacre at Srebenica. Thus, it is opportune to turn to the Judgment's statements on the question of what an organ of state actually is, and to the important distinction that the Court drew between *de jure* and *de facto* organs of state.

The Judgment begins by considering whether it is possible that genocide was committed by a *de jure* organ of the FRY. The Court first established that 'it has not been shown that the FRY army took part in the massacres, nor that the political leaders of the FRY had a hand in preparing, planning or in any way carrying out the massacres' in Srebrenica.[21] In excluding the responsibility of the FRY army in this way, the Court was forced to go much further and examine carefully the relations between the perpetrators of the Srebenica massacre and the FRY: earlier in the judgment, for example, it had concluded, quite significantly, that 'the Respondent was … making its considerable military and financial support available to the Republika Srpska, and had it withdrawn that support, this would have greatly constrained the options that were available to the Republika Srpska authorities.'[22] The Court was also categorical, and in my opinion correctly so, in determining that neither the Republika Srpska nor the VRS were *de jure* organs of the FRY:[23] this conclusion really should surprise no one, as there was no evidence that they formed any part of the state structure of the FRY; even though the Court did recognise that certain payments were made from Belgrade to General Mladić and other VRS

---

21 ICJ, *Bosnian Genocide* case, *supra* n. 1, Judgment, p. 202, para. 386.
22 Ibid., p. 142, para. 241.
23 Ibid., p. 202, para. 386.

officers,[24] this was considered insufficient to make them automatically organs of the FRY. The Court here upheld the test of control, and the test of who the officers in question were receiving orders from; as no evidence to the contrary was submitted to the Court, it was obliged to conclude that they were receiving their orders from the Republika Srpska or the VRS, and not from the FRY. The Court based its arguments, once again, on the customary international law codified in the Articles on State Responsibility, in this case Article 4, which uses the expression 'State organ' to apply to one or other of the individual or collective entities which make up the organisation of the state and act on its behalf.

This leaves us now with the question whether the massacres could have been perpetrated by *de facto* organs of the FRY, in response to substantial submissions by Bosnia to the effect that the Republika Srpska and the VRS were such *de facto* organs. In dealing with this argument, the Court explained that in some cases

> '[it] is appropriate to look beyond legal status alone, in order to grasp the reality of the relationship between the person taking action, and the State to which he is so closely attached as to appear to be nothing more than its agent: any other solution would allow States to escape their international responsibility by choosing to act through persons or entities whose supposed independence would be purely fictitious.'[25]

Such assimilation to the state is to be exceptional, and, as is well known, the test of control established by the Court in the *Nicaragua* case is that of 'complete dependence.' In our present case, the Court concluded that on the basis of the evidence before it, the FRY did not have the requisite degree of control over the perpetrators of the massacres, and could therefore not be held responsible for them.

VIII. Attribution to a State of Genocide Committed by Persons Who Are Not State Organs

Another important question explored by the Court's judgment is the attribution to a state of acts committed by individuals who are emphatically not state organs.[26] This is not the same thing as the transformation of an individual or body into a *de facto* state organ by establishing the required degree of dependence. The Court relied upon its well-established control test in *Nicaragua*, where the Court first affirmed that a state had to have 'effective control' over the activities of individuals in order for these activities to be attributable to it.[27] In so doing, the Court rejected the more permissive test which had been adopted by the Appeals Chamber of the ICTY in the *Tadić* case[28] and which was advocated by Bosnia in its submissions as

[24] Ibid., p. 203, para. 388.

[25] Ibid., p. 205, para. 392.

[26] Ibid., pp. 206-7, para. 396.

[27] Ibid., p. 208, para. 400.

[28] ICTY, *Prosecutor* v. *Tadić*, Case IT-94-1-A, Judgment of the Appeals Chamber, 15 July 1999 (hereinafter, *Tadić*), para. 37.

the correct approach going forward. Thus, the Court finally settled the controversy as regards what response the ICJ would present to the gauntlet thrown down by the ICTY.

The Court explained its reasons for retaining the effective control test and being unable to subscribe to the ICTY Appeals Chamber's view. First, the Court emphasised that the ICTY Appeals Chamber was not called upon in *Tadić* to rule on questions of state responsibility, as its jurisdiction is criminal and not over the conduct of states. While the Court attached the utmost importance to the factual and legal findings of the ICTY in ruling on criminal liability, it could not do so with regard to the ICTY's position on issues of general international law which did not lie within the specific purview of the tribunal's jurisdiction. Second, the Court found the ICTY's 'for-all-purpose' approach with regard to the 'overall control' test to be unpersuasive, emphasising the need for tests carefully tailored for issues different in nature:

> '[A] State's involvement in an armed conflict on another State's territory which is required for the conflict to be characterized as international can very well, and without logical inconsistency, differ from the degree and nature of involvement required to give rise to that State's responsibility for a specific act committed in the course of the conflict.'[29]

Finally, the Court noted that the 'overall control' test would broaden the scope of state responsibility well beyond the fundamental principle governing the law of international responsibility whereby a state is responsible for its conduct and its conduct alone. As the Court explained, the 'overall control' test stretches too far, almost to the breaking point, that connection. My good friend Antonio Cassese has strenuously disagreed with this argument, accusing the Court of 'confining itself to uncritically accepting its previous views.' On my part, I consider that the Court's analysis was carefully undertaken and reflects a correct application of international law as it stands.

IX. Reparation

Finally, I wish to address the question of the reparation which was awarded, or rather, which was not awarded, in that case. Several issues were raised, first and foremost the delicate question of the monetary value which could be assessed as appropriate compensation for the failure to prevent genocide. Bosnia itself had argued that the appropriate remedy for such breaches would be a declaratory judgment under the heading of satisfaction, as such breaches did not lend themselves to 'pecuniary appraisal.'[30] That said, there was some confusion because, in Bosnia's final submissions, it asked for 'full compensation for the damages and losses caused'

---

[29] ICJ, *Bosnian Genocide* case, *supra* n. 1, Judgment, p. 210, para. 405.

[30] ICJ, *Bosnian Genocide* case, *supra* n. 1, Pleadings of the Applicant, CR 2006/11, p. 26 (Pellet); not surprisingly, this argument was picked up by the Respondent, CR 2006/17, p. 43 (Brownlie).

and referred to the 'financially assessable damage' caused by the violation of the acts enumerated in Article III of the Genocide Convention. Thus, the Court was called upon to consider this question in some depth, and did so by considering causality and the question whether 'but for' Serbia's failure to prevent the genocide at Srebenica, it would have occurred. In other words, was Serbia's failure to prevent a *sine qua non condition* for the fact that it happened?

The Court's reasoning rested upon the question of what difference a more decisive stance on the part of Serbia in preventing the commission of the genocide in Srebrenica would have made. Because it held that in fact, the genocide would most probably have been committed anyway by the organs of the Republika Srpska, the Court did not see itself as being in a position to establish any causality of Serbia's behaviour in the resulting dramatic events of those days.[31] Causality of an omission is a particularly difficult question for lawyers, both domestic and international; thus, I wish not to dwell excessively on this point: suffice it to say that the Court's finding that Serbia's omission was not the only cause should not be taken to say that it was no cause at all.

X. Conclusion

Let me conclude by summarising very briefly the points which I consider most relevant in the context of a comprehensive discourse on the prevention and punishment of genocide. What specific contributions has the ICJ made in this regard?

Firstly, the Court has clarified that the Genocide Convention does not only obligate States Parties to prevent and punish genocide but also embodies a prohibition directly addressed at them. The treaty obligation arising in this regard may well be a mere confirmation of an outlawing of genocide by some unwritten, higher law, but at the operational level, so to speak, the 1948 Convention is all we need.

Second, the Court has given the obligation to prevent genocide spelt out in Article I of the Convention a remarkably comprehensive and forward-looking meaning, thus creating an important building block upon which the 'responsibility to protect' in international human rights law will be able to develop and gain sharper contours.

Third, it is the Court's view that a state can be found responsible for having committed genocide or having engaged in any of the other acts or omissions outlawed by the Convention, to the degree that these provisions are applicable to states at all, without a finding by an international criminal tribunal on individual criminal responsibility being a pre-condition.

Finally, the Court has subjected the case of genocide to the rules on state responsibility; that is, to rules to which any element of criminal responsibility or punishment is foreign. I mention this in view of the confusion about so-called 'crimes of states.' As to reparation, the Court resorted to the time-honoured, still generally

[31] ICJ, *Bosnian Genocide* case, *supra* n. 1, Judgment, pp. 233-4, para. 462.

recognised *ancien régime* applicable to classic state-to-state relationships. If the Court had gone beyond a 'mere' finding of breach of a duty of prevention, it might have had the opportunity to be more innovative in this regard. But the submissions of the parties were as unaffected by recent trends concerning more custom-made reparation of human rights violations, as was the judgment of the Court.

Part Six
Historic Cases

THE TRIAL OF ADOLF EICHMANN AND OTHER GENOCIDE TRIALS

Gabriel Bach

The acts of genocide perpetrated by Nazi Germany against the Jewish people, usually referred to as the Holocaust, had been mentioned by international tribunals before the Eichmann trial, and had been referred to in the judgment of the International Military Tribunal rendered on October 1, 1946 at the Nuremberg trials. But it was only during the trial of Adolf Eichmann, held in Jerusalem in 1961 and 1962, that the Holocaust was presented in all its stages and in all its aspects, with the focus fully centered on this terrifying and unspeakable crime. Eichmann was, during the whole period of the perpetration of the Holocaust, including the period of World War II, the head of the Jewish Department of the German Secret Police, the Gestapo, and as such he was in charge of all the steps taken to implement the demonic plan for the so-called 'Final Solution of the Jewish Problem.' After the War, he managed to escape to Argentina and lived there under an assumed name. In May 1960, he was abducted by Israeli agents, taken to Israel, and handed over to the Israeli Police. When, on May 23, 1960, the Prime Minister of Israel, David Ben-Gurion, announced in the Knesset (the Israeli Parliament): 'Adolf Eichmann is under arrest in Israel and will shortly be put on trial,' the impact throughout the country was electrifying. The police investigation, placed in the hands of a special unit established for this purpose, took about nine months to complete. I was at that time the Deputy State Attorney of Israel, and was asked by the Minister of Justice to be in charge of the investigation, and later to appear in the trial, together with the Attorney General of Israel, the late Gideon Hausner. The crimes against the Jewish people with which the accused was charged consisted of all aspects of the persecution of millions of Jews, including their arrest and imprisonment in concentration camps, their deportation to extermination camps, their murder, and the theft of their property. The charges did not, however, confine themselves to Eichmann's participation in crimes against the Jewish people; they also included crimes against other peoples, such as the mass expulsions of Poles and Slovenes; the seizure, deportation to extermination camps, and murder of tens of thousands of Gypsies; and the deportation and murder of some one hundred children from the village of Lidice in Czechoslovakia, in revenge for the killing of Reinhard Heydrich, the notorious head of the SS Secret Police.

C. Safferling and E. Conze (eds.), The Genocide Convention Sixty Years after its Adoption

All the counts related to offences under the 'Nazis and Nazi Collaborators (Punishment) Law' of 1950, a law passed in Israel about ten years before Eichmann was caught and placed on trial. He was defended by two German lawyers of his and his family's choice. The leading defence counsel was Dr. Servatius, one of the advocates who had appeared for some of the defendants at the Nuremberg trials. Until the arrival of his lawyers in Israel, I was in fact the only contact Eichmann had with the outside world, and whenever he wanted to discuss any of his personal problems, he was brought before me.

I intend to share with you some of my reminiscences and personal experiences at the early stages of the investigation and later during the trial itself.

By means of more than one hundred witnesses and some sixteen hundred documents – many of them bearing Eichmann's own signature – the prosecution presented to the Court the full account of all the events related to the Holocaust of European Jewry, or the 'Final Solution of the Jewish question,' as the Nazis called it. In great detail the prosecution furnished the Court with proof of the persecution of the Jews in all its stages: the anti-Jewish legislation; the incitement among the general population of hostility to the Jewish minority; the plunder of Jewish property; and, worst of all, the searching out of Jews in every European country under German occupation and in the satellite states, their imprisonment, under inhuman conditions, in ghettos and concentration camps, where they were harassed and humiliated, and finally, their systematic mass murder, with the aim of completely destroying the Jewish people. The prosecution demonstrated what had happened to the Jews of Europe, country by country, and it proved the personal involvement of Eichmann, as the head of section IVB4 (the Gestapo section for Jewish affairs), in every stage of the heinous operation. In fact the entire scheme was called 'Operation Eichmann' in some of the German documents.

It is rather surprising to me that, even now, about thirty-five years after the trial, in many countries, and on the part of some members of the legal profession, the opinion is still voiced that the Israeli Court was not competent to try Eichmann, or, at least, that it was not a proper forum to do so. A number of reasons are advanced to support this view, and I shall refer to them one by one. Needless to say, these arguments were also put forward by the defence during the trial itself.

First, we hear time and time again that the law under which Eichmann was charged – the above-mentioned law against Nazis and Nazi Collaborators – was passed in 1950, i.e., a long time after the commission of the alleged offenses, and that therefore this was *ex-post-facto*, retroactive legislation which should have no validity.

This argument was rejected by the Court, and rightly so. The principle against enacting criminal laws with retroactive effect is not a rule of law, but a rule of justice. The natural sense of justice is generally outraged by a person being punished for a deed that was not illegal at the time it was committed. The situation with regard to the offenses that were being charged in this case, however, was quite different: the Nazis and Nazi Collaborators Law (like similar laws enacted by various countries after the war) did not introduce new legal norms; all it did was to make it possible to bring persons to trial for committing offenses that were known to be against the law at the time they were committed, in every place in the world, including Germany. Those persons themselves were well aware of the illegality of their acts. Owing to the illegal regime that was in power in Nazi Germany, the perpetrators of these crimes were not punished for them at the time; but it was precisely the sense of natural justice that called for the establishment of a forum where the persons suspected of these crimes could be brought to trial.

We can already read in the famous *Blackstone Commentaries* that 'ex post facto laws were objectionable when, after an action (indifferent in itself) is committed, the legislator then, for the first time declares it to have been a crime and inflicts a punishment upon the person who has committed it. Here it is impossible that the party could foresee that an action, innocent when it was done, should afterwards be converted to guilt by a subsequent law; he had therefore no cause to abstain from it; and all punishment for not abstaining must of consequence be cruel and unjust.'

As Kelsen wrote in his book *Peace Through Law*,[1] 'There is no rule of general customary law forbidding the enactment of norms with retrospective force, so-called ex post facto laws.'

Julius Stone wrote similarly in *Legal Controls of International Conflict*,[2] 'There is clearly no principle of international law embodying the maxim against retroactivity of criminal law.'

The Nazi regime created an arbitrary vacuum in the legal sphere, and justice demanded the institution of a procedure which would make the punishment of the offenders possible. As a matter of fact, the same argument, as to the retroactivity of the law and the charter under which they were charged, was advanced by the defendants in the Nuremberg trials, and was rejected by the International Military Tribunal.

A second charge against the propriety of the trial relates to the fact that the crimes in question were committed outside the territory of Israel and before the state was created. This fact was of no significance in the case. War crimes, crimes of genocide, and crimes against humanity have been recognised by the international community as universal crimes, and every sovereign nation has the right – indeed, the duty – to bring the perpetrators of such crimes to justice. Such crimes have been likened to piracy and the slave trade. It has been held that a pirate is an outlaw, the enemy of all mankind [*hostis humani generis*], whom every nation may in the interest of all capture and punish. The Israeli Law of 1950 under which Eichmann was indicted certainly did not contravene any concept of International Law.

A third argument that is sometimes put forward may be formulated as follows: How is it that an Israeli court, representing the Jewish people, which is the victim of the crimes attributed to the Nazis in general, and to Eichmann in particular, can sit in judgment over this defendant? Is this not contrary to the principle of justice, especially the principle that justice should manifestly be seen to be done?

---

1 H. Kelsen, *Peace Through Law* (Chapel Hill, The University of North Carolina Press 1944), p. 87.

2 J. Stone, *Legal Controls of International Conflict* (New York, Rinehart 1959), p. 369.

Intrinsically, there is of course no merit to this argument. The purpose and normative meaning of criminal law everywhere is that the society against whom a crime has been committed should defend itself against the offender, punish him, and try as far as possible to prevent similar offences in the future. Society – generally the sovereign state, through its courts and other organs – is organised in part to prevent the injured victims of a crime or their families from taking the law into their own hands and punishing the offender in revenge by themselves. This is accomplished by ensuring that the offender is suitably punished by the organs of society as a whole. The fact that a crime is perpetrated against a certain society does not detract from the moral or other right of the courts of that society to judge a person who has tried to harm its interests.

On the contention in the Eichmann trial that the judges of an Israeli court might be influenced by their emotions, the Court stated: 'When a judge sits on a bench, he does not cease to be flesh and blood with human emotions; but he is bidden by law to overcome these emotions. If this were not so, no judge would ever be qualified to sit in judgment in a criminal case evoking strong disgust, such as a case of treason or murder or some other heinous offense.'

In this context, I should like to relate an experience I had during the trial. A professor from a European University asked me about the propriety of the victim trying the offender. Before I could reply, however, he asked me to show him a copy of the indictment against Eichmann. After perusing it, he expressed his surprise that we had charged Eichmann, *inter alia*, also with the murder of Polish, non-Jewish citizens, the Czech children of Lidice, Russian Commissars and Gypsies. 'What have these people to do with you?' he asked, 'why do you not leave the adjudication of those matters to the Polish, Czech, and Russian courts?' I responded as follows: 'Just five minutes ago, you said that according to your opinion, a nation or a people against whom offenses have been committed should not be permitted to judge the perpetrators; but here you seem to find no fault with Polish, Czech, or Russian judges trying the accused for offences committed against their people. What, therefore, is the basis for your opposition and shock when a court of a Jewish State tries a person for crimes committed against the Jewish People?' The learned professor had the decency to blush. He answered in all embarrassment that he would have to think about the matter again, and that off-hand, he could not justify his earlier distinction.

I shall never forget the first moment of the trial, when those judges came into the courtroom – with the Israeli flag and the Israeli emblem behind them – and this man, whose central purpose in life had been to bring about the total destruction of the Jewish People, jumped to attention before the Court. I felt at this moment, more than on any previous occasion, the importance and the impact of the creation of the State of Israel. Any state would have been a proper forum to try one accused of crimes against humanity. However, it was not only proper, but an act of justice, that this man should be tried – with all his rights scrupulously protected – before this Court.

A fourth challenge is sometimes voiced, regarding the abduction of Eichmann from Argentina by Israeli agents. It is argued that the abduction was an illegal act, which automatically invalidated the legality of his detention and the right to bring him to trial.

When this point was raised by the defence, it was rejected; the judges held, basing themselves mainly on English and American judgments, that the method whereby a suspected criminal is brought to trial is of no concern to the court that tries him. In the English case of *Ex parte* Elliott,[3] decided in 1949, the Court heard an application of a British soldier for *Habeas Corpus*. He had deserted from his unit in 1946, was arrested in Belgium in 1948 by two members of the British Military Police, accompanied by two Belgian gendarmes, and brought back to England where he was in custody awaiting trial by court martial for desertion. The applicant's Counsel argued that the British authorities in Belgium had no power to arrest his client and that he was arrested contrary to Belgian law. The Lord Chief Justice dismissed the application and said, in his judgment, that if a person was arrested abroad and brought before a court in this country, charged with an offence which this court had jurisdiction to try, the court had no power to go into the question of the circumstances in which he may have been brought here. In this case, he said, the court martial had jurisdiction to deal with the applicant and the High Court would not interfere.

Similar decisions were handed down by English courts in other cases, and American courts adhered to the same principle. The issue arose frequently in the United States, where suspects were apprehended in one state and brought forcibly into a neighboring state where the suspect was wanted. The US Supreme Court has consistently held that the illegal apprehension of such suspects was no bar to their being tried in the state to which they had been transferred.[4]

Now as to the trial itself. As I mentioned before, I shall try to let you share in some of my impressions and feelings during the traumatic experience of conducting the investigation into these matters, preparing the indictment and appearing as prosecutor, at the trial before the Court of First Instance and later at the appeal. These reminiscences are difficult to reduce to words in cold print. I shall prefer to describe them orally. But some general remarks can also be included in this written outline.

Strange as it may sound, at first it was rather difficult to find witnesses who were prepared to testify at the trial. The reason was that most of the survivors of the Holocaust were reluctant to relate their terrible experiences because for all these many years they had attempted to suppress these memories and pass them into the realm of the subconscious. However, once we succeeded in persuading these people to testify, then one could not stop them and they wanted to tell all the details about what happened to their families and friends. We did not want the trial to go on for

---

[3] [1949] 1 *All ER* 373.

[4] See *Ker* v. *Illinois*, 199 US 436.

too long and therefore we often asked these witnesses to limit their testimony to a particular point that was not covered by the already existing evidence. Often we felt that *we* would be unable to curb the evidence of these witnesses, and with a heavy heart we had to strike some of them off the list of witnesses for this reason.

I am often asked: '"what sort of a man was this Eichmann", and "what made him tick?"' As a general rule I object to defining any person, including an offender, by 'pigeon holing' him as being only a murderer, a robot, a bureaucrat, a sadist or, in genocide cases – a typical Nazi. People are never only something. They are a combination of things and they pass through stages of development. This holds true for Eichmann as well. It seems that when he, as a member of the SS, became an expert on Jewish affairs, and the head of the relevant department in the German Secret Police, the Gestapo, he did this because he thought that this would help him in his career. Then he carried out, efficiently, all parts of the plan concerning the persecution of the Jews and later their annihilation. Then you could trace through the oral evidence and the official documents how this gradually became a form of obsession with him. Maybe it is psychologically understandable, that when for years you deal only with the mass murder of innocent people, men, women and children, then you must either go mad, or by some defence mechanism become obsessed with the idea that you do something which is justified and worth while. One can see how towards the end of the war he became even more fanatical than people like Hitler and Himmler. That does not mean that he was as guilty as those leaders. They were the originators of this hideous scheme, and as such the persons mainly responsible. But for them there were other areas of interest, like the political and military situation. For Hitler those problems were not less important than killing every last Jew, perhaps even more so. But for Eichmann, all his endeavours centered on this one purpose – the liquidation of the Jewish race. Here we had proof, that during the final stages of the war, when the German generals on the Eastern Front were clamouring for reinforcements and for ammunition, Eichmann, by all kinds of tricks and trickery, managed to get priority for his death-trains, knowing that by doing so he was actually harming Germany's war-effort. He told his friends: 'I know the war is lost, but I am still going to win my war.' And then he went to Auschwitz in order to increase the rate of killings from 10,000 a day to 12,000.

When in the final stages of the war, in 1944, Admiral Horthy, the leader of Hungary, who fought on the side of Germany and Italy, wanted to make a separate peace with the Allies, because he thought the war was lost, Hitler came to Budapest to meet him, in order to persuade him, by threats and promises, to continue the fight together with Germany. Horthy finally agreed, but attached some conditions to this, one of those being that the Germans should permit 3,000 Jewish families from Budapest to go to a neutral country, to Switzerland. Hitler agreed, because Hungary's continued support was more important for him then those 3,000 families. In this connection we found in the archives of the German Foreign Ministry a telegram from the German Ambassador, von Veesenmayer, to the Foreign Minister, von Ribbentropp. He described in this telegram the agreement between Hitler and Horthy, including the condition concerning the 3,000 Jewish families, and then he added:

'I have however to inform you, that the local representative of the S.S. Obersturmbannfuehrer Eichmann is very upset about this arrangement. He fears that those 3,000 families might constitute important biological material. They may come to Palestine and may cause there a new cell for the rebuilding of the Jewish race.' Von Veesenmayer added that Eichmann had therefore given instructions to increase the speed of the deportation of the Jews from Budapest in such a way, that until the visas could be arranged for the entry of these people to Switzerland no 3000 Jewish families would remain in Budapest. Here Eichmann was faced with a decision of the Fuehrer Adolf Hitler himself, and he succeeded in thwarting even this order, because he wanted to prevent the saving of a small number of Jews. Documents like that and similar pieces of evidence helped us to explode the 'small cog' theory of the defence, according to which Eichmann was an officer of relatively low rank who merely had to obey orders.

One of the striking features was his pre-occupation with killing Jewish children. Proof of that we found in the notes of the last commander of the Auschwitz camp, named Rudolf Hoess. He was sentenced to death by a Polish court and hanged in 1951, i.e., 10 years before Eichmann's trial. Before he was executed he wrote his auto-biography, which was published in a book called *The last Commander of Auschwitz*. There Hoess relates how they sometimes carried out actions in which they put 1000 children to death on one day. He described how some of the children begged for their lives, and wrote that when he had to push those children into the gas chambers, then his knees often got a bit shaky. But after that he adds: 'I did however always feel ashamed of this weakness of mine after I talked to Obersturmbannfuehrer Adolf Eichmann. Eichmann explained to me that it was especially the children who have to be killed first, because where was the logic in killing a generation of older people and leaving alive a generation of young people, who can be possible avengers of their parents and can constitute a new biological cell for the re-emerging of this people.' This was not devoid of some macabre logic, but I must admit that when 10 minutes after reading this I had to sit opposite Eichmann, who wanted to discuss something with me, it was not without difficulty to preserve a poker face.

During his testimony in Court, Eichmann said that he thought that this was the worst crime ever committed in history. I was asked by the judges and others whether I believed that he honestly meant that. This point could have been important for the sentence which was finally imposed on him. My reply was that this was mere lip service on his part. When I am asked what the basis for this contention was, my answer was as follows: 'I could imagine that even a man like that could theoretically change his mind. His eyes could have been opened between the end of the war in 1945 and 1961 when his trial took place. But here we had proof that in 1956, when he was in Argentina, he was visited by a Dutch fascist journalist called Sassen, who recorded his talks with him on tape. The idea was that he would publish this after Eichmann's death. This was a kind of insurance policy for his family. When Eichmann was caught the journalist sold this material to 'Life' magazine and the transcripts, with Eichmann's handwritten corrections, were obtained by us and submitted to the Court as evidence. There Eichmann enthusiastically describes the trains that pulled towards the death camps almost in lyrical terms ('It was marvellous to watch these trains'). And when he was asked by Sassen whether he ever felt remorse and whether he was ever sorry for what he had done, he replied: 'Yes, I am sorry for one thing, and that is that I was not hard enough, that I did not fight those damned interventionists enough, and now you see the result: The creation of the State of Israel and the re-emergence of the Jewish people there!' And I added, that if Eichmann said this in 1956, eleven years after the end of the war, and now in 1961, five years later, when he is fighting for his life, he suddenly speaks about 'the worst crime in history,' I think we are justified in being sceptical about the sincerity of such a remark.' Eichmann was sentenced to death, his appeal was dismissed by the Supreme Court, by a panel of five justices, and he was executed in 1962. He is the only person who was ever sentenced to death and executed in Israel.

The Eichmann trial achieved the following main purposes:

(a) First and foremost it was an act of real justice, that this man should be tried and convicted by an Israeli court, and receive the severest punishment known in progressive and democratic societies.
(b) This trial triggered a chain-reaction, mainly in Germany, of investigation into Nazi crimes and the conduct of trials against those responsible for the murders and crimes against humanity committed. Also, before that there were prosecutors and teachers in Germany, who wanted to put the guilty persons on trial and teach the facts about the Holocaust in the schools. But they never got the necessary encouragement and budgets to carry out their intentions. Those who were Nazis certainly did not want such activities, but even those who did not approve of the Nazis and the persecution of the Jews did not want to be questioned by their children about those happenings and about the reasons for their not doing anything in opposition. But after the Eichmann trial, which brought the relevant facts into all the homes for hours every day, no one dared to stand in the way of the above mentioned prosecutors and teachers any more.
(c) Until the trial, many people in Israel and especially our youth did not want to hear about the Holocaust. They felt in a way ashamed about what had happened. A young Israeli can understand that you can be killed in action, or even lose a military battle. But he could not grasp how it was possible for millions of people to be slaughtered without offering active resistance.

As one of the by-products of this trial, we proved that there was absolutely no ground for this feeling of shame. We depicted the devilish systems and plans that managed to mislead the victims and made resistance impossible. We showed how all victims of whatever nationality or race were lured to their death by cruel designs and by trickery and deception. And, on the contrary, we also showed that when it became absolutely clear to the Jewish people that death was intended for all of them by the Nazis as the inevitable result, then there came the famous uprisings like the one in the Warsaw Ghetto, where the young Jewish defenders fought with incredible bravery until death, and this was a basis for respect towards the victims and for national pride. As a result, our young people in Israel began to take a greater interest in the history of European Jewry, in Jewish European culture, and in all details of the Holocaust.

I shall briefly mention some facts about the other internationally known genocide trial in Israel which took place recently – the trial against the Ukrainian citizen Demjanjuk, who was extradited by the American judicial authorities to Israel, and charged before an Israeli court for the mass-murder of Jews in the gas-chambers of the notorious Treblinka death-camp. It was alleged that the accused was the person known by the inmates of the camp as 'Ivan the Terrible,' on account of the unspeakable cruelty and sadism that he exhibited towards the victims.

Demjanjuk was identified as being 'Ivan the Terrible' by a number of the survivors of Treblinka. His own evidence, denying all guilt, and denying that he was the Ivan of Treblinka, was rejected as not credible by the judges of the District Court. He was found guilty, and sentenced to death. The accused appealed to the Supreme Court. Actually I should have been one of the judges who sat on the panel of the Court of Appeal in this case, but I asked to be excused. I felt that I was so much associated with the prosecution in the *Eichmann* case, that it would be undesirable for me to sit in judgment in this case.

While the hearing of the appeal was in progress, the following development arose. As a result of the revolutionary changes in the Soviet Union, archives of documents from World War II were opened to the public for inspection. The Israeli State Attorney, who acted as prosecutor in this case, visited the former Soviet Union and detected a large amount of written testimony by German and Ukrainian members of the SS, who were no longer alive. These people testified that they were active in Treblinka, and that there was an Ukrainian guard, known for his cruelty, who was called 'Ivan the Terrible.' Those witnesses also mentioned that the surname of this Ivan was Marchenko. This in itself did not sound very significant, because Demjanjuk, when entering the US, had stated that his mother's maiden name was Marchenko. The assumption was therefore that Demjanjuk and Marchenko were the same person. But then it transpired that those SS guardsmen had identified this Marchenko by pointing at a picture which was not that of Demjanjuk.

This gave rise to serious doubt about the real identity of 'Ivan the Terrible.' The Israeli State Attorney passed this information on to the defence attorney and also handed it to the Court of Appeal as additional evidence. This was clearly his duty, but I think it certainly goes to the credit of the prosecutor that he unhesitatingly did so, although he was of the opinion that the accused had been active in one of the death camps. There was also no doubt that he was trained in a special camp to act as guard in one of the death camps. On account of this new evidence, the Court of Appeal decided to give the accused the benefit of the doubt and acquitted him. Later a petition was brought to the Supreme Court, sitting as the High Court of Justice, in which we were asked to instruct the Attorney General to charge Demjanjuk with criminal activities in another death camp, the Sobibor camp. There was some proof that the accused had been sent to that camp. I myself sat as one of the judges in this case. We rejected the petition. I based this decision on the following grounds:

First of all, the evidence connecting the accused with the Sobibor camp appeared very flimsy, and I did not see any justification for interfering with the decision of the Attorney General, who also based his conclusions in part on this ground.

And secondly, as the prosecutor in the original case had asked the Court of Appeal to find Demjanjuk guilty, in the alternative, for his activities in Sobibor, he had in fact been in jeopardy of such a conviction, and charging him again on account of those allegations would have put him in what is known as 'double jeopardy,' and this is not permitted under our accepted Rules. Demjanjuk was therefore freed, and he has returned to his home in America. Many people in Israel were very unhappy at this result. Of course it is rather disturbing to think that a man who voluntarily underwent training for such bestial crimes and probably was active in this field escaped punishment. But I think the Rule of Law and the reputation of our judicial system as one where justice is scrupulously applied, are more important than that.

Finally, a general remark regarding the genocide trials held in Germany against Nazi offenders. Often severe criticism is voiced against the conduct of those trials and their outcome, and doubts are expressed as to the desirability of continuing with those hearings. The anger and disappointment usually focus on the fact that these cases take a long time, that quite a number of the accused are acquitted, and that, when found guilty, even of acts of murder or sadistic cruelty, they are merely sentenced to a few years imprisonment.

I personally do not share the view that those trials should be discontinued, because in my mind they still are of the most importance. When in many countries, and Germany among them, so-called 'experts' publicly maintain that the Holocaust never took place, that this is a figment of the imagination, or the product of a sinister Jewish-Zionist conspiracy to propagate those false, or at least highly exaggerated, accusations, then the handing down of judgments, one after the other, written by German judges, after painstaking and thorough examination of all the written and oral evidence, is of extreme value in order to put the record straight.

Also, when these German courts, with their characteristic meticulousness, describe in minute detail the terrifying procedures in Auschwitz, Treblinka, Maidanek, Sobibor and the other notorious death camps, then the speedy termination of these trials does not seem all that essential. Also, as far as the accused henchmen are concerned, it seems to me that the most meaningful punishment for these people, who in any case are now in their seventies or eighties, is for them to sit in court and to have to listen to the testimonies of the survivors who bring the committed atrocities to life again. As to the partial acquittals, here it was clear from the start that the longer the time that elapses between the perpetration of those crimes and the conduct of the trials against the people responsible, the larger will be the number of acquittals.

In many cases the relevant witnesses are no longer alive, and even if they are still able to testify, their memories are sometimes not absolutely reliable. Therefore, when pressure was brought to bear on the German government to abolish the Law of Limitation for those murders and crimes against humanity, and such a law was in fact enacted by the German Parliament, then it had to be anticipated that the continued conduct of those trials would necessarily lead to an increasing number of acquittals, owing to the inability to prove the guilt of the accused persons beyond a reasonable doubt. But this by-product certainly does not detract from the advantage of charging those, whose acts can still be proved, before a court, of bringing those facts to light and to the attention of the new generation in Germany and elsewhere, and of seeing to it that those who took part in the atrocities will, as much as possible, not escape public stigma and punishment.

People everywhere have to realise, that if they take part in crimes of genocide or in the commission of unspeakable crimes against humanity, then as long as they live they have to face the apprehension of being apprehended, interrogated, charged before a court of justice and punished for those acts.

THE AUSCHWITZ TRIAL AT THE *LANDGERICHT* FRANKFURT AND ITS IMPORTANCE FOR THE PROHIBITION OF GENOCIDE

Heinz Düx

After the Second World War, this very plain building was erected to serve as a community centre for the Frankfurt Gallus-suburb, in which predominantly less well off residents lived. It is over 45 years ago that in this very building 20 defendants were tried by a jury court before the *Frankfurt Landgericht* (Frankfurt Regional Court), accused of the multiple murders of persons persecuted in the concentration camp at Auschwitz, because of their race, political/world views and religious background. The camp was constructed in 1940 after the Nazi regime invaded Poland, in the Polish town of Auschwitz. My role in this trial was that of the pre-trial judge. That meant that at the commencement of the trial in Haus Gallus my work had already been completed. The German code of criminal procedure in force at the time required a judicial preliminary enquiry for all serious offences, in order to determine whether the accused was to be committed for trial by jury or the proceedings stayed. In the summer of 1961 the prosecution files, which comprised of approximately 50 volumes, were handed over to me. The preliminary enquiry was opened on 9 August 1961. After the in-depth interrogation of all the accused, further questioning of witnesses as well as a private visit to the scene of the crime and the addition of five further defendants to the proceedings, the preliminary enquiry was closed on 19 October 1962. An official inspection of the site of the crime was not possible at the time, due to the cold war between East and West.

Like the venue of the trial itself, the work of the pre-trial judge also took place in a very plain building, namely a rented private house, which was situated next to an erotic establishment, in which the then well known glamorous prostitute Nitribitt was murdered. Her case was also investigated in the same rented building. Such enquiries into ordinary homicide cases were the daily work of pre-trial judges.

The killings in Auschwitz had an altogether unparalleled dimension. They were unique in the history of international crime. They involved the killings of hundreds of thousands of victims by way of suffocation in the gas chambers, phenol injection into the heart, through shootings at the so-called 'black wall' after a court martial hearing of approximately 5 minutes, through medical experiments, through sla-

C. Safferling and E. Conze (eds.), The Genocide Convention Sixty Years after its Adoption

very, through starvation, through battery, through the compilation of a collection of skulls of Jewish-Bolshevist commissioners from the USSR and the like.

Such mass killings are covered by the Statute of the International Military Court of 9 August 1945 under the term 'crimes against humanity and war crimes.' The crime of genocide established by the UN on 9 December 1948 belongs to the category 'crimes against humanity.'

The largest group of genocide victims at Auschwitz were by far the Jewish people. Although originally established in 1940 for Polish nationals, the camp soon became the site for the extermination of Jews from all over Europe.

The trains arrived on a daily basis at Auschwitz with families already demoralised through hunger and thirst. After the unloading of the callously overcrowded freight wagons, the SS singled out those ineligible to work, i.e., the elderly, children, the weak, the sick, and led them directly to the gas chambers. Those eligible to work were subjected to slave labour up to the point of utter exhaustion. Then they too were killed, sometimes by way of a leather injection of phenol, sometimes through the march to the gas chamber.

In 1944, along with the Jews, the ethnic groups Sinti and Roma, as far as they were transported to Auschwitz, were also exterminated. Other nationals, such as for example Soviet prisoners of war, were no better off at Auschwitz. Here all prisoners were equally on death roll. However, it must be said that the largest group to be delivered to Auschwitz were the Jews, and it follows that the greatest number of victims were Jewish.

After the unconditional surrender of the fascist German Reich the Allied Control Council seized power on 8 May 1945 and passed Control Council Law No. 10 on 20 December 1945. This created the legal basis upon which German courts were able to prosecute crimes against humanity and war crimes under the same principles as those applied by the International Military Tribunal in the trial of the major war criminals.

Control Council Law No. 10 however, remained almost completely disregarded by the German courts. What were the reasons for this?

Soon after the defeat of fascist Germany, the Powers composing the Control Council – the USA, the USSR, Great Britain and France – split as the Cold War emerged. Under this disunity, reactionary powers could once again become active in Germany. In this context one must bear in mind: A survey of the German population undertaken by the Allied Powers at the end of 1946 showed that 18 months after the unconditional surrender 80% of those questioned could be depicted as racist and nationalistic. Where people were questioned by a German national the figure was considerably higher. This catastrophic state of affairs was also reflected in the judiciary. In the former British Zone, judges who joined the NSDAP after 1937 as well as *Wehrmachtsrichter* (military judges) were considered to be unimplicated. As if this were not bad enough the so-called 'piggyback' procedure was introduced, which allowed one implicated judge to be appointed for every unimplicated judge in office. In as early as 1948 30% of court presidents and 80-90% of presidents of the *Landgerichte* (regional courts) in the British Zone were former NSDAP members. In 1949 in Bavaria 751 of 924 prosecutors and judges (81%) were former supporters of the NSDAP. In Hamburg a judge, who had been a member of the 6th Chamber in 1940-1941 and had participated in judgments concerning race defilement, was appointed presiding judge of a reparations chamber, responsible for the processing of compensation claims of persons who had been persecuted by the Nazis.

It is not surprising, that under the said circumstances, a tendency had developed towards the end of the 1950s under which proceedings against Nazi criminals were not pursued. In this vein Merten, an SPD member of Parliament during this era, who frequently took part in parliamentary debates, declared in the *Bundestag* (German parliament) 'even a layman can see, that the proceedings against Nazi offenders did not serve justice, but were instead political proceedings' and in his conclusion stated, 'We must put an end to all and every discrimination of Germans ... an end to the legal practice, which bears its foundations in the striving for retaliation and vengeance.'

The climate in the FRG at the time was one of suppression of the Nazi tyranny, which nowadays seems hardly comprehensible. Dr. Hans Globke, the legal commentator of the Nuremberg Racial Laws in 1935, was appointed secretary of state in Adenauer's cabinet. Former NSDAP member Theo Oberländer, who was *Reichsführer des Bundes deutscher Osten* from 1939 until 1945, alleged to have been a member of the unit *Nachtigall* and to have taken part in the shootings of Jews and Polish people, held the post of Minister for Displaced Persons, Refugees and Victims of War[1] between 1953 and 1960.

An application was made to the *Bundesverwaltungsgericht* (Federal Administrative Court) to ban the *Vereinigung der Verfolgten des Naziregimes* (union of those persecuted by the Nazis), an organisation made up of a minority of German nationals who had resisted and fought against the fascist regime. It was only after immense pressure from the foreign press that these proceedings were, after many years, quietly closed on procedural grounds.

Under this political climate massive resistance was put up against Control Council Law No. 10, which codified the principles of international criminal law. Law No. 10 was perceived by the German public as a law 'which does not correspond to our concept of justice.' Another source described this law as 'hardly conceivable under the German concept of justice.' Such comments were made in respectable legal journals such as the MDR and NJW. In 1950, the *Oberste Gerichtshof für die Britische Zone* (the Highest Court of the British Zone), which applied Control Council Law No. 10 on numerous occasions, was accused of 'having distanced itself from the German principles of criminal law.' Subsequently the law was boycotted and not applied, until finally it was officially repealed on 30 May 1956 through *1. Gesetz zur Aufhebung von Besatzungsrecht* (1st Law for the Repeal of Occupation Law).

Under this greatly retrospective mood whereby the German population endeavoured to forget the mass murders of the Nazi regime as quickly as possible, Adolf

---

1 *Bundesminister für Vertriebene, Flüchtlinge und Kriegsbeschädigte.*

Rögner, a former prisoner of the Auschwitz concentration camp, pressed criminal charges against Wilhelm Boger, a particularly sadistic and skilled killer of this extermination camp. Rögner's criminal charges were, in accordance with the zeitgeist at the time, dealt with in a dilatory manner. In a notation the person pressing charges was described as an 'egotistic psychopath.' Nonetheless, the necessity of an investigation could not be denied. Rögner left it to the discretion of the prosecutor whether or not to gather evidence form the International Auschwitz Committee, whose seat at the time was in Warsaw. However, initially no contact was made to the committee. Only after the Secretary General of the committee, Hermann Langbein, personally approached the prosecution in May 1958, did it come to a discussion in November 1958, which advanced the proceedings. In January 1959 a correspondent of the *Frankfurter Rundschau*, Thomas Gnielka, handed over incriminating documents to the Chief Public Prosecutor of Hesse, Bauer. The latter brought about the amalgamation of the investigations concerning Auschwitz at the *Landgericht Frankfurt* in April 1959, through his intervention at the *Bundesgerichtshof* (German Federal Court of Justice).

Bauer strived to finally prosecute the crimes committed in a German extermination camp in a single trial. Of all the members of the German legal profession in the 1950's, which was still tainted by the ideology of the former Nazi regime, Bauer was the one to take this role. Born in Stuttgart in 1903, Bauer was appointed as a judge at the *Amtsgericht* (District Court) in 1930. He was removed from office in 1933 because of his Jewish and socialist background. Thereafter, he was arrested and brought to a concentration camp in Württemberg (Kuberg, near Ulm). In 1936 Bauer was able to emigrate from Germany to Denmark. After the German invasion of Denmark he was rearrested. He was then able to escape to Sweden. Bauer returned to Germany in 1949 and in 1956 he was appointed Chief Public Prosecutor of Hesse.

Due to his past, Bauer was regarded by the numerous supporters of the Nazi regime as a non-person and was met with blatant hostility. Bauer was under no illusion concerning the 'appreciation' of his 'colleagues.' In a lecture he described 'Nazism as a movement of a people, which glorifies authority and the barrack yard drill, rather than human rights and freedom.' In an interview with a Danish newspaper, he spoke of 'the glowing anti-Semitism of the German population below the surface.' Bauer basically described that, which later Daniel Goldhagen, in his book *Hitlers willige Vollstrecker,* accurately depicted as German eliminatory anti-Semitism.

The repeal of Control Council Law No. 10 at the end of the 1950s meant that the offences of crimes against humanity and genocide, stemming from international criminal law, could no longer be applied by the German courts. Hence the crimes committed at Auschwitz could only be prosecuted under the remaining national penal code, the StGB, i.e., § 211, which governed ordinary homicide cases – a legal basis that could not do justice for the prosecution of mass murderers. With this purpose in mind two young prosecutors, chosen by Bauer, were charged with the investigation which was now at long last carried out resolutely. Notwithstanding the prevailing Cold War they established contacts in Poland in order to gather evidence. They also carried out numerous interrogations either personally or by way of legal co-operation. As already mentioned, in summer 1961 they had compiled 50 volumes of files and were able to apply for a judicial preliminary enquiry.

The above mentioned Hermann Langbein directed international attention towards the fact that the political, racial and religious motivated mass murders of the Nazi regime were finally being prosecuted (at least partially, i.e., in relation to the concentration camp Auschwitz). Indeed, on the international forum the public eye was now so intensely focused on the subject matter, that the deniers of the German guilt were no longer able to remove the topic from the daily agenda.

However, it would be wrong to assume that the commenced proceedings could take their course without disruptions. Only a few days after I received the investigation files, two judges of the *Landgericht*, one of whom had a very influential position in the administrative department of the court, approached me with a proposal, which was ostensibly directed at reducing my workload. They thought it would ease my workload, if I were to reject the jurisdiction of the *Landgericht Frankfurt* for at least some of the accused, given that there were so many. Should I follow this advice, I could count on the court administration to cover my back. It was easy to see through their proposal, which was not directed at my workload, but instead was aimed at preventing proceedings that would at long last record the structures of a German extermination camp, over 15 years after the end of the Second World War.

The following attempt to obstruct, or rather to delay the proceedings was also symptomatic. During the investigations it became necessary to send an urgent correspondence to the Soviet Embassy in Bonn. Official channels required the letter to be sent via the Hessian Ministry of Justice, where the letter was held up for days, merely because it contained the term GDR. The ministry insisted that the term SBZ (Soviet Zone) be used instead of GDR. It was foreseeable that the use of this term, which the Soviet Union disliked, could jeopardise the enquiry. After a great deal 'to-ing and fro-ing' the neutral term East Germany was used, so that the correspondence could finally be sent on its way. The ministry official did not, however, neglect to point out that sending the letter was a pointless act, since I could not have expected to receive a reply. However, his prediction failed to come true. During the, then very dramatic phase of the Cold War, irrational anticommunism and the striving to prevent an investigation into the crimes of the Nazis, were cleverly intertwined.

The defendants at the preliminary enquiry came from all social classes and were faces that could be found a thousand times across the county. They came from diverse professions – doctors, dentists, pharmacists, engineers, students, bricklayers, soldiers, voluntary policemen, carpenters, labourers. They were quite unremarkable people, whom one could liken to a 'grey mouse' and portray as petit bourgeois. Had their path of life not led them to Auschwitz, had instead others filled their place there, then these others would have been the perpetrators, because of the wide reaching involvement of the German people in the Nazi regime. The predominant tendency of the accused during questioning was: Trivialisation, inability to remember, directing the blame at others. Some even refused to give evidence and remained silent. The last *Lagerkommendant* (camp commander) at Auschwitz, Richard Baer refused to testify. However, he died in July 1963 due to a circulatory collapse whilst in pre-trial custody at the remand prison Frankfurt-Hammelsgasse.

Of all the defendants who gave evidence, I specifically recall the conduct of the accused Oswald Kaduk whilst he gave testimony. Born in Königshütten, Kaduk had trained to become a butcher, but subsequently worked for the fire brigade. He joined the SS and became a *Blockführer* (head of a prison block) in Auschwitz. Later be became *Rapportführer* (supervisor in charge of all *Blockführer*). He acted in a most compulsive military manner. In response to every question posed to him, he sprang to his feet, took up a military position (Hitler salute, hands tightly pressed against his trousers) and made a statement, articulating in a staccato fashion. When I told him that he need not spring to his feet and take up a military position, he shot to his feet once more and briskly replied *Jawohl* ('yes sir'). In his military frenzy he once even addressed me as *Obersturmführer* (Senior Storm Leader). I was under the impression that his actions were not aimed to provoke. I believe his demeanour sprang from a deeply internalised behavioural pattern. Kaduk's statements relating to the offences he was being accused of were by far more informative than those of his co-accused, who often evaded describing the incidents in question. His defence was based upon the attempt to depict himself as a 'mere servant' in a most inferior position.

According to Kaduk those truly to blame were, for example, Dr. Globke and Dr. Oberländer, whom he explicitly referred to. Kaduk asserted that the higher SS doctors and SS officers had carried out the selection of those to be sent to the gas chamber. He himself had only been responsible for keeping watch like a hawk and ensuring that none of those selected to die sneaked back to the group deemed eligible to work. Kaduk further testified that children who arrived at the camp were gassed immediately, with the exception of those chosen by SS doctors to be subjected to medical experiments. Even though eligible to work, mothers who would not have wanted to be separated from children selected to be sent to the gas chambers, were also gassed.

The Jewish transports 'arrived like hot buns,' said Kaduk. Along with other SS men he transported those condemned to die by the SS doctors and SS officers in a lorry from the arrival ramp to the gas chamber.

He claimed that he had occasionally beaten prisoners, but never killed anyone. With reference to the polish prime minister Jòzef Cyrankievicz, in office in the 1960s and former prisoner at Auschwitz, Kaduk remarked 'if I had had the opportunity I would have done him in.' This revelation quite clearly did not correspond to his pleading that he only ever intended to beat in order to discipline and never had the intention to kill. His attempt to trivialise his actions were rebutted by the testimony of numerous witnesses at the main trial. The jury convicted him for the murder of 1012 people and sentenced him to life imprisonment. Along with Kaduk five other defendants were sentenced to life imprisonment with hard labour. Other defendants received sentences ranging from 14 years to 3 years and 6 months. Three defendants were acquitted.

The highest sentence (apart from the life sentences) of 14 years imprisonment with hard labour was given to *Hauptsturmführer* (SS Captain) Mulka who had the function of *Adjutant des Lagerkommandanten* (adjutant to the camp commander). He was convicted of aiding and abetting common mass murders on four counts, each count relating to the killings of at least 750 people. As already mentioned, Baer the last *Lagerkommendant* (camp commander) at Auschwitz died whilst in pre-trial detention in Frankfurt. His predecessor Höss had been sentenced to death in Poland shortly after the end of the Second World War. He was executed within sight of the camp.

In the proceedings against Höss, Jan Sehn a professor for constitutional and international public law from Krakow presided as pre-trial judge. Whilst conducting my preliminary enquiry in Germany I was in close contact with him. Professor Sehn had visited Frankfurt on several occasions in order to hand over evidence. He also assisted me with my unofficial site visit to Auschwitz. Due to the lack of diplomatic relations between Poland and the FRG at the beginning of the 1960s, my visit could only be undertaken in a private capacity. The purpose of my visit was to view the camp, in particular the buildings of the main camp at Auschwitz, which remained standing. My intention was to put myself in a position in which I could properly understand and accurately assess the statements of defendants and witnesses, especially those accounts concerning the observation of a particular incident from a specific position within the camp. I later gave testimony at the main jury trial about my impressions of the camp during my visits. As a result of my testimony the jury court appointed and instructed a local judge to carry out a further site visit. On my visit to Poland, Professor Sehn had picked me up from Warsaw airport and driven me to Auschwitz. Having arrived, my investigations received the unlimited support of the director of the Auschwitz Museum, Smolen.

Professor Sehn's courteous and accommodating manner was not always reciprocated when he visited Frankfurt to further my investigations. He introduced himself to some of the people, who were to be responsible for the main trial. He expressed to me his surprise and disconcertion at how, despite his professional position, he was patronised and treated like an irksome petitioner, with complete disregard to all international standards of courtesy. I would like to add that he died during one of his official visits to Frankfurt as a result of heart failure.

At the time there was no air connection between Frankfurt and Warsaw. So a Polish aircraft was given special permission to land in Frankfurt in order to transport his body. Despite Professor Sehn's great contribution to the furtherance of the proceedings, the court administration did not consider it necessary to officially pay their last respects to Sehn at the airport. Instead a small group of us turned up to do so. As I recall, the group consisted of Ormand, a lawyer representing a private accessory prosecutor (*Nebenkläger*) in the Auschwitz trial, a prosecutor from the investigation team, which had been established by Chief Public Prosecutor Bauer, the lawyer Reimers, a duty counsel of one of the accused and myself, the pre-trial judge. The ill-treatment, over which Professor Sehn had complained, reflected the zeitgeist at the time, which to a large extent dominated the department of justice.

The investigations undertaken during the preliminary enquiry led to the discovery of further suspects. This in turn led to the opening of new judicial preliminary enquiries. Following the original trial against 20 defendants, to which I have referred to in this lecture, subsequent trials were held, as a result of which three further perpetrators were sentenced to life imprisonment and yet a further three offenders were sentenced to term imprisonment.

In the course of one of the subsequent trials an incident occurred, which one had to expect. I was aware that to conduct diligent and uncompromising investigations during the 1960s, a time when the atmosphere favoured the perpetrators, would result in great resentment towards those carrying out the investigation. In March 1960 a defence lawyer, who was also a member of parliament and belonged to the CDU party, filed a motion requesting my disqualification and withdrawal from the preliminary enquiry. He listed a former *Oberkapo* as an exculpatory witness for his client, who was being held in pre-trial custody at the time. *Kapos* were camp prisoners who cooperated and worked with the SS. The defence lawyer had corresponded with the named *Kapo*. I asked the lawyer to submit the correspondence, in order to examine the possibility of undue interference with the witness. The criminal division responsible for the motion to disqualify and withdraw me from the preliminary enquiry held this measure to be 'inappropriate of furthering the progress of the preliminary enquiry.' Yet 'on the other hand, [the measure was held] capable of supporting the defendant's doubts concerning the impartiality of the pre-trial judge, having regard to the unlimited rights of defence counsel.' Ten lines were all it took to dismiss me from my post of pre-trial judge, on the suspicion of non-impartiality.

I now wish to briefly turn to a particularly morbid subsequent trial. The accused was an anthropologist, who had been a senior SS officer. He had worked with Professor Hirth, who had a post at the University of Strasburg during the Second World War and who committed suicide at the end of the War. Their venture had been to compile a collection of Jewish-Bolshevist commissioners' skulls. Amongst the prisoners at Auschwitz there were also Soviet prisoners of war. The victims were therefore selected from Auschwitz. They were then killed and skeletonised. Thereafter the heads were retained at the University of Strasburg. The project of the two 'scientists' had the quality of the most primitive of primitive horror films. The two scientists had an academic assistant, who had the name Fleischhacker (meat hacker). Like the other defendants from the concentration camp Auschwitz, the scientist who specialised in Jewish-Bolshevist skulls had no sense of wrongdoing. At the main trial he only received a fixed term custodial sentence and not life imprisonment.

All in all one can say that the investigations into the entire Auschwitz complex, given that the setting of the 50s and 60s was very much in favour of the perpetrators, rendered, on the whole, a tolerable result. Without the criminal charges brought by the former prisoner Adolf Rögner, without the important influence of Hermann Langbein of the International Auschwitz Committee and without the resolute initiative of the Hessian Chief Public Prosecutor Fritz Bauer, there would certainly never have been a comprehensive investigation into the crimes committed at Auschwitz. Nonetheless, as already said, Auschwitz is only one detail within the framework of the German fascist crimes.

Looking back at my professional experience up to my retirement in 1989, in particular the field of reparations for fascist injustice, the final balance is not particularly gratifying. I would like to illustrate this by way of two or three examples.

As with the *Auschwitz* case, the Hessian Chief Public Prosecutor also endeavoured to bring about the comprehensive investigation of the Euthanasia cases, in which the highest lawyers of the Nazi State (*Oberlandesgerichtspräsidenten* – presidents of the higher regional courts, and *Generalstaatsanwälte* – chief public prosecutors) had been involved. The highest lawyers of the Nazi State were involved, because at a conference in Berlin on 24 April 1941 they had not opposed the meticulously organised killing operations of the Nazi regime. Furthermore they had subsequently ensured, in their respective jurisdictions, that these killing operations were not impeded through the pressing of criminal charges or the like. An application made to the *Limburg Landgericht* (Limburg Regional Court) for a judicial preliminary enquiry against the lawyers still alive at the time was at first, contrary to the rules, left unprocessed for one year and four months by the judge responsible. Following the death of the chief of prosecutions Fritz Bauer on 30 June 1968, the then commenced proceedings against the judicial representatives of the Nazi State dragged on without the occurrence of anything much worth mentioning, until 1970. Then an application to discontinue the proceedings was made to the *Limburg Landgericht*. In a decision dated 27 May 1970 the *Limburg Landgericht* granted the application. The decision was only nine lines long.

On 6 June 1972 the jury court in Frankfurt acquitted a so-called euthanasia doctor accused of having killed 4696 people. The role of this doctor consisted of the following: He had to identify the persons transferred form the psychiatric hospitals of the former German Reich to the death facility Sonnenstein near Pirna and then choose an appropriate false cause of death. Thereafter the unsuspecting patients were led into a gas chamber disguised as a shower room, where, under the medical supervision of the euthanasia doctor, they were poisoned with carbon monoxide. The relatives of the victim were informed of the patient's death by way of a so-called letter of condolence from the euthanasia doctor, specifying the fabricated cause of death. The letters of condolence were signed by the doctor using an alias. On 20 March 1974 the *Bundesgerichtshof* (German Federal Court of Justice) confirmed the acquittal. The accused had stated that 'those patients selected to be killed, were utterly stupid beings leading a decomposed existence in a pitiful state.' He claimed only ever to have come across such patients during his work. He regarded the use of an alias as unnecessary with regards to the victims. As far as the relatives of the victims were concerned, he considered the measure to be based on good will. He alleged not to have known that the main purpose of the killings was based on a cost-benefit-ratio. The jury court considered this defence not to have been disproved. The *Bundesgerichtshof* followed the same reasoning and stated that the defendant's claimed to have primarily thought he was committing an act of compassion was consistent with the findings of the jury court. The construction of a theory of compassion strongly suggests a perversion of criminal justice and an obstruction to the punishment of someone who was a willing executioner of the Nazi ideology of elimination.

The deficiency in confronting and coming to terms with Nazi atrocities becomes blatantly obvious if one looks at the compensation awards made to victims. There was never any question of full compensation in accordance with the German civil law. Thus, for example a sum of 150 DM was awarded for one month imprisonment in a concentration camp. Entire groups of victims were excluded, such as forced labourers, people who were sterilised, conscientious objectors and homosexuals. Over 40 years after the end of the Nazi tyranny, in 1987, 1989 and 1995, expert hearings took place in the *Bundestag* (German parliament). This finally led to the award of hardship payments to the forgotten victims. However, at this point in time thousands of victims had already died.

None of the judges, who sat at the *Sondergerichte* (Nazi special courts) or the *Volksgerichtshof* (Nazi People's Court) and unscrupulously imposed death sentences en mass in their fascist disorientation, were ever punished for perverting the course of justice. Only few proceedings of this kind were instigated after 1945. They were all stayed. Not until the 1990s, during the proceedings against a former GDR judge for the perversion of justice, did the *Bundesgerichtshof* declare, in an *obiter dictum*, that a legal error had been committed in failing to prosecute and punish the Nazi judges for perverting the course of justice. This rather late insight had no legal consequences for the former Nazi judges, since in the 1990s all perpetrators in question were already deceased.

Bearing in mind these circumstances one may ask what significance the Frankfurt Auschwitz trials had. One must conclude that thanks to the dedication of those persons I have already mentioned on numerous occasions in this paper, the Auschwitz trials in the 60s represented a breakthrough of the reactionary spirit of the German Federal Republic at the time. The fact that there was international and national press coverage of the trial led to the far-reaching impact of the issues covered by the proceedings. The protagonists of the 1968 student movement once again enquired into the role of their fathers during the Nazi regime. The atrocities committed at Auschwitz, which were made public by virtue of the Frankfurt proceedings, may have been a causal factor.

In the Frankfurt Auschwitz trial the crime of genocide had to be prosecuted, due to the lack of alternatives, on the basis of the principles of ordinary criminal law. In the legal history of the FRG the trial represents a single event, which should under normal political circumstances have taken place far earlier and alongside numerous other proceedings against the Nazi perpetrators. The significance of the trial was the breakthrough of a wall of silence and the desire to forget, which had been erected in front of the mass atrocities in order to protect the perpetrators – a matter which one should always take into account at events remembering the trial. The proceedings put an end to the era of euphemisms and aposiopeses regarding the mass atrocities of the Nazi regime. This and only this is the simple conclusion which can be drawn from this trial.

After the trial gained a fair degree of historical importance, some, who had initially rejected the proceedings due to sympathy towards the perpetrators, suddenly used the trial for their advantage in matters of foreign policy. Hence one should take notice of the accurate assessment of the *Zentrum der Organisation der Holocaust-Überlebenden* (Centre for Holocaust Survivors) in Israel with regard to Germany's will to make reparations. The centre asserts: The German conduct 'is primarily based on pragmatic political, rather than noble or moral considerations.' The conduct of the FRG 'served German foreign policy as opposed to true rehabilitation.' This assessment of the German readiness to make reparations, applies likewise to the pursuance of criminal investigations in order to come to terms with the crimes of the Nazi regime. Amongst the majority of the institutions involved as well as the majority of the German population there was a profound lack of willingness to bring those responsible to justice and to make reparations to the victims.

THE NUREMBERG TRIAL 1945–1946

Whitney R. Harris

In all of history, the twentieth century, and particularly the first half of those hundred years, witnessed the gravest inhumanities and killings that man has ever perpetrated on man. It is hard to believe that the long road of civilisation which man had trod since the dawn of history could have led to the dreadful conflicts of World War I, from 1914 to 1918, and of World War II, from 1939 to 1945. The tragedies of these wars passed from the battlefields of Verdun, where thousands of soldiers died in miserable muddy trenches under unremitting rifle and cannon fire, to Hiroshima and Nagasaki, where hundreds of thousand of civilians were pulverised by atom bombs. There must be an end to war, or there will be an end to civilization. The great trial of 1945-1946 held in Room 600 of the Palace of Justice, in Nuremberg, Germany, was man's first effort to put tyranny on trial. More than half a century has passed since the Nuremberg trial at the end of World War II, the most devastating of all the wars of ancient or modern history.

On October 30, 1943, President Franklin Roosevelt, Prime Minister Winston Churchill and Premier Joseph Stalin stated in the Moscow Declaration that Germans would be held individually responsible for crimes committed by them in course of the war. The leaders declared that at the time of the granting of any armistice those officers and men and members of the Nazi Party who were responsible for, or took a consenting part in atrocities, massacres or executions, would be sent back to the countries in which their deeds had been committed in order that they might be judged and punished according to the laws of the liberated countries, and that others, whose offenses had no particular geographical location, would be punished by joint decision of the governments of the Allies. The statement concluded: 'Most assuredly, the three Allied Powers will pursue them to the uttermost ends of the earth and will deliver them to their accusers in order that justice may be done.'

Germany, unable to match the military strength of its opponents, surrendered to the Allies on May 7, 1945. Five days earlier United States President Harry Truman had formally designated Supreme Court Justice Robert H. Jackson as the representative of the United States in drafting a protocol for the trial of the leading Nazis and as its chief of counsel in preparing and prosecuting charges against them before an international military tribunal. On his first visit to London in that capacity, shortly after his appointment, Justice Jackson received the assurance of Lord Chancellor Simon that the British government would support an international military trial of the major alleged German war criminals.

C. Safferling and E. Conze (eds.), The Genocide Convention Sixty Years after its Adoption

Representatives of the United States, Great Britain, France and the Soviet Union met in London on June 26, 1945 for the purpose of drafting a covenant for the trial of the major alleged German war criminals. Agreement was reached on the establishment of an international military tribunal composed of four members representing Great Britain, the United States, France, and the Union of Soviet Socialist Republics. An indictment was drafted charging the commission of crimes against peace, war crimes, crimes against humanity, and a conspiracy to commit these crimes. For purpose of administration occupied Germany was divided into four zones, each under the control of one of the major Allies. Berlin, the declared repository for Allied documents, was in the Soviet Zone; Nuremberg was in the American Zone.

Agreement having been reached on the selection of the major German defendants to be tried and the charges to be brought against them, a decision had to be reached on the place of trial. The Soviets strongly urged Berlin, which seemed a logical choice as the former capitol of Germany. Justice Jackson conferred with the United States Commissioner for Germany, General Lucius Clay, who suggested as a possible alternative, the historic City of Nuremberg, the principal city within the United States Zone of Occupation, despite severe damage which it had sustained by Allied shelling in the last days of the war. Justice Jackson visited Nuremberg and examined its Palace of Justice. Although heavily damaged in the last hours of the war, he found that it had substantial advantages including a courtroom on the sixth floor which could be enlarged to suit the needs of the four judges and their alternates, the twenty-four defendants and their counsel, the prosecuting attorneys, witnesses, interpreters and court personnel. Moreover, the wall separating Room 600 from the adjoining room could be removed to provide additional space for visitors. The prison facilities in the basement and lower areas were more than adequate to provide for the detention of the defendants and the use of prison personnel.

A more serious problem was the lack of adequate communication facilities. The trial had to be conducted in the languages of the defendants and the prosecuting powers. Witnesses would be called who spoke other languages. All testimony had to be translated into the four principal languages of the trials. This demanding problem was solved by the use in court of translators and the installation of devices to enable the translation of spoken testimony into the four principal languages of the trial.

The city of Nuremberg was in ruins. The patient Pegnitz flowed its ways through stone and rubble. Fallen brick façades of buildings blocked many passageways. Women filled iron carts with bricks and rubble and pushed them down openings in the blockaded streets. Only the front façade remained standing, miraculously, of the *Frauenkirche*.

Germany was in ruins, its people in despair, and in this aura of desperation the trial of the alleged major German war criminals of World War II proceeded in the once beautiful Palace of Justice in the noble medieval city of Nuremberg.

Tribute must be paid to the principles of law declared by the International Military Tribunal in the Palace of Justice on the first day of October 1946, and to the judges and trial counsel, prosecutors and lawyers for the defense, whose dedication to the cause of justice ended in a judgment condemning aggressive war, war crimes and crimes against humanity committed in war and criminalising the conduct of leaders of nations responsible for these crimes.

The genesis of the Nuremberg trial was the Moscow Conference of October 1943, at the conclusion of which a statement was issued by President Roosevelt, Prime Minister Churchill, and Premier Stalin declaring the determination of the three powers to hold Germans individually responsible for crimes committed by them in course of World War II. The statement warned that at the time of any armistice to any German government, those German officers and men and members of the Nazi Party who were responsible for or took a consenting part in atrocities, massacres or executions would be sent back to the countries in which their deeds had been committed in order that they might be judged and punished according to the laws of the liberated countries and that those whose crimes encompassed more than one country would be tried by decision of the Allies.

The International Military Tribunal was established by agreement of the four major allied powers at the end of the war for the purpose of bringing to justice those leaders of Nazi Germany. The tribunal consisted of four judges and their alternates. The presiding judge was Lord Justice Lawrence of Great Britain. Other judges were Mr Francis Biddle of the United States, Professor Donnedieu de Vabres of France, and General I.T. Nikitchenko of the Soviet Union.

The chief prosecutors were Justice Robert H. Jackson of the United States, Sir Hartley Shawcross of Great Britain, General R.A. Rudenko of the Soviet Union, and M. François de Menthon of France. The final draft of the indictment was signed by the chief prosecutors in Berlin on October 6, 1945.

I served as an officer in the United States Navy throughout World War II. Towards the end of the war I was assigned for special duty with the Office of Strategic Services, or OSS, and was put in charge of the investigation of war crimes in the European Theatre. While on this assignment I came in contact with the small European staff which had been assembled by Justice Jackson in London. I was invited to join the prosecution team and transferred to Nuremberg in August, 1945.

The trial began on November 20, 1945 with the reading of the indictment. The next morning the twenty defendants then present in court entered pleas of not guilty. There followed one of the foremost forensic speeches in legal history – the Opening Statement for the United States, eloquently delivered by Justice Jackson:

> 'The privilege of opening the first trial in history for crimes against the peace of the world imposes a grave responsibility. The wrongs which we seek to condemn and punish have been so calculated, so malignant and so devastating, that civilization cannot tolerate their being ignored because it cannot survive their being repeated. That four great nations, flushed with victory and stung with injury, stay the hand of vengeance and voluntarily submit their captive enemies to the judgment of the law is one of the most significant tributes that Power has ever paid Reason.'

Justice Jackson declared that what the defendants stood for would be patiently and temperately disclosed. 'We will give you undeniable proofs of incredible events,' And he described the crimes of the Hitler regime as 'the fruits of the sinister forces that sit with these defendants in the prisoner's dock.'

He acknowledged the problem of credibility posed by trial of the accused before an *ad hoc* tribunal of the victors.

> 'Unfortunately,' he observed, 'the nature of these crimes is such that both prosecution and judgement must be by victor nations over vanquished foes. The world-wide scope of the aggressions carried out by these men has left but few neutrals. Either the victors must judge the vanquished or we must leave the defeated to judge themselves …'

After referring to the failure of the latter course at the end of World War I, he counseled:

> 'We must never forget that the record on which we judge these defendants today is the record on which history will judge us tomorrow. To pass these defendants a poisoned chalice is to put it to our own lips as well. We must summon such detachment and intellectual integrity to our task that this trial will commend itself to posterity as fulfilling humanity's aspirations to do justice.'

Justice Jackson did not contend that judicial remedies alone could prevent future wars, but he urged the importance of holding statesmen accountable to the law. 'And let me make clear,' he added, 'that while this law includes and, if it is to serve a useful purpose, it must condemn, aggression by any other nations, including those which sit here now in judgement.'

The aggressions ordered by Adolf Hitler were open and obvious. It was only a matter of locating witnesses and documents to prove his assault upon Poland on September 1, 1939 which began the long series of military assaults which, with the support of Italy under Mussolini, brought the nations of Europe, other than Great Britian and the Soviet Union, to submission.

Crimes against humanity, particularly Jewish genocide, were more difficult to prove. From the admission to me by Otto Ohlendorf to the killing of 90,000 Jews in the year 1941 by *Einsatzgruppe D*, to the confession to me by Rudolph Hoess to the murder of two and a half million Jews in Auschwitz Concentration Camp, the evidence of these incredible crimes against humanity by the Nazi barbarians became part of the record of this blackest page of modern history.

Of all the evidence introduced over the ten-month period in the trial of the major war criminals at Nuremberg, the most dramatic was a three minute exchange between the witness, Otto Ohlendorf, the chief of *Einsatzgruppe A*, and the Soviet judge, General Nikitchenko. This was that interchange in open court:

> Question: In your testimony you said that the Einsatz-Groups had the object of annihilating the Jews and the commissars. Is that correct?
> Answer: Yes.

> Question: And in what category did you consider the children? For what reason were the children massacred?
> Answer: The order was that the Jewish population should be totally exterminated.
> Question: Including the children?
> Answer: Yes.
> Question: Were all the Jewish children murdered?
> Answer: Yes.
> In this brief exchange between the Soviet judge and the witness Ohlendorf the consummate evil of the Hitler tyranny was exposed.

At eleven minutes past one o'clock on the morning of October 16, 1946, the white-faced former Foreign Minister, Joachim von Ribbentrop, stepped through the door into the execution chamber which had been constructed in the basement of the Palace of Justice, and faced the gallows on which he and the others condemned to die by the tribunal were to be hanged. His hands were unmanacled and bound behind him with a leather thong. Ribbentrop walked to the foot of the thirteen stairs leading to the gallows platform. He was asked to state his name, and answered, 'Joachim von Ribbentrop.' Flanked by two guards and followed by the chaplain, he slowly mounted the stairs. On the platform he saw the hangman with the noose of thirteen coils and the hangman's assistant with the black hood. He stood on the trap, and his feet were bound with a webbed army belt. Asked to state any last words, he said: 'God protect Germany, God have mercy on my soul. My last wish is that Germany's unity be maintained, that understanding between East and West be realized and there be peace for the world.' The trap was sprung and Ribbentrop died at 1:29.

In the same way, each of the remaining defendants to receive a capital sentence approached the scaffold and met the fate of common criminals. After the executions the body of each man was placed upon a simple wooden coffin. The body of Hermann Goering was brought in and placed upon its box, there to be photographed with the others.

In the early morning hours two trucks, carrying the eleven caskets, left the prison compound at the Palace of Justice, bound for a Munich crematory. There, during all of that day, the bodies were cremated. It was reported that in the evening the eleven urns containing the ashes were taken away to be emptied into the river Isar. The dust of the dead was carried along in the currents of the stream to the Danube – and thence to the sea.

The other seven, who were sentenced to varying terms of imprisonment, were brought to Spandau prison in the British sector of Berlin, the only prisoners in a prison built to house six hundred inmates. The first to be released was Hitler's successor, Admiral Karl Doenitz, and the last was Rudolf Hess, who managed somehow to commit suicide on August 17, 1987, forty-one years after the final judgment of the tribunal. With his death the Hitler tyranny ended.

In *Tyranny on Trial* I concluded the chapter on the Judgment of the International Military Tribunal with these words:

'The tyrant and his chief cohorts were gone. They had sought to achieve greatness in history. But they inscribed their names in sand, and clean waters fell upon the beach and washed them out. They had intended to establish a new order for Europe. But they built upon pillars of hate, and what they stood for could not stand.
Hitler had taken the best that was Germany and that was in Germany, and corrupted it to his evil purposes. He took the loyalty of the German people and led them into endless, hopeless wars; he took the creativeness of the German mind and set it to devising horrible instruments of mass murder; he took the bravery of youth and commanded them to die upon far and frozen battlefields; he took the nobility of the German spirit and sullied it with wicked persecutions. In all this he was aided and abetted by men eager to share his hours of triumph. They shared, too, his guilty ways and his personal shame. With Hitler, they erred, and for their errors they paid a just and deserved penalty. Because they turned from the final result could not have been otherwise …'

'Truth, crushed to earth, shall rise again; Th' eternal years of God are here, But Error, wounded, writhes in pain, and dies among its worshippers. The tyrant is dead, and gone the evil of his reign. Germany, crushed to earth, shall nobly rise again.'[1]

---

[1] W.R. Harris, Tyranny on Trial, 3rd edn. (Dallas, Southern Methodist University Press 1999), p. 488.

LIST OF CONTRIBUTORS

Jürgen Aßmann serves as legal advisor to the national Co-Prosecutor at the Office of the Co-Prosecutors, Extraordinary Chambers in the Courts of Cambodia, located in Phnom Penh.

Justice Gabriel Bach was prosecutor in the trial against Adolf Eichmann, and has appeared in dozens of other internationally known criminal and civil cases, representing Israeli interests before foreign courts and tribunals and at international conferences. From 1982 until 1997 he was a judge of the Israeli Supreme Court.

Prof. Dr. Thorsten Bonacker is Professor of Peace and Conflict Studies at the Philipps-University of Marburg. He is also a member of the International Research and Documentation Centre for War Crimes Trials.

Prof. Dr. Antonio Cassese is Professor of International Law at University of Florence. From 1993-1997 he has been the ICTY's first president; since 2009 he is President of the Special Tribunal for Lebanon.

Prof. Dr. Eckart Conze is Professor of Modern and Contemporary History at the Philipps-University of Marburg and Deputy Director of the International Research and Documentation Centre for War Crimes Trials.

Prof. Dr. Jost Dülffer is Professor emeritus for Contemporary History and International Relations at the University of Cologne.

Dr. Heinz Düx worked as permanent judge at the District Court of Frankfurt am Main from 1961 to 1966. His work focused on the investigations for the Auschwitz trial and for trials concerning euthanasia. In 1967 he became judge at the Higher Regional Court Frankfurt am Main, heading the division responsible for compensation cases. He retired in 1989.

Dr. Wolfgang Form is co-ordinator of the Research and Documentation Centre for War Crimes Trials in Marburg.

Prof. Whitney R. Harris became a member of the American prosecution staff at Nuremberg at the end of World War II. He presented the case against the defendant, Ernst Kaltenbrunner, and prepared the case against the Gestapo und SD.

Dr. h.c. Hans-Peter Kaul is the International Criminal Court's first German judge and the Second Vice-President of the ICC.

Dr. Stefan Kirsch appeared as defence counsel before the International Criminal Tribunal for the Former Yugoslavia (ICTY) in The Hague as well as before the International Criminal Tribunal for Rwanda (ICTR) in Arusha, Tanzania. His name has also been included in the List of Counsel at the International Criminal Court (ICC).

Margaret Patten Knowlan is associate legal officer for the Chambers at the ICTR, Arusha.

Prof. Dr. Henning Radtke is Professor of Criminal Law, Criminal Procedure and International Criminal Law at Leibniz University of Hannover.

Prof. Dr. Herbert R. Reginbogin is Professor in the Department of International Relations at the European University of Lefke, Northern Cyprus.

Prof. Dr. Christoph Safferling is Professor of Criminal Law, Criminal Procedure, International Criminal Law and Public International Law at the Philipps-University of Marburg and Director of the International Research and Documentation Centre for War Crimes Trials.

Prof. William A. Schabas is Director of the Irish Center for Human Rights at the National University of Ireland, Galway.

Matthias Schuster worked as a junior lawyer for the State of Berlin and as Research Fellow at Humboldt University in Berlin for Prof. Dr. Gerhard Werle. After interning at the ICTR and the ICTY, Mr Schuster joined the ICTY in 2006 as Associate Legal Officer in the Appeals Chamber.

Dr. Anja Seibert-Fohr heads the Minerva Research Group at the Max Planck Institute for Comparative Public Law and International Law in Heidelberg.

Judge Bruno Simma has served as judge at the International Court of Justice since February 2003. He is Affiliate Overseas Professor of the University of Michigan Law School in Ann Arbor and was from 1973-2003 Professor of International and European Law at the University of Munich.

Prof. Dr. Ulrich Wagner is Professor of Social Psychology at the Philipps-University of Marburg and Deputy-Director of the Center for Conflict Studies at the Philipps-University of Marburg.

Judge Inés Weinberg de Roca was elected as a judge of the ICTR and appointed to the joint Appeals Chamber of the United Nations International Criminal Tribunal for the former Yugoslavia and Rwanda in 2003, to the Trial Chamber in 2005. She is Professor of Private International Law at the Law Faculty of the University of

Buenos Aires, of Public International Law and Regional Integration, of Private International Law, and of Economic Law at the Universidad Argentina de la Empresa.

Dr. Annette Weinke is research assistant of the Independent Historians' Commission appointed by the German Foreign Minister in 2006 to investigate the history of the German diplomatic service during the Nazi regime and in its aftermath.

Prof. Dr. Moshe Zimmermann is an Israeli historian and publicist. He is Head of the Richard Koebner Center for German History at the Hebrew University of Jerusalem.

INDEX

MIX
Papier aus verantwortungsvollen Quellen
Paper from responsible sources
FSC® C105338

If you have any concerns about our products,
you can contact us on
ProductSafety@springernature.com

In case Publisher is established outside the EU,
the EU authorized representative is:
Springer Nature Customer Service Center GmbH
Europaplatz 3, 69115 Heidelberg, Germany

Printed by Libri Plureos GmbH
in Hamburg, Germany